THE ENCYCLOPEDIA OF
EROTIC LITERATURE
PART ONE

THE ENCYCLOPEDIA OF EROTIC LITERATURE

PART ONE

C. J. Scheiner

BARRICADE BOOKS INC.
NEW YORK

Published by Barricade Books Inc.
150 Fifth Avenue, New York, NY 10011

Printed in Great Britain

Library of Congress Cataloging-in-Publication Data

Scheiner, C. J.
The encyclopedia of erotic literature/ by C. J. Scheiner.
p. cm.
Published simultaneously in England under title: The essential
guide to erotic literature.

ISBN: 1-56980-084-7
1. Erotic literature—Encyclopedias. I. Title.
PN56.E7S35   1996
809'.933538—dc20
                                                    96-19124

CIP

First Printing

Introduction

This book is not a history of erotic literature. Nor is it a bibliography of erotica. It is rather an anthology of extracts from specific works of erotic literature which I find are exemplars of the numerous functions which erotica serves.

Erotica is, and should be, fun. Since time immemorial, sexually explicit literature has served the multiple purposes of education, aphrodisia *and* entertainment. In just the recent past it has been recognised by scholars, academics and social researchers that this self-same material is also a valuable and legitimate source of primary reference. While this acceptance should in no way diminish the pure joy of erotica, it does expand its cultural significance and acknowledge its redeeming social value.

Not that there is anything wrong with pure and simple entertainment. I hope that my readers will find the following texts pleasurable. However, as has been recognised by formal academia, erotic literature does have much more to offer, and in acknowledgement of this, there has been created a formal academic discipline, called erotology, under which the scholarly study of erotic material is classified. This present work was in fact first created to be a course curriculum for graduate study, and was amended for the purposes of a broader, less pedantic audience.

Erotology is a multidisciplinary field. Its primary concern is the collection and investigation of all manner of expression concerned with sex. This includes not only the actual physical act of procreation, but the attitudes towards it, the social and cultural controls on it, the depictions of it in art and literature, the psychology and physiology (i.e. mind and body) at all levels of physical and mental complexity to explain the instigation and successful completion of copulation, and the artifices (aphrodisiacs) used to promote sexual activity. Erotology concerns itself with the real and tangible, as well as the symbolic and surrogate. Art, science, law, economy, criminology, theology, sociology, medicine, linguistics, ethnology and history are just a few of the 'major' academic disciplines that are readily identifiable as being concerned with the subject matter of erotology. Since the primary inborn, genetic instinct of the human being is successfully to reproduce its species, it is obvious that no element of human life is without sexual elements. It is the understanding of the evolution and expression of these sexual elements that is the foundation of erotology.

The largest fund of primary erotological source material is the collective sum of human activity throughout the entirety of history. The libido is the primary mental drive of the organism, to which all other drives and instincts, including the will to survive, subserviate themselves. Therefore, everything that mankind has ever done has at some time been done with a sexual connotation, or in an attempt to enhance the frequency, efficiency or pleasure of sexual activity. Most of this material has been lost due to lack of documentation, and even that which has been recorded in word and picture and archetypal memory is too vast to analyse in full. The purpose of this project is to create a defined collection of written literature (as opposed to material that survives only in the oral tradition or in non-verbal forms of expression) that will serve as an introductory text to the varied forms of erotological material. Additionally, the material will be for the most part limited to original works, rather than compilations of earlier material, of sufficient length to be considered equivalent to the modern 'novel', although both fiction and non-fiction is included.

The 'literature' of erotology is without calculable bounds and stretches from the beginning of physically recorded language. If 'a picture is worth a thousand words', then symbolically, this literature extends back in time to the earliest drawings of *homo sapiens*, since the earliest uttered verbal communications of mankind are now lost to history. Over the millennia erotological representations have been in the form of spoken and recorded words, physical actions, pictures, music, dance, sculpture, 'art' of every sort, written words, photographs, movies, videos, and every other form of communication that has ever existed, or with the assistance of science and technology, ever will. The 'literature' of erotology, the written words, have been in the form of puns, one liners, jokes, riddles, acrostics, novels, short stories, anecdotes, epigrams, anagrams, ballads, songs, plays, drama, poems, fiction, non-fiction, captions, etc. In other words, every form of prose and verse has been applied to matters of sexual expression. Even mixed media, such as rebuses, have their place in the canon of erotology.

This particular book is limiting itself to what might be generically referred to as 'formal' erotic literature. By my own subjective definition this means works that have been printed and are equivalent in length to what we commonly refer to as a 'novel'. This in no way makes a value judgement as to the validity or scientific importance of ephemeral and shorter material, nor claims any superiority of one form over another for the purposes of erotological research. This decision is simply made to allow the creation of a specific original contribution to the field of erotology that will have the defined purpose of being used as an introductory text to this specific aspect of erotology. It should be remembered that as early as the fifteenth century, Antonio Beccatolli scoured the extant writings from ancient Greek and Roman times, and excerpted all found references to sexual practices. This unpublished manuscript was rediscovered in the nineteenth century by Friedrich Karl Forberg, who edited and expanded the text, added his own commentary, and published it in Latin in 1824 as *Hermaphroditus* by Panormitae. This work is best known to the world today under the title of its English translation, printed by Nichols and Smithers in 1887: *The Manual of Classical Erotology*.

For this book, selections from the *œuvre* of erotic literature have been arranged chronologically, and were chosen to be representative of the function and form of erotic literature through history. This anthology is not exhaustive in scope, nor is it meant to be. The selections demonstrate the various themes and styles that have been penned and preserved for us as erotic literature, and are extant for evaluation and analysis. While most pieces are fiction prose, allowances have been made for the various forms of literature that predominated at different periods of time. Non-prose pieces and non-fiction considered to be seminal examples of erotica were included if they equally represented the popular form of literature of their times.

The titles that have been chosen for this guide are all classics of erotica. They express in fact or fantasy the psychological and cultural content of the sexual psyche of the society that produced the text. As much as some wish to believe that the content of sexually explicit writing, and erotic literature in particular, is all fantasy, the truth is that this genre expresses the 'nuts and bolts' of daily social life, the unglamorous tasks of daily living, that is most often omitted from the conventional, 'official', formal literature of the day. Where else is to be found the historical record of personal hygiene and copulation and conception and birth, sexual colloquialisms (slang), actual sexual practices as opposed to the expressed morality of the age, libidinal fantasies, venereal health concerns, undergarments, fetishes, aphrodisiacs, and the homeopathy and folklore and distortions of the sexual impulse? This literature may be *sub rosa*, but it is from the underbelly of the mind that the motivating forces behind civilisation arise.

The original incarnation of this work, as a course curriculum, was intended to present to the academic, professional and lay communities a body of work which demonstrated what erotology was, in terms of being a serious and indispensable research discipline for all other academic disciplines to borrow from, since it is a unique repository of vital information on the physical and psychological 'facts' that have been suppressed, censored, bowdlerised and otherwise omitted in true form from other genres. Throughout history, until the mid twentieth century, it has been the rare exception where overtly explicit sexual material, visual or otherwise, has been allowed to be openly published, even in the scientific and serious medium of dissertations or studies. For example, when the extremely important and massive collection of English ballads known as *Bishop Percy's Folio* was being prepared for publication during Victorian times, the editors had to remove those pieces with sexual content, and privately publish them separately as the infamous 'fourth volume'. When the compilers of the great Oxford English Dictionary, the largest etymological and lexicographical undertaking in history, decided against including sexual slang and 'dirty words' in their 'complete' reference, it fell to John S. Farmer and William Henley to gather these common terms and privately publish their eight-volume result, *Slang and Its Analogues*, as a proper supplement to the *Oxford English Dictionary*.

Since this current book is meant to be published and widely distributed, certain unfortunate realities of our times had to be considered to avoid limitation of its distribution. Current national laws for the most part place limitations on even written depictions of sadomasochism, bestiality, anal sex, paedophilia (sex with persons under the age of legal consent) and incest. Suspected 'intent' (a purely subjective, capricious and arbitrary assessment, usually made by individuals with no special expertise in the subject matter being considered) is paramount in the decision to censor and suppress material. We are aware that all the 'banned' sexual topics are in fact descriptions of activities that occur naturally and frequently in the real world, with different levels of social and legal acceptability at different geographic locales and times in history. To discuss sexual life or sexual literature without reference to these forbidden behaviours is like trying to describe what a stew is, without any mention of the vegetables! Additionally, as mores change over the centuries, what was usual and acceptable at one time, becomes criminal at another. Current national laws make the age of sexual consent sixteen. Yet when the average lifespan for the human being was twenty-five, and not seventy-five as today, this limitation could have doomed the human species. The Old Testament reflected this when it pronounced a female ready for marriage (legal sexual intercourse) when menstruation began. This thinking is still prevalent in parts of our world today, but not in Europe or the United States. Equally, flagellation, which we contemporarily classify as a form of sadomaso-chism, was once widely and openly practised, especially for its aphrodisiac effects. Revisionist thinking and George Orwell's *Nineteen Eighty-Four* aside, the authentic writings of bygone times do not change spontane-ously to suit our current mores and laws.

To falsify or rewrite literature to satisfy temporal, and soon to change, moral and legal proscriptions is a crime against honesty, integrity and the scientific foundation upon which all proper research must be conducted. To do so would also defeat the entire purpose of this project, which is to present historical *evidence*, in the form of a body of literature, that is truthful and valid primary material for analysis to discover sexual truths that have been preserved for us over the millennia.

Practical considerations must be maintained. The extant library of erotic literature is so vast that 'mild' and legally acceptable depictions of most sexual activity (except 'kiddie porn') exist, and those have been specifically chosen for inclusion here. Where stated ages of characters would contravene legal statutes, yet the descriptions of the characters clearly indicate them to be mature, consenting adults, the ages have been simply omitted. The latitude I am allowed in making the excerpt choices to achieve the stated goal is immense. Perhaps at a later date another curriculum, to be strictly limited to recognised professionals as defined by law, will be compiled to make available for serious scientific research erotological material felt to be inappropriate for the general public, but still of extreme and vital importance to our understanding of the history, forms and expressions, social attitudes and control of actual acts and fantasies that are now considered psychopathological and sexually criminal.

Erotology, the study of things erotic (i.e. concerning sexual stimulation and activity), is solidly based in the sociology of its time. The importance of written erotological material as a research tool is that it accurately reflects the actual *sub rosa* actions and thoughts of the culture, society, or population that produced and read it. From four-thousand-year-old Egyptian papyri recording sexual dreams (replete with incest and genital mutilations) to the current 'bestsellers' list, with examples like *American Psycho*, we see that very little has actually changed in the way human beings think about and act out the sexual impulse. We know that the natural mechanisms of human reproduction, as well as the inborn instincts and neural reflexes controlling it, have not altered. Equally, the symbolic expressions of sexual thoughts and acts have altered little since the beginning of recorded history. Mankind has remained, in Freud's words, the same polymorphous perverse creature that was created by millions of years of evolution that defied any concept of morality or social control. The proof is in the records erotologists discover and elucidate. Erotic literature purely reflects the society from which it emanated; it does not shape or change it, as is the purpose of philosophical and theological texts. History researches actions, philology researches literature and language, philosophy studies thought, teleology and ontology study the origins and meanings of reality. Erotology studies all of these in their service of the libido, the life-force principle that directs mankind to preserve its species and culture.

Erotology is not abstract. It is not a hypothetical science; without people, it cannot exist (unlike mathematics, biology, physics and sciences that objectively exist, irrespective of the existence of living, breathing, conscious human beings). The richness and value of erotic literature is enhanced and more apparent when the facts of its creation are known, as well as the social circumstances in which it was nascent. The bibliography of the work is necessary for understanding the social implications of the text, and vice versa.

That is the explanation for the form I have chosen in which to present this work. Classic, representative examples of erotic literature have been chosen, and arranged in chronological order. A socio-critico-bibliographical preface is given to establish a social context for the excerpt which follows. The excerpt has been extracted from the full text of the work and may have been slightly edited (but never censored or bowdlerised or changed in context) to satisfy current standards for international distribution.

CONTENTS

1   *Sonetti Lussuriosi*, Pietro Aretino, c.1527   13

2   *The Dialogues of Luisa Sigea*, Nicholas Chorier, c.1660   23

3   *Fanny Hill*, John Cleland, 1748–49   33

4   *Gamiani, or Two Nights of Excess*
    Alcide, Baron d'M— (Alfred de Musset), 1833   54

5   *Letters produced in the Divorce Case Cavendish v. Cavendish
    and de la Rochefoucault*, 1859   62

6   *Nunnery Tales*, 1866-8   72

7   *The Ups and Downs of Life*
    Captain Edward Sellon, 1867   83

8   *Pauline the Prima Donna* I
    Wilhelmine Schroeder-Devrient (?), 1868   91

9   *Pauline the Prima Donna* II
    Wilhelmine Schroeder-Devrient (?), 1875   103

10 *The Romance of Lust*
    William Potter and Friends, 1873–6   114

11 *The Pearl*, 1879   126

12 *The Pearl: Christmas Annual*, 1881   136

13 *The Boudoir*   146

14 *The Autobiography of a Flea*, Stanislas de Rhodes, 1887   155

15 *My Secret Life*, 'Walter', 1888-94   167

16 *Parisian Frolics*, Adolphe Belot, 1889–4   187

17 *The Simple Tale of Susan Aked*, c.1892   198

18 *Teleny*, Oscar Wilde *et al.*, 1893   212

19 *Lascivious Scenes in the Convent*, 1898   225

20 *Wide Open*, Jem, 1899   238

21 *The Initiation of Aurora Trill*, 1903   248

22 *The Confessions of Marie Carey*
      George Reginald Bacchus, 1902   259

23 *The Romances of Blanche la Mare*
      George Reginald Bacchus, 1903   271

24 *The Story of Nemesis Hunt*
      George Reginald Bacchus, 1906   282

25 *Josefine Mutzenbacher*, Felix Salten, 1906   292

26 *Sadopaedia*, J. P. Kirkwood, 1907   301

27 *James Grunnert*, Werner von Bleichröder (?), 1908   313

28 *The Way of a Man with a Maid*, 1908   326

29 *Life on Board a Yacht*, 1908   338

    Bibliography   348

    Notes   350

I

Sonetti Lussuriosi

PIETRO ARETINO *c.* 1527

We don't know for sure what the first printed erotica was, although it certainly could not have predated the invention of the printing press in 1450. Many examples of the earliest printing have been lost to history, and are known today only from past references that have survived. Many incunable items were never even recorded for posterity, particularly small and ephemeral ones, such as pamphlets and single-sheet broadsides. This should not surprise us, since even today a great amount of erotica – be it paperback books, privately issued posters or flyers or chap books, printed gimmicks and ephemera of all sorts – disappears without a trace on a daily basis.

The earliest printed erotic work we have evidence for is the 1527 printing of Aretino's *Sonnets*, known in the original Italian as *Sonetti Lussuriosi*. This is an excellent place to start any discussion of erotological aspects of literature, since the sonnets' history is so fascinating and well documented. Additionally it clearly demonstrates the inter-relationship of erotic literature with art and law and politics and censorship, and even critics now and then, 450 years ago.

In the May 1989 issue of the *New York Village Voice Literary Supplement*, there was a review of the book *I Modi* by Dr Lynne Lawner. Dr Lawner's book discussed specific items of sixteenth-century sexually explicit art by the Italians Giulio Romano and Marcantonio Raimondi, and the equally explicit sonnets written to accompany them by Pietro Aretino, which together had come to be known over the years colloquially as 'Aretino's Postures'.

The reviewer remarked that *I Modi* (as he chose to call the illustrated sixteenth-century first edition of Aretino's work) was 'the premier strokebook of Western culture'. This is a rather crass insult of the lowest order, especially since no matter what one thinks of the content and craftsmanship of *I Modi*'s text and art, reference was still being made to the first illustrated printed erotic book in Western civilisation. While certainly no Gutenberg Bible, it was none the less a milestone in the history of man and his mind.

To set the record straight, a brief history of the work in question is called for. About 1523 Giulio Romano, the main *protégé* of the then recently deceased Raphael, drew sixteen scenes of human sexual intercourse on the walls of the Sala di Costantino, in the Vatican. Legend has it this was done in anger over Pope Clement VII's slowness in paying for the commissioned art he was finishing, in his capacity as Raphael's successor. Equally Romano could actually have been commissioned to paint erotic scenes as Raphael and his students had already done for the bathroom of Cardinal Bibbiena in the Vatican Palace in 1515. Whatever, Marcantonio Raimondi was called upon to make copperplate engravings of this art (which are correctly called *I Modi* [The Manners or Postures]). The art historian Vasari reported that Raimondi was directed to make twenty engraved plates, indicating that perhaps he was also to make copies of other sexually explicit art Romano was known to have painted. (Numerous artists of the time did such erotic work, usually on mythological themes or under the broad heading of 'Loves of the Gods'. Raimondi is himself responsible for a large *œuvre* of erotic and sexually explicit engravings). The *Sedici Modi* (sixteen postures) appeared for sale in 1524, and aroused the ire of Cardinal Giberti, who ordered all copies of the plates and prints destroyed and had Raimondi imprisoned; Romano had previously escaped to Mantua. In 1525, Aretino, a scabrous wit and confidant of the rich and powerful, saw a set of Raimondi's sixteen engravings, and wrote a series of matching graphic sonnets to suit them. Entitled *Sonetti Lussuriosi* (Wanton Sonnets) these appeared in print, illustrated, by November of 1527, according to one of Aretino's own letters. There is no physical description of this 1527 book, except for Aretino's remark that the sonnets appeared at the foot of each page, below their corresponding illustrations.

The reviewer further stated of this (in)famous and legendary work: 'yet only a few years ago it was thought to be lost forever'. How could this be? Under the titles of *Sonetti Lussuriosi*, *Corona di Cazzi* (The Crown of Cocks) or *Dubii Amorosi* (Dubious Love), Aretino's text was reprinted in 1556, 1735, 1757, 1779, 1792, 1864, 1865, 1882, 1904, 1921, 1926 and many more times since, and probably several other times before. It had been translated into many languages (with Oscar Wilde getting undue credit for the first English translation!). The text had in fact expanded over the years from sixteen to thirty-one sonnets attributed to Aretino, and had appeared in print accompanied by various illustrations, few matching what are now known to be the *Sonetti*'s original artwork. As for the Romano/Raimondi art, both the Bibliothèque Nationale and the Vienna Museum have a single complete etching from the 1524 printing. The British Museum also has nine fragments from the 1524 prints, with a provenance traceable to 1775. J. T. Smith's 1829 biography *Nollekens and His Times* reports that Mr Nollekens had a set of the original prints, and that his confessor forced him to destroy them. The French sculptor Gerard had eleven original prints which *c.*1808 were sold via Samuel Woodburn to an English duke; these were reported burned after his lordship's death, however not before tracings of them had been made, which in 1843 were seen by Count de Waldeck, who himself in 1858 produced a suite of twenty pen-and-wash drawings (sets now in the British Museum and the Bibliothèque Nationale) which he claimed were based on a set of the original Raimondi engravings he had seen in a Mexico City convent! (Actually not so impossible when one considers the number of Europeans in Mexico before the overthrow and execution of the Emperor Maximilian in 1867.) As ten of the Waldeck pieces exactly correspond to the earliest known *Sonetti* art, the Count must have seen at least some originals or excellent copies of Raimondi's work. And finally, as of 1929, we have had a genuine sixteenth-century woodcut-illustrated example of this fabulous book.

What was thought to be lost could only have been an actual copy of the genuine first edition of the *Sonetti*, with illustrations based on the Romano paintings. The great bibliographers Brunet, Graesse and Ebert all mention that in 1781 the Dresden Royal Library destroyed a copy of the Aretino sonnets, which contained 'engravings'. Was this a 1527 'first' edition, or a later copy with tipped-in plates? The question became academic with the discovery of a unique surviving genuine sixteenth-century edition, described by Max Sanders in 1929, and for years in the collection of the late Walter Toscanini, and now in the library of a European collector. This is the Rosetta Stone for the Aretino mystery, yet Kendrick insultingly dismissed this important tome by pronouncing, sight unseen, 'without doubt an early-sixteenth-century product, Toscanini's prize [is] a crude rip-off . . . '! He wrote further concerning the 1524 Raimondi engravings, 'before long a second edition appeared containing pictures and poems together', obviously what the reviewer believed to be a different genuine first edition of the *Sonetti*, predating the Toscanini volume, although no one has ever produced an actual copy of such, or even a description that would not equally fit the 1929 find!

The former Toscanini copy, when rediscovered, was bound with three other *c.*1531 Italian pornographic works. The typography, paper and style of the 1929 find are consistent with a 1527 production date for the *Sonetti*. The primitive printing of the illustrations (woodcuts which are reversed right to left from the Raimondi originals), as well as the crude printing of the text below them is all in keeping with the surreptitious printing of a book still being actively condemned. It has long been a practice for *sub-rosa* publishers to reproduce pornographic art by tracing the original and cutting the tracing directly into a new block for their own use. Hence the images become reversed.

A further indication of the contempt in which the reviewer held this entire matter was his description of bibliophiles as 'those rare, quaint creatures who drool over books as precious objects'. Equally stupid was his conclusion: 'Whatever Giulio's and Marcantonio's intentions may have been, Aretino's were explicit: just as the artists' presumed lust turned him on, so the combination of pictures and poems aims to turn on the reader, to encourage performance of the engraved and sonnetised acts.'

A reading of the facts concerning this wonderful story make the primary players' intentions quite clear. Romano was either acting out of pique or just doing his job. Raimondi wanted to make some money. Aretino, in one of his letters, clearly states that he dashed off the sonnets as *jeux d'esprit* (i.e. for fun). In the same letter he states that the Raimondi engravings made him feel 'the same inspiration which moved Giulo Romano to draw them'. That may have been anger (over the hypocrites who had caused the art's suppression, or patrons who failed to pay promptly) or it could have been for the mere wit of it; certainly lust was not Romano's incentive for drawing the original *I Modi*. To accuse Aretino of having, in Kendrick's words, 'used a book as a sexual instrument' is to fail to understand the man Aretino. His vitriolic pen and scathing social commentary had earned him the title of 'Scourge of Princes' and at least one assassination attempt. Aretino was to the Renaissance what John Wilmot (the Earl of Rochester) was to Restoration England – a *bon vivant*, companion and intimate of the highest and lowest society, and a man who was at his most effective in verse, obscene if necessary.

To attempt to reduce Aretino's *Sonetti Lussuriosi* and its attendant art to 'a book as a sexual instrument' is an act of cultural vandalism. It ignores its original historical context. Its explicit sexuality sharpened its bite as social criticism, and added to its enjoyment as sophisticated entertainment. The most appropriate comment on Kendrick's criticism of *I Modi* is the motto of the British Order of the Garter: *Honi soit qui mal y pense* (Shame on him who thinks evil of this).

Here follow excerpts from Aretino's *Sonnets*, which are in the form of on-going dialogues between lovers.

from *Sonnetti Lussuriosi*

Sonnet 1

Fuck me, dearest, one quick fuck,
Since we were born to fuck,
And you adore cock, like I love cunt,
And a world without cock play is a meaningless nothing.

And if fucking were possible after death,
I'd demand that we fuck ourselves to death,
So as to fuck Eve and Adam,
Who 'died the dishonest death'.

Yet had those miscreants never fallen,
By not eating the Apple of Tradition
Lovers still would lust on earth.

But let's shut up; satisfy my lust;
Fill me to the core with your cock,
For that is the nature of all animals.

Let's go to it, let's take care of your cunt,
And don't leave out my balls, which will testify to our
    ecstasy.

Sonnet 2

Press your finger into my arsehole, dearest,
And put your cock in me little by little.
Lift up my leg, make a fancy move,
And pound me worthy of your reputation.

This is indeed a worthier banquet,
Than sitting by the fire eating garlicky bread,
And if my cunt isn't good enough for you,
Then why not try a little sodomy?

I'll take you cunt-wise this time,
But next time in your arse; cock in cunt *and* arse will go,
With beastly furious delight we'll play.

It is a foolish dim wit
Who doesn't realise it a waste of time
Unless a thing concerns fucking.

So I'll settle in your pretty box
And remain until I'm done,
No matter how much you try to uncock me.

Sonnet 3

This cock is priceless,
You'll not find a royal jewel more endearing.
This cock would satisfy a Queen,
And is more valuable than gold.

Save me cock, I am dying,
Touch me to the very womb,
To such an end a small prick is useless
Properly to serve a cunt.

Such true words, my patroness,
Whoever tries to fuck a cunt with a small prick
Deserves an ice-water enema.

A small prick should only fuck an arse,
But those with a macho one like me
Need a big juicy cunt.

But we are insatiable,
So take cock any which way we can
And have our fun, both front side and back.

Sonnet 4

Put your leg on my shoulder,
And stick my cock in your cunt,
And while I gently move in and out,
Draw me tightly to your breast.

And if I slip from cunt to arse,
Call me whatever vile names you wish,
Since I know that difference as well
As a stallion knows what to do with a mare in heat.

My hand will keep your cock in place,
Lest it slip, but you'd know that
By the dirty look on my face.

They say only one enjoys a bum-fuck,
While its shared enjoyment the other way ,
So let's do it that way, and quickly.

Like Hell, my dear, I'm in no rush,
I wouldn't leave this screwing
Even to save the King of France.

Sonnet 6

My cock is in your cunt, and your arsehole is in my
    sight,
And I look at your arse and see how fat it is.
Think me a maniac if you wish,
Since I have my hands where my feet should be.

If you think this mode of fucking worthy
Of but beasts, it doesn't bother me,
Because it makes it just as easy also to fuck you,
With your chest clasped to mine;

I long to fuck just by the letter,
With your arsehole tantalised by a thousand touches
From my fingers, and cock, and tool,

So you shall reveal in grand delight,
That none shall have such sweet gratification,
Not Ladies, nor Duchesses, nor even the Queen,

And immediately at the finale
You'll applaud my masterful skills,
Although my then small prick will bother me.

Sonnet 7

Where are you straying, kindly say,
To the back or front to give pleasure?
Perchance I slip it to the rear,
Would you be unhappy if you were cocked up the arse?

My dear Lady, no, but because the cunt satisfies
The cock, may not a smaller penetrator
Work on your bottom, so I don't appear
To be gratifying myself like a Fra Mariano?

But if you prefer to be stuffed with cock up your arse,
Rather than with less grand contents,
Then satisfy yourself with me as you wish.

Squeeze it with your hand, place it behind,
You won't hurt yourself by accident,
But it may hurt a bit at first,

And I declare to the deities,
As I feel my cock in your hand,
I'll die if we don't end in a real fuck.

The Dialogues of Luisa Sigea

NICHOLAS CHORIER c.1660

Printed erotica as we know it today did not suddenly materialise *de novo*. Rather, 'dirty books', as they are wont to be called, are the product of tens of thousands of years of erotological evolution and technological advances. The very first erotica is lost to us in history. Whether it was a drawing or a mere scratching on stone or bark or in earth or sand we can only guess.

We know from extant objects and records that long before the printing press and Aretino's *Sonnets*, erotica was created, collected and produced commercially. Prehistoric wall drawings and erotic figurines survive from the age of cave men. The Roman emperor Tiberius collected erotic art, and especially loved 'old' Egyptian papyri that his agents scoured the known world to find (or had made to his order). The erotic art and artifacts from turn-of-the-millennium Pompeii and equally from twelve hundred years later (which demonstrated the rediscovery of the nude and erotic human form in the Renaissance) are further proof that erotica had not changed much in content or form over those centuries.

Then as now there was censorship and a sense of 'pornography', that is art or literature felt to be morally unacceptable or legally indictable because of its sexual content. The ancient Greek plays of Elephantis and Aristophanes were censored because of their licentiousness and open sexuality. Numerous ithyphallic objects from past times were destroyed, or sequestered in secret and restricted collections if their value as cultural heritage was recognised and appreciated.

The author Walter Kendrick in his May 1989 *New York Village Voice Literary Supplement* essay on Aretino's *Sonnets* stated that 'it was the middle of the eighteenth century when the modern concept of pornography was born'. This is obviously not true, as already discussed, although that is the time when the modern concept of the erotic novel was developed.

Prior to the 1700s, erotic literature appeared exclusively in written forms not as common to us today. Sex appeared in the Greek dramas, the songs of Bilitis, the poetry of Sappho, the scabrous epigrams of Martial and Juvenal, the histories of Suetonius and Petronius, the legends and myths of ancient deities and heroes, and the erotic fertility rites of all cultures.

Contemporary with Aretino's 1527 erotically illustrated sexual sonnets, there were long erotic verses and character libels, such as the *c.*1531 *La Puttana Errante*, *Il Manganello*, *La Zaffetta* and *Processus contra ser Catium Vinculum.*

The seventeenth century saw a new form for erotica, the dialogue, that is back and forth conversation between characters, usually an older instructing woman and a younger female eager to learn the secrets of love. These early-seventeenth-century dialogues frequently occurred in the setting of a brothel. The most famous of these were *La Retorica delle Puttante* (1642), a 1650 prose version of the earlier mentioned *La Puttana Errante*, *L'Ecole des Filles* (1655) and *Aloisae Sigeae* (1660). All of these were translated quickly into other languages, including English.

Of all these, the latter, known in English translation as *The Dialogues of Luisa Sigea*, was a high, or rather a low, point in the concept of pornography. Where the other works were matter of fact and instructive, even to the point of emphasising romance, sexual ecstasy, mutual physical satisfaction, and genuine erotic emotional warmth, *Luisa Sigea* took a different turn. Written *c.*1659 in Latin by the French lawyer and author Nicholas Chorier, it presented itself to be an erudite translation by the great Dutch historian Joannes Meursius of a lost Spanish manuscript by a woman named Luisa Sigea. (This subterfuge was quite necessary as just four years before the author of *L'Ecole des Filles* had been sentenced to death *in absentia*, hung and burned in effigy with copies of his book, and had his property confiscated because of his erotica). Chorier obviously sought to avoid a similar fate.

The Dialogues of Luisa Sigea was in the form of seven extended conversations between an older (twenty-six year-old) married woman, Tullia, and her soon-to-be-married young naïve friend Ottavia. It contained not only 'marriage manual' information, but a great deal of erotic fantasy material as well, especially of a perverse and mean-spirited sexual nature. Atypical of earlier erotic works, the speakers here not only discussed sexual matters, but acted out the sex, between themselves and with the aid of additional male lovers. Like a modern soap opera, sexual improprieties concerning parents and relatives and close friends were disclosed in a most shocking manner. There were strong sadistic tones to this work, and it well foreshadowed the grimness of Victorian pornography of two centuries later.

One wonders if the impetus and inclination of *The Dialogues of Luisa Sigea* were purely the machinations of a single mind, the author's, or more universally reflected a growing pan-European libertinism that was developing after the fall of decades of Puritan hypocrisy. Whatever the case, written erotica lost its innocence and was never the same again.

Here is an episode from *The Dialogues of Luisa Sigea* in which Tullia recounts her wedding night with her husband Callias, and gives a lecture of seventeenth-century sex facts so that Ottavia will know what to expect from her fiancé, Caviceo.

◁ from *The Dialogues of Luisa Sigea*

OTTAVIA: Ah! Ah! Ah! Tullia, how thou didst throw thyself madly upon me! Oh, had the gods but changed thee into a man!

TULLIA: Thy husband will, in the very same way, throw himself upon thee stretched with outspread thighs. He will besiege thy mouth with kisses; he will suck these plumpy paps; he will press his breast against thy breast; he will squeeze and shake thee all over, but much harder than I could, as he is both stronger and far more lustier than I am. There will arise such agitation that the bed in which thou wilt be lying will creak, aye, and even the very floor. The first night Callias deflowered me, he went at it with such impetus, rushing upon me with so much bodily force, that my bed was heard straining by those who were sitting up feasting to my marriage in the next room. See how I fared in that struggle, out of which I nevertheless came victorious.

OTTAVIA: What will become of me if I chance to encounter so rude a champion? For when thou wast handed over to Callias's enjoyment, thou wast older and thy person more developed than I am now. I clearly see there is a dreadful torture awaiting me.

TULLIA: I will not deny, Ottavia, that thou hast to endure a lot of hardships. Were I to deny it, I would of course be making a sham of thy inexperience.

OTTAVIA: Carefully teach me whatever it behooves me to know. What will that suffering be like? How keen will it be, and how long will it last? Of course I would rather it were quick for a while, than moderate and enduring.

TULLIA: No. Except the first night, thou wilt feel no pain. All suffering in love, if thou knowest how to bear it, is light.

OTTAVIA: To be sure I shall bear it, and I hope courageously and resolutely. What else would I do? But now what will I have to endure?

TULLIA: The Latins and our contemporaries generally call that part of our person, about which we have already spoken, *vulva*, *cunnus*, *fregna*, *fica* and *potta*. *Vulva*, as if they meant valve; *cunnus* from *cuneus*, a wedge, because great force must be exerted to drive into it on the first assaults. I have read in an old grammarian that the lips which enclose it are called *cadurda*. Into this spot Caviceo will first thrust his huge lance with all his might. He will in this moment cause thee great suffering, but shortly after, still greater joys.

OTTAVIA: May the joys speedily, very speedily, make the pain be forgotten!

TULLIA: Thou beholdest its marvellous structure. It first bulges out with a certain protuberance, which a light down covers. Do not fancy it is concealed between the thighs for shame's sake, of which it is utterly devoid, but it is set there for use. They style this protuberance the hillock of Venus. Whoever has once climbed it, my dear Ottavia, prefers it ever after to the Parnassus, Olympus or the sacred hills.

OTTAVIA: That I had a climber as pleasant as thou art! I should not then have to envy Parnassus its Apollo or Olympus its Jupiter.

TULLIA: There are two slits, the one under the other, through which this hillock opens to a full coition. They call the first, the large one; the second is the interior one. The former is suitable for bringing forth. We are indeed, Ottavia, workshops in which the human race is manufactured. If it were narrower, the foetus, on seeing the light of day, could not be extended without horrible suffering. It must be both extended and dilated. When youths are allowed to make free with this place, they fancy women are really as wide inwardly as they are at this outer gate, and I have seen some that were stupefied, the jacks. But the inner one is narrower. I have already stated that the lips which cover the edges of the broader slit are called *cadurda*. Inside this slit, namely, the more hidden one, there are wings. They are very prominent in me. These they call nymphs. But in maidens, such as thou art, there rise four sorts of little valves under the wings. These stop up the way to the uterus, which man, in his first encounters, does not free to his lustful desire without a deal of force and trouble.

OTTAVIA: I anticipate it. The severity of the whole pain will consist in that effort thou hast been speaking of.

TULLIA: Allow me to finish my description. As these four membranes are joined together, they end in a pipe somewhat in the shape of a clove. But they do not run, as if drawn, over the cross route of the uterus. Being erect, they shoot forwards towards the outer gate of the garden. They occasionally gape, however, in an upward direction.

The excretions which nature forces out of our bodies are ejected by this route. But I have forgotten to speak about the clitoris. This is a membranous body situated almost at the bottom of the pubis, and resembles a kind of cock. It stiffens up, as if it were a cock, at any amorous desire. It inflames rather sensible-natured women with so keen an itching that, if excited unto pleasure by drawing the hand near it, they generally spill of their own free will, without awaiting a rider. Of course I have experienced this pretty often whilst Callias is sprinkling me with his lubricities, whilst he is fondling me and toying with the thing itself. A copious, dewy sap falls from my garden into his hands whilst he is playing too freely in these localities. Hence the rich harvest of gibes he has to fling at me, and the wide plain for jesting. But how can I help it? He breaks out in loud mirth. I simply laugh. I chide him for his anger, he rebukes me for my wantonness. We are each the laughing-stock of the other. While thus bickering, he bounces in good earnest upon me, lays me flat whether I will or no, bestrides me stretched on the bed and, playing the wag because my garden had dropped that moisture, he gives me back a lot out of his own, that I may not have to complain for having lost any through his fault.

OTTAVIA: You are both leading a happy life and full of delights. You amply suffice for each other's happiness.

TULLIA: Well, that road extending from the entrance to the bottom of the garden is called the sheath. The rod is introduced into it the moment the woman receives the shock. Doctors termed it, at one time, collar, neck of the uterus; at another, bosom of pudency. It envelops, squeezes and sucks the virile member once driven into and set in this sheath. It is, Ottavia, a kind of tube through which the human race passes from the utter darkness of nothing to the light of day.

OTTAVIA: Thou describest the thing so well that methinks I behold in person all that is concealed in my innermost bowels, as if it were placed before my eyes.

TULLIA: This inner slit, friend, and that winding passage which precedes it are narrower in thee than in me. Well, now, I loathe thoroughly to scrutinise these things with steadfast gaze. Spread thy legs out as wide as ever thou canst conveniently do so.

OTTAVIA: Here. They are open. What design hast thou then upon me with these naughty eyes of thine? Thou art pulling these lips over on each side with thy fingers. What dost thou see inside?

TULLIA: Sweet maid! I behold a flower. Whoever will see it will prefer it to every other flower and smell.

OTTAVIA: Ah! Tullia, pray do withdraw thy lewd hand. Take away that cursed finger, which thou art sticking into me.

TULLIA: I pity thee, precious conch, fitter for conceiving Venus than was that conch out of which we are told Venus sprang! Under what lucky auspices Caviceo was born, he to whom a new Venus will spring from this conch!

OTTAVIA: And still thou sayest thou pitiest me.

TULLIA: Aye, I behold thee going to be lacerated in a deplorable way.

OTTAVIA: What will become of it? Why dost thou wonder?

TULLIA: Thy garden is opened by a very small gate, and it presents a narrow inlet. I fear that there devolves on Caviceo a task which, however acceptable it be, will be more burdensome than pleasing. Thou hast seen his catapult with which he is to cleave this redoubt of thine?

OTTAVIA: I have not seen it but, by Castor, I have felt it. It is such as they figure the club of Hercules: fat, stiff and of respectable length.

TULLIA: Thy mother told me that he was admirably well furnished, so she is exceedingly glad of it. She thinks there is not a single man in our town better set off than he. I answered her, while thus bragging, that my husband's dagger was eight finger breadths in length. She replied that he is a man of nothing at all compared to Caviceo. She pities and at the same time envies thee thy lot. She congratulates thee exceedingly on it. She says that Caviceo's tool is eleven inches long and as thick as thy arm at the place it is joined to the hand.

OTTAVIA: O prodigy! And he will forcibly drive the whole of this monster into my person? Can I endure it? My heart is already sinking, as it occurs to my mind how many calamities are awaiting wretched me.

TULLIA: Yet do not lose heart. Callias yields it in length to Caviceo, but as to thickness, Caviceo certainly does not surpass Callias. For thou seest this arm of mine?

OTTAVIA: I do, by Pollux! I should be blind if I did not see it.

TULLIA: His dagger swells out as big as this when it gets angry with me. Well, now this dagger fits nicely in my sheath.

OTTAVIA: I should like then to know what that victorious and fulminating sheath of thine resembles.

TULLIA: Fleas differ not more widely from chicks than mine from thine. Here it is: inspect, view, explore.

OTTAVIA: Throw thyself on the bed and get upon thy back, for I can not see properly when thou art seated.

TULLIA: I am stretched. Examine everything closely. It will be of use to thee as well as a pleasure for me.

OTTAVIA: I behold a chasm! It is like the one which engulfed Curtius, swallowing him down loaded with his arms and mounted on his steed! I shall put my hand to it and pull the edges aside. I am pleased with putting my finger in, since it is that of Venus, to run it over all this plain, however vast it is, and ascertain its breadth, depth and ease for the rod. Well! It would suit Priapus himself! Or anybody else better supplied than Priapus. But a nasty wind rises to my nose. What bad-smelling flowers this garden of thine bears! Venus herself would be most displeased to have a garland or a crown made for her out of them.

TULLIA: Thou art merry, dear maid, and art jesting. Thou, too, wilt be as I am now. Within a few months after, thou wilt have an immense opening, as thou beholdest in me. This lower fundament of thy uterus will gape, as mine is gaping now. Thou, whose breathing is as pure in this mouth as in the other, wilt stifle my nose with a noxious smell, and thou wilt infect my hand if it touches thee. These are the inconveniences of marriage, they are the over plus of our pleasures. Aye, it will be so, doubt it not.

OTTAVIA: How may that be? I long to know.

TULLIA: When that member of man has developed to its full size, it penetrates our person with such rage that it sullies, contaminates and pollutes the whole locale.

OTTAVIA: But be not unmindful of thy questant. I am coming to the question. Now, those women who love and have had experience brag in different tones of that virile part which is so intractable and hasty.

TULLIA: None has tasted it without loving it.

OTTAVIA: I shall be therefore mad in love with it when I have tasted it?

TULLIA: Wonderfully so. The Latins call it *veretrum, mentula, penis, phallus, taurus, machaera, pessulus, peculium, vas, vasculum, pomum, nervus, hasta, trabs, palus, muto, verpa, colei, scapus, caulis, virga, pilum, fascinum, cauda, mutinus, noctuinus, columna* – titles taken partly in their proper sense, partly in a figurative sense. Outside the venereal act, man's nerve lies inert and hanging, but for this act it stiffens, swells out, rages, increasing to such a size that it first strikes into us desperate awe. It soon causes maidens a keen pain, but afterwards the supreme voluptuousness of the deflowered one, which by far surpasses the fear.

OTTAVIA: I am ignorant of the voluptuousness, nor do I care to know the suffering. I feel but the fear.

TULLIA: Below the rod and adhering to its basis, there is a little purse. They call it scrotum. It is covered over and concealed by many crisped and shaggy hairs. The witnesses of manhood reside within it, and these are the beneficent witnesses of men's love towards us.

OTTAVIA: I have neither seen nor heard of these witnesses. Explain what they are like.

TULLIA: They are two balls, not too small either, not quite round, but extremely hard. The harder they are, the more suited they are for pleasure. Owing to their being two, the Greeks call them *didyms*, and many great heroes have borne this name. There were some to whom nature, in her munificence, discerned one more, so that they had three. Lucky are the wives they possess! For there is in the windings of the testicles a sort of fabric of that ambrosial dew, which charms us so graciously and cures so wonderfully the wounds which the virile member made on entering our person, so that they hurt us no longer. I am indebted to this dew for my little daughter. I also owe it all my joys. The human race is indebted to it for its existence. They commonly call it seed and sperm, the one of Latin and the other of Greek origin. Once this seed is cast into the female furrow, it is soon formed into a man. Of all animals, man casts out the greatest supply of seed, but those who have three operators engaged at it, as, for instance, Fulvio, the brother of my friend Pomponia, flood of course the woman with a still greater quantity than those who have only two.

OTTAVIA: Perhaps Caviceo has also three. He thus sprinkled me all over with a shower of that dew, almost up to the navel, wetting my shift.

TULLIA: It would be shameful of a lusty youth enamoured of thy beauty, friend, to offer a libation to thee and thy love, leaving thy vases dry. Let me go on with the remainder. This frothy, white, slimy liquor – the spittle of the virile member – is conveyed from the very spot it is cooked in, to the extreme top of the rod, and is then shot out with such impetuosity that it flies three feet away from him who shoots it. Therefore, when the work is achieved, after much digging, it is cast so promptly into the bottom of the uterus that there are no women, unless they are of perfectly benumbed nature who, once they are drenched by this burning shower, do not feel a sharp itching of voluptuousness. Ottavia, I cannot sufficiently describe in words this enjoyment you will feel. Thou wilt tell it to thyself in a few hours' time.

OTTAVIA: It is from the extreme end of the rod these milky rivers flow? I shall not indeed deny that he had a head, he who ceased to reside among the Lampascians because he was too largely supplied, or rather to be near the goddesses, as I have learned from thee. But I was not even aware there was a head on men's members. I did not know that each man has two heads, fool that I am.

TULLIA: And these would be perfectly happy and fortunate, and would enjoy supreme glory among heroes, had they also three feet! They call the extreme part of the penis, being oblong, head, *balanus*, glans. If thou squeezes it between the tops of thy fingers, far from doing it the slightest harm, thou wouldst cause the most pleasing sensation. When thou wilt be burning, excited by thy lover, thou wilt induce Caviceo to satisfy thy Venus by no shorter way, even were he taken up by thoughts exceedingly remote from like desires. And this head of Priapus is covered with a cap. They call it the prepuce. He scarcely ever takes it off, unless it be to salute and present himself bareheaded at his lady's court.

OTTAVIA: Thou art amazing, nor would I be ever satiated on listening to thee. Would to God it may be so likewise with Callias sleeping beside thee!

TULLIA: My eyes are closing with sleep. Dear Ottavia, I am no good for bearing such prolonged vigilance as you require of me. And thou toldst me what thou hast said, only after having hinted that I was dozing during the conversation we had about these questions of what pertains to man and wife.

OTTAVIA: Pray, be not sleepy, friend. Listen to one who is beguiling thee so pleasantly.

TULLIA: By thy Venus and mine, as also by Caviceo's! Thou has greater need of sleep than I. Tomorrow night thou wilt not sleep a wink, in the midst of Caviceo's embraces, kisses, squeezes and madness. Repose thy body, so tender, so soft. Prepare thyself boldly to meet this strife.

OTTAVIA: I shall do as thou wishest, but I care more about thy health than my own. Go asleep now.

TULLIA: Give me a kiss. It will be my *viaticum* for rest.

OTTAVIA: I offer thee my mouth, lips and my whole person. Take of me whatever pleasures thou wilt.

TULLIA: O the kisses that Jupiter would envy me! O the delightful embraces! O the seducing handlings! Allow me to fall asleep so, with my mouth laid between thy paps, one hand placed upon thy garden, the other grasping those hard and compact thighs. When I shall be freed from sleep, I shall resume my discourse, and with the same truthfulness as I began, I shall finish what remains over and above, darling maid, my lady.

OTTAVIA: Thou hast more to say than is necessary. Hold thy tongue and go asleep. Do what thou art doing.

~ 3 ~

Fanny Hill

JOHN CLELAND 1748–9

The most famous erotic novel in the English language is without doubt John Cleland's *Memoirs of a Woman of Pleasure*, more popularly known as just *Fanny Hill*. Since its first London publication in 1748–9, it has been more frequently reprinted, illustrated, translated, and prosecuted than any other erotica in recorded history. It was even the first book banned in the USA (Commonwealth *v.* Holmes, 17 Mass. 336 [1821])! The book's true origin is a bit obscure, as is the life of the author, who was born in 1707, entered college (Westminster School) at thirteen, graduated and served as a British consul in Izmir (Turkey), and then went with the East India Company to Bombay, before trouble with certain officers in India forced him to return to England, where he had difficulty finding work to support himself. It is said that he sold his erotic novel *Fanny Hill* to the publisher Fenton Griffiths in 1748 to raise money to get himself out of debtors' prison. The book may however have been written ten years or so prior to that, as the records of The Most Ancient and Puissant Order of the Beggar's Benison, an eighteenth-century Scottish sex club for gentry, noted that in 1737, on St Andrew's Day, '*Fanny Hill* was read' before the assemblage. Legend has it that Cleland originally wrote the book to win a wager that he could write an erotic novel without the use of even a single obscene or tabooed word. If this anecdote is true, Cleland would have won the bet.

Within one year of the first printing of *Memoirs of a Woman of Pleasure* (1748–9), a warrant was issued for the arrest of the author, who in the meanwhile had abridged the book to remove a sodomy scene that was thought to have started the novel's legal troubles. This reissue appeared in 1750 under the title of *Memoirs of Fanny Hill*. Brought before the British Privy Council, Cleland pleaded poverty as his only motive for writing the book, and supposedly was given a government pension for life on the condition that he never again author such a volume. Cleland apparently kept his pension until his death in 1789 for his later novel *Memoirs of a Coxcomb* and his translation into English of *Maria Brown* caused no outcries of moral indignation.

What is it that has made *Fanny Hill* such a classic? It certainly was not the first erotic book in English – the Restoration period of a century before had seen a plethora of erotic and obscene books, not the least being Pallavacino's *The Whore's Rhetorick* (1683), and John Wilmot's *Sodom* (1684). Less objectionable bawdy and licentious works preceded Cleland's novel by a score, including Defoe's *Moll Flanders* (1722) and Fielding's *Tom Jones* (1749). *Fanny Hill* can't even be considered the first English 'modern novel', as Richardson's *Pamela* (1740) has received this honour. Thousands of erotic, obscene and pornographic novels have followed Cleland's yet his remains the most famous.

In the strictest etymological sense, *Fanny Hill* is a 'pornographic' book, for it satisfies the definition of being 'writing by or about prostitutes' (from the Greek *porne* = prostitute and *graphos* = writing). Yet, as already noted, it contains no obscene or objectionable words. It is a fairly typical eighteenth-century English novel in construction, being in the form of two long letters purporting to tell the history of the narrator and chief protagonist, Francis Hill.

The basic story is the oldest romantic plot in history – boy meets girl, boy loses girl, boy finds girl again and lives happily ever after. However, here the story is told from the woman's perspective. Fanny is an unsophisticated country girl who, when orphaned, travels to London to seek employment. Unbeknownst to her, she is engaged by a lecherous bawd who tries to sell Fanny's virginity to a particularly loathsome creature. This fate is escaped with the aid of a handsome young man, with whom Fanny falls in love, and lives with until he is shanghaied by his own father. To support herself she becomes a rich man's mistress, but is sent packing when she is caught in bed with her footman, an act of revenge on her part for finding her lover in bed with her maid! Back in London she takes up life in a stylish and well-kept brothel, where she forms close friendships with the madame and her fellow working girls. They share with each other their sexual experiences and life stories, and here Fanny observes and participates in the entire gamut of eighteenth-century sexual life. She finally retires to the country with her considerable savings, platonically befriends an old gentleman who dies and leaves her his vast estate, and as a wealthy woman finds her first love, just recently returned from years overseas. They marry and settle into domestic felicity.

The importance of *Fanny Hill*, beyond its entertainment value, is that it is one of the finest examples of erotic realism in the English language. Its sex scenes are numerous, and quite detailed, without being coarse or vulgar. Its characters are not the products of hyperbole; they are completely believable in their humanness. Their actions and motivations and reactions are those of any normal person in the same social and economic situation. They have their foibles, but their virtues as well. Above all the protagonists have compassion. They have human needs and they exercise them as nature, if not the law, meant them to. Sexual performances do not strain credulity. Youth has vigour the old lack; the array of sexual preferences displayed in the brothel (fetishes, flagellation, sadomasochism, etc.) are the exact same interests we know still exist today. Cleland needed not be a trained psychiatrist like Krafft-Ebing to present the *psychopathia sexualis* of his day, he needed only to be a careful observer and an accurate recorder of daily life. And that he was.

In Cleland's novel are scenes of utter hilarity, e.g. humorous activity emanating from self-deluded individuals attempting feats of sexual proficiency beyond their physical capabilities. Equally there are scenes of grim, dark sexual reality, e.g. episodes of sadomasochism (that cannot be printed here) and the infamous homosexual sodomy scene that caused the book's first prosecution in 1749.

John Cleland's *Memoirs of a Woman of Pleasure* is a literary classic, as relevant to modern readers as it was to its original audience nearly 250 years ago. Erotic realism – the ability accurately and honestly to portray human sexual experience – is what sets *Fanny Hill* apart from the bulk of erotic, 'sexy' and pornographic fiction penned through the ages. On the title page of the 1750 second edition of *Fanny Hill* the author placed the following words: 'If I have painted Vice in its gayest Colours, if I have deck'd it with Flowers, it has been solely in order to make the worthier, the solemner Sacrifice of it to Virtue.' This is an apt epitaph for a novel that recounted the good, the bad and the ugly (physically and philosophically) of eighteenth-century English sexual life.

We present here episodes from the experiences of Francis Hill. The first occurs while she is being kept as the mistress of an older gentleman, with an affliction quite similar to that of a recently disgraced television preacher (the Jimmy Swaggart sex scandal), a peccadillo that drives her in frustration into a spontaneous *liaison* that

causes concern among her friends – 'safe sex' not being the concern of
the present generation exclusively. The second episode involves perhaps the first description in fiction of the medical condition known as
'adrenogenital syndrome', in which diminished intellectual capacity is
coupled with hypertrophied sexual endowment. The last selection
from *Fanny Hill* reprints one of the book's lighter moments, when
Fanny, living in a brothel, espies the madame of the establishment, a
woman well beyond her physical prime, who has decided to treat
herself to the services of a handsome and well-endowed soldier. The
scene is not only comic, but so stimulating that it induces the voyeur to
masturbation, further voyeurism, and a lesbian encounter.

⌒ from *Fanny Hill*

I was now restored again to my former state of a kept mistress, and
used punctually to wait on Mr Norbert at his chambers whenever he
sent a messenger for me, which I constantly took care to be in the way
of, and managed with so much caution, that he never once penetrated
the nature of my connections with Mrs Cole; but indolently given up
to ease and the town dissipations, the perpetual hurry of them hindered
him from looking into his own affairs, much less to mine.

In the meantime, if I may judge from my own experience, none are
better paid, or better treated, during their reign, than the mistresses of
those who, enervated by nature, debaucheries, or age, have the least
employment for the sex: sensible that a woman must be satisfied some
way, they ply her with a thousand little tender attentions, presents,
caresses, confidences, and exhaust their inventions in means and
devices to make up for the capital deficiency; and even towards
lessening that, what arts, what modes, what refinements of pleasure
have they not recourse to, to raise their languid powers, and press
nature into the service of their sensuality? But here is their misfortune,
that when by a course of teasing, worrying, handling, wanton postures,
lascivious motions, they have at length accomplished a flashy enervate
enjoyment, they at the same time light up a flame in the object of their
passion, that, not having the means themselves to quench, drives her
for relief into the next person's arms, who can finish their work; and
thus they become bawds to some favourite, tried and approved of, for a

more vigorous and satisfactory execution; for with women, of our turn especially, however well our hearts may be disposed, there is a controlling part, or queen-seat in us, that governs itself by its own maxims of state.

Mr Norbert, who was much in this ungracious case, though be professed to like me extremely, could but seldom consummate the main joy itself with me without such a length and variety of preparations as were at once wearisome and inflammatory.

Sometimes he would strip me stark naked on a carpet, by a good fire, when he would contemplate me almost by the hour, disposing me in all the figures and attitudes of body that it was susceptible of being viewed in; kissing me in every part, the most secret and critical one so far from excepted that it received most of that branch of homage. Then his touches were so exquisitely wanton, so luxuriously diffused and penetrative at times, that he had made me perfectly rage with titillating fires, when, after all, and much ado, he had gained a short-lived erection, he would perhaps melt it away in a washy sweat, or a premature abortive effusion, that provokingly mocked my eager desires: or, if carried home, how faltered and unnervous the execution! How insufficient the sprinkle of a few heat-drops to extinguish all the flames he had kindled!

One evening, I cannot help remembering that, returning home from him, with a spirit he had raised in a circle his wand had proved too weak to lay, as I turned the corner of a street, I was overtaken by a young sailor. I was then in that spruce, neat, plain dress, which I ever affected, and perhaps might have had, in my trip, a certain air of restlessness unknown to the composure of cooler thoughts. However, he seized me as a prize, and without farther ceremony threw his arms round my neck, and kissed me boisterously and sweetly. I looked at him with a beginning of anger and indignation at his rudeness, that softened away into other sentiments as I viewed him: for he was tall, manly carriaged, handsome of body and face, so that I ended my stare, with asking him, in a tone turned to tenderness, what he meant; at which, with the same frankness and vivacity as he had begun with me, he proposed treating me with a glass of wine. Now, certain it is, that had I been in a calmer state of blood than I was, had I not been under the dominion of unappeased irritations and desires, I should have refused him without hesitation; but I do not know how it was, my pressing calls, his figure, the occasion, and if you will, the powerful combination of all these, with a start of curiosity to see the end of an adventure, so novel too as being treated like a common street-player, made me give a silent consent; in short, it was not my head that I now obeyed. I suffered myself to be towed along as it were by this man-of-war, who took me under his arm as familiarly as if he had known me all his lifetime, and led me into the next convenient tavern, where we were shown into a little room on one side of the passage. Here, scarce allowing himself patience till the drawer brought in the wine called for, he fell directly on board me: when, untucking my handkerchief, and giving me a snatching buss, he laid my breasts bare at once, which he handled with that keenness of lust that abridges a ceremonial ever more tiresome than pleasing on such pressing occasions; and now, hurrying towards the main point, we found no conveniency to our purpose, two or three disabled chairs, and a rickety table, composing the whole furniture of the room. Without more ado, he plants me with my back standing against the wall, and my petticoats up; and coming out with a splitter indeed, made it shine, as he brandished it, in my eyes; and going to work with an impetuosity and eagerness, bred very likely by a long fast at sea, went to give me a taste of it. I straddled, I humoured my posture, and did my best in short to buckle to it; I took part of it in, but still things did not go to his thorough liking: changing then in a trice his system of battery, he leads me to the table and with a master-hand lays my head down on the edge of it, and, with the other canting up my petticoats and shift, bares my naked posteriors to his blind and furious guide; it forces its way between them, and I feeling pretty sensibly that it was not going by the right door, and knocking desperately at the wrong one, I told him of it: – 'Pooh!' says he, 'my dear, any port in a storm.' Altering, however, directly his course, and lowering his point, he fixed it right, and driving it up with a delicious stiffness, made all foam again, and gave me the *tout* with such fire and spirit, that in the fine disposition I was in when I submitted to him, and stirred up so fiercely as I was, I got the start of him, and went away into the melting swoon, and squeezing him, whilst in the convulsive grasp of it, drew from him such a plenteous bedewal, as, joined to my own effusion, perfectly floated those parts, and drowned in a deluge all my raging conflagration of desire.

When this was over, how to make my retreat was my concern; for, though I had been so extremely pleased with the difference between this warm broadside, poured so briskly into me, and the tiresome pawing and toying to which I had owed the unappeased flames that had driven me into this step, now I was grown cooler, I began to apprehend the danger of contracting an acquaintance with this, however agreeable stranger; who, on his side, spoke of passing the evening with me and continuing our intimacy, with an air of determination that made me afraid of its being not so easy to get away from him as I could wish. In the meantime I carefully concealed my uneasiness, and readily pretended to consent to stay with him, telling him I should only step to my lodgings to leave a necessary direction, and then instantly return. This he very glibly swallowed, on the notion of my being one of those unhappy street-errants, who devote themselves to the pleasure of the first ruffian that will stoop to pick them up, and of course, that I would scarce bilk myself of my hire, by my not returning to make the most of the job. Thus he parted with me, not before, however, he had ordered in my hearing a supper, which I had the barbarity to disappoint him of my company to.

But when I got home, and told Mrs Cole of my unplanned adventure, she represented so strongly to me the nature and dangerous consequences of my folly, particularly the risks to my health, in being so open-legged and free, that I not only took resolutions never to venture so rashly again, which I inviolably preserved, but passed a good many days in continual uneasiness, lest I should have met with other reasons, besides the pleasure of that encounter, to remember it by; but these fears wronged my pretty sailor.

* * *

One morning then, that both Mrs Cole and Emily were gone out for the day, and only Louisa and I (not to mention the housemaid) were left in charge of the house, whilst we were loitering away the time, the son of a poor woman, who earned very hard bread indeed by mending of stockings, in a stall in the neighbourhood, offered us some nosegays, ranged round a small basket; by selling of which the poor boy eked out his mother's maintenance of them both: nor was he fit for any other way of livelihood, since he was not only a perfect changeling, or idiot, but stammered so that there was no understanding even those sounds his half-dozen animal ideas, at most, prompted him to utter.

The boys and servants in the neighbourhood had given him the nickname of Good-natured Dick, from the soft simpleton's doing everything he was bid at the first word, and from his naturally having no turn to mischief; then, by the way, he was perfectly well-made, stout, clean-limbed, tall of his age; as strong as a horse, and, withal, pretty-featured; so that he was not, absolutely, such a figure to be snuffled at neither, if your nicety could, in favour of such essentials, have dispensed with a face unwashed, hair tangled for want of combing, and so ragged a plight, that he might have disputed points of show with any heathen philosopher of them all.

This boy we had often seen, and bought his flowers, out of pure compassion, and nothing more; but just at this time as he stood presenting us his basket, a sudden whim, a start of wayward fancy, seized Louisa; and, without consulting me, she calls him in, and beginning to examine his nosegays, culls out two, one for herself, another for me, and pulling out half a crown, very currently gives it to him to change, as if she had really expected he could have changed it; but the boy, scratching his head, made his signs to explain his inability in place of words, which he could not, struggling, articulate.

Louisa, at this says: 'Well, my lad, come upstairs with me, and I will give you your due,' winking at the same time to me, and beckoning me to accompany her, which I did, securing first the street door, that by this means, together with the shop, became wholly the care of the faithful housemaid.

As we went up, Louisa whispered to me that she had conceived a strange longing to be satisfied, whether the general rule held good with regard to this changeling, and how far nature had made him amends, in her best bodily gifts, for her denial of the sublimer intellectual ones; begging, at the same time, my assistance in procuring her this satisfaction. A want of complaisance was never my vice, and I was so far from opposing this extravagant frolic, that now, my curiosity conspiring with hers, I entered plump into it.

Consequently, as soon as we came into Louisa's bedchamber, whilst she was amusing him with picking out his nosegays, I undertook the lead, and began the attack. As it was not then very material to keep much measures with a mere natural, I made presently very free with him, though at my first motion of meddling, his surprise and confusion made him receive my advances but awkwardly; nay, insomuch that he bashfully shied, and shied back a little; till encouraging him with my eyes, plucking him playfully by the hair, sleeking his cheeks, and forwarding my point by a number of little wantonnesses, I soon turned him familiar, and gave nature her sweetest alarm: so that aroused, and beginning to feel himself, we could, amidst all the innocent laugh and grin I had provoked him into, perceive the fire lighting in his eyes, and, diffusing over his cheeks, blend its glow with that of his blushes. The emotion in short of animal pleasure glared distinctly in the simpleton's countenance; yet, struck with the novelty of the scene, he did not know which way to look or move; but tame, passive, simpering, with his mouth half open, in stupid rapture, stood and tractably suffered me to do what I pleased with him. His basket was dropped out of his hands, which Louisa took care of.

I had now, through more than one rent, discovered and felt his thighs, the skin of which seemed the smoother and fairer for the coarseness, and even the dirt of his dress, as the teeth of Negroes seem the whiter for the surrounding black; and poor indeed of habit, poor of understanding, he was, however, abundantly rich in personal treasures, such as flesh, firm, plump, and replete with the juices of youth, and robust well-knit limbs. My fingers too had now got within reach of the true, the genuine sensitive plant, which, instead of shrinking from the touch, joys to meet it, and swells and vegetates under it: mine pleasingly informed me that matters were so ripe for the discovery we meditated, that they were too mighty for the confinement they were ready to break. A waistband that I unskewered, and a rag of a shirt that I removed, and which could not have covered a quarter of it, revealed the whole of the idiot's standard of distinction, erect, in full pride and display: but such a one! It was positively of so tremendous a size, that prepared as we were to see something extraordinary, it still, out of measure, surpassed our expectation, and astonished even me, who had not been used to trade in trifles. In fine, it might have answered very well the making of a show of; its enormous head seemed, in hue and size, not unlike a common sheep's heart; then you might have trolled dice securely along the broad back of the body of it; the length of it too was prodigious; then the rich appendage of the treasure-bag beneath, large in proportion, gathered and crisped up round in shallow furrows, helped to fill the eye, and complete the proof of his being a natural, not quite in vain; since it was full manifest that he inherited, and largely too, the prerogative of majesty which distinguishes that otherwise most unfortunate condition, and gave rise to the vulgar saying that 'a fool's bauble is a lady's playfellow'. Not wholly without reason: for, generally speaking, it is in love as it is in war, where the longest weapon carries it. Nature, in short, had done so much for him in those parts, that she perhaps held herself acquitted in doing so little for his head.

For my part, who had sincerely no intention to push the joke further than simply satisfying my curiosity with the sight of it alone, I was content, in spite of the temptation that stared me in the face, with having raised a Maypole for another to hang a garland on: for, by this time, easily reading Louisa's desires in her wishful eyes, I acted the commodious part, and made her, who sought no better sport, significant terms of encouragement to go through stitch with her adventure; intimating too that I would stay and see fair play: in which, indeed, I had in view to humour a newborn curiosity, to observe what appearances active nature would put on in such a natural.

Louisa, whose appetite was up, and who, like the industrious bee, was, it seems, not above gathering the sweets of so rare a flower, though she found it planted on a dunghill, was but too readily disposed to take the benefit of my cession. Urged then strongly by her own desires and emboldened by me, she presently determined to risk a trial of parts with the idiot, who was by this time nobly inflamed for her purpose, by all the irritation we had used to put the principles of pleasure effectually into motion, and to wind up the springs of its organ to their supreme pitch; and it stood accordingly stiff and straining, ready to burst with the blood and spirits that swelled it . . . to a bulk! No! I shall never forget it.

Louisa then, taking and holding the fine handle that so invitingly offered itself, led the ductile youth, by that master-tool of his, as she stepped backwards towards the bed; which he joyfully gave way to, under the incitations of instinct, and palpably delivered up to the goad of desire.

Stopped then by the bed, she took the fall she loved, and leaned to the most gently backwards upon it, still holding fast what she held, and taking care to give her clothes a convenient toss up, so that her thighs duly disclosed, and elevated, laid open all the outward prospect of the treasury of love: the rose-lipped overture presenting the cockpit so fair, that it was not in nature even for a natural to miss it. Nor did he: for Louisa, fully bent on grappling with it, and impatient of dalliance or delay, directed faithfully the point of the battering piece, and bounded up with a rage of so voracious appetite, to meet and favour the thrust of insertion, that the fierce activity on both sides effected it with such pain of distention, that Louisa cried out violently, that she was hurt beyond bearing, that she was killed. But it was too late: the storm was up, and force was on her to give way to it; for now the man-machine, strongly worked upon by the sensual passion, felt so manfully his advantages and superiority, felt withal the sting of pleasure so intolerable, that maddening with it, his joys began to assume a character of furiousness, which made me tremble for the too tender Louisa. He seemed, at this juncture, greater than himself; his countenance, before so void of meaning, or expression, now grew big with the importance of the act he was upon. In short, it was not now that he was to be played the fool with. But, what is pleasant enough, I myself was awed into a sort of respect for him, by the comely terrors his motions dressed him in: his eyes shooting sparks of fire; his face glowing with ardours that gave another life to it; his teeth churning; his whole frame agitated with a raging ungovernable impetuosity: all sensibly betraying the formidable fierceness with which the genial instinct acted upon him. Butting then and goring all before him, and mad and wild like an overdriven steer, he ploughs up the tender furrow, all insensible to Louisa's complaints; nothing can stop, nothing can keep out a fury like his: with which, having once got its head in, its blind rage soon made way for the rest piercing, rending, and breaking open all obstruction. The torn, split, wounded girl cries, struggles, invokes me to her rescue, and endeavours to get from under the young savage, or shake him off, but alas! in vain: her breath might as soon have stilled or stemmed a storm in winter, as all her strength have quelled his rough assault, or put him out of his course. And indeed, all her efforts and struggles were managed with such disorder that they served to entangle, and fold her the faster in the twine of his boisterous arms; so that she was tied to the stake, and obliged to fight the match out, if she died for it. For his part, instinct-ridden as he was, the expressions of his animal passion, partaking something of ferocity, were rather worrying than the kisses, intermixed with eager ravenous love-bites on her cheeks and neck, the prints of which did not wear out for some days after.

Poor Louisa, however, bore up at length better than could have been expected; and though she suffered, and greatly too, yet, ever true to the good old cause, she suffered with pleasure and enjoyed her pain. And soon now, by dint of an enraged enforcement, the brute-machine, driven like a whirlwind, made all smoke again, and wedging its way up, to the utmost extremity, left her, in point of penetration, nothing to fear or to desire: and now, 'gorged with the dearest morsel of the earth' [Shakespeare], Louisa lay, pleased to the heart, pleased to her utmost capacity of being so, with every fibre in those parts, stretched almost to breaking, on a rack of joy, whilst the instrument of all this overfulness searched her senses with its sweet excess, till the pleasure gained upon her so, its point stung her so home, that catching at length the rage from her furious driver and sharing the riot of his wild rapture, she went wholly out of her mind into that favourite part of her body, the whole intenseness of which was so fervidly filled, and employed: there alone she existed, all lost in those delirious transports, those ecstasies of the senses, which her winking eyes, the brightened vermilion of her lips and cheeks, and sighs of pleasure deeply fetched, so pathetically expressed. In short, she was now as mere a machine as much wrought on, and had her motions as little at her own command, as the natural himself, who, thus broke in upon her, made her feel with a vengeance his tempestuous tenderness, and the force of the mettle he battered with; their active loins quivered again with the violence of their conflict, till the surge of pleasure, foaming and raging to a height, drew down the pearly shower that was to allay this hurricane. The purely sensitive idiot then first shed those tears of joy that attend its last moments, not without an agony of delight, and even almost a roar of rapture, as the gush escaped him; so rapturous too for Louisa, that she kept him faithful company, going off, in consent, with the old symptoms: a delicious delirium, a tremulous convulsive shudder, and the critical dying: Oh! And now, on his getting off, she lay pleasure drenched, and regorging its essential sweets; but quite spent, and gasping for breath, without other sensation of life than in those exquisite vibrations that trembled still on the strings of delight; which had been too intensively touched, and which nature had been so ravishingly stirred with, for the senses to be quickly at peace from.

As for the changeling, whose curious engine had been thus success- fully played off, his shift of countenance and gesture had even something droll, or rather tragicomic: there was now an air of sad repining foolishness, superadded to his natural one of no-meaning and idiotism, as he stood with his label of manhood, now lank, unstiffened, becalmed, and flapping against his thighs, down which it reached halfway, terrible even in its fall, whilst under the dejection of spirit and flesh, which naturally followed, his eyes, by turns, cast down towards his struck standard, or piteously lifted to Louisa, seemed to require at her hands what he had so sensibly parted from to her, and now ruefully missed. But the vigour of nature, soon returning, dissipated the blast of faintness which the common law of enjoyment had subjected him to; and now his basket re-became his main concern, which I looked for, and brought him, whilst Louisa restored his dress to its usual condition, and afterwards pleased him perhaps more by taking all his flowers off his hands, and paying him, at his rate, for them, than if she had embarrassed him by a present, that he would have been puzzled to account for, and might have put others on tracing the motives of.

* * *

Hitherto I had been indebted to the girls of the house for the corruption of my innocence: their luscious talk, in which modesty was far from respected, and their description of their engagements with men, had given me a tolerable insight into the nature and mysteries of

THE ENCYCLOPEDIA OF EROTIC LITERATURE

their profession, at the same time that they highly provoked an itch of florid, warm-spirited blood through every vein: but above all, my bed-fellow Phoebe, whose pupil I more immediately was, exerted her talents in giving me the first tinctures of pleasure: whilst nature, now warmed and wantoned with discoveries so interesting, piqued a curiosity which Phoebe artfully whetted, and leading me from question to question of her own suggestion, explained to me all the mysteries of Venus. But I could not long remain in such a house as that, without being an eye-witness of more than I could conceive from her descriptions.

One day, about twelve at noon, being thoroughly recovered of my fever, I happened to be in Mrs Brown's dark closet, where I had not been half an hour, resting upon the maid's bed, before I heard a rustling in the bed-chamber, separated from the closet only by two sash doors, before the glasses of which were drawn two yellow damask curtains, but not so close as to exclude the full view of the room from any person in the closet.

I instantly crept softly, and posted myself so, that seeing everything minutely, I could not myself be seen, and who should come in but the venerable mother Abbess herself! handed in by a tall, brawny young horse-grenadier, moulded in the Hercules style: in fine, the choice of the most experienced dame, in those affairs, in all London.

Oh! How still and hush did I keep at my stand, lest any noise should balk my curiosity, or bring Madam into the closet!

But I had not much reason to fear either, for she was so entirely taken up with her present great concern, that she had no attention to spare to anything else.

Droll was it to see that clumsy fat figure of hers flop down on the foot of the bed, opposite to the closet door, so that I had a full front view of all her charms.

Her paramour sat down by her: he seemed to be a man of very few words, and a great stomach; for proceeding instantly to essentials, he gave her some hearty smacks, and thrusting his hands into her breasts disengaged them from her stays, in scorn of whose confinement they broke loose, and sagged down, navel-low at least. A more enormous pair did my eyes never behold, nor of a worse colour, flagging, soft, and most lovingly contiguous: yet such as they were, this great neck-beef eater seemed to paw them with a most uninvitable lust, seeking in vain to confine or cover one of them with a hand scarce less than a shoulder of mutton. After toying with them thus for some time, as if they had been worth it, he laid her down pretty briskly, and canting up her petticoats, made barely a mask of them to her broad red face, that blushed with nothing but brandy.

As he stood on one side, unbuttoning his waistcoat and breeches, her fat, brawny thighs hung down, and the whole greasy landscape lay fairly open to my view; a wide, open-mouthed gap, overshaded with a grizzly bush, seemed held out like a beggar's wallet for its provision.

But I soon had my eyes called off by a more striking object, that entirely engrossed them.

Her sturdy stallion had now unbuttoned, and produced naked, stiff and erect, that wonderful machine, which I had never seen before, and which, for the interest my own seat of pleasure began to take furiously in it, I stared at with all the eyes I had: however, my senses were too much flurried, too much concentrated in that now burning spot of mine, to observe anything more than in general the make and turn of that instrument; from which the instinct of nature, yet more than all I had heard of it, now strongly informed me I was to expect that supreme pleasure which she had placed in the meeting of those parts so admirably fitted for each other.

Long, however, the young spark did not remain before giving it two or three shakes, by way of brandishing it; then he threw himself upon her, and his back being now towards me, I could only take his being engulfed for granted, by the directions he moved in, and the impossibility of missing so staring a mark; and now the bed shook and the curtains rattled so, that I could scarce hear the sighs and murmurs, the heaves and pantings that accompanied the action, from the beginning to the end; the sound and sight of which thrilled to the very soul of me, and made every vein of my body circulate liquid fires: the emotion grew so violent that it almost intercepted my respiration.

Prepared then, and disposed as I was by the discourse of my companions, and Phoebe's minute detail of everything, no wonder that such a sight gave the last dying blow to my native innocence.

Whilst they were in the heat of action, guided by nature only, I stole my hand up my petticoats, and with fingers all on fire seized, and yet more inflamed that centre of all my senses: my heart palpitated, as if it would force its way through my bosom. I breathed with pain; I twisted my thighs, squeezed, and compressed the lips of that virgin slit, and following mechanically the example of Phoebe's manual operation on it, as far as I could find admission, brought at last the critical ecstasy: the melting flow, into which nature, spent with pleasure, dissolves and dies away.

After which, my senses recovered coolness enough to observe the rest of the transaction between this happy pair.

The young fellow had just dismounted, when the old lady immediately sprung up, with all the vigour of youth, derived, no doubt, from her late refreshment, and making him sit down, began in her turn to kiss him, to pat and pinch his cheeks, and play with his hair: all which he received with an air of indifference and coolness, that showed him to me much altered from what he was when he first went into the breach.

My pious governess, however, not being above calling in auxiliaries, unlocked a little case of cordials that stood near the bed, and made him pledge her in a very plentiful dram: after which, and a little amorous parley, Madam set herself down upon the same place, at the bed's foot; and the young fellow standing sidewise by her, she, with the greatest effrontery imaginable, unbuttons his breeches, and removing his shirt, draws out his affair, so shrunk and diminished, that I could not but remember the difference, now crestfallen, or just faintly lifting its head: but our experienced matron very soon, by chaffing it with her hands, brought it to swell to that size and erection I had before seen it up to.

I admired then, upon a fresh account, and with a nicer survey, the texture of that capital part of man: the flaming red head as it stood uncapt, the whiteness of the shaft, and the shrub growth of curling hair that embrowned the roots of it, the roundish bag that dangled down from it, all exacted my eager attention, and renewed my flame. But, as the main affair was now at the point the industrious dame had laboured to bring it to, she was not in the humour to put off the payment of her pains, but laying herself down, drew him gently upon her, and thus they finished, in the same manner as before, the old last act.

This over, they both went out lovingly together, the old lady having first made him a present, as near as I could observe, of three or four pieces; he being not only her particular favourite on account of his performances, but a retainer to the house.

As soon as I heard them go downstairs I stole up softly to my own room, out of which I had luckily not been missed; there I began to breathe more free, and to give loose to those warm emotions which the sight of such an encounter had raised in me. I lay me down on the bed, stretched myself out, joining and ardently wishing, and requiring any means to divert or allay the rekindled rage and tumult of my desires, which all pointed strongly to their pole: man. I felt about the bed as if I sought for something that I grasped in my waking dream, and not finding it, could have cried for vexation; every part of me glowing with stimulating fires. At length, I resorted to the only present remedy, that of vain attempts at digitation, where the smallness of the theatre did not yet afford room enough for action, and where the pain my fingers gave me, in striving for admission, though they procured me a slight satisfaction for the present, started an apprehension, which I could not be easy till I had communicated to Phoebe, and received her explanations upon it.

Next morning, Phoebe could not hear my recital to the end without more than one interruption by peals of laughter, and my ingenuous way of relating matters, did not a little heighten the joke to her.

But, on her sounding me how the sight had affected me, without mincing or hiding the pleasurable emotions it had inspired me with, I told her at the same time that one remark had perplexed me, and that very considerably.

'Aye!' says she, 'what was that?'

'Why,' replied I, 'having very curiously and attentively compared the size of that enormous machine, which did not appear, at least to my fearful imagination, less than my wrist, and at least three of my handfuls long, to that of the tender small part of me which was framed to receive it, I could not conceive its being possible to afford it entrance without dying, perhaps in the greatest pain, since you well knew that even a finger thrust in there, hurt me beyond bearing . . . As to my mistress's and yours, I can very plainly distinguish the different dimensions of them from mine, palpable to the touch, and visible to the eye; so that, in short, great as the promised pleasure may be, I am afraid of the pain of the experiment.'

Phoebe at this redoubled her laugh, and told me that she never heard of a mortal wound being given in those parts, by that terrible weapon, and that some she knew younger, and as delicately made as myself, had outlived the operation; that she believed, at the worst, I should take a great deal of killing; but that at a certain age and habit of body, even the most experienced in those affairs could not well distinguish between the maid and the woman, supposing too an absence of all artifice, and things in their natural situation; but that since chance had thrown in my way one sight of that sort, she would procure me another, that should feast my eyes more delicately, and go a great way in the cure of my fears from that imaginary disproportion.

On this she asked me if I knew Polly Philips. 'Undoubtedly,' says I, 'the fair girl which was so tender of me when I was sick, and has been, as you told me, but two months in the house.'

'The same,' says Phoebe. 'You must know then, she is kept by a young Genoese merchant. He met casually with this Polly once in company, and taking a liking to her, makes it worth her while to keep entirely to him. He comes to her here twice or thrice a week, and she receives him in the light closet up one pair of stairs, where he enjoys her in a taste, I suppose, peculiar to the heat, or perhaps the caprices of his own country. I say no more, but tomorrow being his day, you shall see what passes between them, from a place only known to your mistress and myself.'

You may be sure, in the ply I was now taking, I had no objection to the proposal, and was rather a tip-toe for its accomplishment.

At five in the evening next day, Phoebe, punctual to her promise, came to me as I sat alone in my own room, and beckoned me to follow her.

We went down the back stairs very softly, and opening the door of a dark closet, where there was some old furniture kept, and some cases of liquor, she drew me in after her, and fastening the door upon us, we had no light but what came through a long crevice in the partition between ours and the light closet, where the scene of action lay; so that sitting on those low cases, we could, with the greatest ease, as well as clearness, see all objects (ourselves unseen), only by applying our eyes close to the crevice, where the moulding of a panel had warped, or started a little on the other side.

The young gentleman was the first person I saw, with his back directly towards me, looking at a print. Polly was not yet come: in less than a minute though, the door opened, and she came in; and at the noise the door made he turned about, and came to meet her, with an air of the greatest tenderness and satisfaction.

After saluting her, he led her to a couch that fronted us, where they both sat down and the young Genoese helped her to a glass of wine, with some Naples biscuits on a salver.

Presently, when they had exchanged a few kisses, and questions in broken English on one side, he began to unbutton and, in fine, strip unto his shirt.

As if this had been the signal agreed on for pulling off all their clothes, a scheme which the heat of the season perfectly favoured, Polly began to draw her pins, and as she had no stays to unlace, she was in a trice, with her gallant's officious assistance, undressed to all but her shift.

. When he saw this, his breeches were immediately loosened, waist and knee bands, and slipped over his ankles, clean off; his shirt collar was unbuttoned too: then, first giving Polly an encouraging kiss, he stole, as it were, the shift off the girl, who being, I suppose, broke and familiarised to his humour, blushed indeed, but less than I did at the apparition of her, now standing stark naked, just as she came out of the hands of pure nature, with her black hair loose and a-float down her dazzling white neck and shoulders, whilst the deepened carnation of her cheeks went off gradually into the hue of glazed snow: for such were the blended tints and polish of her skin.

This girl could not be above eighteen: her face regular and sweet-featured, her shape exquisite; nor could I help envying her two ripe, enchanting breasts, finely plumped out in flesh, but withal so round, so firm, that they sustained themselves, in scorn of any stay: then their nipples, pointing different ways, marked their pleasing separation; beneath them lay the delicious tract of the belly, which terminated in a parting or rift scarce discernible, that modestly seemed to retire downwards, and seek shelter between two plump, fleshy thighs: the curling hair that overspread its delightful front, clothed it with the richest sable fur in the universe: in short, she was evidently a subject for the painters to court her, sitting to them for a pattern of female beauty, in all the true pride and pomp of nakedness.

The young Italian (still in his shirt) stood gazing and transported at the sight of beauties that might have fired a dying hermit; his eager eyes devoured her, as she shifted attitudes at his discretion: neither were his hands excluded their share of the high feast, but wandered, on the hunt of pleasure, over every part and inch of her body, so qualified to afford the most exquisite sense of it.

In the meantime, one could not help observing the swell of his shirt before, that bolstered out, and pointed out the condition of things behind the curtain: but he soon removed it, by slipping his shirt over his head; and now, as to nakedness, they had nothing to reproach one another.

The young gentleman, by Phoebe's guess, was about two and twenty; tall and well-limbed. His body was finely formed, and of a most vigorous make, square-shouldered and broad-chested: his face was not remarkable in any way, but a nose inclining to the Roman, eyes large, black and sparkling, and a ruddiness in his cheeks that was the more a grace; for his complexion was of the brownest, not of that dusky dun colour which excludes the idea of freshness, but of that clear, olive gloss, which glowing with life, dazzles perhaps less than fairness, and yet pleases more, when it pleases at all. His hair being too short to tie fell no lower than his neck, in short easy curls; and he had a few sprigs about his paps, that garnished his chest in a style of strength and manliness. Then his grand movement, which seemed to rise out of a thicket of curling hair, that spread from the root all over his thighs and belly up to the navel, stood stiff and upright, but of a size to frighten me, by sympathy for the small tender part which was the object of its fury, and which now lay exposed to my fairest view; for he had, immediately on stripping off his shirt, gently pushed her down on the couch, which stood conveniently to break her willing fall. Her thighs were spread out to their utmost extension, and discovered between them the mark of her sex, the red-centred cleft of flesh, whose lips vermilioning inwards, expressed a small ruby line in sweet miniature, such as Guido's touch or colouring could never attain to the life or delicacy of.

Phoebe, at this, gave me a gentle jog, to prepare me for a whispered question: 'Whether I thought my little maidenhead was much less?' But my attention was too much engrossed, too much enwrapped with all I saw, to be able to give her any answer.

By this time the young gentleman had changed her posture from lying breadth- to length-wise on the couch; but her thighs were still spread, and the mark lay fair for him, who now kneeling between them, displayed to us a side view of that fierce erect machine of his, which threatened no less than splitting the tender victim, who lay smiling at the uplifted stroke, nor seemed to decline it. He looked upon his weapon himself with some pleasure, and guiding it with his hand to the inviting slit, drew aside the lips, and lodged it (after some thrusts, which Polly seemed even to assist) about half-way; but there it stuck, I suppose from its growing thickness: he draws it again, and just wetting it with spittle, re-enters, and with ease sheath'd it now up to the hilt, at which Polly gave a deep sigh, which was quite another tone than one of pain; he thrusts, she heaves, at first gently, and in a regular cadence; but presently the transport began to be too violent to observe any order or measure; their motions were too rapid, their kisses too fierce and fervent for nature to support such fury long: both seemed to me out of themselves: their eyes darted fires: 'Oh! . . . oh! . . . I can't bear it . . . It is too much . . . I die . . . I am going . . .' were Polly's expressions of ecstasy: his joys were more silent: but soon broken murmurs, sighs heart-fetched, and at length a dispatching thrust, as if he would have forced himself up her body, and then the motionless languor of all his limbs, all showed that the die-away moment was come upon him; which she gave signs of joining, by the wild throwing of her hands, closing her eyes, and giving a deep sob, in which she seemed to expire in an agony of bliss.

When he had finished his stroke, and got off from her, she lay still without the least motion, breathless, as it should seem, with pleasure. He replaced her again breadth-wise on the couch, unable to sit up, with her thighs open, between which I could observe a kind of white liquid, like froth, hanging about the outward lips of that recently opened wound, which now glowed with a deeper red. Presently she gets up, and throwing her arms round him, seemed far from undelighted with the trial he had put her to, to judge, at least, by the fondness with which she eyed, and hung upon him.

For my part, from that instant, adieu all fears of what man can do unto me! They were now changed into such ardent desires, such ungovernable longings, that I could have pulled the first of that sex that should present himself by the sleeve, and offered him the bauble, which I now imagined the loss of would be a gain I could not too soon procure myself.

Phoebe could not, however, be unmoved at so warm a scene; and drawing me away softly from the peeping hole, for fear of being overheard, guided me as near the door as possible.

There was no room either to sit or lie, but making me stand with my back towards the door, she lifted up my petticoats, and with her busy fingers fell to visit and explore that part of me, where now the heat and irritations were so violent, that I was perfectly sick and ready to die with desire; that the bare touch of her finger, in that critical place, had the effect of a fire to a train, and her hand instantly made her sensible to what a pitch I was wound up, and melted by the sight she had thus procured me. Satisfied then with her success, in allaying a heat that would have made me impatient of seeing the continuation of the transactions between our amorous couple, she brought me again to the crevice, so favourable to our curiosity.

On our return we saw everything in good forwardness for recommencing the tender hostilities.

The young foreigner was sitting down, fronting us, on the couch, with Polly upon one knee, who had her arms round his neck, whilst the extreme whiteness of her skin was not undelightfully contrasted by the smooth glossy brown of her lover's.

But who could count the fierce, unnumbered kisses given and taken? I could often discover their exchanging the velvet thrust, when both their mouths were double-tongued, and seemed to favour the mutual insertion with the greatest gust and delight.

In the meantime, his red-headed champion, that had so lately fled the pit, quelled and abashed, was now recovered to the top of his condition, perked and crested up between Polly's thighs, who was not wanting, on her part, to coax and keep it in good humour, stroking it, with her head down, and receiving even its velvet tip between the lips of not its proper mouth: whether she did this out of any particular pleasure, or whether it was to render it more glib and easy of entrance, I could not tell; but it had such an effect, that the young gentleman seemed by his eyes, that sparkled with more excited lustre, and his inflamed countenance, to receive increase of pleasure. He got up, and taking Polly in his arms, embraced her, and said something too softly for me to hear, leading her withal to the foot of the couch and taking delight to slap her thighs and posteriors with that stiff sinew of his, which hit them with a spring that he gave it with his hand, and made them resound again, but hurt her about as much as he meant to hurt her, for she seemed to have as frolic a taste as himself.

But guess my surprise, when I saw the lazy young rogue lie down on his back, and gently pull down Polly upon him, who giving way to his humour, straddled, and with her hands conducted her blind favourite to the right place; and following her impulse, ran directly upon the flaming point of this weapon of pleasure, which she staked herself upon, up-pierced, and infixed to the extremest hair-breadth of it: thus she sat on him a few instants, enjoying and relishing her situation, whilst he toyed with her provoking breasts. Sometimes she would stoop to meet his kiss: but presently the sting of pleasure spurred them up to fiercer action; then began the storm of heaves, which, from the undermost combatant, were thrust at the same time, he crossing his hands over her, and drawing her home to him with a sweet violence: the inverted strokes of anvil over hammer soon brought on the critical period, in which all the signs of a close conspiring ecstasy informed us of the point they were at.

For me, I could bear to see no more; I was so overcome, so inflamed at the second part of the same play, that, mad to an intolerable degree, I hugged, I clasped Phoebe, as if she had the wherewithal to relieve me. Pleased however with, and pitying the taking she could feel me in, she drew towards the door, and opening it as softly as she could, we both got off undiscovered, and she reconducted me to my own room, where, in the agitation I was in, I threw myself down on the bed, where I lay transported, though ashamed.

Phoebe lay down by me, and asked me archly if, now that I had seen the enemy and fully considered him, I was still afraid of him? Or did I think I could come to a close engagement with him? To all which, not a word on my side; I sighed, and could scarce breathe. For my part, I now pined for more solid food, and promised tacitly to myself that I would no longer be put off with this foolery of woman to woman.

~~~ 4 ~~~

Gamiani, or Two Nights of Excess

ALCIDE, BARON D'M —
(Alfred de Musset) 1833

Gamiani, or Two Nights of Excess by Alcide, Baron d'M—, is one of the greatest French erotic classics of all time. Since its first publication in the nineteenth century, the book has never been out of print. Louis Perceau's 1930 census of post-1800 French erotica found forty-one separate editions of *Gamiani* since its initial appearance; the next most popular erotic title had only seventeen reprints during the same period.

To what does this book owe its constant popularity? Surely mystery, celebrity, scandal, and the incredibly perverse nature of the tale all contribute. The first edition of *Gamiani* was an oversized quarto volume of twenty-six pages plus two illustrated title pages, one for each part of the book. The text was a lithographic facsimile of a calligraphic manuscript of unknown hand. In addition there were twelve exquisite but anonymous full-page illustrations of a most pornographic nature.

Despite the title pages giving the publication information as Brussels, 1833, the book's true origins and first publication were clouded in mystery. False information about erotica was (and still is) common for purposes of evading the law. Years of research have revealed most of *Gamiani*'s secrets. The author of the book is most certainly Alfred de Musset (1810–57), the famous French Romantic author and poet. The art has been attributed to Grevedon and Deveria, both nineteenth-century illustrators renown for their erotic work. The book's characters and activities were based on celebrities of the day, about which more will be said. There are two stories as to how the book came into print. One goes that de Musset wrote the pieces as amusement for a dozen friends, and had a few copies printed in Paris for them. An alternative, and more likely story, is that the manuscript fell into the hands of an unscrupulous publisher who had the book printed in Brussels about 1835.

What is certain is that *Gamiani* is an obscene *roman-à-clef*, and one of the most vituperous, misogynistic pieces ever penned. Written as an act of spleen against a single woman, the disdain and hatred of women in general that it shows drips like poison venom from the author's pen. The catalyst for *Gamiani* was de Musset's affair with Amandine Aurore Lucie, *née* Dupin, the Baronne Dudevant, better known to the world and history under her *nom de plume* of George Sand (1804–76). This talented and scandal-plagued authoress and poet was infamous for her masculine propensities, including her physiognomy, attire (top hat and tails) and even her choice of lovers and pseudonym.

A strange couple indeed. A woman who wears the trousers keeping company with one of the great romantics of French literature, who was not only six years younger than herself, but decidedly effeminate in temperament. It is a matter of history that the two travelled to Italy in the winter of 1833–4, when de Musset was twenty-three years old. They separated in Venice, according to the biographers after a rather fierce row, precipitated by de Musset's jealous reaction to Sand's other amours. George Sand then allegedly spread rumours that de Musset was a poor lover, and often impotent; de Musset retaliated by writing *Gamiani*, in which he sought to expose and defame the morals and private life of the woman who had jilted him. Special attention was given to Sand's supposed tribadistic, sadomasochistic and bestial predilections.

Musset's novel opens with Baron Alcide (Musset) spying on Gamiani (George Sand) who is engaged in lesbian sex with her young friend Fanny. Alcide joins in the orgy, and the three then decide to retell erotic episodes from their lives. What follows are scenes of depravity and perversity not often found in erotica, and what is most remarkable is that women are the instigators and perpetrators of the sexual acts. Tribadism, sodomy, rape, flagellation, religious sacrilege, bestiality (with a variety of animals including a dog, a donkey and an ape), and even necrophilia are reported.

Gamiani is more than a litany of *psychopathia sexualis*. Though the author is writing in revenge for a perceived personal wrong, he is also reacting to a world, imagined or otherwise, where women were the aggressors and dominant sex. His attack on a single woman becomes an indictment of all women and their sexuality. While hyperbole must enter some of the more outrageous accounts, what was penned was based on first-hand experience and observation. Perhaps unintentional, even unconscious, is the frequent juxtaposition of death and sensuality in *Gamiani*. Time after time Thanatos (the death force) appears simultaneously with Eros (the life principle).

De Musset was, of course, not the first author to introduce these psychosexual elements into fiction. These same themes were paramount in the eighteenth-century writings of Donatien Alphonse François, Comte de Sade. Nearly fifty years before *Gamiani*, the infamous Marquis de Sade was penning 'philosophical romances' – novels of amorality and societies of inverted moral standards and total debauchery. Women were for de Sade also the instigators of the grossest infamies, and he too based his novels on historical facts.

This philosophical relationship of death and sexual ecstasy has received even greater attention in the twentieth century, as the writings of Freud and the author/philosopher Georges Bataille have tried to demonstrate how this seemingly contradictory alliance of psychological factors can contribute explanations for such complex human activities as war and sadism.

An erotic novel, a psychosexual case study, a philosophical treatise, muckraking journalism, an act of revenge in prose, *Gamiani* is all these and more. It is a work of depth far beyond its simple narrative, as evidenced by its appeal to every generation of the last one hundred and fifty years. That is its quality as a classic, as it continues to educate and inform all who read it.

From *Gamiani*

Midnight sounded and the salons of the Comtesse Gamiani still shone in a flood of light.

The rounds and quadrilles continued animatedly to the intoxicating sounds of the orchestra. The *toilettes* were marvellous, the jewels sparkled.

Gracious, assiduous, the mistress of the ball seemed to enjoy the success of her carefully planned fête, announced at great expense. She was observed to smile agreeably to all the flattering words, to the customary phrases that each one prodigally used in payment for his presence.

Withdrawn in my habitual role of observer, I quickly judged the Comtesse Gamiani as a woman of the world, but it still remained absolutely for me to dissect her moral being, to carry the scalpel into the regions of her heart; and I know not what strange and unknown emotion withheld and stopped me in my examination. I felt an infinite pain to analyse the background of this woman's existence, whose conduct nothing explained.

Still young and with an immense fortune, pretty in the eyes of a great number, this woman was without relatives, without intimates, was alone in the world. Alone, she spent an existence capable in all appearance of supporting more than one sharer.

Many a tongue had criticised, ending always by slandering, but, in the absence of proof, the Comtesse remained absolutely impenetrable.

Some applauded her as a woman without a heart, without temperament; others supposed her a spirit profoundly wounded, who would in the future avoid cruel deceptions.

Desiring to resolve my doubts, I placed under contribution all the resources of my logic, but all was in vain; I never arrived at a satisfactory conclusion.

I was about to quit the subject when, behind me, an old libertine raised his voice in an exclamation: 'Bah! She is a tribade.'

The word was like a sudden flash of lightning. Suddenly all fit together logically and was satisfactorily explained. There was no longer a possible contradiction.

A tribade! The word rings in the ears in a strange manner. Then it raises in you I know not what strange images of unknown voluptuousness, lascivious to excess. 'Tis a luxurious rage, an infuriated lubricity, a horrible pleasure which remains forever unachieved.

Vainly I tried to put these ideas aside, but these ideas had moved my imagination to visions of debauchery. Already I saw the Comtesse nude, in the arms of another woman, with hair unbound, panting, broken and still tormented by an aborted pleasure. My blood was on fire, my senses confused, and I fell on a sofa like one in a faint.

Overcoming my emotions, I calculated coldly what I must do to surprise the Comtesse, what I must do at any price. I decided to watch her during the night and, for that purpose, to hide myself in her bedchamber.

The glass door of a clothes closet faced the bed. I perceived the advantage of that position and, screening myself with some of the costumes and garments hanging there, I resigned myself silently to await the hour of her retirement.

I was hardly hidden when the Comtesse appeared, calling her maid, a young girl of a brown tint and striking figure.

'Julie, I will do without you this evening. Go to bed. And if you hear sounds in my chamber, do not disturb yourself. I wish to be alone.'

These words almost presaged a drama. I applauded my own audacity.

Little by little the voices from the salon died out; the Comtesse remained alone with one of her friends, Mlle Fanny B. Both were soon in the chamber, and before my eyes.

FANNY: What terrible weather! The rain is falling in torrents, and not a carriage to be had anywhere.

GAMIANI: I am as desolate as you, but unfortunately my carriage is at the repair shop.

FANNY: My mother will be worried.

GAMIANI: Have no fear, my dear Fanny. Your mother is informed; she knows that you will pass the night with me. I offer you my hospitality.

FANNY: In truth, you are too good. I will only cause you trouble.

GAMIANI: Say, rather, a real pleasure. It will be an adventure to divert me. I would not send you to sleep alone in another chamber. We will remain together.

FANNY: Why? I will only keep you from sleeping.

GAMIANI: You stand too much on ceremony. See, we will be like two young friends at boarding school.

A sweet kiss reinforced this tender effusion.

GAMIANI: I will help with your undressing. My maid has retired, but we can do without her. How you are built! I admire your figure.

FANNY: You find it good?

GAMIANI: Ravishing!

FANNY: You flatter me.

GAMIANI: Oh! Simply marvellous! It is enough to make one jealous. What exquisite whiteness!

FANNY: As for that, I am no better than you. Frankly, you are whiter than I.

GAMIANI: Don't think it. Take off everything like me. What! Embarrassed? One would think that I was a man . . . There, look in that glass. See yourself so fair. You well deserve a kiss on your forehead, your cheek, your lips. You are *belle* throughout, everywhere.

The Comtesse's lips passed lasciviously, ardently, over Fanny's body. Surprised and trembling, Fanny submitted without understanding. They were a delicious couple, full of grace, of lust and lascivious abandon and fearful modesty. One would have said it was an angel, a virgin, in the arms of a *bacchante in furore*.

What beauties placed before my sight! What a spectacle to arouse and excite my senses!

FANNY: Oh! What are you doing! Stop, Madame!

GAMIANI: No! No! My Fanny, my life, my joy. You see, you are too beautiful! Oh! I love you! I love you! . . . I am crazy!

Fanny was smothered with kisses. Pressed and enlaced, the Comtesse carried her to the bed in her ardent embrace and laid her there.

'Fanny, be mine, all mine! Come, be my life! It is pleasant! How you tremble! Ah, you yield! Yes, embrace me, my little one, my love! Press me closer. How beautiful you are in your pleasure! Lascivious! You spend! You are happy! Oh God!

Then passed a strange spectacle. The Comtesse, her eyes aflame, hair unbound, rolled and twisted on Fanny, whose senses became active in their turn. Both renewed their bonds, their *élan*, smothering their sighs and cries with fiery kisses.

The bed creaked beneath their furious lunges.

The Comtesse became delirious. The pleasure killed her but did not satisfy. Furious, quivering, she leaped to the centre of the chamber, where, rolling on the carpet, she excited herself by lascivious poses, crazily lubricious, provoking with her fingers all the excesses of pleasure.

This sight succeeded in making me lose my head.

For an instant, disgust, indignation had dominated me, I wanted to show myself to the Comtesse; to load her with the weight of my disgust. But the senses were stronger than reason. The flesh triumphed, superb, quivering. I was giddy, like a fool. I presented myself – naked, all afire, purple – to the fair Fanny.

She had hardly the time to comprehend this new presence when I felt her slight, supple body tremble under me, act and respond to each of my thrusts. Our tongues met, burning, pointed; our souls melted into a single one.

FANNY: Oh! My God, good!

At these words the fair one stiffened sighed and then fell back, at the same time inundating me with her favours.

'Ah! Fanny!' I cried loudly. 'Wait . . . to you! Ah!'

And in my turn I thought I was rendering up my life.

What excess! Exhausted, lost in Fanny's arms, I had felt nothing of the Comtesse.

Recalled to herself by our cries and sighs, transported by a furore of envy, she had thrown herself upon me to tear me from her friend.

This double contact with bodies sweating pleasure, all burning with lust, ravished me still further, redoubling my desire. Fire ran throughout me. But I remained firm, victorious, in the power of Fanny; then, without losing any advantage of my position in this strange disorder of three bodies, mixed, crossed, intermingled the one in the other, I succeeded in firmly seizing the Comtesse's thighs and holding them spread above my head.

'Gamiani! Lean forwards and support yourself on your arms!'

Gamiani understood me and I could at leisure place my active, devouring tongue on her burning part.

Fanny, crazed, abandoned, amorously caressed the palpitating breasts which swung above her.

GAMIANI: What a fire you light! It is too much for me! Mercy! Oh, what lubricious play!

The Comtesse's body fell heavily to one side.

Fanny, still more exalted, threw her arms around my neck, enlaced me, pressed me.

FANNY: Dear friend! Be mine! All mine! Slow a little . . . stop! . . . ah! . . . now quicker . . . come now! Oh! I feel . . . I swim . . . I . . .

And we remained like that, the one extended on the other, rigid, without movement, our half-open mouths pressed tightly together and hardly exhaling our exhausted breath.

Little by little we recovered ourselves. The three of us got up and regarded each other stupidly for a moment.

Surprised, ashamed of her transport the Comtesse covered herself in haste. Fanny hid herself under the covers; then, like an innocent who discovers her fault when it is irreparably committed, she began to weep; the Comtesse did not wait to criticise me.

GAMIANI: Monsieur, this is certainly a miserable surprise. Your action is that of an odious spy, an infamous villain! You make me blush.

I tried to defend myself.

She replied: 'Oh, Monsieur! Know that a woman never pardons one who surpasses her in her weaknesses.'

I did my best to reply. I declared that an unhappy passion, irresistible, that her coldness had rendered desperate, had reduced me to this ruse.

'And further,' added I, 'could you believe, Gamiani, that I would ever abuse my temerity? Ah no! That would be too ignoble. Never in my life will I forget the excess of our pleasures, but I will guard the memories for myself alone.

'If I am culpable, think of the delirium in my heart, or, rather, hold but the thought of the pleasures that we have enjoyed together, and that we may enjoy again at another time.'

Then addressing myself to Fanny, the while the Comtesse turned her head aside in feigned desolation: 'Mademoiselle, should you sorrow in your pleasure? Ah! Think only of the sweet felicity that united us but a moment ago and which will remain in our memories like a happy dream, one that belongs but to you and to you alone.

'I swear to you that I will never sully the memory of my happiness by confiding it to others.'

Insensibly we soon again found ourselves all three enlaced, disputing with toyings, kisses and caresses.

'Oh, my fair friends, let no fear trouble you. Give yourselves without reserve . . . as if this night were the last . . . to joy . . . to lust.'

And Gamiani cried: 'The die is cast; to pleasure. Come, Fanny. Kiss me, dear one. Let me suck you, clear to the marrow. Alcide, do your duty . . . Oh, the superb animal! . . . What treasures!'

'You are envious, Gamiani. Let it be yours. You disdain this pleasure, but you will bless it when you have tasted it. Remain lying and shove forwards that part I must enter . . . Ah, what beauties! . . . What a posture! Quick, Fanny, straddle the Comtesse. Be firm . . . too hard, too quick, Gamiani! . . . Ah! . . . You skirmish with pleasure.'

The Comtesse acted like one possessed, more occupied with Fanny's kisses than with my efforts. I profited by her disturbing movements to lean Fanny backwards on the Comtesse's body and to enter her with vigour. In an instant we were all three melting with pleasure.

~ 5 ~

Letters produced in the Divorce Case Cavendish v. Cavendish and de la Rochefoucault

1859

Many modern adult-oriented magazines, such as *Forum* and *Penthouse Letters*, collect and print the sexiest real letters imaginable. These sort of publications did not invent this genre, but in fact follow in a grand tradition that is over two centuries old in the realm of the English-language mass-media magazine. The dawn of the Industrial Revolution and with it the advent of semi-automated printing presses, made it economically possible to print diverting, inexpensive, ephemeral material on a weekly or even daily basis. Simultaneously, social reforms, specifically those geared to reduce illiteracy, produced a new and ever growing readership, eager for any new amusements publishing entrepreneurs could offer them. Soon pictures, first in the form of woodcuts, and then metal engravings, and finally lithography (eventually in colour) added a new dimension to the simple printed word. To be successful, then as today, you had to be entertaining as well as informative. The common news – politics, foreign wars, local disasters, and the weather – wasn't enough to grab and hold the potential reader's attention. You had to offer something the reader would want to take home to read, something that would make him buy the paper, rather than just borrow someone else's. Then, as today, gossip, scandal, sex and violence are what did this best. The racier the headlines, the bigger the readership, and the bigger the publisher's profits.

Of course scandal-mongering did not originate in the eighteenth century. It is the oldest and most prevalent form of communication entertainment we have. After the necessary tasks of daily living are finished, what else fills so much of our leisure time? In pre-history and in the oral tradition (as evidenced from studies of still primitive and illiterate native cultures, yet to be tainted with modern electronics), sexy gossip was a frequent and major element of daily conversation. The great epics that survive from the ancients, such as *The Iliad* and *The Odyssey* are filled with eroticism and scandal of a political and sexual nature. Four-thousand-year-old Egyptian papyri and Babylonian clay tablets contain the same, as of course does the Bible. Suetonius's turn-of-the-millennium *Lives of the Twelve Caesars* is an example *par excellence* of this muckraking. The fourteenth-century *Canterbury Tales* and *Decameron*, with all their naughtiness, were in fact just written records of alleged social conversations. Until the *c.*1450 invention of the moveable-type printing press, by Gutenberg, these all remained available only as expensive and closely guarded handwritten manuscripts and hence (except for the Bible) accessible to only a very few wealthy and educated (literate) individuals. So it stayed until Gutenberg, at which time the small merchant middle class was allowed a peek into the shenanigans of history. And not until the mid-eighteenth century could the 'masses' have such access to popular reading.

Newspapers were fine for the news and editorials, but the thirst for entertainment led to the creation of the mature magazine as we know it today. Ostensibly at first 'news' publications, and protected from prosecution as such, the real intent of some of the more daring of them was obvious. Rereading today the eighteenth- and early-nineteenth-century English weekly 'catch-penny' magazines (they cost but a penny or two, hence their name), such as *The Crim Con Gazette, The Bon Ton Gazette, The New Bon Ton, The Bon Ton Magazine, The Rambler, The Rambler's Magazine, The New Rambler's Magazine, The Ranger's Magazine, Paul Spry, The Ferret, Peter Spy, The Pearl, The Cremorne, The Boudoir*, etc., one finds that except for the spellings of words and the archaic language, they read literally the same as our modern scandal tabloids. Lurid descriptions of brutal murders, domestic violence, illicit affairs among the gentry and rapes perpetrated on poor domestics filled the pages. Perhaps most *risqué* of all the printed 'news' were the salacious crim. con. (i.e. criminal conversations entered as evidence in divorce hearings). The kinky allegations of celebrated recent divorces, such as that of the Pulitzers, had nothing on what our great-great-great-great-great-great-great-grandparents could read in reports of the notorious marriage dissolutions of their own times.

'Grub Street journalism' – named for the area in London where the scandal sheets originated – developed as a separate journalistic tradition.

All semblance of 'legitimate' news was slowly replaced with more and more titillating gossip and 'gut smut'. Racy short stories and excerpts from sexy and banned books were added to the pages to pad the non-fiction fare. The evolutionary culmination of this trend was achieved in *The Pearl* (1879–81), which was a pornographic Victorian monthly magazine whose sole purpose was erotic entertainment.

The trend in 'adult' mass-market magazines has since that time tended back towards the eighteenth-century model. Once again factual news, including matters of sexual health, are an integral part of the format. Audience participation, in the form of letters to the editor, letters to advice councillors or letters sharing personal experiences, has been found to boost popularity, so letters have become an important part of the modern adult magazine. Technology has allowed for more and better photo-illustration, hence the final product as we currently have it.

The Cavendish Divorce Letters are an example of a potential 'letters'-type submission which were written in the mid-nineteenth century. As first published, they contain excerpts from sexually explicit letters written in 1859 between the Count de la Rochefoucault and his married mistress, Mrs Chichester, wife of Lord Cavendish, while the Count was an *attaché* to the French Embassy at Rome. The French-language originals of these letters were discovered when, during the course of divorce proceedings, the cuckolded husband broke into his wife's davenport. A sworn notary's translation was made and given to the magistrate, who felt they were too licentious and scandalous to be read in open court. H. S. Ashbee, who recounts this story (*Catena*, 1885, pp.185–8), tells that the judge instead took the letters home with him to read! It was noted that the adulteress was a woman of about forty-five years of age, with several children, but of an apparently lascivious, lustful and randy temperament, and not unlike so many of her age, then and now, who provoke an extremely strong sexual infatuation in men of a younger age.

It is an almost poetic irony that the same law that tries to suppress sexually explicit fiction and prose, compels the same to be made publicly available when it is evidence or testimony in legal proceedings. As part of the official record, unexpurgated and unedited material becomes public domain, printed in the legal records for the lawyer, the scholar, and the prurient equally to divine. No wonder the Holywell Street publishers (the nineteenth-century London district roughly equivalent to New York City's 'porno' 42nd Street area) printed up such testimony whenever they could for sale to the masses. Our own copy of the text is taken not from its first printed appearance in 1876 as the final pages of the erotic novel *The Romance of Lust*, but from a separate *c.*1891 offprint of just the letters, an offprint attesting to their continued popularity.

How much of de la Rochefoucault's letters are fact and how much are imagination and fantasy could perhaps best be answered by modern 'letters' writers, whose epistles are so integral a part of so many magazine publications today.

from *The Cavendish Divorce Letters*

When I shall have undressed my adorable little mistress it will be nine o'clock. She will be mad with desire, delirious from passion and rapturous excitements, her maddening look, exciting in the highest degree, will arouse all the strength I possess, and enable me to exhaust her so completely that she herself will attain the height of happiness. The greater the refinement and delicacy of my caresses, the greater will be your happiness; the more languishing your eyes become, the more will your pretty mouth unclose itself; the more your tongue becomes agitated, the more will your bosoms, firm and soft as velvet, become distended and their nipples grow large, red and appetising. Then will your arms grow weaker, and then will your angelic legs open themselves in a voluptuous manner, and then, seeing ourselves reflected on all sides in the mirrors, shall I take you in my arms in order to excite you with my hand, whilst your own rosy fingers will similarly excite me with vigour, and I shall suck your divine nipples with passion. When the agitation of your little legs, of your lovely little *derrière*, of your head, and those murmurs of pleasure prove to me that you are at the point of emission, I shall stop and carry you to a piece of furniture made to sustain your head, your back, your bottom and your legs, and having secured an opening sufficiently wide to allow my body to pass erect between your legs, I shall fuck you with frenzy with my enormous and long member, which will penetrate to the mouth of your womb. Being squeezed by your pretty legs, which will bring me closer to you, I shall wriggle my strong pretty member, which you love, with more vigour than ever; my testicles will touch your little bottom, and this contact will provoke such an abundant flow of the essence of love in your little cunt that I shall be as wet as if I were in a bath.

How I fear to leave off here! But we shall see. Do not write to me by the night post, it is useless! It is true that when I am near you in a carriage I have difficulty in remaining quiet. Oh, no, do not alarm me by your insatiability, my desire is much greater than yours, there is not the slightest comparison to be drawn between us from a physical point of view, but as far as our moral nature and hearts are concerned we can rival each other.

1:30 I was most annoyingly interrupted by the luncheon bell, and afterwards I played a game of Fourreau (a game all the fashion at Verteuil), and here I am again. I have just refused to accompany my father and mother on a drive in the neighbourhood, so that I shall be able to write to you more at length.

You tell me that you like the little costume, but that is all you say, and you give me no details as to liking the colours, length and shape. I believe, my treasure, my jewel, that your bosoms will be white, swollen and soft as velvet, and it is very nice of you to tell me that my hands will have difficulty in containing them and putting their ruby tips to my mouth.

You are quite right in saying that you will develop my virility, it is you who have made my member what it is now. I repeat, on my word of honour, perhaps you will not like to hear these details, but, nevertheless, I shall say it. You are the first woman in the world who has stimulated that essence which flows from my prick, which your kisses have rendered so pretty, and it is you who have plucked the flower of my virginity. Never have I had any other woman, and whatever may be the misfortunes to which I may be destined, it will always be an immense and ineffable happiness to me to think that I have given and lost it through the luscious draughts you offer. It is, and it will be, perhaps, the greatest blessing, and the only consolation of my life. But before God it is a great one, and my enjoyment has not been such as one can expect to find in this world. I do not believe that even he who had the pleasure to rob you of your virginity was as pure as myself, and as for voluptuous pleasures, if there be any greater than that which I know, I promise you never to learn or seek it. I do not wish to have any other woman spoken of, they all disgust me, even to look at them. You know it, and you know that there is nothing, absolutely nothing, in you to disgust me, but all that belongs to you maddens me, and I love and adore all. It has become a madness, and you know it, for when you are kind you acknowledge at least the idea by letter.

In you everything appears different and pure. The purity which reigns in your every feature, the excess of refinement which exists in your whole body, your hands, your feet, your legs, your cunt, your bottom, the hairs of your private parts, all is appetising, and I know that the same purity exists in all my own desires for you. As much as the odour of women is repugnant to me in general, the more do I like it in you. I beg of you to preserve that intoxicating perfume; but you are too clean, you wash yourself too much. I have often told you so in vain. When you will be quite my own, I shall forbid you to do it too often, at most once a day. My tongue and my saliva shall do the rest.

If it is necessary, let the doctor examine you, and mind he does not fall in love with you. I bet he has never before seen anything so seducing, so pretty or so perfect. It is to be hoped that the irritation you speak of does not proceed from the size of my member.

I would lavish the following caresses upon you, angel of my delight, were I a little calmer. I had a dream, such as it was, about it last night, and only remember it just now by way of explanation of my mad excitement of this morning. I saw you as I was asleep, you were by my side frigging me with your fingers of love, and you heard me say to you, 'I see you there.' You were as lovely as Venus, your lusciousness and lasciviousness were at their very height, your body was completely perfumed for my enjoyment so that I might lick you. You had painted the most seductive parts of your person. Your shoulders were white, your rosy bosoms revealed themselves through a rose-coloured gauze trimmed with bows of the same hue. Your thighs, as well as your navel and your heavenly bottom, were revealed through a heavenly gauze, your legs were clad in rose-coloured stockings. The sperm flowed; how much I needed the release! This is true, for my testicles were swollen in an alarming manner.

Oh, my child, my pretty little mistress, if you only knew how much I suffer from the excessive heat, and the privation in which I live! Without exaggeration, my testicles are enormous. My member is as large, straight and stiff as my arm. I am mad with desire for you. I had the unhappy idea of going to bed again. My mind was full of this dream I had had, and of which you were, of course, the subject. Then I thought of the caresses which you would have been obliged to submit to. And at last, in consequence of your letter of yesterday, a mere half sheet, so pretty at the beginning and at the end, but yet quite beside the question, I found myself engaged in the act of rubbing myself with frenzy, and of stroking myself and of frigging my prick until I was exhausted, before I could discharge the merest drop. That was too much for me, and now I desire you like a madman. If a delicious half sheet does not arrive by the Embassy bag, I know not what will become of me. I have had an emission. I am saved. I feel myself so relieved. You have forbidden my going with other women. You are determined that I shall not have a discharge with anyone but yourself, and that I fuck no one but you. Oh! How I love you.

It is two o'clock in the morning, I have violated and worked you well, kissed, frigged, licked and sucked you, obliged you to yield to desires the most debauched, the most shameless, during the whole of the afternoon. All the afternoon, too, I have got you to suck my member and my testicles. I have made you pass your tongue between my toes and under my arms. I have got you to paint your body. I was almost on the point of getting you sucked and licked by a pretty maid, perfectly naked, between your legs, but you withdrew from my delirium.

I have had discharges from jealousy. I have discharged at least forty times, and when, after having left you to go to my club, I returned home, and finding you fast asleep from exhaustion, I awakened you and insisted upon your frigging me with your rosy fingers, all the while licking my parts. You implore me. You are wearied, but I am intractable. You must do it in order to excite yourself as much as I am myself excited. I suck your breasts with frenzy. The sucking that I have given your bosoms, and the fear you have lest I should fetch a girl to violate you with her breasts in your cunt, filling your womb with her nipples to excite your senses, stimulates you unbearably. And then you hear a voice whose sound alone so pleasingly tickles your womb, saying to you, 'My pretty mistress, I implore you to abandon yourself to me. I will love you so fondly. I will be so kind and gentle, I am so handsome, I will do all you can possibly wish. I know so well how to have and suck a woman, my member is enormous, it is beautiful, rose-coloured, large, long, hard and vigorous. Yield yourself to me.'

Tell me if you like this one.

When you are ready you will call me so that I may come and say my daily 'How do you do.' You will begin by taking my prick out of my trousers, then, half opening your gown, you will lift up your pretty chemise with one hand, and will pass your other arm, soft as satin, round my neck. I shall embrace you tenderly, then I shall lick your snow-white shoulders and your bosoms, which seem to be bursting from the imprisonment of your rose-coloured stays embroidered with lace. I shall lick between your legs, over your divine little bottom, your nymph-like thighs being at that moment on my knees. Then you will place your angelic little feet, with your stockings on, one after the other in my mouth. After this you will send me into the dining room, in order to get rid of the servants, and, by this time, filled with an amorous and impassioned languor, each of your movements will breathe forth the frenzy and voluptuousness of passion.

There will be only one chair, and the table will be laid for only one person. We shall each of us have only one hand free, I the right, and you the left. Then you will sit upon my left leg, which you have found means to make naked; you will have unfastened your gown in such a way that it will hang down behind, and your right hand will caress and stroke my enormous prick, which you will have taken between your legs without putting it into your angelic cunt, whilst my left arm will wind itself round your lovely waist in order to bring you still nearer to me.

After breakfast, which will have lasted till half-past twelve, and which will have given you strength, we will go into the little rose-coloured boudoir. I shall place myself in a low narrow chair, and as I shall be very much excited by your enchanting looks, my enormous member will come out of its own accord from its prison, and you will sit astraddle upon me, introducing, with the greatest difficulty, my pretty and vigorous prick into your pretty girl-like cunt. You will wriggle about from sheer enjoyment, then stop your movements every time I tell you I am on the point of discharging, so as to increase my desires and my transports of happiness.

Then in half an hour's time you will get up and place yourself upon the sofa, whilst I, at your desire, shall slip off all my clothes. Then you will get up from the sofa and take off your dressing gown, only keeping on what you have underneath. In my turn I will stretch myself on the sofa, getting every moment more delirious with passion, for your dress, betraying the delicious outlines of your figure, without revealing it entirely, will render me almost beside myself, and will make my prick so long and so stiff that you will hardly be able to sit on its point. And then, as I introduce it into your delicious cunt, in spite of its size, I will force from you sighs and murmurs of rapture. At last, when once seated, fucked by my manly and powerful prick, you will throw yourself backwards. I should lean my enraptured legs against your bosoms, in order that you might lick my feet, while you would pass your amorous and divine legs, softer, whiter, and more rose-tinted every day, over the whole breadth of my chest, placing your tiny goddess-like feet in my mouth. As our desires would augment at every moment, you would allow me, would even ask me, to take off your garters, your pretty stockings and your slippers, in order to procure me the luxury of licking every part of your body, and of realising in the most perfect manner the intense enjoyment arising from the contact of the most delicate, the most woman-like, the most voluptuous portion of your body. My hands would frig your little love of a member, my manly prick would kiss your celestial womb and my thighs would caress your delicious bottom. When I have worked you in this way for an hour, ceasing every moment you were on the point of emission, I should, as I withdrew my member, let you at last discharge, and, pressing my mouth to this delicious font, allow an immense stream of love to flow into my mouth, which, suddenly and as if by enchantment, would find itself in the place of my member, while your bosoms would be covered with that white essence which would escape from my amorous member.

Every day after dinner, reclining voluptuously on a couch, you would snatch a few moments of repose while I was taking off all my clothes. When I had finished, and when I, filled with love, had shown myself to your contemplation, you would give up to me your place upon the sofa, and, assuming the most seductive, the most coquettish and the most graceful attitudes, you would come and play with my member, whose vigour would arise solely from the sight of your pretty costume, which, I am convinced, would render you more delicious than the most graceful fairy. You would love me so deeply that I should cease to have any power of will. You would have exhausted me, sucking me completely dry, nothing would remain in my prick, which would be more full of desire, more enormous, and stiffer at every moment. My languishing eyes, gentle as love itself, surrounded by large dark blue circles caused by your look, your tongue, your bosom, your cunt, your member, your heavenly little bottom, your legs, your fingers and your angelic little feet, would tell you how complete was my happiness, my intoxication, my ecstasy, and my faint, exhausted but happy voice would give you the same assurance, murmuring with rapture in your ears – 'Oh! How I love you, my lady love, my divine little virgin. Caress me yet once more, again, still again, it is a dream. Thank you, oh, thank you, and yet again. Oh, I am in heaven, do not pause, I implore you, suck me harder than ever, lick me well. Oh! What rapture! Ask me what you will, it shall be yours. You are my mistress, no other but you in the whole world can transport me in this way. Frig me with your knees. Oh! Oh! Oh! I am going to discharge!'

Then, more full of passion than any woman had ever been, and enraptured as you listened to my voice, completely beneath your sway, you would raise your little coquettish petticoat, and pressing your dear little loves of calves more closely together, for you would be on your knees, you would frig me in this manner, with greater vigour than ever, sitting down every now and then upon your tiny little heels, in order the better to release my beautiful prick, perfectly straight and rudely swollen and inflamed with passionate desires sprung from between your divine thighs, as soft as satin, and as white as snow, to better introduce the wet tips of your lovely and velvet-like bosoms into the seductive little hole of my member. My knees, raised slightly behind, would gently caress your bottom, so as to give you some little satisfaction in your turn. And at last, unable any longer to retard the moment of emission, you would bend forwards, resting upon both your hands, to increase my desire, and keeping yourself back a little distance from me, while your petticoats would now cover my head, and act almost like an electrical conductor upon me, you would intoxicate me with the perfume exhaled from your legs, from your member, from your cunt, from your bottom, and you would slake my thirst and complete the celestial transport by shooting, with eager rapture, between my burning lips some of that woman's nectar which you alone possess, and which, emanating from you alone in the world, is worthy of the gods.

You cannot form any idea of my excitement at this moment. I hope you will like this, and will answer me prettily. Am I sufficiently in love? And do you believe that there will be another woman in the whole world beside yourself for whom I shall have any desire? Oh, how wild is the longing that I have for you at this moment, and this nectar I have spoken of, from whom else could I care for it, could I endure it even, whilst from you evoking what mad delight! Tell me, do you believe this? You know it perfectly well, I am sure; these are not mere words. Tell me that you will discharge into my mouth again when I ask you. I am now going to try to sleep, but what chance have I of doing so with this love that consumes me? I must await your pretty letter of tomorrow morning, for it is that alone which will excite the flow and stream.

Someone is coming. Adieu!

~ 6 ~

Nunnery Tales
1866–8

If Guinness records were ever given for erotica, *Nunnery Tales* would certainly get the prize for the fastest paced novel with the most non-stop sex activity. By the end of the book's second paragraph the reader already knows almost all there is to know about the main characters, and by the end of the second page the stage has been credibly set for the libertinism that has already started and continues unabated for the next four hundred pages! Perhaps not since Robert Louis Stevenson's *Treasure Island* has a work of fiction got into the action so quickly.

The plot of *Nunnery Tales* is simple. Augustus is the seventeen-year-old son of a French aristocrat who has fled to England to escape the wrath of the French Revolution's *sans culottes* (literally 'no underwear') rabble. With his mother, the boy (now dressed as a young lady and called Augustine) seeks refuge in a convent, where his aunt is the Abbess. The two arrive just as a novice is to receive chastisement from Father Eustace, the local confessor. The punishment is totally secular and overtly sexual, to the joy of the penitent, whose crime had been the use of a candle to assuage her sexual urgings. The female disguise fools no one, but it is decided that Augustus/Augustine can remain as long as there are no complaints from the convent residents. Not only is there no outcry but what follows is an orgy of the most amorous and arduous sex imaginable, punctuated only by episodes of storytelling, in which the various players recount their own sexual histories.

Nunnery Tales first appeared in Victorian England. It was published in three volumes in 1866, 1867 and 1868 by the notorious pornography publisher William Dugdale. The author is to this day still unknown. Although the great erotica bibliographer H. S. Ashbee noted the book to be poorly printed, filled with typographical errors, of 'no tone or character' and consisting of orgies of only the lowest kind, the book has

THE ENCYCLOPEDIA OF EROTIC LITERATURE

been reprinted frequently in English, and has gone through several editions in French and German.

The structure of *Nunnery Tales* appears familiar, as well it should, as it is derivative of many works of erotica that preceded it. The novel takes place during the terrors of the French Revolution, and is a series of stories and orgies told and performed to pass the time by the inhabitants of a convent and their aristocratic guests. It is reminiscent of Geoffrey Chaucer's classic fourteenth-century *Canterbury Tales*, which, with its several salacious episodes, e.g. the Miller's scatological story and the randy recitation by the Wife of Bath, is also a collection of short stories told to pass the time, but here by a group of religious pilgrims on their way to Canterbury Cathedral during the time of a grievous plague. Next is Boccaccio's 1527 *Decameron*, a collection of a hundred ribald stories told over a ten-day period by ten young men and women for their own entertainment. *The Heptameron* by Margaret of Navarre in the same century is again a collection of licentious tales, here told to pass time within castle walls while the Black Death scourged Europe. Even more similar is de Sade's *The 120 Days of Sodom*, in which again refugees from the French Revolution spend their days in a non-stop sexual frenzy.

In *Nunnery Tales*, the tellers in turn recount their own past sexual experiences, and the stories are each interrupted by explicit descriptions of the lustful activities the tales induce from the audience. On a scale of one to ten, *Nunnery Tales* must rate next to zero for erotic realism. The novel is in fact pure male fantasy. The perpetual virility of the male characters is nothing short of superhuman. Although the fornication is non-stop, the males' potency never wanes or droops. The ever-ready sexual tumescence defies the natural laws of human biology and physiology. No other erotic novel, not even the legendary *Romance of Lust*, has as much constant sexual activity.

The novel's recurring themes, beyond sexual intercourse in its myriad variations, are also from the male sexual *id*. Voyeurism, transvestism, female masturbation, lesbianism, dildo fetish, defloration mania, gentle sadomasochism, and an endless supply of willing sexual partners is the psychiatric stuff of daydreams. The anticlerical theme is also an attempt at wish fulfilment. Not vicious, as in *Gamiani*, *Maria Monk*, or even *The Autobiography of a Flea*, it serves as a symbolic statement of the author's defiance of conventional authority. The characters act contrary to the accepted moral and religious laws, though never sadistically as in de Sade's *120 Days*. The strongest defiant point is made by the surrogate violation of the incest taboo, as those with the religious titles of 'father', 'mother', 'sister' and 'brother' all consort sexually. More concretely, it is discovered that several of the characters are in fact related in the manner indicated by their religious forms of address.

Nunnery Tales is not an attempt accurately to describe the actual activities of any religious group. The author did no homework; the descriptions of the mechanics of order life are all wrong. Further, there is no pretence at great writing. As Ashbee accurately pointed out, *Nunnery Tales* has no character or plot development. The tone of the book is an almost monotonous recitation of superhuman sexual excesses. Augustus, in turn, has sex with each and every sister in the convent. Episode follows episode, and not one is integral to the overall integrity of the novel. None are meant to be. Base (basic) human sexual activity is presented to the reader purely for its entertainment value. What the author wanted, and achieved, was erotic entertainment that came directly from and appealed directly to the fantasy life that we all have within us. In the words of the publisher himself, in *Nunnery Tales* 'every stretch of voluptuous imagination is here fully depicted, rogering, ramming, one unbounded scene of lust, lechery, and licentiousness'.

Here then is the opening sexual scene from *Nunnery Tales*.

⟅⟆ from *Nunnery Tales*

We were most cordially welcomed by my aunt, the Lady Abbess of St Claire, who however could not help lamenting the necessity which there was for us to take refuge with her – I noticed that she stared at me with great curiosity and whispered apart to my mother. The answer that she received seemed to be only partly satisfactory, as she shrugged her shoulders and slightly smiled as she glanced at me: 'I do not doubt your stepdaughter's discretion, but I hope that she will recollect that she is Mademoiselle de Ermenonville and will behave as becomes her rank and sex!' This was addressed to me with very pointed emphasis, but all my reply was a low sweeping curtsy at which feminine performance my mother could not repress her smiles. 'But my dear Henriette,' commenced the abbess, 'I fear that I must treat you inhospitably, turn you out of the room, in fact, for I am momentarily in expectation of the arrival of Father Eustace.'

'Oh, I know him very well indeed,' replied my mother, appearing to me rather confused, 'and there is no necessity for me to leave the room unless you want a very private interview with him, Agatha!'

'None of your badinage,' replied the abbess, tapping her sister's cheek, 'the father is coming here on duty.'

'Those handsome young monks are always on duty,' muttered my mother. But here we were interrupted by a tap at the door, and as the abbess gave the necessary permission, a tall, handsome young nun entered who, first making a lowly obeisance to the superior and a slighter recognition of the two ladies unknown (my mother and myself), remarked, 'I have come holy Mother, to receive my punishment.'

'You have done well to keep your time punctually, daughter Emilie,' replied the abbess, not unkindly. 'It shows some degree of penitence and though the degree of the penance must rest in a great manner with Father Eustace, yet I think I can promise that you will not be treated very severely. But stripped you will have to be, so you had better begin to undress yourself at once in order to save time.'

'Will these ladies remain to be spectatresses of the proceedings?' asked Emilie, alluding to my mother and myself.

'Why, it is rather unusual to allow strangers to be present,' replied the abbess, 'but as these ladies are my sister and niece, I think I may venture to grant them the privilege.'

'Certainly, I should like it of all things,' replied my mother; 'I have a great curiosity to see what penance Father Eustace, whom I know very well, will impose on a fine girl such as Sister Emilie. Pray what fault has she been committing?'

'Oh, dear Lady Agatha, pray don't tell your sister,' exclaimed Emilie. 'I should die of shame!'

'Nonsense, my child,' replied the abbess. 'Proceed with your disrobing yourself, and then go and kneel down upon that buffet in the corner and repeat one of the penitential psalms to get yourself into a proper frame of mind before the arrival of Father Eustace.'

(I may mention here parenthetically that I had on my first entrance into the room remarked this so-called 'buffet' and wondered what its use was! It was a sort of low divan, provided with pillows and cushions, and covered with black velvet. On this black velvet altar then, which set off the dazzling whiteness of her skin most charmingly, the beautiful Emilie knelt down as a victim for sacrifice, and having spread her legs, proceeded to her devotions or what we presumed to be such. She was stark naked with the exception of her slippers and stockings; her massive locks of black hair, escaping from their cincture, hung over her snowy shoulders).

I was not altogether without experience in women's charms. For instance, I was more than intimate with a pretty *grisette*, a seamstress who lived on the top floor of a house in the Rue Joubert. She was very sweet and loving and lively, and appreciated my fucking her in the most flattering style. Also a young housemaid, a particular favourite of my mother, who, while making her ladyship's bed one day was astonished, but not disagreeably I fancy, to find her petticoats thrown up from behind abruptly, and a hot, stiff cock thrust violently up her cunt between her buttocks. But never in all my youthful experience had I seen such a sight as was presented by the young novice, Emilie – while I was devouring with my eyes, her varied charms, the swell of her bust, partially concealed by her posture, her long graceful legs, and above all her delicious cunt, looking like a knot of black moss pierced with vermilion and placed between two large cushions of satin texture and snowy whiteness.

Surely Father Eustace can never be such a brute as to flog that lovely rump, I thought to myself. As these reflections were passing through my mind, my aunt was informing my mother regarding the fault for which Emilie was to suffer. It appears that, in consequence of the young lady complaining about being poorly, she was allowed an extra quantity of candle in her sleeping apartment, where the lady abbess was kind enough to visit her in the middle of the night – when, to her intense consternation, instead of finding her young patient wrapped in slumber or restless with pain, her young *protégé* was lying partly uncovered with her legs lasciviously spread open as far as they could go, a large candle rammed about nine inches up her cunt, which she was working most furiously and heaving and wriggling her rump about as if she were possessed of a devil! Of course any attempt at concealment or excuse was utterly useless, as Lady Agatha was an eyewitness of the transaction; indeed, at the very minute of her entering the apartment, the natural result took place, and Mademoiselle Emilie sunk back upon the pillows in a half-fainting state, leaving her candle to drop out of its moistened sheath at its leisure.

Emilie, on being scolded, retorted on her with some impertinent remarks about handsome young confessors and the superior's special privileges, etc. All this my aunt retailed to my mother in a half whisper, not altogether unheard, however, by the beautiful culprit on the cushions, who, as I could perceive as I closely watched her, could hardly restrain her laughter. She is not much afraid of Father Eustace, thought I, and I was right.

In he came at length, but before paying any attention to his penitent, he saluted the lady abbess with what I suppose he considered a 'holy kiss', and then turned to my mother with delight and surprise: 'Good

Heavens, my dear Madame de Ermenonville, what brings you here? And who is this – this – young lady?'

This he said with some emphasis, and I saw in a moment that he had found me out. But my mother prevented any outbreak at the moment; she drew him on one side and spoke to him in a whisper. This conversation was not long and ended in his saying, 'Then, Henriette, will you promise? If so, I will not only keep the secret, but do my best for you in the bargain!'

This agreement was ratified by a half-dozen kisses given and taken, which somehow seemed to me hardly to be very holy ones. But I supposed my mother knew best – she remarked, 'Now I think, Father Eustace, that poor girl has been on her knees awaiting her penance long enough, and in common charity you ought to inflict it, whatever it is, only don't be too severe upon her!'

I may say here that he was a very good-looking man, indeed but for his unbecoming dress he would have struck any observer as being downright handsome. But a brown serge gown, open in the front and merely fastened by a girdle, is not a becoming costume, and what seemed strange to me was that he had on no breeches, or other garments of any description. But I very soon found that this was intentional, and not neglectful. Turning round and regarding with lustful complacency the lovely posterior and private charms displayed by the kneeling girl, he briefly asked the abbess if she had confessed her sin and promised repentance. Being answered in the affirmative he remarked he would not use the rod but would merely whisper forgiveness and pour in a little holy oil, after which the young sister might consider herself absolved and purified. Nothing could be milder in the way of penance than this, and to my astonishment as he knelt down to approach his face to the novice's white buttocks, his frock became a little open in front, and a most monstrous standing prick became undisguisedly exposed to view – it was a powerful machine, with a huge purple knob! As it was quite clear to me how all this penance would terminate, I could not help thinking that Mademoiselle Emilie would find it rather a different affair to the tallow candle.

His whispering forgiveness, as he called it, consisted of his putting his tongue up the private little treasure and gently sucking it. When he fancied he had it sufficiently opened and lubricated for his purpose, he proceeded to administer what he denominated his holy oil, this was effected simply by ramming his enormous cock into the orifice from which he had just taken his mouth and, to make use of a common expression, he began to fuck the lovely girl in dog fashion. She on her part bore it very well, much better than I could have considered it possible; after two or three natural exclamations such as 'Ah!' and 'Oh!', produced by the weapon at first forcing an entrance, she seemed to reciprocate his forceful shoves, and I particularly noticed that she bent down so that by looking under her belly, she could see Father Eustace's entire performance and the noble tool that he was working with. My mother I dared not look at, but as I stood in one corner with my arms round my aunt's waist, I could not for the life of me help resting the other hand upon her well rounded arse, and she never so much as whispered an objection, so she must have been feeling something rather queer. And there was a prominence exhibited in the front of my frock such as no girl could exhibit except indeed she had pocketed a cucumber or a rolling pin.

His fair penitent was the first to give in, which she showed by sinking down from her sturdy kneeling posture until she was all but prostrate on her belly; the confessor of course stuck to her in this position almost simultaneously with her own transport. In two or three minutes he gently withdrew himself, warmly kissing her plump charms and assuring her of entire absolution and complete forgiveness.

Then he turned to my mother and, looking towards me in a very expressive way, said that he wished to talk with her on a certain subject privately. My aunt said her room was at her sister's service, and she would stay and help Emilie to dress.

'It is too much honour for me, dear lady,' said Emilie. 'Perhaps this young lady would lend me a little assistance; she looks very good natured, and I should so like a glass of wine, kind lady Agatha, for I feel very much exhausted!'

'Naturally, my child,' responded my aunt, 'I will give you one.' So saying, she left the room, turning round as she did so with rather a quaint expression on her face, as if she were rather uncertain as to what the upshot of my assisting Emilie to dress might lead to.

'Dear Mademoiselle,' she remarked, 'you are as kind and loving as if you were a young man and not a young lady!'

'Perhaps,' said I, in a bantering tone, 'you would have no objection if I were a young man?'

'Well,' she replied, 'I should like such a brother as you, or a cousin . . . '

'Or a lover,' I hinted.

'After the scene you have just witnessed, my kind friend, it would be useless for me to affect any prudery, or even modesty; of course it was the duty of the abbess to be present, but I think it was rather too bad of her to inform you and your mother of my fault and allow you to witness my punishment.'

'Don't apologise, sweet Emilie,' I replied, kissing her. 'It was a very pretty sight indeed, a most luxurious spectacle; pray did the holy father hurt you at all?'

'Why, no,' she replied, 'as long as the penance lasted I rather enjoyed it, but now I do feel rather inflamed and sore.'

'Permit me,' I replied, 'to wipe your secret charms dry with my cambric handkerchief. I will do it gently, and you will find yourself much more comfortable.'

Without waiting for her permission, I knelt down before her and, taking up her undergarments, proceeded to dry the delicate lips of her little moss rosebud and the adjacent parts. As I predicted, she found great comfort from this operation and was profuse in her gratitude. While I on my part protested that it was a pleasure to do such a delicate piece of service to such a splendid girl as herself.

Now, this complimentary remark of mine led to unforeseen results. Emilie immediately replied that such a compliment from me was very valuable inasmuch as I was one of the finest and tallest girls she had ever seen and that she was sure I was well made. So saying, she endeavoured, as lascivious girls will do, to feel my person and, as may readily be imagined, felt something quite unexpected. In fact, as I have before stated, my silk frock stuck out in front of me in a most strange and prominent manner.

'Good Heavens! What is this? Have you a dildo strapped on?' she exclaimed in a low tone. 'You had better look and see,' I answered, laughing!

Without a word more she, in her turn, went down upon her knees and, to her surprise and delight, found situated among the usual correct articles of ladies' underclothing, such as silk stockings, cambric chemise, ornamental petticoats, etc., an article not at all down in the list of a lady's *toilette* (except indeed when it is artificial!). She found a fine prick with its usual globular attendants in a fiery state of stiffness and thoroughly ready for work. She instantly grasped it with delight, and the consequences would inevitably have been that she would have found herself on her back on the divan from which she had just arisen from her pleasing penance; but a light footstep was heard in the corridor, and she dropped my petticoats just in time, as my aunt, her superior, entered the room, bringing in some wine.

'I have brought you in some refreshment as I promised, my child, but upon my word you don't seem to require it – you have got quite a colour in your cheeks, thanks, I presume, to the kind attentions of my niece Augustine. But mind, my dear niece, I do not approve of even young ladies being too affectionate; it sometimes leads to nonsense, if not to mischief.' This was of course meant as a broad hint for me to be careful, but the mischief was half done already!

'But, dear Lady Mother, pray may I not take Mademoiselle Augustine to some of our sisters to introduce her? They will be glad to see a fresh face and hear some news about society.'

'Hum, ha,' replied my aunt, apparently not much liking the proposition. 'Well, I grant permission on strict conditions that you do not neglect chapel or any of your other duties and that you bring my niece to my room after vespers, as she must sup with her mamma and me.'

'Your commands shall be punctually obeyed, Madame,' replied Emilie. Making a low reverence and taking me by the hand, we quitted the room together.

As we went down the corridor, she broke into a short laugh and said, 'The lady abbess is quite jealous; she guesses some thing about you, and if it had not been for my happy idea of introducing you to the other novices, I should not have been able to enjoy the pleasure of your society, certainly not alone But I will bring you into the company of Louise and Adele, who are pretty, playful girls, and almost as lascivious, if they knew how, as the Lady Abbess herself, and that is saying a good deal. By the by, I hope you do not consider it immoral to sleep with your aunt, for she most certainly will make you do so tonight, and she will, if all accounts are true, give you such a specimen of voluptuous and even obscene lust, as you never had any idea of – the scene you lately witnessed in the penance chamber is nothing to what you would experience. But here we are at one of the young ladies' apartments and here are my young friends.

'Adele and Louise, my dears, here is Mademoiselle Augustine Ermenonville, whom the superior has allowed me to bring here as an addition to our society this afternoon.' Here both the pretty girls who had been sitting at embroidery frames rose from their seats and kissed me warmly.

'We had better make the most of her society, for her aunt the lady abbess fancies there is something manly in her appearance, and she intends her to sleep with her tonight and you know, girls, what the consequence of that will be; she will be too much exhausted for us to have any fun with her tomorrow!'

'Adele knows,' said Louise. 'It is a pleasure which I have yet to learn.'

'Tell us all about it, dear Adele,' said I. 'It will amuse me greatly.'

'Since it is so, I will tell you,' said the sweet girl, 'though I am rather ashamed. The lady superior reported herself ill and nervous, and wishing someone to stop in her room all night, made selection of me. I gladly consented, taking it as a compliment, and repaired to the lady's apartment, where I found her already in bed; she desired me to undress and come to bed, leaving the lamp burning. I had no sooner lain down beside her, than she thrust her hand between my thighs and shoved a couple of fingers into my private parts and began working me, to my consternation, for I knew nothing about such lustful games. She had not continued this long before she altered her position and knelt down, if you can understand my description, with her belly upon my breasts, her fat rump resting on my face and the lips of her cunt applied to the lips of my mouth. She then desired me to shove my tongue into her orifice and work it well in, and I, though more than half smothered, was obliged to comply and do my best to give her pleasure. I must acknowledge that she did her best to reciprocate, as according to our relative positions her head naturally fell between my thighs and she put her tongue into me as well as she could; of course she could not do me the justice that I did her, but she did enough as I very soon found out. And as for my holy superior, whether I did my duty by her or not may be judged from the fact that in a few minutes, after some convulsive lifting and wriggling on her part, my mouth was filled and my face and throat drenched with a warm, oily liquor. Then she lazily rolled off me and lay for a few minutes with her naked legs on the pillow and her person completely exposed. I, on my part, thought it advisable to get a towel and wipe my face and her rump.

This done, she wanted her medicine, which I found on tasting to be neither more nor less than curaçoa. After this stimulant she went to sleep, and I hoped for a quiet night's rest. But I was never more mistaken in my life, for about two o'clock in the morning I was awakened by her kissing me, which I took as an honour, though I was sorry to be disturbed. She then asked me if I was a virgin, and on my assuring her of the fact, she proceeded to satisfy herself by thrusting her finger up me as far as it would go. Finding an obstacle, she announced her intention of taking my maidenhead. How she intended to do this I hardly knew, but I was speedily enlightened, for stripping off her only garment, her chemise, she took out of a drawer a curious thing that seemed like a thick ivory ruler, about nine inches long, partly covered with red velvet. This apparatus had an elastic appendage shaped like a ball, which she filled from a vial and the whole machine was firmly strapped round her front and bottom by a strong bandage.

She proceeded to shove this instrument up me, forcing my virgin barrier. Indeed, I am certain that my exclamations and half-suppressed cries of pleasure gave her the utmost delight. When she began to find from my movements and unmistakable signs that I was reciprocating her proceedings, she placed one hand under her buttocks and, squeezing the ball before mentioned, spouted a strong jet of warm, milky matter right up into me as far as my kidneys, I should think – and the performances were concluded for that time.

'But she was not satisfied with this, for before I left her in the morning, she desired me to fasten the machine upon myself and roger her strongly and well as she had done me. I was very clumsy in strapping on the curious instrument, but she assisted me, and I may safely say that she assisted me also in the actual performance, for when I had got this thing which she called a dildo fairly rammed into her, I began to push the best way I could, but I might almost have saved myself the trouble, for clasping me round the waist, she heaved herself up so vigorously that she more than met me halfway. At length, giving one fearful wriggle, she screamed out, "Milk, Adele, milk!" At first I hardly knew what she meant, but recalling my presence of mind, I remembered what she had done. Imitating her action as well as I was able, and squeezing the ball, I injected the precious fluid into her as far as it would go. When she recovered herself, she kissed and dismissed me with thanks and benedictions. And now that is my story; what do you think of it, dear Louise? You may depend upon it, it is just what you will have to endure. As for you, Mademoiselle Ermenonville, you will catch it this very night!'

'Thank you, Mademoiselle Adele,' I answered, 'but I carry a safe-guard about with me that will prevent my "catching" it, and if dear Louise here is guided by me, she shall not have her sweet little morsel of virginity taken by a hard ivory dildo wielded by a lustful woman; she shall yield it up gently and lovingly!'

Here I appealed to Emilie, who was in my secret and who answered promptly, 'Certainly, dearest Augustine, and I have no doubt that these two young ladies will be only too happy to meet you here tomorrow after our breakfast hour, and receive your instruction and account of the night's transactions.' She then reminded me that it was time for me to keep my appointment with my aunt, and that I should be punctual, or risk losing the privilege of visiting the fair, young sisters.

7

The Ups and Downs of Life

CAPTAIN EDWARD SELLON, 1867

Captain Edward Sellon's *The Ups and Downs of Life* is the rarest 'erotic autobiography' ever printed. Only a single copy of the 1867 first edition is known to exist, and it is currently in a private European collection, where ironically it is housed with the only other known printed copy of the text! What makes this book so extraordinary is not so much its rarity, but its sexual content. The author was not only a military man of many talents and numerous exotic and dangerous adventures, but also a self-confessed total libertine with no regard for conventional sexual morality. He spoke and wrote candidly of his sexual exploits, and in so doing gave an unparalleled picture of Victorian mores and practices, as well as views of a 'gentleman's life' in nineteenth-century India and England.

In brief, Sellon was born moderately well off in 1818, and at the age sixteen went with the army to India. After active participation in local sex life, including innumerable adulteries (one leading to a duel to the death), he returned to England in 1844 to an arranged marriage that failed quickly. While his wife was faithful, he could not be, his greatest weakness, perhaps brought back from India, being a penchant for young girls. After several reconciliations, and stints as a mail driver, fencing master, acclaimed expert on Indian sexual customs and author and illustrator of pornographic novels (mostly autobiographical), he finally ostracised himself completely from polite society with a particularly outrageous sexual indiscretion he recounts completely in his autobiography. He finally took his own life in 1866, at the age of forty-eight.

The text of *The Ups and Downs of Life* speaks for itself. It has no pretensions to being great literature. Sellon's talent was in narrative, plain and simple. He spoke of things he knew first hand. His accounts of colonial army life, sexual dalliances among the gentry, and Indian sexual practices and worship (more fully presented in his still classic monogram *Annotations on the Sacred Writings of the Hindus*, 1865), tell us what Victorian censors laboured to hide – the TRUTH. Sellon's translation from the Italian to English of Boccaccio, his non-erotic novel about the Mahratta War, and his other ethnological treatises show us that the man was more than the scamp and consummate rake he presented himself as. What he tells us of his times sheds a new perspective on a period of history known for its strict morality, and hypocrisy. For that alone we owe Sellon an eternal debt of gratitude.

⌘ from *The Ups and Downs of Life*

I read the whole affair in the newspapers at the time, and soon forgot the adventure in the gaieties of Cannanore. My reputation had preceded me, and on my arrival I found myself caressed by all the ladies, and my society sought after by the men. I had a happy knack of telling a droll story, and could set a whole mess-table in a roar at something I had said, without allowing any smile to appear on my own lips. It is a great secret in telling a funny anecdote, or giving vent to a witticism, for so sure as the narrator or wit smiles at his own joke, his listeners will compose their countenances into gravity, and if he adds, as some really witty fellows do, 'Not bad that, eh?' then woe to him, he will at once be voted a bore, and never more listened to.

I now commenced a regular course of fucking with native women. The usual charge for the general run of them is two rupees. For five, you may have the handsomest Mohammedan girls, and any of the high-caste women who follow the trade of a courtesan. The 'fivers' are a very different set of people from their frail sisterhood in European countries; they do not drink, they are scrupulously clean in their persons, they are sumptuously dressed, they wear the most costly jewels in profusion, they are well educated, they sing sweetly, and they generally decorate their hair with clusters of clematis, or the sweet-scented bilwa flowers. They understand to perfection all the arts and wiles of love, are capable of gratifying any tastes, and in face and figure they are unsurpassed by any women in the world.

They have one custom that seems singular to a European; they not only shave the *mons Veneris*, but take a clean sweep underneath it, so that until you glance at their hard, full, and enchanting breasts, handsome beyond compare, you fancy you have got hold of some unfledged girl. The Rajputani girls pluck out the hairs as they appear with a pair of tweezers, as the ancient Greek women did, and this I think a very preferable process to the shaving.

It is impossible to describe the enjoyment I experienced in the arms of these sirens. I have had English, French, German, and Polish women of all grades of society since, but never, never did they bear a comparison with those salacious succulent houris of the Far East.

But, although immersed in this voluptuous debauchery, I did not entirely neglect my fair countrywomen. I found time to go to balls, routs, and dinner parties; I found time even for hunting and shooting.

What an exciting, jovial life it was!

Amongst the ladies of the cantonment was one who more particularly took my fancy. She was the wife of a Major T—, of His Majesty's Dragoons, a lovely blue-eyed blonde of twenty-two, blooming and fresh as a daisy. Her husband was sixty if he was a day, and most incontestably to prove himself an arse, had married her from a Hammersmith boarding school some five years before, that is, when she was seventeen. She had then seen nothing of the world, and hardly knew what love was. But the major was her guardian, and thus secured to himself both her person and fortune, which was considerable. To this sweet creature I paid such marked attention that we soon understood one another. She the more readily accepted the intrigue as my extremely youthful appearance, to a certain extent, disarmed scandal, and she wished to draw off from the public eye her real *cavalière servente*, Captain M—, by whom she had had a child, which passed for the major's. Indeed, Major T— was very fond of the little fellow, and devoutly believed he was of his own begetting.

The major was a great invalid, and had a separate room, but seldom essaying to perform his marital duties, and signally failing when he did try. This was the state of things when I set my wits to work how I might seduce this beautiful but artful woman. I used to pass hours at her house nearly every day, hold the silk she wished to wind, turn the leaves of her music book while she played or sang at the piano, and make sketches in her album, and everything that lovers could say to each other we had said. I had had my hand down her breasts and up her clothes many times, and she would sit with me on a sofa with her hands in my trousers, manipulating for half an hour at a time.

Occasionally the poor major would look in, seem pleased to find me there, instead of Captain M— (whose presence always made him uneasy; I could not tell why, as he was not of a jealous nature), and would accost me with, 'Ah, little S—, there you are again, making love to my wife, you young dog!' and he would laugh good-naturedly and slap me on the back. And wily Mrs T— would say, 'Oh yes, he's a good little boy, and as long as he is so he shall be my knight and wear my colours.' Poor old major, if he had only known, but he did not know, and hadn't the shadow of a suspicion of me! *Tant mieux*.

Now it happened that one day I had dropped in as usual, when Mrs T— told me, with an arch look, that the major was gone down to the Presidency on an affair of business and would not be back for a week and that, it being the native festival of Huli, she had allowed all her servants to go and see the show, except the gardener, whom she would now tell to deny her to any visitors who might call. She went into the veranda and gave him her orders and returned to me. I threw myself into her arms. 'Not yet, not yet, my dear boy,' said she. 'I must first go over the bungalow and see if those rascals have fastened the doors and jalousies, for in their absence some scoundrel might enter the premises and rob the house, and – and . . . ' She burst into a laugh.

'We might be surprised,' said I, completing the sentence.

'Good,' said she. 'That is just what I mean.'

We secured the jalousies and doors, and carefully searched all the rooms. Satisfied that all was safe, I went with her into her chamber, when having double-locked the door, 'Now, my dear love,' said she, 'do what you like. I am all your own!' In a minute we were both naked, sporting on the bed. Then for the first time I had a full expansive view of that lovely woman. I revelled in the woman's cunt with its luxurious fringe of fair locks that curled above, on the sides, and beneath it. I never saw so much hair on a woman before, she had quite a forest under her arms. It was a novelty to me, and pleased me. I entwined my fingers in it, I combed and parted it, and overcome by an irresistible lust, ended by gamahuching her, to her great delight. I had so wriggled about that at length I got astride of her with my rear pressed down on her glorious bubbies, and felt them rise and fall as she panted with desire. Presently she grasped my thighs and, raising me up, took my pestle in her mouth, and sucked it with such ardour that I feared every minute she would either bite it off or swallow it whole. Suddenly she stopped, exclaiming, 'Oh, 'tis too much! I cannot bear it another instant. Turn round! Put it in! Fuck! Fuck! Oh fuck me!' I lost no time in complying. Then she clasped me with such strength, she murmured forth such lascivious words, she did such lascivious things, she quite frightened me. Why, this woman, said I to myself, is a perfect

Messalina. We were both so wrought up that in ten minutes our climax
came. Gods, how she ground her teeth, how she bit and pinched. And
then we lay both panting, quite exhausted.

At length recovering a little, she wiped her beautiful face with her
handkerchief saying faintly, 'Give me the eau de cologne off the
dressing table, and open a bottle of claret. You will find some in the
cooler in the corner of the room.'

She deluged her fair body with the eau-de-Cologne, and then
playfully threw a quantity over me. We soon finished the delicious cool
wine, and so to bed again.

I begged her to kneel up that I might have a full view of her hinder
beauties. She complied at once. Oh, what an enchanting prospect was
before me. Imagine a skin white as alabaster, a slender waist, a Spanish
back with a delicious fall in it, over which meandered her waving
golden hair; imagine hips of enormous size terminating in a bottom the
largest, the most dimpled, and the whitest I had ever beheld, supported
on thighs, so rounded, so symmetrically proportioned, so altogether
ravishingly exquisite, that an angel of light could not have withstood
such temptation. I stooped down and buried my face in those hills of
snow; then, rising up, I slipped with ease into her mossy grotto, and at
it we went again. She jutted her puss towards me to meet my thrusts;
she reached down between her legs, and felt my wand as it went in and
out; she toyed with the balls of Cupid, and soon brought forth another
sweet shower.

'Oh, you're a man! A man!' she said. 'More charming by far than
M—, who shall have me no more. Sweet boy-faced fellow, I am thine
forever.' And she sank fainting on the bed.

When she had a little recovered, 'What,' said I, 'have you done with
little Jack?' (her son).

'Oh,' said she, 'Mrs B— so often asked me to let the little man pass
the day with her children that I could not refuse, you know.'

'Ah, I see. Bright idea, wasn't it, today?'

'Very.'

'Hark! What's that?' And she sat wildly up in the bed.

'Somebody trying the door of the entrance hall, and violently, too,'
said I, coolly.

'Up, quick, my love! Do not wait to dress. Gather up your clothes,
and get out of the window. Run down to the border of the *tank*. Hide
yourself among the trees. Dress there. Take the boat. Flee! Quick,
begone.'

I grasped my clothes, and to unfasten the jalousie door, to spring out (fortunately we were in a one-storey house), to run like a madman across the lawn at the back of the house and to gain the grove of trees, was the work of an instant. But even as I fled I heard a tremendous crash. The front doors had been burst open, but I knew her door was double-locked. I knew, before the intruder could make that yield, she would have time to put the bed in order, to close the jalousies, to cast on her *robe de chambre*, to put out of sight the claret bottle and the glasses, and I was content. I dressed myself and, unmooring a little sailing skiff, which the major kept for his diversion on the lake, I leapt in and, hoisting the sail, was soon a hundred yards from the shore. Then, indeed, I turned my head and saw a man running at full speed down the jetty. By the time he reached it I had gained another fifty yards. He raised a gun to his shoulder, and whiz, crack, came a shot slap through the sail and about a foot above my head. 'Well aimed, old fellow,' said I, jeeringly to myself. 'Before you load the gun again I shall be out of reach.' But load again he did and, that rapidly, crack went another shot, but it only splashed harmlessly in the water, fifty paces astern of me. 'Well, to be sure,' said I, 'you're a paladin, my fine fellow, whoever you are, but you're not the major. He could never have run like that.'

Concluding that my enemy would mount a horse and gallop along the bank after me, I made for the shore at once, and starting off through a belt of jungle, the track of which I knew quite well from having often had a day's sport there, I reached my bungalow half dead with the heat, for it was barely three o'clock, the hottest part of the afternoon.

I drank some brandy and soda water, and after I was cooled a little, I took a tepid bath. Nobody was at home but my *choera*, a pretty little boy about twelve years of age. This boy, Muniah his name, was very fond of me and once, when I was ill, nursed me with the greatest tenderness. 'Boy,' I called. In the Madras Presidency all servants answer to the name of Boy, even if old grey-headed men. I addressed my haughty, high-caste *dubash* as 'boy' occasionally, just to keep him in his right place, though sometimes I called him by name, in compliment to his superior attainments and his caste. In Bengal, servants are called by '*qui hie?*' – 'who waits?'

'Boy,' said I. Muniah appeared.

'Muniah,' said I (a great compliment, he not being of high caste). He made me a low, a gratified, salaam. 'Do you know where I went this morning?'

'Yes, sir. My gentleman went to Mrs T—.'

'How do you know that?'

'I heard master tell the bearers to take palanquin there.'

'Very good,' said I. 'Now mind, pay great attention to what I am going to say. If any sahib asks you where I went this morning, you must say that I have not been out, that I am not well. Do you understand?'

'Quite understand, sir.'

'That's all right. Now bring some brandy and water. Bring a light and a cheroot.'

I lay down on my cot and smoked. Presently I heard the galloping of a horse at speed. The horse was snorting as if distressed. The rider pulled up with a jerk at the door.

'Is your master at home?' roared the voice of Captain M—.

'Yes, sir.'

'When did he come in?'

'Master has not been out this morning,' said the boy, innocently.

'Not been out? You lie, you pig.'

'No, sir, I tell truth. Sahib not well. Sahib not been out at all since yesterday.'

'Very odd,' said M— in English. 'Can I see him?'

'Hullo! Is that you M—?' said I from within. 'Come in, old fellow. Glad to see you.'

He entered. He looked heated and troubled, and was covered with dust and his horse's foam. He beheld me in an immaculate clean cambric shirt and striped silk pajamas, languidly lolling on my cot, smoking, my face pale and unheated. He was evidently staggered.

'And you really have not been out this morning, S—?'

'Out? By Jove! What should I go out for in this broiling sun, and I as seedy as be damned? Oh, those blasted fellows of the dragoons, they sewed me up damnably with their bad wine. You know, old fellow, we always give our guests good wine.'

M— winced and bit his lip. I surveyed him with the utmost nonchalance. From head to foot, he was a powerful ruffian and could have made mincemeat of me.

'But, my dear fellar,' said I, with a fashionable drawl. 'What the devil's the matter with you? You look so deucedly excited. Is anything up?'

'Up? Yes, by God, something is up!' cried M—, dashing his fist down on the table. 'And curse me if I don't fathom it.'

'Ah, really!' said I, with the most imperturbable coolness as I blew out a cloud of smoke. 'Try a cheroot, old fellar!' and I handed him my case.

M— took the case and lit a cheroot. While pulling at it, he suddenly raised his eyes. They met mine. What he read there, I don't know, but he gazed at me long and fixedly, without saying a word. 'Now is the time of trial,' thought I, and I continued steadily to meet his threatening

fierce eye, with an expression half curious, half languid, my brows
slightly raised, and a cynical smile (I felt it must be cynical) on my lips,
from which ever and anon issued volumes of smoke.

'Damn it,' cried M—. 'Either you are really seedy and have not been
out of your bungalow, as you say, or you are the most perfect specimen
of duplicity and coolness I ever met.'

'You flatter me,' said I, with a faint smile.

'Flatter you? By Jove! Look here, old fellar, if you have been out of
the house, you have been to Mrs T—'s, and if I thought you had been
there, I'd kill you,' he roared out fiercely.

'Now, my dear M—, pray talk any rhapsody you please, but have a
little mercy on my nerves!' said I coolly, but to say truth I was in a most
damnable funk.

'Then you really have not been out today?' said he, cooling a little.

'Captain M—,' said I, rising and making him a bow, 'when I tell a
gentleman one thing, I don't mean another. If you think I'm a liar, say
so like a man, and I shall know how to avenge myself for the insult!' I
bent upon him a look so fierce and defiant that the strong man cast
down his eyes; in the boy of seventeen he had found his match.

'But, sir,' I went on, 'as you have done me the honour to mention the
name of that most virtuous lady, whose husband's friend I am, may I be
permitted to enquire, supposing I had been there this morning, what
business is it of yours? You are not her husband or the friend of her
husband. Nay, he detests you, and I tell you that it is currently reported
you are the father of her child. Now, mind you, I pry into no man's
secrets. It's nothing to me one way or other, but if you, undermining
the affections of that lady for her husband, have seduced her, very ill it
becomes you to fall foul of any lovers, other than yourself, that she may
have. You have seemed to imply that I am one. Look upon me. Look
upon yourself,' and I pointed to a mirror. 'Would a woman who would
choose a stalwart cavalier like you, condescend to a mere boy like me?'

He seemed convinced and took leave, saying, 'Forgive me, S—, I am
sorry I offended you, but you don't know how much I love that woman.'

'My dear M—, she has deceived her old, confiding husband, and
believe me, she will deceive you. There are no bounds to women.
When once they fall – they fall. There's no chaining them up. It's the
common lot! Good morning. Oh, by George, how precious hot it is,'
and I ran in from the veranda.

He galloped off in the sun. 'Now that fellow will run his thick head
against a stone wall and get the poor woman into trouble. By Jove, he
will,' thought I.

8

Pauline the Prima Donna 1

WILHELMINE SCHROEDER-DEVRIENT (?)
1868

German erotic literature is stereotyped as being mainly sadomasochistic. It also has a reputation for being cold, morose and pathologically
obsessive in sexual temperament (as extremely evident in *James Grunnert*,
one of the only three original German erotic novels well known in
English translation). Even the fanciful elements in the popular *Josephine
Mutzenbacher* are ascribed to the fact that the author was actually
Austrian, and a children's-story writer. There is a happy exception to
this generally depressing pattern in German erotica. Imagine crossing
the delicate, feminine (charming if you will) style of an Anaïs Nin
(*Delta of Venus, Little Birds, White Stains . . .*) with the frank, insightful,
descriptive pedanticism of 'Walter' (*My Secret Life*) and you would
wind up with the book we know as *Pauline, the Prima Donna; or
Memoirs of an Opera Singer*. This is the most famous, beloved and
reprinted original German erotic novel of all time. It is to the Germans
what *Fanny Hill* is to the English, Aretino's *Sonnets* are to the Italians,
and *Gamiani* is to the French; a national literary erotic classic.

The first volume of the first edition of this two-volume work
appeared in 1868 as *Aus den Memoiren einer Saengerin* (Reginald
Chesterfield: Boston). The introduction was dated 'Dresden, 1851'.
The book was obviously not an American production, rather it was the
handiwork of the notorious pornography publisher August Prinz, who
worked out of the Verlagsbureau in Altona (Germany). A second
volume was issued by the same publisher seven years later. The book
was an instant success, no doubt due in part to the allegation that it was
the actual sexual autobiography of one of Europe's great nineteenth-
century opera divas, Wilhelmine Schroeder-Devrient. Hayn and
Gotendorf's massive eight-volume bibliography of German erotica
noted twelve reprints of this work prior to 1910, and Dr Paul Englisch

(the twentieth-century German equivalent of the great English erotica bibliographer H. S. Ashbee) in 1927 noted six additional ones – this despite being placed on the German forbidden-book list as early as 26 October 1877! Bibliographies note three partial French translations of the book prior to 1940, as well as one complete translation by Blaise Cendrars with editing by Guillaume Apollinaire. The first English translation was dated, probably correctly, 1898, and being 'Printed for the erotica Biblion Society of London and New York' was almost certainly the work of Charles Carrington in Paris with help from H. S. Nichols. This first English translation was sadly incomplete, and contained episodes from mainly the first of the original volumes. (C. R. Dawes stated that the work, entitled *Pauline, the Opera Singer; or Memoirs of an Opera Singer*, was actually a translation from a greatly abridged earlier French translation of the book and not from the original German). A fuller, but still not complete translation was commissioned and issued by the Olympia Press in Paris in 1960, as *The Prima Donna*, with an introduction signed 'Jacques Sternberg' but no attribution as to the translator or source of the text. This English-language translation is more poetic than the first, and less American in idiom. It also eschews the simple and direct use of 'obscene' words, in favour of descriptive phrases. While this does not make the book any less erotic, it does decrease the temperature of the prose.

Poor as these translations are, they are sufficient to let the English reading world see what all the fuss was about (the identity of the author aside). Here are the frank and candid sexual memoirs of a nineteenth-century woman, recounting, at the request of an old friend (a doctor who had done her a great personal service), the deepest and most secret sexual thoughts and feelings and motives she has experienced in her life, so as to 'fathom the secret motives which become the cause of some many and varied actions of us women, for which even the most enlightened of men in vain seek for an explanation'.

The alleged author, Wilhelmine Schroeder-Devrient, was born in 1804 and died in 1860. She was a charismatic and celebrated artist during her lifetime, and not a little controversial. Kearney, in his *History of Erotic Literature*, describes the diva as a mercurial singer who dazzled Beethoven with her performance of Léonore in the composer's *Fidelio* (1822). She knew Goethe, who wrote poems to her, and took an active role in the 1848 German Revolution. Her love affairs, marital break-ups, and sharp tongue were notorious, so much so that an obscene novel about her (*Abenteuer der Saengerin Wilhelmine*) appeared two years after her death. A legitimate biography was published one year later.

It is not unreasonable to think that an opera star could live the rapacious sexual life described in *Pauline*. Rather it is to be expected. One need only consider the tempestuous existence of Maria Callas, and her celebrated affairs, most notably with Aristotle Onassis, to realise this. *Pauline the Prima Donna* reads with a definite female touch. Here is a heroine who presents herself as a clever person, thirsting for knowledge, highly amorous by nature, and yet still with enough self-control to curb her passions so as to attain her ultimate goals of personal freedom, recognition and professional success in her chosen field. In addition she is ever cognisant of the pitfalls unique to her sex in a society that is male oriented and dominated.

The English text of this book shows the author to be sincere, plain spoken, and not a little naïve. She recognises early and often the difference between mere reproductive physiology and sex. For the author sex is beautiful, sex is without shame, sex is a pleasantry to be engaged in with tenderness and caring and expressions of sentiment. Sex for Pauline is ROMANCE, and she rails against sex that is without love or with animosity.

In addition to romance, other recurrent (and rather feminine) erotic themes of this book are: erotic literature and its influence on women (with the injunction that it is 'poison' for any woman without a mate), voyeurism, lesbianism as an effortless extension of female friendship, masturbatory devices, the importance of a career for a woman, and contraception. This latter theme is returned to more often than in any other erotic autobiography, and merits several extended excursuses on the various techniques and appliances available in the nineteenth century for both women and men.

Pauline the Prima Donna, in both its English translations, is a thoroughly plausible and believable book. It does not strain credulity. We can believe that these are the innermost secret feelings of a vibrant and artistic woman. It would of course take a woman to know if the presented facts on female sexual physiology, psychology, curiosity and emotional development are true. For example, is Pauline correct when she says that feminine modesty is not a natural phenomena, but must be taught? Is female masturbation as prevalent and pleasurable as she says? One element in *Pauline* does seem, at least to the male mind, a bit out of place. That is the relative female penchant for the flagellation and sadomasochist activity the heroine presents. One would like to believe that this is a real account, worthy of academic consideration, but in the light of this and several other items one must question whether *Pauline the Prima Donna* is a genuine candid sexual autobiography.

That question will be answered in the second part of this essay. In the meanwhile, here is an excerpt from Pauline's life, in which her amorous temperament gets the better of her with her music instructor.

~~~ from *Pauline the Prima Donna* I

I had lots of opportunities to make gentlemen friends. I was just at my best, and being considered good-looking, there were plenty of young men who longed to pay their respects to me. But I had sense and my ambition was to become an artist first before I gave myself up to the enjoyment of life. I therefore refused all overtures of admirers, and my old chaperon was delighted with my morality and virtue.

She had no notion that I could enjoy myself secretly, and I only partook of my secret pleasures in moderation. I forgot to tell you that Marguerite made me a present of the book which I saw her reading that night when I watched her through the peephole. Its title was *Félicie, ou mes Fredaines*.

This book would have been sufficient to teach me what really is the centre, the axis of the whole of human existence, if I had not had practical and tangible illustrations.

I derived great pleasure from reading it, but once very narrowly escaped it being seen by my musical instructor.

He had arrived rather sooner than expected that day, and as I left my seat on the sofa to greet him, his eye caught sight of the volume partly hidden by my pocket handkerchief.

'Ah, Mademoiselle Pauline,' he remarked, 'what book are you studying; may I glance at it?' stepping towards the sofa.

'No, indeed, you may not, Signor; it is only for ladies, and lent to me by a friend.'

He was too polite and gallant a gentleman to seem curious, but a certain twinkle of his eyes told me he made a shrewd guess as to its nature.

I have said that he was a very charming man, this instructor of mine, but I did not want his love or any gallantry on his part. My soul was filled with aspiration to proficiency in the career I had marked out for myself. I wanted him to inspire me with his genius; success might bring love and gratitude on my part, but at present – no!

However, we may propose, but cannot always dispose of what is to be. His manner appeared gradually to change towards me. There seemed such tenderness and pathos in his voice as we sang together. One day he startled me by exclaiming, 'Mademoiselle Pauline, could I but throw my soul into yours, what progress we should make, and what fame it would bring us both, as pupil and master; one day you will be a Queen of the Stage, but it is slow, so slow, when there is no union in our souls.

'My heart is drawn to you, Pauline; only give me a little hope, and let the love of your musical art be a closer bond between us than that of pupil and teacher.'

My eyes fell, and my head drooped on his shoulder; presently his quivering hands drew my face to his, and he imprinted long, luscious kisses on my passive lips – and the fire coursed through my veins. I had expected, and yet dreaded, the love of this fine, handsome man – as great in his profession as he was well-made and good-looking.

'Oh, Signor, you unnerve me, it is so sudden! Besides, you are married.'

'Bah! That is nothing in this city. Every Viennese lady has her *liaison*; besides we can have our fill of love without risk to your position or reputation. Prudence – prudence! That is all we require.'

'Ah, Signor, then you must teach me what prudence is,' I said, bashfully looking down, and pretending to be unable to look him in the face.

'We shall progress rapidly; within twelve or eighteen months you will make your début, and your fame will be my reward, but love shall stimulate us as nothing else will.'

He sank upon the sofa and drew me upon his lap; I appeared passive in his hands, which caressed first my face and then found their way to my bosom.

'What glorious globes!' as he pulled aside the slight muslin which hid them from his view; 'I must kiss those beautiful strawberry nipples; your agitation tells me too truly what a voluptuous girl you are: how I love you, dearest Pauline! Queen of my heart! I will kiss you all over, even the most sacred parts. you must refuse me nothing.'

My face was crimson – I caught a glimpse of it in the mirror opposite to us. 'Oh, spare me, Signor, I can refuse you nothing, but let me first tell you my secret: two years ago I was raped by my cousin, so I am not a virgin, as you might expect. I've never seen him since. It was a dreadful outrage, and I hated him for it.'

'Never mind, my darling, it will only make my love greater for you; but we must be prudent – then we can feast on love, with safety. It is only the rough animal-like lover who does mischief; you will find me like a bee, gathering the honey without spoiling the flower.'

His invading hands were now transferred to a lower region. Gently placing me on the sofa, he knelt by my side, raising my skirts little by little, and dwelling on each charm as it was displayed to view.

'What a pretty foot my Pauline has got!' – caressing and kissing the calves of my legs – 'your silk stockings, garters and pretty lace-trimmed drawers, all tell me of your refined nature. Nothing so enchants a lover as to find the approaches to the temple of Venus hidden by delicate lingerie; this is indeed a scented garden, but the real aroma of the centre of love drives me wild with desire; I can't stop; I – I – I burst! Oh, Pauline, darling, pity me!'

I knew well enough what had happened to him, but resolved that he should teach me and think me comparatively innocent. Presently his trembling fingers found the spot, gently parting the silky hair which curtained the longing gap. His touch was electric, squeezing and softly rubbing the sensitive clitty, and passing along the stiff, cord-like connection between that and the entrance to my longing cunt, which was swimming in spend. His slow approach had so worked up the intensity of my excitement, it was quite impossible to restrain myself.

'Ah, love! How delicious; I must have every drop of the cream of life, which you cannot keep back, and the more you give way to pleasure the better I shall love you.'

His lips were glued to my gushing fanny and one arm was passed beneath my bottom so as to present the object of his ardent attentions more readily to his warm lips, the touches of which and the darting of his tongue thrilled every nerve in my body.

I threw my legs around his neck and nipped him between them in the intensity of my emotion; the very essence of my life seemed to gush from me in constant spasmodic emissions, his moustache and beard being drowned by the copiousness of my long pent-up vitality. How eagerly he sucked every drop of 'Love's nectar', as he called it.

Pressing my hands on his dear head, I kept his lips to the charmed grotto, until his furiously amorous sucking fairly exhausted me and I lay in a motionless lethargy of dreamy bliss. Presently his hot kisses covered my face, every part, forehead, eyes and lips, as he called me every endearing name he could think of, such as, 'My queen, my pet, my love, my own Pauline!'

Then, 'Have I made you taste the true pleasure, did your very soul seem to flow out to me?'

'Indeed, you have, Signor. I never felt such heavenly feelings before; and is that indeed love?'

'Yes, my pet; but you have yet greater ecstasies to experience, and it shall be my pleasure to impart them to you.'

'But, dearest,' I said, 'did you have the same blissful sensations, did your soul mingle with mine?'

'Not exactly, darling, I was too intent on giving you pleasure. But next time, perhaps.'

'Ah! You have not then felt the same as I did. What can I do for you, to make you feel the same? It is not love, unless the pleasure is equal. Tell me – tell me, what can I do? I must make you happy! Now – now, not another time,' throwing my arms round his neck and covering his face with kisses, as amorous as his had been. 'I could kiss you all over, to make you feel the same delirium of pleasure as you gave to me.'

Our tongues met in fiery osculations, and I sucked his quite into my mouth, to his evident delight.

One of his hands guided my impatient fingers till they touched his torch, which he had already released from his trousers. Nervously grasping the thick, firm, soft-skinned column, which throbbed under my pressure, he guided my hand to move up and down upon it, making it swell bigger and bigger every moment, till, parting my willing thighs, he introduced the head of his instrument between the burning lips of my cunt; giving a suppressed sigh, I felt it glide slowly – up – up – up – till I had him to the roots of his hair.

The sense of possession was delicious beyond expression, especially as it was the first time I had felt the real live article actually within me; the folds of the innermost recesses of my cunt clung convulsively and tenaciously around the jewel of love. He was only still for a moment or two, then gently withdrawing a little, he thrust in again till the head of his affair seemed wedged right up at the top of my womb. My flood gates opened again, and ravished his throbbing prick with another effusive emission of love's creamy essence.

What an epicure he was. His motions were so slow, the gentle in and out action drove me wild with lust. I longed to scream out, 'Faster, quicker! Fuck me well now, you darling!' as my dear Marguerite had taught me was the true way of spurring on one's lover.

'How lovely that feels, dearest,' I sighed softly, as if I was dreaming.

'Wait a bit, darling, till I go quicker, then you will experience the very acme of voluptuous delight. I move gently to prolong the pleasure – presently I shall get so fiercely excited, it will make me work like a steam engine, till we both die away in a delirium of ecstasy. But we must be careful; you may dissolve and melt away as often as you can, it only gives me greater enjoyment. But if only a drop or two of the male seed spurts from me within you, your womb may suck it up, and our mingled juices might create a baby, and bring disgrace on my darling love, so I have to be careful, and withdraw at the critical moment, in order to avoid that fearful risk. Only a brute would gratify himself to such a dangerous extent.'

Gradually working up the speed, I was presently fucked to my heart's content. Responding with all my energy, clasping his body to mine with all the strength of my nervous arms, we both heaved and writhed with erotic passion, and a final emission made me fairly squeal, so intense was the pleasure. It was almost an agony of delight, more in fact than I could endure for a moment longer, so that I actually pushed him off me (and as he afterwards said, only just in time to save impregnation, as he was quite lost to every sense of the prudence which he had been dilating upon to me), receiving his spurting emission all over my belly, as it shot almost up to the globes of my bosom.

'Now, darling,' he said, as we recovered our composure, and rearranged our dress, 'it is useless to think of pursuing your studies today, our hearts are in too much of a tumult for that, so I shall content myself with merely indicating what you are to read and practice till I see you again.'

Thus for a while he sat by my side, turning over the leaves in a listless fashion, and I could see that his thoughts (as well as my own) were thoroughly *distrait*. Every now and then he would imprint warm kisses on my lips, and I could see his prick was bursting and rampant in its confinement.

'Do you suffer, dearest?' I said, almost under my breath. 'Is the poor darling hard again? Do you know, I should so like – yes, like . . . but I blush to say so.'

'My pet, what is it? You need not blush for anything you say to me – everything, words or actions, should be free and unrestrained between us. What is it, darling?"

'Only a kiss, a little kiss,' I said, blushing deeply.

'But surely you don't blush like that for thinking of a simple kiss.'

'Not on your face or lips, my love. You know you have kissed, sucked and swallowed the essence of my life. I must do the same to you, or you won't believe I love you, and, unless you surrender that to me to fondle and do as I like with it, you don't love me as I should like to be loved.' I placed my hand on the swelling object, and proceeded to unbutton his trousers. He passively allowed me to have my way, as, with burning cheeks, I was really so ashamed of my precocity, but, led away by intense lust for further enjoyment, could not restrain myself.

When the proud object of my wishes presently stood up between my grasping fingers in all its glory, the sight made me beside myself, quivering all over. My cunt gave down a copious discharge, which it was impossible to keep back.

'Kiss it, darling, I know how you feel, let me have the soft bites of your pearly teeth, whilst one hand gently caresses and plays with the bag below, which is the reservoir of my vitality.'

Sinking on my knees before him as he sat on the sofa, I buried my face in his lap, fondling the dear object by the side of my burning cheeks, nibbling the white soft-skinned column with my lips, and now and then putting the head in my mouth, where I moulded it with my tongue, and sucked a little, but not too fast, as I wished to prolong my pleasure as long as possible. All the while my own thighs were deluged by continuous emissions, so worked up were my feelings that it seemed as if nothing would stop it.

'Now, darling, suck quick and fast, take it all in and don't lose a drop,' as he thrust it right up to my tonsils, and a sudden spasm (which I could feel originated in his precious balls) distended his prick to an enormous size, quite filling my mouth, whilst a veritable flood of sperm was ejected down my throat or frothed about my eager lips, as I sucked and swallowed all I could get, till he sank back quite exhausted on the sofa.

'Now I know we truly love each other, Pauline. Nothing but real abandon would nerve you to do that, which is the sincerest proof a woman can bestow on her lover.'

'And have I made you taste the uttermost delight, my Felix, my own dearest man? Love me always as you have today, and see how true I shall be to you.'

He left me after many endearments, but sleep was banished from my eyelids for that night – it was the first experience I had had of the real thing, which had troubled my mind for years past.

I tossed about, opening my thighs and feeling if there was any perceptible difference in the parts his affair had visited, and I thrilled alternately hot and cold as I dwelt on all the incidents of the delightful afternoon, never to be forgotten as long as I should live.

When he came again on the third day, my duenna was out of the way, and I arranged we should thoroughly enjoy ourselves. It was an early spring day, almost as warm as summer, so I received him *en déshabillé.* My blonde hair falling over my shoulders, with only a dressing gown of dark blue silk, secured by a sash, and underneath a simple chemise, drawers, stockings and garters, with my feet in delicate Indian slippers.

'Felix, how I longed for your coming! Come to my arms, you dearest of men,' as I opened my dressing gown and clasped him to my almost naked body, and could feel his stiff prick as he pressed against my belly. 'Ah! Is it so with you, my love?' as my hand felt outside his trousers. 'Off with everything today, there is no fear we shall be disturbed for an hour or two, but first take a glass of wine, it will do us good for – what do you call it, Felix?'

'My dear, it is a very rude word, but not between real lovers such as we are. Fucking is the name when I put it into you, gamahuching when we suck each other – do you like those words, Pauline? I think we ought to use them to each other, they add zest to our conjunction, and spur us on to our utmost endeavours. You should know mine is called a prick, whilst your darling slit is a cunt; do you love to feel my prick in your cunt, isn't it nice when we both shoot out the essence of our being? Let us do everything today, fucking, gamahuching and tonguing; every part of us is for love; but let us be careful and prudent, then we shall have nothing to blame ourselves for, and this delightful *liaison* is likely to last. What do you say my dear?'

'Anything to add to our transports; whatever you teach me, you will find a willing pupil; and I now pledge you in this glass of sparkling wine even to outdo you in rude ideas, now we are for each other.'

'Well done, dearest pet, here's long life and happiness to your cunt, may it never live to want a good prick!'

I almost tore off his coat, waistcoat and trousers. 'There,' he said, 'we shall do now; it is a little too rude to be quite naked, don't you think so?' as I threw off my dressing gown. 'A little clothing – especially delicate and refined lingerie – adds a piquancy to enjoyment. When one has a lady quite naked, it is a little too sensual; she ought only to be a rustic or a maidservant. Still, sometimes I will admit that after considerable preliminaries, a final tableau of naked charms is very agreeable.'

I hugged him again to my bosom, and he carried me to the ever convenient sofa (what tales such articles of furniture could tell).

Rolling up my chemise right under my chin, he stood with his standing prick in his hand, contemplating the beauties of my person, gently frigging himself as he gazed on me.

'Felix, darling, don't keep me in suspense like that, when you know I am burning for you to possess me again. Come, sir, do your duty, fuck my cunt without further delay!' I exclaimed impatiently.

Leaning over me, he buried his face between the marble globes of my bosom, kissing me between them, then quickly transferring his lips to each of my nipples, one after the other, then again to the centre of my bosom; it made me wriggle with a delightful thrilling sensation, and I was raging with desire as he still tantalised me by letting the head of his rampant engine just touch the panting lips of my cunny.

'Oh, oh! Let me have it quick, you excite me so, how you fire my blood from tip to toe!' as I tried my best to catch hold of Mr Cock, but he drew back, and went on driving me mad with his dalliance, until I had spent over and over again, and he shot his sperm all about my belly, making my bush quite clotted with the thick creamy essence of his manhood.

He had scarcely uttered a word during this play, although all the time I was calling him every endearing name I could think of and begging him to fuck me.

'Now, love, he at last said, when our emotions had subsided a little, 'we shall be safer. The first fuck is always dangerous – the man, in fact both, are so eager for it that the precaution of withdrawing is likely to be forgotten, especially as the female always holds him as tight as possible at the ecstatic moment.

'When she has once had a good spend, there is not much risk afterwards. Now I am going to show you what I call the lazy style of enjoyment.'

Then getting between my legs he lay over me rather on my right side, and with my left thigh between his, gently inserted his still glowing prick into my eager cunt, so that his balls were squeezed against my thigh, proceeding to fuck with long drawn in-and-out slow strokes, and however much he excited and made me spend, and inundate his prick with my love juice, he prolonged his own pleasure indefinitely, till he thought fit to give me the *coup-de-grâce* by a few rapid movements, which made me heave with delight.

'Felix! Felix! I have never felt such sensations before, don't withdraw, let me experience the heavenly joy once more, then I feel as if I could die in your arms.'

Twice more did he shoot his very life into me and after that we discarded every vestige of clothing, and he showed me how to ride *à la* St George, impaling myself on his stiff weapon, as he lay on his back, and riding up and down on it, till we achieved a rapturous emission. I fell forwards on his body, quite exhausted for the time.

He visited me regularly three times every week, and I advanced rapidly in proficiency.

Love spurred me on, and most of the time I had to myself I studied assiduously. He was very careful in his intercourse with me, always insisting upon using a French letter, as he called it, for every first fuck, fearing prudence might be forgotten in our too ardent enjoyment.

The warmth of my temperament seemed to increase every time he had connection with me, and the lustfulness of my nature developed daily.

He was not enough for me, especially as after a little while his prudent carefulness would not allow him to go to such extremes as we had at first, and he would only really spend inside me after using the thin skinny safeguard, which I did not like, as the shooting of his hot sperm up me gave the most intense pleasure.

Then as a wind-up I had always to ride St George, as he said that no girl could be impregnated that way, as she must lie on her back for the womb properly to receive the male seed.

∽ 9 ∽

Pauline the Prima Donna II

1875

As noted, *Pauline the Prima Donna* is one of the most famous and continually popular volumes of German erotica. Purporting to be the genuine sexual memoirs of the famous nineteenth-century diva Wilhelmine Schroeder-Devrient, it is potentially one of the most important primary documents on Victorian female sexuality we have, a female analogue to *My Secret Life*. The question to be begged is whether *Pauline* is in fact authentic. The available English translations of the text certainly indicate it to be a well-written, sincere, and plausible account of psychosexual development in a nineteenth-century woman artist. A reading of the entire German original, however, indicates otherwise.

One of the earliest reviews of *Pauline* was by H. S. Ashbee in his 1877 *Inde Librorum Prohibitorum*. Obviously working from the German originals, he noted its two volumes to be extremely dissimilar both in style, content and physical printing. While not confirming the authorship, or noting how the attribution came about, he indicated the book to be the affirmed memoirs of 'the celebrated and notorious Frau Schroeder-Devrient'. Ashbee wrote that the autobiography was in the form of letters sent to an old friend, a doctor, among whose papers they were found after his death by a nephew who edited and sold them for publication. Episodes from the singer's life were presented, but it was her love/sex life and not her musical career that was the focus of these epistles, with her physical and emotional development exposed in the greatest of detail. 'The book is certainly as much a psychological study as it is a collection of the most lascivious episodes,' stated Ashbee. The book he deemed fairly well written and thoroughly readable, with the first volume being better as it had an element of *naïveté*, and was without the impossible sexual activities and sadistic, perverse behaviour that abounded in the second. Ashbee summarised the contents of the complete German text as follows: Volume I followed her life until at seventeen she lost her virginity, and accepted an engagement in Frankfurt (one year after her début in Vienna). Volume II took her to Pest where she seduced a young gentleman and then formed a *liaison* with a woman familiar with the myriad debaucheries available in that capitol of Hungary. She commenced a life of lesbian sadomasochism, complete with episodes of flagellation, capital punishment and orgies straight out of de Sade's novel *Justine*. Rekindling an amorous interest in men she engaged in scenes of group sex, sodomy, bestiality, sacrilege, scatology, necrophilia, vampirism and prostitution, all prior to being orphaned at the age of twenty-seven! She continued with various lovers, including an English lord who willed her a tidy sum upon his death. Pauline abruptly ends the memoirs, indicating that she has told all that transpired prior to her meeting the doctor to whom these letters were sent.

The burning question is, can these memoirs be genuine? Those with access to the complete German text seem not to be of that opinion. Ashbee notes that the book had to have been written a great deal from personal observation owning to the accuracy of many of the details given, including those of locations no longer existing at the time of the book's publication, but that 'blunders' abounded also, as did scenes that seemed lifted directly from the novel *Justine*. Clowes's 1884 bibliography *Biblioteca Arcana* states this work to be the 'pretended autobiography' of Schroeder-Devrient, very obscene, and strongly resembling Sade in description. The German bibliographer Hayn notes the work to be of the utmost lewdness, with 'masses' of folly, exaggeration and lies.

The greatest research on the background and authorship of *Pauline* was done in the 1920s by Dr Paul Englisch. His research showed conclusively that the two volumes of *Pauline* could not be the exclusive work of Schroeder-Devrient. Using internal evidence, such as stated ages at given times and lengths of stays in various cities, he found inconsistencies with the known facts about Schroeder-Devrient's life. For example, the introduction to the first volume, dated Dresden, 7 February 1851, states Pauline's age to be then thirty-six, making her birth year 1815 (rather than the 1804 of the real diva); in addition the real diva spent 1851 in Russia not Dresden. In a second place, the authoress states that her mother was twennty years older than she; Sophie Schroeder (Wilhelmine's mother, and an actress herself with a notorious sex life) was born in 1781, now making Pauline's birth year 1801! The real Wilhelmine lost her father in 1818, and her mother outlived her by eight years, making it impossible for the heroine to declare herself orphaned at twenty-seven. Many more chronological errors can be found.

More telling of course is the inclusion of episodes that occurred after the death, in 1860, of the supposed authoress. As noted before, many of the more outrageous and perverted episodes related in the second part of the book are simply impossible to have occurred as written and seem to be lifted directly from other novels, including *Justine*, *Gamiani* and *Fanny Hill*. One particular orgy scene has been identified as having been taken nearly word for word from another *c.*1860 German pornographic novel.

These incongruities are overpowering. Yet there are still a great number of accurate facts in *Pauline*, details that could have only come from first-hand observation or participation. It is known from letters written to C. G. Carus (1789–1869), a doctor in Dresden and a long-time intimate friend of the diva, that the two had discussed the writing of a memoir. Wilhelmine even mentioned that she was putting her papers in order to this end. Despite this, it was Dr Englisch's educated and considered opinion that the autobiography was not genuine, and the author of at least part of the first volume was the publisher of the book, August Prinz, who specialised in this type of erotica. The second volume was judged the work of a different hand, very likely one of Prinz's house porno authors.

Is *Pauline the Prima Donna* a complete work of fiction, a *roman à clef* with great liberties taken, a genuine manuscript that was misread in spots and continued by a second hand, or the autobiography of someone other than Wilhelmine Schroeder-Devrient? The complete truth will never be known for sure. It seems most likely however that August Prinz wrote or had written, perhaps by a woman, an erotic novel based loosely on the life of the famous opera singer. He could have been motivated by the success of a *c.*1862 pornographic novel about her, and may even have had access to her papers and the letters written to the Dresden doctor. Mixing fact with fiction made it easier to imply a famous authoress to promote sales. The great success of the first volume probably induced Prinz to commission a continuation. This second volume borrowed heavily from the most popular erotic fiction of the day, which accounts for its obscene nature being distinct from the sexual insightfulness of the first volume.

It is sad to realise that so potentially valuable a piece of 'erotic realism' is at the very least partially bogus. Although the bubble is burst, that is no reason not to enjoy the entertainment to be afforded by Pauline and her friends. Here is an excerpt from the life of the narrator's close girlhood friend, Marguerite, a recitation that will not suffer from *Pauline the Prima Donna*'s not being an authentic autobiography.

〜〜　from *Pauline the Prima Donna* 11

Marguerite entered and went about her business; in the small sitting room she packed the things for the return journey, and finally laid the breakfast. Now followed the sign of Marguerite for the Count to open his bedroom door and to enter the bedroom of the Baroness.

The latter was terrified to see him enter, but he heeded not; he threw himself on the bed and covered the Baroness with the most amorous kisses.

She was not able to utter a word about this rash and foolhardy proceeding, but she pointed to the door of the sitting room, where Marguerite could be heard fumbling about. The Count took the hint; he got up, went to the door and pretended to put the bolt on; he then returned to the bed and begged the Baroness to let him have once more, before her departure, the greatest favour she could bestow on him. She had been so very nice the previous night; he was beside himself with the desire to have her once more, and a refusal would make him ill.

Whilst saying this, he was busy uncovering her – his member was ready, covered with the skin, in order not to lose time, and the Countess, anxious to get rid of her unexpected visitor, at once opened her thighs and led the point of the iron rod to the entrance of her charming grotto.

At first the Count worked silently, then came a deep sigh, a sign for Marguerite to enter through the door which the Count had not bolted.

Marguerite appeared dumbfounded, speechless, when her eyes fell staring on the spectacle on the bed: the Baroness, her thighs high up, the finely shaped legs across the shoulders of the Count, who seemed in full possession of the much coveted trench.

She could not possibly feign so much fright, with all her acting, as the Baroness experienced in reality, for her honour, her position, her very existence was at stake.

Professedly enraged, the Count jumped up and ejaculated some curse in Russian, at the same time telling the Baroness they both would be lost if he did not murder Marguerite, and thus silence her forever, adding, 'She must not leave this room before we are safe.'

Marguerite professed to be frightened, and as if ready to fly for her life. The Count, however, stopped her, by putting his back against the door, and ordering her to remain. With all this the Baroness was more dead than alive. Suddenly the Count seemed to have an idea, that there was only one way of silencing this girl without proceeding to extremes: she must be made a willing helper between them. 'Pardon me, Baroness, whatever I may be doing, I do for your sake and your safety,' and saying so, he clutched Marguerite round the waist and carried her to the bed, where he laid her down beside the Baroness, who was still lying with her thighs bare. The Count raised Marguerite's clothes, and as she happened to have no drawers on, the whole of her charms were at once in full view.

'Look at me, Baroness,' he said, 'how I shall pierce this maiden cunt,' and with one jump he was on the top of her, and brought his fleshy stiletto to the mouth of the grotto. Marguerite acted, as well as she could, as if to frustrate his plans, and yet she brought her cunt into such a position so as to facilitate the ingress, and seeing the prick covered with the skinny bag, she apparently gave way, overpowered by the strength of a man, and though begging the Baroness to assist her against the rude thrusts of the Count, she experienced the most delicate sensations in this encounter. There were two reasons why she felt so jolly: first, because she had outdone the Baroness, who was obliged to see her maid receive on her own bed what had been destined for her cunt, and second, because the Count fucked her most gently and lovingly.

Not satisfied to have the Baroness a looker-on, he insisted on her assistance. He begged her to comfort the girl; to tell her not to make so much noise, to lie quietly, to open her thighs wide, and when once the knob had gone in an inch, assure her that the other six inches would not hurt so much.

The Baroness did all this, and more. With one hand she held apart the thighs, and with the other she got hold of the Count's prick, and every time this was withdrawn to give a fresh fuck, the Baroness guided it to the mouth of the hairy grotto. At last there was an opening, the point stuck in this hairy heaven. The Baroness became excited, and begging the girl not to resist any more, she encouraged the Count by saying, 'Fuck her, my beloved; draw her virgin blood, and let me see how you pierce this maiden cunt.'

The Count could not keep it in any longer, one more violent effort and his prick disappeared within the depth of Marguerite's belly, who also felt the excess of delight of which she gave unmistakable signs by heaving her bottom upwards and by those funny contortions of the body which can only be brought about by the most lustful sensations.

When all was over, the girl lay down exhausted, and closing her eyes seemed asleep. The Count had risen, and after dressing himself he knelt down before the Baroness, hugging and kissing her and telling her that he had only demeaned himself in fucking Marguerite for their own safety, that he had made a great sacrifice in doing so, for her sake, more than his own, and now, with such an intimacy established, she should do her best to gain the full confidence of the girl.

Fondly embracing the Baroness, and throwing a stolen glance at the still nude figure of Marguerite, the Count retired to his own apartment.

The Baroness approached the bed of the lass, who just then opened her eyes, and asking her whether she felt better, she begged permission to withdraw the skinny bag from her cunt, and on holding it up she told her that she might be proud. The Count must have felt very happy – only once had she seen the bag so full of cream; that was when he for the first time fucked her. The discharge had never been so copious since, in fact she believed that this bag's contents surpassed her own first, but then, she told the girl, 'You were a maid, a virgin an hour ago; that may have added to the Count's pleasure, whereas with me, the road was made.'

It was a moment of triumph for Marguerite, when the Baroness condescended to wipe the blood from her thighs with a fine Balosle handkerchief, and with a sponge which she used to wash her face with she washed the maid's cunt.

The Baroness, having everything to lose, tried her best to win the good graces of her maid. She confessed to the whole of the intrigue between the Count and herself. She promised to provide for her, she begged her pardon for the rudeness and violence of the Count, she craved for her indulgence, and painted the future in such glowing colours, until Marguerite at last seemed pacified; she forgave the Count's behaviour, and now, as things were as they were, and could not be altered, she had made up her mind to assist as much as possible in this little love affair.

With this promise, the ice was broken, and with it a curious relationship arose amongst these three people. The Count had no idea of the previous intimacy of these two women, but he had experienced so much pleasure in his connection with Marguerite, her fresh and youthful form, and the tightness of her maiden cunt, that he preferred fucking her to the Baroness, of which he gave ample proof when he chanced to be alone with her. On the other hand, Marguerite professed great dislike for the Count, and declared if she was made to take part in the lustful performances of the Baroness and her lover, she would only do that to heighten the pleasure of her mistress.

The latter had no idea of the secret understanding that existed between them and considered it a great act of devotion that Marguerite promised to assist her, and for this she was grateful. She loaded her with presents, she treated her as her best friend and even promised her that if she should ever get rid of her aversion for the Count, she would do her best to persuade the Count to fuck her, if she ever felt any longing for his prick.

The last few days at Morges passed as usual, and then followed the visit to Geneva for shopping purposes. Marguerite was the first to find an opportunity to slip into the Count's bedroom, and there to receive the first fruits of their labours.

Then evening came, and at an early hour the Count appeared before the Baroness, this time in Marguerite's presence. The meeting was most cordial; the Baroness sat on the Count's lap, and whilst kissing each other, the Baroness touched the sausage-shaped appearance of his trousers, whilst the Count groped below the petticoats behind. This was a kind of *hors-d'oeuvres*, to sharpen the appetite.

The Count then gently laid the Baroness on her back, and without any further ceremony, entered her lustful sanctum, his prick well covered, and after a few fucks, he discharged his ammunition, uttering the most endearing terms.

Marguerite could not cease telling me what a pleasure it was, when more than two persons became intimate with each other, especially as was the case with her, where the Baroness was hard worked by being made to believe that her maid was only the passive partner in the business.

The two understood each other. As often as the Baroness went to Geneva, so often did Marguerite visit the Count, who became more and more enamoured of her, and who became her lover, as he was passionate, not only because she was a fine made, well-educated young woman, but also because he had had the privilege of being the first to ascend the throne of her virginity. He tried hard to persuade her to allow him to have his pleasure in full; he drew a glowing picture of the extreme bliss it would be for both, if she would allow him to discharge his marrow at the height of the crisis within the folds of her heavenly charm with a prick uncovered, what a blissful sensation it would be for her, to feel the warm flow of sperm moisten the innermost parts of her recess. But in spite of all persuasion and all promises that he would provide for the child, if such a contingency should arise, Marguerite resisted all temptation, and she told him that she felt quite satisfied, when she felt the spurting of this wonderful sap, without tasting its moisture entering her womb. When in the afternoon they had thus, undisturbed, enjoyed themselves, then came in the evening the little play in the rooms of the Baroness, who felt particular pleasure in having Marguerite as spectator. They tried their gambols in every possible way.

Marguerite had to lie across the Baroness in such a manner that her arse was elevated, and showed her cunt from behind. The Count would then mount the Baroness, and after lodging his prick in her hairy grotto, would bring his face into contact with Marguerite's lovely buttocks, then putting his tongue into her mossy crevice, he would suck her one way, whilst the Baroness was busy sucking the virgin nipples of the youthful breast that were hanging like ivory balls over her face.

She gave me a most lively description of the blissful sensations she experienced when the crisis came, how she felt a stream of nectar ooze out of her queen of charms, which the Count sipped with smacking lips, and then finally discharged his own essence of love into the craving gorge of the lustful Baroness. Marguerite further described to me how, on other occasions, the Count would have her sit by the bed, whilst he made the most elaborate preparations to fuck the Baroness.

Destitute of all clothing himself, like a statue of Hercules, his prick sticking out horizontally like a rod of iron, his large balls showing from below in a firm bag well covered with long hair, he would lift the Baroness in his arms, then lay her down gently and undress her so carefully as if she had been made of biscuit china, until he came to the last covering, a chemise of the finest linen, with the most costly embroidery, and lifting this artfully, he would peep under and call to Marguerite.

'See here the cunt of your mistress, how firm the hairy lips, how they are parted, as if they want to speak the language of love, what a beautiful crimson, how longing they look, behold the eyes of Venus, swimming in a fluid of lust.'

Marguerite then set to work. She fiddled with one or both hands amongst the hair of that greedy slot; she then rubbed the prick of the Count, fondling the balls. Then grasping the rod and opening the lips, she would put it in gently, and whilst the Count kept on putting it in and drawing it out, she would rudely clutch it and, moist and slippery as it was, she would suck it and return it to the yawning gap.

All this she described to me as causing her immense pleasure. The snow-white surging alabaster hemispheres; the fair hair of the Baroness issuing from the sacred temple; this mount longing for the olives; the fiery redness of the officiating priest, craving to bring his sacrifice into this holy temple; the black hair of the priest mingling with the fair hair of the goddess, and to see all this, to see how with every second the pleasure increased, to hear how first the Count eulogised his darling's tight and hairy cunt, and how the Baroness admired the swollen prick, which appeared more swollen on account of her own swollen cunt, and when finally they poured forth their elixir of love simultaneously – verily it was a time of bliss not easily forgotten; in fact, the description of it to me now gave her pleasure. I had put my hand between her thighs, and I felt distinctly a fluid moistening the palm of my hand.

As is mostly the case, when one has too much of a good thing, one gets tired of it; so it happened with the Count: being able to revel between two lusty women who could not get enough prick, he got cooler and cooler; the cock refused to stand, and at last he disappeared without any particular leave-taking.

From this moment the Baroness tried to shake Marguerite off, the latter took the hint, and the two ladies separated.

Marguerite had some money given to her by the Count and the Baroness and with this she went to live with a relation who instructed her in the Russian language, her object being to go to that country and take a place as governess.

But the change of life had been too sudden, and she could not feel happy. Having been used to the intercourse with the Count and to the manipulations of the Baroness, now missing both caused her sleepless nights and exciting dreams.

The remedy which she tried with her own hands was but a poor substitute, and in vain did she look for a friend who would have acted to her with the same precaution as the Count.

A girl will not admit the knowledge of things which might degrade her in the eyes of a man. She kept quiet, and for a whole twelve months, she subdued her feelings amongst books and maps, whilst at night the most voluptuous dreams replaced the fucks of reality.

At last she had an opportunity to become intimately acquainted with several young ladies at some baths; great friendship sprang up between them, then came confidential whispering between two, then another was taken into the secret, and finally the fourth was made acquainted with the naughty whisperings of the lot. Everyone of them wanted to know and to learn, though one knew quite as much as the other.

They looked upon Marguerite as their pupil; whilst she knew more than all of them together, this was one way of satisfying her desires, but she longed for more and she succeeded in getting it.

She became acquainted with a brother of one of the young ladies, a handsome young man of high birth, in fact, a perfect gentleman. From the first moment he set eyes on Marguerite, he did all he could to get into her good graces.

This young admirer, whose name was Charles, had received his education in the house of a country pastor. He was a most moral young man – there was modesty in every word and action – but he soon felt the companionship with Marguerite giving him a peculiar pleasure. As regards Marguerite herself, she was delighted with the prospect of having the gradual development of her admirer's manifestations of love, and she, in her turn, felt the first signs of love in her heart.

No wonder then, when, for the first time he pressed his lips to hers, she felt the lips of her womanly treasure expand; she felt all power of resistance had flown and the timid embraces of her lover drove her to frenzy. She could not help showing signs of encouragement and the innocent young man soon found out, by natural instinct, that the acme of bliss was not reached with a nice kiss.

Marguerite, who had had so many experiences, derived particular pleasure from the manoeuvres of her lover. For her it was especially piquant to see the young man fumble about to reach the goal of his smouldering desires. He took her on his knees, he kissed her and hugged her, and inadvertently he would place his hands on her round bosoms, then place them in her lap, giving a gentle push as if by accident, and finish up by looking at her high-buttoned boots and admiring her ankle. He would then press her against himself, and Marguerite could feel the throbbing of his prick, and when he did let go, the indication of moisture was plainly visible on the outside of his light trousers.

But at every meeting Charles became more daring, and when the next time they met he had the audacity to put his hands under her petticoats and pat her lovely thighs. Marguerite, instead of resisting this rude attack, rather encouraged it by giving him a lovely kiss. This served as a signal for the assault; like lightning his hand grasped the mount; in an instant he had his trousers down, and putting Marguerite flat on her back, he raised her petticoats, looked at the haven of bliss, and brought his point to the brink of the trench.

Marguerite, forgetting all danger in the excitement of blissful sensations, did all she could to guide the prick into her cunt, and once it was in she felt the full force of the discharge of hot semen, which caused her to disgorge her own fluid of love, to the indescribable pleasure of both.

Entirely carried away by her feelings, she forgot herself entirely; like an electric shock, she felt the powerful jet of a hot stream penetrate to the farthest end of her womb, and mingling her seed with the sperm of her lover, the mischief was done.

Her womb had sucked it all in, and in vain did she resist the repetition of this blissful operation.

Her monthly flower did not appear; to the world her honour had fled, her future was spoiled; but from the moment she was certain of her condition, she allowed her lover all the privileges of marriage to his heart's content.

For three months she herself enjoyed these carnal connections, but then came a chapter of misfortunes. Her guardian, who had the custody of her money, became bankrupt and fled to America; her lover, Charles, became ill and died; she was turned away when her condition became known, and after two years of misery she lost her child. It was soon after that she got a situation as governess.

IO

The Romance of Lust

WILLIAM POTTER AND FRIENDS 1873–6

The six hundred and eleven pages of *The Romance of Lust; or Early Experiences* first saw the light of print in London, in four stout volumes, over the years 1873–6. It was published by a shady, mysterious man known at the time as 'D. Cameron', most certainly a false name that was an intentional pun. It was printed in only a hundred and fifty sets, most of which were destroyed about 1879, upon the death of the man for whom the novel had been privately printed.

The great Victorian bibliographer H. S. Ashbee knew this erotic book well, and wrote of it contemporaneously in his 1885 erotica bibliography *Catena Librorum Tacendorum*. Ashbee, as the definitive authority on the erotica of his day, bears repeating. Of *The Romance of Lust* he wrote that it was far better written than most books of its ilk, but that its contents were 'pungent' and the language never moderated and for the most part employing the 'grossest' words where ever possible. The hero, Ashbee reported, performed feats of sexual endurance in a superhuman fashion, and had from the beginning of his sexual career at the age of fifteen, the ability to be 'every moment ready for the fray'. The themes of the novel included incest (male and female), sodomy and flagellation; in addition the novel contained 'scenes not surpassed by the most libidinous chapters of *Justine*' (by the Marquis de Sade). To make matters worse, Ashbee pronounced the episodes improbable, impossible, and 'as a rule, too filthy and crapulous'!

The author of *The Romance of Lust* was left unidentified. However, Ashbee did indicate that the novel was the work of several individuals, and as such was as 'orient pearls at random strung, woven into a connective narrative by a gentleman'. The identity of this latter culprit was made all too easy to discover. He was described as a well-known collector of erotic pictures and *bric-à-brac*, who composed *The Romance of Lust* while on a trip to Japan. In addition, this 'gentleman' had spent the period from December 1875 to April 1876 in India, and had died at Catania on 16 January 1879, at the age of seventy-four. No need to run to the Records Office for this research; Ashbee himself, in the introduction to *Catena*, kindly supplied the biography of one William S. Potter, who was born in 1805, collected 'erotic pictures, engravings, photographs and *bric-à-brac*', and travelled extensively. To settle any final doubts, Ashbee also added footnotes and an index listing that referred the Potter biography directly to the review of *The Romance of Lust*.

Despite his rather negative review of *The Romance of Lust*, Ashbee seems to have had a fondness for it. He did not rip it totally to shreds as was his wont with books that failed to please him. Perhaps it was the author, a fellow businessman, traveller, collector and 'gentleman', who evoked his sympathies. Whatever, future bibliographers and critics of erotica were not content to let Ashbee's critique remain unamended. C. R. Dawes, who inherited Ashbee's mantle as doyen of English erotica, added (in his unpublished 1943 *A Study of Erotic Literature in England*) that *The Romance of Lust* did not have 'characterisation' as a strong point; Henry Miles in *Forbidden Fruit: A Study of Incest in Forbidden Literature* (Luxor Press: London, 1973), noted that Potter's characters recognised no social prohibitions, and hence transgressed all the boundaries of sexual priority that are generally recognised by a moral society.

The most adroit analysis of this novel is by Professor Steven Marcus. In his 1964 book *The Other Victorians* this scholar describes the book's plot as a constant 'juxtaposition of human bodies, parts of bodies, limbs, and organs' rather than the presentation of any real relationships between human beings. The novel, he notes, is clearly a fantasy; the sex is intricately described, yet controlled and mechanical, as if it were meant to be a blue print, rather than a piece of fiction. *The Romance of Lust*, he writes, 'comes as close as anything I know to being pure pornotopia in the sense that almost every human consideration apart from sexuality is excluded from it'.

For a work of erotica, is this praise or damnation? Incest, sodomy, homosexuality, voyeurism, flagellation, scenes beyond the excesses of *Justine* totally devoid of morality – these are what we are told are the themes and nature of *The Romance of Lust*. Certainly we must be speaking of one of the most repulsive, horrific novels of all time, a literary creation too disgusting to read, a work that would turn the reader's stomach at every page.

In truth, this is not what *The Romance of Lust* is. In the works of de Sade we are horrified and revolted because the 'sinning' is expressly exercised for the outrage it evokes from the victims and society at large; in *Justine* the actors seek specifically to violate what they recognise as the code of human moral conduct. The characters in *The Romance of Lust* neither acknowledge, nor even recognise any moral boundaries. It is hence amoral, and simply an expression of the primal urge of polymorphous perverse sexuality that Freud wrote of in his classic psychoanalytic text *Three Theories of Sexuality*. The reader may not espouse the actions of Potter's characters, but what they do is no more disgusting than say an infant happily playing in a mud puddle. Messy perhaps, but certainly no threat to the fabric of civilisation. Sade can evoke thoughts and feelings of horror; *The Romance of Lust*, perhaps because of its length, instead evokes fatigue and occasional boredom.

Choice of theme and previous reservationsaside, there is still one major criticism of *The Romance of Lust* as a whole. Though known to be the work of multiple authors, the scenes are woven together in a less than seamless fashion; it is just too obvious to discern where the different contributions were joined. Some prose reads literally like the fast flowing narrative in *My Secret Life* (and hence the theory at one time that Potter was the mysterious 'Walter' who authored that massive sexual autobiography) while other sections meander through every possible permutation of sexual connection a specific scene could allow for. In one case we have an author with too much to say in too little space, in the other case we see a literary draughtsman laboriously at work, organising and reorganising the ponderous minutiae he has set himself to explore.

One can wonder what William Potter was trying to achieve with *The Romance of Lust*. It was certainly not written for any commercial success, what with only 150 sets printed, and those apparently not for general sale. Was the book for his private amusement, and that of a few like-thinking friends (such as those who contributed to its prose)? Was it simple wish fulfilment on paper, a catharsis for impulses or fantasies he knew could not be acted out by a man of his station? Was it Potter's attempt to play out all the possible combinations of its extended themes of incest and sodomy, much as de Sade's *120 Days of Sodom* was an attempt to describe, better yet catalogue, all the sadistic perversions that played in the infamous Marquis's libido? This we will never know. The book, however, stands on its own, and judging from its continued popularity, strikes a sympathetic cord in many.

Here then is an excerpt from *The Romance of Lust*. The protagonist/ narrator has just taken new lodgings, having gone off to college and having had to leave his coterie of summer-time orgiasts. Let the reader decide how many hands were responsible for this bit of authorship.

from *The Romance of Lust*

I concluded my last volume by saying that I had taken lodgings in
Norfolk Street, Strand, for the convenience of being near King's
College. It was at the house of a Mrs Nichols: tall, powerfully built,
masculine, but a kind and motherly looking widow of fifty-two, an
attentive and bustling landlady, looking herself to the better cooking,
and having a plain cook, who was also a general servant, to help her
downstairs, and two nieces to do the waiting and attendance on her
lodgers upstairs. The younger was there alone when I entered the
lodgings; her elder sister had had what they called a 'misfortune', and
was then in the country until she could be unburdened of it. She was
expected back in about six weeks. Meanwhile, as winter was not the
season, I was the only lodger, and the younger had only me to attend
to. Her name was Jane and she was but a little thing, but very well
made, good bubbies and bottom, which I soon discovered were firm
and hard, projecting fully on both sides. She was fairly good-looking
but with a singular innocent manner of freedom about her that made
me imagine she had as yet had no chance of a 'misfortune'. In a week
we became intimate, and after often praising her pretty face and figure,
I snatched a kiss now and then, which at first she resented with an
attractive yet innocent sort of sauciness. It was in her struggles on these
occasions that I became aware of the firm and hard bosom.

Up to this time my flirtations were without ulterior object, but the
reality of the attractions of these hidden charms raised my lustful
passions. I gradually increased my flatteries and caresses, and squeezed
her bubbies, when I sometimes drew her on my knee and was kissing
her, and as at first she resisted my drawing her to my knee, I took
occasion to lay hold of her buttocks, which I found more developed
than I could have supposed. Gradually her resistance to these little
liberties ceased and she would quietly sit on my knee and return the
kiss I gave. Her dress would be a little open in front, so from feeling her
bubbies outside, I gradually got to feeling their naked beauty inside. I
now thought I could attempt greater familiarities, so one day when I
had her seated on my knee with one arm round her waist, I pressed her
to my lips, and while so engaged, whipped my free arm up her

petticoats, and before she had become aware of the movement, had got my hand upon her mount, a very nicely haired one. She started up to a standing position, but as I held her close, clasped round the waist, she could not get away, and her new position enabled me the easier to get my hand between her thighs and thus to feel her charming, pouting little cunt. I began attempting to frig her clitoris, but, stooping, she drew her cunt away, and looking at me with a droll, innocent expression of alarm, and with a perfect unconsciousness of the import of her words, cried, 'Oh! Take care what you are at. You don't know how a lodger this last summer suffered for seizing me in that way and hurting me very much. I screamed out, aunt came up, and, do you know, he had fifty pounds to pay for his impudence.' I could not but smile at the extraordinary innocence of the girl.

'But I do not hurt you, dear Jane,' said I, 'and don't mean to do so.'

'That was what he said, but he went on in a most horrible way, and not only hurt me very much, but made me bleed.'

'It would not be with his hand, you see I only gently press this soft hairy little thing. I am sure that doesn't hurt you.'

'Oh, no! If that was all I should not mind it, it was when he pushed me on the sofa, and pressed upon me, that he hurt me terribly, and you must take care what you are about, or you, too, will have to pay fifty pounds.'

There was a curious air of innocence in all this. It was evident to me the fellow had got into her, and broken her hymen with violence, and then her screams had prevented his finishing his work. Her manner convinced me that she was really not aware of the consequences, or rather had not as yet really had her sexual passions aroused.

'Well, my dear Jane, I neither intend to hurt you nor make myself liable to pay fifty pounds, but you will not refuse me the pleasure of feeling this nice little hairy nest. You see how gentle I am.'

'Well, if you will do me no more hurt than that I shan't refuse you, because you are a nice, kind young gentleman, and very different from the other rough fellow, who never chattered with me and made me laugh as you do. But you must not push your fingers up there, it was something he pushed up there that hurt me so.'

I withdrew my finger, and as, at my request, she had opened her thighs a little, I felt and caressed her very nice little cunt, and with a finger pressed externally above her clitoris. I could see that she flushed and shivered on feeling me there. However, I did no more than gently press and feel all her hairy mount and fat, pouting cunt; she said I must let her go, or her aunt would be coming up.

The first step was now gained. Gradually I progressed further and further, felt her charming bare arse as she stood before me, got her to let me see the beautiful curls she had got on her cunt, then came to kissing it, until at last she opened her thighs and let me tongue it, to her most exquisite delight. I made her spend for the first time in her life, and soon she came to me for it.

I had gradually introduced a finger up her cunt while licking her clitoris and exciting her so much that she was unconscious of my doing it; then two fingers, and after she had spent deliciously, I made them perform an imitation of a throb, which made her jump and ask what I was doing. I asked if she did not feel that my fingers were inside of her sweet cunt.

'You don't say so. It was there I was so hurt.'

'But I do not hurt you, dear Jane?'

'Oh, dear no, it makes me feel queer, but it is very nice.'

'Well, now you know that I have two fingers inside, I will use my tongue again against your charming little clitoris, and work the fingers in and out.'

I did so, and she soon spent in an agony of delight, pressing my head down hard on her cunt, and crying, 'Oh! Oh! It is too great a pleasure!' and then dying off, half insensible. Another time I repeated this she told me not to forget to use my fingers. Having made her spend twice, I took her on my knee and told her that I possessed an instrument that would give her far more pleasure than tongue or finger ever possibly could.

'Indeed?' said she. 'Where is it? I should so like to see it.'

'You won't tell?'

'Oh, no!'

So, pulling out my stiff-standing prick, she stared in amazement. She had really never seen a prick, although it was evidently a prick that had deflowered her, for with my fingers I had explored her cunt and found no hymen there. I put her hand upon it; she involuntarily grasped it firmly.

'This enormous thing could never get into my body. Look, it is thicker than all your fingers put together, and only two fingers feel so tight.'

'Yes, darling, but this dear little thing stretches, and was made to receive this big thing.'

As I was exciting her clitoris with my finger, she grew evidently lasciviously inclined, so I said, 'Just let me try, and if it hurts you I will stop; you know I am always gentle with you.'

'So you are, my dear fellow, but take care not to hurt me.'

She lay down on the bed, as I desired, with feet up and knees laid open. I spat on my prick, and wetted the knob and upper shaft well, then, bringing it to her cunt, well moistened by my saliva in gamahuching her, I held open the lips with the fingers of my left hand, and half buried its knob before getting to the real entrance underneath.

'Don't flinch, dearest, I shall not hurt.' And I got it well over the knob, and buried it one inch further.

'Stop!' she cried, 'it seems as if it would burst me open, it so stretches me.'

'But it does not hurt you, dearest?' I had immediately stopped before asking the question.

'No, not exactly, but I feel as if something was in my throat.'

'Rest a little, and that will go off.' I slipped a finger down on her clitoris, and as I frigged it she grew more and more excited, giving delicious cunt pressures on my prick, until it gradually made its way by the gentle pushing I continued to make without other movements. It was more than half in when she spent. This not only lubricated the interior, but, the inner muscles relaxing, a gentle shove forwards housed it to the hilt, and then I lay quiet until she recovered from the half-fainting state her last discharge had produced. Soon the increased pressures of the inner folds showed that her passions were awakening afresh. She opened her eyes and, looking lovingly, said I had given her great pleasure, but she felt as if something enormous was stretching her inside to the utmost. Had I got it all in?

'Yes, dearest, and now it will be able to give you greater pleasure than before.' I began a slow withdrawal and return, frigging her clitoris at the same time, for I was standing between her legs. She soon grew wild with excitement, and, nature prompting her, her arse rose and fell almost as well as if she was mistress of the art. The novel combination of prick and finger quickly brought on the crisis. I, too, was wild with lust, and we spent together, ending in an annihilation of all our senses by the extreme ecstasy of the final overpowering crisis. We lay panting for some time in all the afterjoys. Dear Jane begged me to give her some water, as she felt quite faint. I withdrew, still almost in a standing state, got her some water, helped her up, seated her on the sofa and kissed her lovingly as I thanked her for the exquisite joy she had given me. She threw her arms round my neck, and with tears in her eyes told me I had taught her the joys of heaven, and she should always love me, and I must always love her, for now she could not live without me. I kissed and dried her eyes, and told her we should in future enjoy it even more when she got accustomed to it.

'Let me see the dear thing that gave me such pleasure.'

I pulled it out, but it was no longer at the stand, and this surprised her. I explained the necessity of its being so, but said she would quickly see it rise and swell to the former size if she continued to handle it so nicely. It rose almost before I could say as much. She fondled it, and even stooped and kissed its ruby head. We should quickly have got to another bout of fucking if the ringing of the call bell had not brought us to a sense of its imprudence; so after arranging her hair and dress, she hastily descended with some of the breakfast things.

Of course, so good a beginning led to constant renewals and Jane quickly became extremely amorous, and under my instruction a first-rate fucker.

A month after I had taken up my residence at Mrs Nichols's, Jane's sister arrived. Ann was a much finer woman than Jane: broad-shouldered, with a wide-spread bosom, which, in afterdays, I found had not suffered by her 'misfortune', but then she had not suckled it. Her hips were widely projected, and she was grand and magnificent in her arse. Naturally of a very hot temperament, when once she had tasted the magnificent weapon I was possessed of, she grew most lasciviously lustful, and was one of the best fuckers I ever met with. Jane was fair. Ann was dark, with black locks and black hairy cunt – a very long cunt, with a small tight hole in it, and above it a wide-spread projecting mount, splendidly furnished with hair. Her clitoris was hard and thick.

On her first arrival Jane was much afraid Ann would discover our connection and we took every precaution, although I, in my heart, wished this might occur, for as she occasionally waited on me, I grew lecherous upon one whose charms, even covered, excited me greatly. One morning I overheard Mrs Nichols tell Jane to put on her bonnet and go to Oxford Street on some errand; I knew thus that Ann would attend on me, and there would be no chance of interruption from Jane, so I determined to come at once to the point. We had become on friendly, chatty terms, and when she had laid breakfast I asked her to help me on with my coat, which done, I thanked her and with one arm round her waist drew her to me and kissed her. 'Hallo!' said she, 'that is something new,' but did not attempt to withdraw. So giving her another kiss, I told her what a glorious woman she was, and how she excited me, just see. I held one of her hands, and before she was aware, placed it on my huge prick, that bulged out of my trousers as if it would burst its way through.

She could not help squeezing it, while she cried, 'Goodness, gracious! What an enormous thing you have got!'

Her face flushed, her eyes sparkled with the fire of lust that stirred her whole soul. She tried to grasp it.

'Stop,' said I, 'and I will put it in its natural state into your hand.'

So pulling it out, she seized it at once, and most lasciviously gazed upon it, pressing it gently She evidently was growing lewder and lewder, so I at once proposed to fuck her, and thinking it best to be frank, and put her at her ease. I told her that I knew she had had a 'misfortune' but if she would let me fuck her I should be on honour to withdraw before spending and thus avoid all chance of putting her belly up.

She had become so randy that she felt, as she afterwards told me, she could not refuse so splendid a prick of a size she had often dreamed of, and longed for.

'Can I trust you?' said she.

'Safely, my dear.'

'Then you may have me – let me embrace that dear object.'

Stooping, she kissed it most voluptuously, shivering at the same time in the ecstasy of a spend produced by the mere sight and touch. She gave one or two ohs, and drawing me to the bed by my prick threw herself back, pulling her petticoats up at the same time. Then I beheld her splendid cunt in all its magnificence of size and hairiness. I sank on my knees and glued my lips to the oozing entrance, for she was one who spent most profusely, her cunt had the true delicious odour, and her spunk was thick and gluttonous for a woman.

I tongued her clitoris, driving her voluptuously wild. So she cried, 'Oh! Do put that glorious prick into me, but remember your promise.'

I brought it up to that wide-spread, large-lipped, immense cunt. I fully expected that, big as I was, I should slip in over head and shoulders with the greatest ease. So you may imagine my surprise to find the tightest and smallest of entrances to the inner vagina I almost ever met with. It was really with greater difficulty I effected an entrance than I had with her little sister, whose cunt presented no such voluptuous grandeur. It was as tight a fit as Jane's was to me on our first coition. Tight as it was, it gave her nothing but the most exquisite pleasure. She was thoroughly up to her work, and was really one of the most voluptuous and lascivious fuckers I have ever met with, excellent as my experience has been. I made her, with fucking and frigging, spend six times before I suddenly withdrew my prick, and pressing its shaft against her wet lips, and my own belly, spent deliciously outside. Shortly after it rose again, and this time after making her spend as often as before, for she was most voluptuously lustful, when I withdrew, she suddenly got from under me, and seizing its shaft with one hand, stooped and took its knob between her lips, and quickly made me pour a flood of sperm into her mouth, which she eagerly swallowed and sucked on, to my great delight.

We should have had a third bout but for the necessity of her going down to her aunt.

I breakfasted, then rang to take away. Again we had a delicious fuck, and a fourth when she came to make the bed and empty the slops. This fourth time I begged her to kneel on the sofa, and let me see her gloriously grand arse, and when I had to retire I would show her a way that would continue both our pleasure. So after fucking her from behind, and making her spend far oftener than me, I withdrew, and pushing it up between the lips over the clitoris, with my hand round her waist, I pressed it tightly against her cunt and clitoris, and continued to wriggle my arse, making her spend again as I poured a flood all up over her belly. She declared it was almost as good as if inside of her cunt.

It soon happened that both sisters knew of the other enjoying me, and it ended in their slipping down separately, from their attic, where both slept, to my room, and we had the most delicious fucking and gamahuching sessions ever.

Ann was by far the finest and the most lascivious fuck, but little Jane had a certain charm of youth and also of freshness, which got her a fair share of my favours.

We carried this on for several weeks until use made us careless and noisy.

The aunt, when no lodgers occupied the room, slept overhead, and, probably being sleepless one morning, when it was early daylight, heard our voices, came down and surprised me in the very act of gamahuching Jane, who stood above me and presented her cunt to my lecherous tongue. A loud exclamation from her aunt roused us up at once.

'Get to bed, you dreadful hussy.'

She fled without a moment's hesitation.

Mrs Nichols then began to remonstrate with me on the infamy of my conduct. I approached the door to get my shirt, for I was stark naked. But Mrs Nichols, who had only her short shift on, which not only allowed the full display of very fine, firm and ample bubbies, but not falling below the middle of her thighs, showed remarkably well-made legs and small knees, with the swelling of immense thighs just indicated, turned and kissed me with vigour.

My stiff-standing prick in full vigour, and if anything, still more stimulated by the unexpected beauties shown by Mrs Nichols, I was yet more surprised when she turned upon me and, seizing me round the waist, pushed herself forwards, and before I could recover, she had hauled up her 'cutty sark', revealing a most magnificent arse, and placed me into her cunt – before I could recover from the surprise of the attack.

There was no one who could hear but the girls, and they knew better than to interrupt me. I kept fucking away, and passing an arm round her body, with my finger I got to her clitoris, which sprang out into considerable proportions. My big prick and the frigging of her clitoris produced their natural result. She grew even more full of lust. I felt her cunt pressures, and knew how her passions were rising. Speedily, she began to cry, 'Oh, oh,' and breathed hard, and then most gloriously wriggled her splendid arse, and as I spent she too was taken in the delicious ecstasy of the final crisis. She lay throbbing on my delighted prick until it stood as stiff as before. I began a slow movement, and she made no resistance, except crying out, 'Oh! Dear. Oh! Dear,' as if in spite of regrets, she could not help enjoying it; indeed, at last she said, 'Oh! What a man you are, Mr Roberts; it is very wrong of me to do this, but I cannot resist enjoying myself. It is years since I did such a thing, but as you have done it, it makes me wish you would do it again. Let us change position and carry on.'

'Very well, but you must throw off this tiresome chemise, or I won't withdraw.'

As her lust was so excited, she made no objection, so withdrawing we stood up. She drew her shift over her head, and displayed a far more splendid form, with an exquisitely fair and dimpled skin, than I could have thought possible.

'My dear Mrs Nichols, what a fine perfect form you have got. Let me embrace you in my arms.'

She was nothing loath, flattered by my praise. She laid hold of my cock with one hand, and closely clasped me with the other arm, while I threw an arm and hand round her truly magnificent arse, and with my other hand pressed on a wonderful pair of bubbies as hard and firm as any maid of eighteen. Our mouths met in a loving kiss, our tongues exchanged endearments in each other's mouths.

She said, 'You have made me very wicked. Let me have this enormous and dear fellow again.'

I said I must first gaze on all her beauties, especially on her gorgeous and enormous bottom. She turned herself round in every way, delighted to find that I so ardently admired her.

She then lay down on her back, and spread wide her legs, and called to me to mount and put it in.

'First I must kiss this beautiful cunt, and suck this superb clitoris.'

Her mount was covered with closely curled brown, silky locks; her cunt was large with grand, thick lips and well-haired sides. Her clitoris stood out quite three inches, red and stiff. I took it in my mouth sucked it, and frigged her cunt with two fingers, which went in with the greatest ease, but were nipped tightly the moment the entrance was gained, and I frigged and sucked until she spent madly with absolute screams of delight. I continued to suck and excite her, which quickly made her cry out, 'Oh, darling boy, come and shove your glorious prick into my longing cunt.'

I sprang up and buried it until our two hairs were crushed between us. She held me tight for a minute without moving, then went off like a wild bacchante, and uttered voluptuous, bawdy expressions: 'Shove your delicious prick further and harder. Oh, you are killing me with delight. Harder! Harder!'

She was a perfect mistress of the art, gave me exquisite pleasure, and, I may add, proved afterwards a woman of infinite variety, and became one of my most devoted admirers. Our intrigue continued for years, while her age, as is the case with good wine, only appeared to improve her. Her husband was not a bad fucker, but having only a small prick, had never stimulated her lust as my big splitter had just done.

We had on this first occasion three other good fucks, which she seemed to enjoy more and more.

As I had previously fucked the girls pretty well, my prick at last refused to rise and perform. We had to stop fucking, but I gamahuched her once more after again posing her and admiring her really wonderfully well-made and well-preserved body. She had a good suck at my cock, without bringing him up again.

At last we separated, but not before she made a promise that she would sleep with me that night, and a glorious night we had. I had the more difficult task of reconciling her to my having her nieces. I used to have them one night, and sleep with her the next.

~ II ~

The Pearl

1879

The Pearl is the quintessential Victorian erotic magazine and the greatest erotic periodical of sexual prose and verse in history. The usually impeccably correct English erotobibliographer H. S. Ashbee noted in his 1885 *Catena Librorum Tacendorum* that *The Pearl* was limited to a hundred and fifty sets, sold by the publisher, in three bound volumes of 192 pages each, with thirty-six obscene colour lithographs added in. It sold for the then princely sum of £25 (more than the annual salary of the average worker of the time). One such copy, supposedly from the private collection of King Wilhelm III of Holland, was offered for sale in the United States in 1977 for $2,500. However, as the following excerpt demonstrates, this presentation most likely represented the publisher binding up unsold copies of the individual monthly issues for high-society sale, for in fact *The Pearl* first appeared in eighteen issues, one a month, from July 1879 through to December 1880.

The Pearl described itself as 'A Monthly Journal of Facetia and Voluptuous Reading'. According to Ashbee's bibliography, the publisher claimed this work to be 'without exception the grandest and best erotic work ever published in the English language', a boast possibly proved by *The Pearl* having stayed in print continuously since its original publication, though with continually changing imprints. The first editions stated themselves to be printed at Oxford on the University Press; in actuality they were printed in London. When this printing was sold out, a complete reprint of the text by Auguste Brancart appeared in Belgium about 1890, the imprint altered to 'London. Printed for the Society of Vice. 1879'. This was followed by an undated *c.*1910 Rotterdam reprint by Berge, marked 'London – Paris. Printed for the Society of Vice'. A *c.*1933 New York reprint, allegedly by Vincent Smith, claimed to be 'London. Printed for the Society of Vice. 1880', to throw off the police. Since the 1960s nearly a dozen soft-cover reprints have appeared worldwide. In addition, partial reprints of it have appeared since 1879. The Bibliothèque Nationale even has odd fascicles of a turn-of-the-century French printing meant only for English-reading tourists.

In total, *The Pearl's* 576 pages contained six full novels in serial form, along with many novel excerpts, short stories, ballads, poems, acrostics, songs, jokes, anecdotes, riddles, limericks, letters, puns, facetia, gossip, nursery rhymes, erotic literary parodies, irreverent spoofs, and sex trial reports (Crim. Con.). The unifying feature was blatant sex and a sense of frivolity. The language was coarse, bawdy, explicit or simply obscene to the fullest, and the themes covered the gamut of human sexual conduct and misconduct. Flagellation, homosexuality and bisexuality were more prominent than in most Victorian erotica.

The following excerpt from the final issue of *The Pearl* is not the best example of fine writing to be found in that periodical. However, it gives an interesting overview of the range of material contained in *The Pearl*, as well as references to itself. Perhaps unintentionally it refers to 'the last issue' of *The Pearl*. Readers will recognise that the style, themes, and scenes are very similar to the Edwardian novel *The Initiation of Aurora Trill*, written by a New Zealander, so the reference to an Australian in this excerpt is perhaps slightly biographical.

from *The Pearl*

You didn't know Steve Broad? More's the pity! A jollier, better-hearted and manlier fellow never pissed against a wall. He was my constant chum. From the time we occupied the same diggings in Camden Town, till he went to Australia, we were altogether.

Damon and the other fellow, the Siamese twins. Castor and Pollux were not more inseparable. Old Jack Falstaff said Prince Henry and Poins loved each other because 'their legs were both of a bigness'.

Shall I whisper the secret, or one of the secrets, of our attachment? Our pricks were both of a length, and our arseholes the same gauge. Don't infer too much from that admission, it was not often that – but, there, I will tell you a story of Steve Broad that will show you the sort of fellow he was.

Steve had a pal, Alf Nugent, and he and Alf had lived together as chums. Alf occasionally received a visit in his lodgings from a pretty sister, Lettice or, as they called her, Letty Nugent, a charming little blonde, with, oh, such shoulders; a mouth humid and peachlike; and a pair of eyes that could entice the bark off a tree.

It was not long before Steve and Letty struck an acquaintance.

Steve could make love like a Romeo.

Letty was as 'willing' as Barkis, and the brother Alf was not one to spoil sport, so the three got on charmingly together.

Alf often gave a pleasant little party. I was invited. Steve had made my acquaintance in the city and took me there. I introduced a young lady, Kitty Marshall, and Alf brought his *inamorata*, Nellie Grover. The six of us formed a pleasant little gathering and rare fun we had.

Let me sketch for you one of our social meetings, after a *recherché* supper prepared by the nimble hands of Letty Nugent, who turned out every article as palatable as Ruth Pinch's steak pie.

The table was cleared of all but wines and fruits. The couches were drawn up to the fire, and the six of us would go in for a little fun.

Steve would warble in his rich, manly voice a jolly song, such as:

> There's a thing that bears a well-known name,
>   Though it is but a little spot,
> Its smell sets my heart and my brain in a flame,
>   And its touch makes my prick grow hot.
> 'Tis the sweetest thing this world can show,
>   To praise it, can't be wrong;
> 'Twill set your blood in a fervid glow,
>   Make your prick grow stiff and long.
> 'Tis a woman's cunt. Her glorious Fan,
>   Oh, a cunt is the pride of an Englishman.
>
> That cunt will not be treated with shame,
>   But calls for proper respect;
> And though mostly fit for a fucking game,
>   Yet it sometimes in mourning is decked.
> Then beware how you go with the darling then,
>   Or perhaps sorely punished you'll be;
> For cunt won't be the sport of men,
>   When it wants its privacy.
> For caprice is part of cunt's own plan,
>   To enhance its joy to an Englishman.

But when cunt is ready, I give you the tip,
  No half-hearted play can it stand;
It likes to be fondled with tongue and with lip,
  And shuns not the touch of your hand.
But the glorious Prick sets Miss Cunt in a thrill,
  She loves a prick long, thick and firm;
And she'll wriggle and pant till you madly fill
  Her bang full of glowing sperm.
You may frig and gamahuche, and try every plan,
  But fair fucking's the pride of an Englishman.

Of course a song like this was well received, and quickly followed by a practical illustration.

My little lady Kitty Marshall warmly defended gamahuching, and so did I. Lying Kitty down on the couch and parting her beautiful legs, I displayed to the others a cleft that an angel would think it a new joy to suck. Soon all six of us were engaged in an amorous orgy, and Steve, who certainly could boast the most magnificent priapus that ever adorned a man, took pretty little Letty in his arms and gave her what you may call an 'exhibition fuck'. His balls knocked against the entrance of her lovely quim, and at last she wriggled and panted and hugged him into a spend. He poured such a libation into her that we could see it overflow, and they mutually lay entranced until we revived them with some glorious wine.

Steve soon got to be really in love with Letty. He proposed marriage to her and had the full consent of her brother Alf and the promised consent of her father. It was arranged that on the return of Alf and his sister to their home in the country, Steve should come on a visit and get the old boy's consent.

The old gentleman cordially invited him, to get a look at him.

The time came.

Alf and Letty went home, and Steve was soon to follow.

At last the day arrived, and he went.

After packing up his traps, bidding his landlady goodbye and giving the slavey a farewell grind on the kitchen dresser, he took himself down to the station, booked for Pairbank, and was soon seated alone in a snug, first-class carriage.

Alone! Yes, all but for a delightful companion – the last number of *The Pearl* – with which, and his favourite meerschaum, Steve wiled away the time as station after station flew past.

It was a beautiful morning, but he heeded not the aspect of the country, so thoroughly was he absorbed in the doings of Lady Pokingham and Miss Coote.

All this excited his imagination until he got in an almost furious state, not knowing how to ease his torment, and only wishing that he had a companion to accompany him on the journey, whether male or female.

After a short while, the train stopped at Bellevue, and a young lady got into his carriage. She carried a rather large bundle, which she placed under the seat, and then sat down.

Steve's heart bounded as he noticed her light flowing hair, her airy step and her lithe figure. But she was closely veiled, and as yet he could not see her face, but the lovely swell of her bosom, the creamy whiteness of the little bit of her throat that was visible, convinced him she was young and quite lovely.

The train sped on.

Modestly the young lady kept her veil down, and Steve thrust *The Pearl* in his pocket and was soon deep in *The Times*.

Oh, how that veiled fall piqued him. Again and again he cast his eyes to it, over *The Times*, but the veil was still down.

'Does the draught annoy you?' said Steve pleasantly, pointing to the partly open window.

'Not at all, thank you,' replied a sweet voice behind the veil.

Something in the voice thrilled Steve through. He had heard it before – he felt sure. He was more anxious than ever to see the face of the young woman it belonged to.

At last they passed a certain station. With a sigh of relief, she threw up her veil and finally turned her pretty face towards our hero.

'Good heavens! Kate, is it really you, my love?'

'Why, Mr Broad, who would have thought of seeing you? Oh, I am so glad. You know that odious old lawyer they wanted to marry me to? Well, I am positively flying from him, and until I passed this station, I felt sure they would pursue me. That is why I kept myself veiled. Now I am quite out of my trouble, I think, for I have got a disguise which I shall put on. I tried all I could to get into an empty carriage, but the guard assured me there was not one, but now you can help instead of hinder me.'

Let me tell you now that Steve and the lady were old friends. They had met first at some private theatricals. Steve made love to her in the character of a French count on the stage, and in his own character of an English ladylover off it, and, off the stage, he managed to make a first appearance in Kate's delicious cunny. In fact he took her maidenhead, and many a delightful love-fuck they had enjoyed until Kate decided to go abroad, and now the two had met again under such strange circumstances.

'Let me tell you quick,' said Kate. 'I am engaged to Paul Jellocombe. You remember him? Well, love, you won't be jealous when I tell you we are going to be married as soon as ever I am of age. I have escaped from home and mean to stay with Paul's friends until a few weeks elapse, when I shall be my own mistress. Now for my plan. I have eluded them so far, but for fear they should telegraph to the station and stop me, I have brought a disguise, and now, quick, help me put it on. You shall be my lady's maid.'

Before Steve had time to get his breath, the charming, volatile, impulsive girl took off bonnet and cloak, undid her dress and whipped it off round her feet, exposing a lovely pair of white shoulders and two glowing breasts, small for her size, but round, firm and polished as marble. Steve's hungry eyes feasted on them.

If Steve's priapus had before been excited, it was now delirious.

Jumping from his seat he helped her take off her garments until she came to her drawers.

'Stop, sir, that will do,' said Kate. 'I don't want any further undressing. No! No! Don't be foolish, I can allow no liberties now. Quick, I know this line well. You have only just time to turn me into a middy before we get to the next station.'

Stooping as she spoke, she undid the bundle at her feet, and quick as her nimble fingers could move, and with Steve's assistance, she was soon dressed as a middy. Her light hair was cleverly tucked up, a short crisp wig assumed, her cap stuck jauntily on her head. She looked as smart and trim a middy as ever saluted the quarter deck.

The transformation was completed. The train stopped at a station, and they both jumped out and hurried for refreshments.

The rollicking, jovial style of Kate, her walk and gait, showed her well fitted to play her part. She was indeed no mean actress.

Soon they were back in the carriage, which Steve adroitly secured for themselves by puffing a tremendous cloud of smoke into the eyes of an old lady who would fain have entered it.

Steve took the pretty middy on his knee.

'Well, Kate, love, this is quite an adventure, and I tell you it is a long way to the next station, and as it has been one of the great ambitious of my life to fuck a midshipman, this is too good an opportunity to let pass.'

Kate offered no resistance. Thrusting his hand into the bosom of her jacket, he first felt her round and polished breasts, squeezed her nipples and fired her blood with his wanton touches and the hot, burning kisses he printed on her lips. Then, unbuttoning his trousers, he allowed his splendid staff *d'amour* to display itself before her.

'Oh, Steve, how it has grown since I saw it last,' said Kate mischievously as she took it in her hand.

'Yes,' said Steve, who could not resist a pun. 'I have heard him groan for a taste of your darling cunny. Come, let me feel how that is getting on.'

As he spoke he slid his hand into her trousers and felt her moist and mossy cunt, tickled her clitoris and roused all her warm passions.

As the train sped on, they abandoned themselves totally to all that their warm, impassioned natures could suggest.

Steve knelt down on the floor of the carriage and, opening wide Kate's firm and polished thighs, pressed his hot lips to her creamy cunt and gamahuched her until she spent in a delirium of pleasure.

And then, when all his feelings were worked up to such a pitch of excitement that he could no longer contain himself, he laid her supple form over the seat. Getting into her from behind, he thrust his prick to the very hilt in her reeking cunt. One, two, three thrusts and, as he clasped her tightly to him, with a convulsive thrill he poured out his manly balm in an ecstasy of shuddering enjoyment.

'Hey! Stop that, you infernal scoundrels. Oh, you dirty rascals! How dare you do that!'

In a sudden bewildered start of alarm, they looked around to see a red, round, indignant face, ornamented with a bristly white moustache and surmounted by a tuft of white hair that made the upper part of the head look like an infuriated cockatoo. His face was peering on them through a window in their compartment, which, being concealed by a curtain the same colour as the carriage lining, they had not noticed.

The passenger in the next compartment was prompted to draw his curtain, and his restless, listless curiosity was rewarded by seeing Steve repeatedly ram his hungry prick into Kate's writhing, clasping cunt.

In a minute Steve had filled his lover's cunt. Then he and Kate had arranged their costume and were sitting down, whilst the passenger continued to glare at them, muttering subdued imprecations and swearing he would charge them as soon as they arrived at the next station.

Without turning his head, Steve whispered to Kate to get out at the next station, to bolt through, ask for the high road and leave him to detain the old boy until he could join her.

Quick as thought, as they neared the station, Steve bolted out and, using a railway key he always carried, locked the compartment in which the old man was alone. He and Kate dashed through the station before the fat, old duffer could cause them to be stopped.

Quickly as they could, they made for the country, and there they had a parting rural fuck which they thoroughly enjoyed.

There is really something delightful in a rural, alfresco fuck. The music of the birds. the babbling of a stream nearby, the fresh air fanning your face and invigorating your frame, seems to me always to give great zest and vigour to the performance. I know for myself the thrusts I give are more vigorous, the sperm I spend more copious, and the thrill always more delicious when I have a glorious country fuck in the open air.

'Goodbye. I am sure it will not be long before I see you again,' said Kate. 'And married or not, remember that there is always a loving, dear, affectionate, little cunny to welcome you whenever you see me.'

'Farewell,' said Steve. 'and be sure my prick will always stand your true friend.'

So they parted.

A hearty welcome awaited Steve at the hands of Alf Nugent and his charming sister Letty.

They were alone in the house, their father being expected shortly, so they made him quite free.

After a jolly meal, which his walk gave him an appetite for, Alf said, 'Now, Steve, let me show you our very own private boudoir.'

Following him, Steve soon found himself in a most tastefully furnished little room. A pianoforte stood in one corner. Other musical instruments were about the room. Splendid pictures of a voluptuous character adorned the walls, and a glorious couch that seemed fit for a seraph to recline on stood the chief object of attraction.

'And now,' said Alf, 'before my father comes home – and he will not be long, he had only some slight business in the town – I must tell you that Letty is dying for a fuck.'

Steve was quite reinvigorated. After Alf left the room, it took but a little time for him to undress the lovely girl and lay her on the soft couch.

In a few moments Steve was on her, and his prick buried to the hilt in her luscious cunt. He quickened his strokes, and soon a shiver shook their bodies as Letty and he both melted in a glorious spend.

'Hark!' they heard Alf cry. 'What is that! A carriage as sure as I live. It must be father. Look, Steve, from the window. Who is it?'

Steve looked out.

'It is an old gentleman coming up the garden walk, Alf. Is that man there your father?'

Alf peered out. 'Yes.'

'Then, for heaven's sake, don't let him see me. I must disguise myself. I cannot stop now to tell you now, but something must be done to destroy my identity, or I am done for. Quick, Letty, go down and meet your father. Alf and I will join you presently.'

Letty soon disappeared, though burning with curiosity. She was a docile creature, and did as she was bid.

'Now, Alf,' said Steve, 'your guv'nor saw me in the railway carriage fucking a lovely girl, but as I was having her backwards, and she was disguised as a sailor – a tale hangs to it, but I can't tell you now – I expect he thought I was doing a bit of back-door work, and as he may be a particular old boy, he must not know me again.'

Steve was a young man of decision and although it cost him a sigh, his beautiful whiskers were soon sacrificed. His tact and skill soon changed his whole appearance, and when he descended to join Letty and Mr Nugent but for a sign from Alf, Letty would not have known him, much less did Mr Nugent recognise the bold Fucker of the Railway Train.

That's how Steve Broad managed to lose his whiskers.

And a curious sequel hangs to the story.

After dinner, when the gentlemen were alone, the old gentleman began telling them the following: 'A very curious circumstance happened to me this morning. When in a railway train I happened accidentally to look through the window of the compartment and saw a young man actually in the act of indecency with a midshipman. The rascals escaped by locking me in the carriage. However, in the carriage he had left, the young villain dropped a book. I took charge of it. As I had no spectacles, I did not look close at it, but as it doubtless contains some clue to the rascal, look at it for me.'

Steve saw in a moment it was *The Pearl*, but knowing no clue to his identity was in it, he just glanced at it and handed it back, advising Old Nugent to look at it more closely in the privacy of his chamber.

The old chap retired presently for his afternoon's nap, taking the book with him, and soon after they heard peals of laughter from his room. Then he was heard walking up and down. Soon his voice was heard calling Patty, his favourite servant.

Alf and Steve peeped through the keyhole after she entered the room and saw him showing her the pictures and reading passages from the book. Then, taking her in his arms, he laid her on the bed and, raising his shirt-tail, he displayed a prick, stalwart and strong. In a few moments it was lodged in her creamy cunt.

In the evening Old Nugent called Letty and Steve, joined their hands, and said, 'Bless you my children, a delightful little work I have been reading today has put fucking in such a beautiful light that I at once give you my consent to commence it as soon as possible. I have quite altered my opinion about that young fellow I saw and am convinced that to give his prick a treat is the first duty of every man at all times. I propose now that your nuptials shall be celebrated by a glorious fucking tournament.'

This was done. Happiness was the lot of them all that evening.

Old Nugent never found out Steve's escapade. He died soon after and left them a heap of money. So amorous was the old boy to the last, that they had to send for the servant to toss him off before they could get the lid on the coffin.

Kate married and is quite happy, and I long to see Steve and have another laugh with him over how he lost his whiskers.

~~~~ 12 ~~~~

The Pearl
Christmas Annual 1881

Nearly all readers of erotica are familiar with *The Pearl*. Much less known is that four supplements to it were published also. The first three, *Swivia*, *The Haunted House* and *The Pearl: Christmas Annual*, appeared for December 1879, 1880, and 1881 respectively. They were poorly printed, about sixty-four pages each, illustrated with five or six coloured lithographs, and were entirely independent of the original *Pearl* volumes. The final offering, *The Erotic Casket Gift Book for 1882* was a mere twenty pages and seemed to have contained odd bits the publisher had had no room for previously, and hoped finally to use to his financial gain. Despite their size, each of these four was offered for sale at £3 3s!

This was a rather sad and ignoble end for a once truly great erotic periodical publication, for *The Pearl* was the apogee of over one hundred years of journalistic evolution in England that is perhaps little understood today. Magazines, adult or otherwise, as we currently know them are a relatively recent phenomenon. It took the advent of the Industrial Revolution, with its increasing literacy and decreasing printing costs, to open the way for popularly directed and priced periodicals. These filled a new entertainment niche that newspapers could not. Meant for a more restricted market, and depending less on advertising revenues, they could print 'common' material which wide-circulation formal publications could not. Starting in the 1780s, with such names as *The Bon Ton Magazine*, *Rambler's Magazine*, *The Ranger's Magazine* (and numerous variations thereon), these catchpenny publications contained gallant and semi-erotic fiction, accounts of fashion, gossip, scandals, theatre notes, biographies of celebrities, 'amatory adventures and folly', anecdotes about royalty, crim. con. (i.e. criminal conversations, or reports of sex crime trials), sexual anthropology and ethnology (in the form of reports on marriage customs and mating rites around the world), and readers' letters on flagellation, home discipline, prostitution, gambling, and 'sin' in general. They carefully avoided outright pornography and obscenity, although some had lists of actual Covent Garden 'women of pleasure'.

By the 1830s, particularly due to the publishers Jack Mitford and William Dugdale, this genre of periodicals, still with the same basic mix of entertainment, became more sexually explicit. The letters, fiction, trial reports, and humour became stronger and more graphic, and *double entendres* increased. It was a logical extension that someone would finally discard all the socially acceptable cover material and just leave the sex, which was what the publications were actually bought for, in a totally unexpurgated fashion. *The Pearl* was the Victorian culmination of this evolution. In the twentieth century we have seen the same process as 'licentious' publications such as the popular *Broadway Brevities* were followed by 'smutty' adult weeklies like *Tattle Tale* and finally anything-goes papers like *Screw*.

The following excerpt is from *The Pearl: Christmas Annual 1881*. Possibly written by the publisher himself, with no small degree of self-promotion, it lacks many of the fine touches exhibited by *The Pearl* in its prime, yet still makes entertaining reading.

∾ from *The Pearl: Christmas Annual*

It took a day or two for Madame Coulisse to rig me out with all new clothes; she actually sent me to another milliner to have my things made in the best possible fashion. Then one Sunday afternoon she took me and two of her young ladies for a drive in Hyde Park, during which I noticed several gentlemen stop and speak to her in a low tone, as they looked at me rather significantly. This was her market; I was sold to advantage before we drove back to the house.

The same evening, about ten o'clock, Madame sent for me to her boudoir. She had previously told me to make myself look my very best, as she expected to be able to introduce me to a very nice gentleman during the evening (of course keeping to herself the fact of having sold my maidenhead for a couple of hundred pounds).

Upon entering I saw a fine aristocratic-looking man seated by her side on a sofa.

'Allow me, milord, to introduce Mlle Vanessa. Have you ever seen a prettier little thing? I warrant her genuine.' Then, turning to me, 'This gentleman, Vanessa, wishes to honour you with his love. Be as good a girl as you promised, my dear, and you will have nothing but happiness to look forward to in my house,' saying which she vanished from the room and left me *vis-à-vis* with his lordship, who rose, kissed my lips and drew me to his side on the sofa.

'So, my dear, you are willing to make love with me. Look, if I am pleased I shall give you these sovereigns,' he said, showing me a handful of gold. 'When I make love I don't like crying and sulks, it takes it all out of me.'

I blushed awfully, but when he kissed me again I gave him a little one in return, as I clung round his neck and promised to try and please him.

'Ah, then you know a little, my dear?'

'Yes, Madame has told me it might hurt a little but will give great delight afterward. I – I want to be a woman, sir!'

'And so you shall. Let us undress and try what yonder spring bed will do for us, by Jove! I'll take you and keep you if you please me, Vanessa; I want a girl no one has ever had.'

We were both soon reduced to a state of complete nudity, except stockings and garters. After lifting me on the bed, he jumped up beside me and began to examine all my charms: first my firm round little bubbies, then my mound, but the spot below was too attractive for him to linger long before he put his finger there.

It made me wince a little – the passage was too narrow and tender.

'You love!' he exclaimed, his eyes almost darting fire as he spoke, whilst I actually saw his manly affair quite suddenly lift its head, which had up to then been only partially erect. 'You love! You're a real virgin, are you not? How I shall love you, Vanessa! Now, be good, and bear a little discomfort for the sake of the pleasure to come, then I will pay the old bitch her money and take you away. I won't leave such a jewel in her care for a moment; she would sell you again before tomorrow night. No, darling, you must belong to me alone!'

Then, raising my buttocks, he put a pillow under my bottom and, getting between my legs, his fingers gently opened the lips of my pussy. Pointing the head of his moderate-size dart of love to the entrance, he pushed as far as it would go. Feeling the obstruction of my hymen, he paused for a moment, then thrust suddenly and fiercely. He effected his purpose at once, so that my defloration was complete, and he was buried to the roots of his hair.

Presently he began to move, thrusting slowly in and out, with a poking kind of motion. Then I felt his warm juice spurt right up into my vitals. I soon began to feel some pleasurable sensations, which increased as he went on again, till I began to meet him with all the ardour of my warm temperament, now fairly aroused for the very first time to the true joys of womanhood.

How we struggled, lovingly and yet almost furiously, to get more love from each other. My champion was a good man, and his size just suited me. We swam in delight three times before he was compelled to rest.

Then, embracing me most tenderly, he sponged my parts till he had cooled them and removed all trace of the havoc he had committed. I really loved him for his tender kindness, and when he made me dress and took me in his carriage, in spite of all Madame's protestations that she would not have me taken away, I threw my arms round his neck and sobbed tears of gratitude.

We went to a fine hotel, and the next day saw me installed as his mistress in a pretty suite of chambers at the West End, near Belgrave Square.

I do not want to mention his name, but shall simply call him my lord. He was so kind to me and, I believe from the first, almost loved me to distraction. He got French, English and musical governesses for me, and took the greatest possible pleasure in seeing me do the honours of his table when a friend or friends visited at our chambers, but it was not to last long, only two brief happy, happy years, and then all was blown to the wind.

He had a bosom friend, a Mr Gower, who spent hours with him every day. They were partners in everything. Gower was a much younger and handsomer man than his lordship, and being so often in his company, sometimes he would call and catch me alone, and wait for my protector.

My God! What an oily tongue that serpent had! How he flattered me and led me on till I really loved him as much as his friend. It was rank adultery. I felt I must have him, and that he would soon ask me to be unfaithful to my protector, to whom I owed my happiness, my all; still I knew I would yield – I had a fancy and couldn't help myself.

At last the fatal promise was given, but we had to wait for an opportunity for the feast of love we were to taste on the sly.

Ours were the only inhabited chambers in the house at night, and his lordship seldom left me to sleep alone.

At last the chance came. My protector had a great match on at Newmarket, but Mr Gower was too ill to go with him. As soon as he had left I gave my servant a holiday for the night, and about eight o'clock in the evening my paramour came. I was careful to put up the chain to the street door: his lordship had a latch key, and my guilty conscience told me there was just a chance of his return, although extremely improbable.

How lovingly we walked up the stairs together, after a long, luscious kiss behind the street door. I had prepared a nice little cold collation with plenty of champagne, for I must admit having always had a great partiality for the sparkling fizz.

He bore me to the sofa in a perfect transport of impatience, raised my clothes and, kneeling down, printed hot, burning kisses on the sensitive spot itself till I fairly begged him to give me a better proof of his manhood.

Our first conjunction was far too impassioned to last long; we came together at once in a flood of bliss, but he kept his place, and soon almost drove me out of my mind by the thrilling effects of his thrusts. He was a little bigger than his lordship and filled me up so tightly that it seemed most exquisite. However, this second turn came to the usual delicious ending, then we sat down to supper. I must confess he was allowed to pledge me so frequently in bumpers of champagne that I got quite lecherous, threw off my clothes, made him undress and then persisted in sitting on his lap with his fine John Thomas buried to the hilt in my crack.

At last we went to bed and then commenced a regular battle of love. My champion was quite my equal in lust; how we joined and grappled in our love struggles, each one unable to subdue the raging fires of the other, or even quench the constantly increasing flame of desire.

'Hark! I hear a key in the street door,' I whispered in alarm, 'It must be my lord returned. What shall we do?'

The craven-hearted coward was frightened in a moment and would have been caught where he was had I not had the presence of mind to shove him into a closet on the landing and throw his clothes after him. The bell was ringing furiously and the knocker made a fearful din. So, kicking all the debris of the supper under the table and only leaving my own plate and glass, I at last put on a wrapper and let him in.

'What a time you were, Vanessa. There's been an accident on the line, so I returned to town, and shall go in the morning again.'

'Yes, love, I couldn't help it – I was fast asleep. The fact is I've drunk a whole bottle of fizz to myself, dearie,' I replied with a feigned yawn.

'Zounds, girl! What a state the bed is in!' he exclaimed, noticing it for the first time. 'Who have you had here?'

'No one, love. Pray don't look so cross, I have been tossing about for hours thinking of you, and only a little while ago fell off to sleep and had a frightful nightmare, dreaming we had been captured by brigands. They tied you to a tree and were just drawing lots to see who was to have your little girl, when your knocking and ringing put an end to it. Wouldn't it have been awful to have really been true?'

'Then I suppose, Vanessa, that I'm the brigand to have you, now that I've got in,' he said, his face relaxing into a smile as he began to throw off his clothes. 'I wanted you awfully a little while ago, when our train was blocked on the line, and that is the cause of my coming back for a bit of love.'

'Then, love, come to bed quickly. I do want you so. You will divert my thoughts and cool my hot blood,' I said, hoping to distract his attention and prevent notice being taken of the debris under the table, and more especially as I fancied I heard my gallant sneaking downstairs at the moment.

Throwing off his clothes, he carried me to the bed with an impetuosity quite unusual to him. As he laid me upon my back and got between my readily opening legs, my hand guided his impatient courser to my love mark, which, notwithstanding all its precious battering and the fright I had had, was again in a tremor of longing expectation. My blood had been so fired by the champagne that my lubricity was perfectly unquenchable. I felt as if I could have engaged a dozen lusty men, one after the other, at that moment.

The insertion of a second priapus in my excited affair was an unexpected pleasure as it glided slowly up the well-lubricated sheath. If he had not been especially amorous he must have noticed that I was not nearly as tight as usual on a first penetration. My arms clasped him closely to my body, and our lips met in hot, burning kisses. I sucked his tongue into my mouth in the most lascivious manner, while my legs crossed over his buttocks with all the abandon of a perfect bacchante.

Almost in an instant, before he had given more than three vigorous thrusts, I felt the warm rush of his seed up into my very vitals, which had such a thrilling effect on me that my own emission instantly flowed in response to his; the floodgates of love mingled their flow in the most ecstatic manner.

Without for a moment relaxing in stiffness, his weapon kept its place in my hot, throbbing sheath and soon commenced another course (it must have been the heat of my vagina, which infused, or rather, kept such strength in him, for it was quite unusual). His swollen and eager courser plunged forwards in the most vigorous manner and so worked up all the lubricity of my nature that, quite forgetting everything else, I fancied it was my paramour still in my arms and just at the moment of coming, I murmured, 'Oh, Henry! Oh, Gower, I shall die! You kill me with love, you darling!'

He sprang from my embrace as if a serpent had stung him, exclaiming, 'Vile wretch, that's it, is it? He must have been here when I came! Ha! What's this, his watch, by God!' as he caught a glimpse of the chain peeping from under the pillow, and thrusting his hand under brought out the damning evidence of our guilt. After cursing and berating me for my indiscretion, he threw me out of the house.

Having no place else to go, I went to Gower's home and related my tale of woe. No doubt feeling guilty for his part in this, he took pity on me and found me a place to stay for the night. The next day I received a cheque for two thousand pounds from him, along with a note suggesting I relocate to Naples, where he had some friends.

By Gower's advice I determined to go to Naples for a few months, so in a few days I found Mlle Zara, a ladylike person who undertook to be my chaperone during the journey for a salary of ten pounds per month, and all expenses paid.

Captain Beard, the commander of the vessel, was a regular lady's man and had been so very kind in his enquiries about me during the first few distressing days of the voyage. I now noticed he eyed my every movement, and as I knew he had a spacious cabin all to himself, as well as being a handsome middle-aged man, he was exactly the sort of fellow who could please a thoroughly lecherous girl, as I only too well knew myself to be.

I gave him every possible encouragement, and if eyes can speak, plainly told him what I wanted.

When not on duty he continually attached himself to me, played draughts with me, or brought out books for me to read, among others, *Moths* by Ouida.

The evening after leaving Gibraltar I was reading on deck. Just as it was getting dusk, I found him by my side.

'Well, Miss De Vere' (that was the name I had assumed), 'what is your opinion of Ouida as an authoress?'

'Ah, Captain Beard, you must be a naughty man to give me such a book to read! There is very little left to tell, and that can be imagined!' I replied.

'I'm sure it's a highly proper book.'

'Then, sir, I'm sure you have worse in your cabin library. How I should like to have a rummage there when it is your watch on deck,' I said laughingly.

'Hem! So that's your opinion, is it, Miss De Vere? Well. I will tell you in confidence that I have a really naughty book called *Fanny Hill* which an old maiden lady I once had for a passenger left behind in her cabin. The stewardess brought it to me, and of course I told Mrs Robins that I should burn it, but it was too good to be destroyed.'

'For shame, sir! Mind no one hears you telling me, but you really have excited my curiosity, Captain, and you know nothing is scandalous unless found out,' I said, archly. 'Now, couldn't you lend me that book to read? *Sub rosa*, of course!'

'Why!' he ejaculated with a laugh, 'I can lend you *Sub Rosa* itself. It is a magazine, but only the first three numbers have come out yet. There is a hitch of some sort about the publication; you know that sort of thing often gets seized by the police in England. It is rather free and funny, but nothing compared to *The Pearl*.'

'*The Pearl*? What is that, a book?'

'Yes, the most extraordinary magazine ever brought out in parts. I have it complete for the eighteen months it came out, plates and all, but it's too bad for a young lady to look at.'

'What a naughty man you are to mention things and say I mustn't see them, but I must, sir! I'm not afraid and can take care of myself. Still, captain, dear, I might perhaps go as far as a kiss, if you promise to behave yourself. Now will you let me see them?'

'You are such a dear young lady, I haven't the heart to refuse, but you know it's awfully imprudent, even with an old fellow like me, who has to set a good example to all the passengers and crew. Why, if they once thought me even the slightest bit immoral I should have to give up the ship – it would not be thought safe for single ladies or young wives without their husbands to go on my vessel. Luckily we have no gamblers on board, for they often sit up all night and spoil every chance of even an innocent lark. After eleven o'clock there won't be a soul stirring. You can then slip into my cabin and look at the books and pictures I will leave on the table. My watch isn't up till twelve, then I can join you and explain anything you might like to know. Dear Miss De Vere, you have made my heart all aflutter only to think of the kiss you promise. I must leave you till then, or they may say I'm having a flirtation with you. *Au revoir!*'

On plea of a headache I kept on deck, and did not return at the same time as did Mlle Zara and the other two young ladies who occupied our cabin. As soon as I found all clear, I slipped into the captain's room, which was a most comfortably furnished place, roomy, with a good-size table under a brilliant swing lamp at one side, whilst at the other was his berth with the curtains closely drawn. Several small books with very unpretending covers lay upon the table and at once attracted my attention, so I sat down for a good look over them. The first I took up had a curious frontispiece of a gentleman holding his cocked hat partly in front of a laughing face, whilst his open breeches exposed the delight of life in all its rampant glory. An extraordinary thrill passed through my whole frame as I caught sight of it, and caused me to exclaim to myself almost *sotto voce*, 'How I should like to see the real thing at this moment!'

'You have your wish, darling!' someone said in reply, which gave me quite a start, as I thought it must be one of the young officers or a passenger. To my great astonishment, there was the captain getting out of his berth, with nothing but his shirt to cover his nakedness. 'What a fairy you must be, Miss De Vere: you wished, and, presto! here it is, all alive and real!' he said as he raised his shirt to expose a fine-looking ladies' toy to my astonished gaze.

'Pray, sir, for heaven's sake! Cover up that dreadful-looking thing!' I said in a loud whisper.

'It's only that to an old maid, not to a delightfully voluptuous-minded pretty girl as I guess you to be, darling. You can't look me in the face and say truthfully that you are a stranger to the delights of sexual intercourse?'

'No, captain, I don't wish to pretend to such squeamish morality. According to my code of morals, love is very nice and a proper thing to indulge in between discreet people; it is only immoral and scandalous when found out. I would never have encouraged you, as I know I have, had I not believed you to be a very prudent man with a reputation to preserve.'

'Your remarks show more wisdom than I would have expected in one so young. Besides, do you not find that we middle-aged men of the world know better how to please the ladies and prolong the pleasure than young men who are so impetuous that everything is over almost before you begin to realise its pleasures? This is *Fanny Hill*, the celebrated book that everybody has heard of, but so few seen, because it is so difficult to purchase, as shopkeepers who risk selling such books are liable to two years' imprisonment,' he said, taking a book from the table and drawing me on his lap. We sat on the couch at the end of the cabin, where I sat on his knee as he turned over the leaves and pointed out all the variety of enjoyment depicted in the numerous and luscious plates.

My whole frame quivered with emotion, and I could feel his frightfully stiff affair throbbing under my bottom as I sat on his lap, and hardly resisted his busy hands as they were rapidly unfastening every part of my dress.

My head dropped on his shoulder as I whispered faintly, 'Oh, do let me go; it is too bad to have let me see such things!' Yet I never made any effort to get away from him. He glued his lips to mine and tipped the velvet so delightfully that my tongue involuntarily responded to the loving challenge. At the same moment a blissful shudder, which ran through my body, must have let him know that the critical moment had arrived in spite of myself.

'My God, darling, I have made you come!' he said, laying me gently back on the sofa, 'I must kiss you till you come again, and suck up every drop of the pearly nectar of love as it distils from the petals of your rosebud.'

Almost quicker than I can write it he had turned up my skirts and found the critical spot. My legs opened mechanically at the first touch of his lascivious tongue at the entrance of my crack.

Good heavens! How he tickled my clitoris as I came again and again. My very soul seemed to melt into his mouth under the combined titillation of his tongue, fingers and long beard.

At last I begged him to get up and let me have him in the orthodox fashion, but he first divested himself of his shirt and pulled off everything from me till I was as naked as he was. Then, throwing himself upon me, his mouth sought not my lips, but the little strawberry nipples of my firm orbs of love. The ravenous manner in which he sucked and almost devoured them was so exciting that I threw my legs over his buttocks. With my right hand I took hold of his modest affair, which had been resting and palpitating on my belly, as if afraid to go near my Venus's wrinkle.

How I burned to feel it inside me. His ardent attentions to my titties shot such a flame of desire to the very tips of my toes that it was impossible to delay any longer. My hand guided the head to my slit, and a slight upward heave of my bottom sheathed it to the hilt at once, as my plentiful emissions had so lubricated the passage.

Both of us seemed driven into a lustful fury by the previous long and loving dalliance. The floodgates were opened, and my copious emission so delighted him that I was quite afraid his cries of ecstasy would be heard by someone.

'You darling, you love! How delicious, you make me come in a moment! My God! There it is! For heaven's sake, do something to me – pinch me – put your hand on me. Ah! Ah!! Oh!!! I'm done for, love!' he moaned as he almost fainted.

It was nearly daylight before he allowed me to leave, and we repeated our revels the two following nights. When I finally went ashore at Malta he insisted upon my taking all I wished for of his vast collection of erotic books and pictures.

~ 13 ~

The Boudoir

Despite its sad demise, it is hard to say enough about the classic Victorian monthly *The Pearl*, and its creators. What had set it above the rest of Victorian erotica was not only the sheer volume and diversity of its texts, and the ephemeral nature of many of them, but the overall quality as well. The writers and editors were obviously highly educated and sophisticated, if not somewhat cynical, and could be considered the cream of Victorian pornographers. Humour and entertainment in the absence of hypocrisy were *The Pearl*'s goal, as noted in the editor's explanation for the title: 'at last our own ideas have hit upon the modest little "Pearl" . . . especially in the hope that when it comes under the snouts of the moral and hypocritical swine of the world, they may not trample it underfoot and feel disposed to rend the publisher, but that a few will become subscribers on the quiet. To such better disposed piggywiggies, I would say for encouragement, that they have only to keep up appearances by regularly attending church, giving to charities, and always appearing deeply interested in moral philanthropy, to ensure a respectable and highly moral charac-ter . . . ' (The application to the then Prime Minister Gladstone was all too obvious.)

While some of the pieces in *The Pearl* were reprints of earlier erotic works, most were original contributions or translations (and soon reprinted by others). The names of *The Pearl*'s contributors are mostly unknown but can be conjectured in an educated fashion. The poet Swinburne definitely contributed several long verse pieces on flagella-tion (e.g. 'Charlie Collingwood's Flogging' and 'Frank Fane – A Ballad'). Other pieces were extremely similar to *Cythera's Hymnal* and *The Index Expurgatorus Martialis* (both with contributions by F. P. Pike, G. A. Sala and Captain Edward Sellon), *The Romance of Lust* (by William Potter and friends) and *The Mysteries of Verbena House* (by Sala and J. C. Reddie). Ashbee in his erotica bibliography noted that *The Pearl*'s publisher was also an editor and part author, who had a history of publishing round-robin collaborative erotic works, including the last two mentioned above. It seems logical then that this publisher accepted contributions from his old friends, and from them created a magazine, *The Pearl*, that suited their personal tastes and whimsies.

The name of the publisher of *The Pearl* is still only a partially solved mystery, and a true bibliographical puzzle. Ashbee's annotations in his own copies of his bibliographies (1877–85) and in notes pencilled into his own volumes of erotica now in the Private Case, indicated the publisher to be named 'D. Cameron', also known as 'W. Lazenby'. Apollinaire *et al.*'s *L'Enfer* bibliography (1913) noted that 'Cameron' was a false name. Ongoing research has yet to identify the publisher's true name, although his connections with numerous erotica authors and titles are established. After *The Pearl* and its four supplements, he published two more erotic magazines, *The Cremorne* (three issues in 1882) and *The Boudoir* (six issues in 1883) before his publishing career was suddenly ended, presumably by arrest and imprisonment on obscenity charges.

To honour this publisher *extraordinaire*, whatever his name, here is an excerpt from 'D. Cameron's' final literary erotic effort, *The Boudoir*.

⟋⟍⟍ from *The Boudoir*

As Mr Capias finished the account of the seduction of the milliner's girls, they were already entering London and were soon set down at the noted La Belle Sauvage Inn, Ludgate Hill. A hackney coach was called and Capias easily persuaded Polly to go with him to his chambers in the Temple. It was yet early in the day, so after a good breakfast provided by the housekeeper they lay down to rest on his bed till the evening, when he expected a friend for supper.

'Now darling,' exclaimed the young barrister, throwing aside his clothes, 'undress yourself and let us enjoy without restraint those delicious pleasures which the accident to the coach interrupted and of which we afterwards in the gypsy tent had only a rough taste. Ha, what exciting charms! Let me caress those swelling orbs of snowy flesh which I see peeping from your loosened dress. What a difference there is in titties. Some girls have next to nothing, others are so full they hang down like the udders of a cow, and then again, some of the finest have no nipples to set them off. Yours, my love, are perfection. Let me kiss them, suck them, mould them in my hands!'

This attack upon her bosom almost drove Polly wild with desire. Her blood tingled to the tips of her toes as she heaved with emotion and sighed, 'Oh! Oh! Oh!'

He had gradually pushed her towards the bed and presently, when her back rested on its edge, one of his hands found its way under her clothes to the very seat of bliss.

'What a lovely notch. I had scarcely time to feel what a beautiful fanny you had when I was so hot for the bliss in the gypsy tent. Now, darling, we can enjoy everything in perfection and increase the delights of fucking with such preliminary caresses as these, which will warm the blood till, maddened, you beg me to let you have it at once, and my excited prick revels in your spending gap. And to think that I'm the first, that I am the one who took your maidenhead last night.'

She was spending profusely and begged with sighs of delight for him to satisfy her irresistible longings.

'Not with your things on, dear. Off with them quick. See what a glorious stand I have. There. Caress it. Press it in your hand.'

He had taken off everything and helped her to do the same. Then he tossed her on to the bed and was between her open legs as they stretched wide to receive him. He toyed with her for a minute or two, letting the head of his engine just touch between the warm, juicy lips which were so anxious to take him in.

'Ah, you tease! Do let me have it!' she almost screamed, heaving up her bottom to try and get him farther in. 'Oh, do! Don't tease me so.' Then, with a deep sigh, she cried, 'I'm coming again! Oh! Oh!'

He awfully enjoyed this dalliance, but at length took pity on her languishing looks and slowly drove in up to the hilt, till his balls flapped against the soft, velvet cheeks of her rump.

'I like to begin slowly,' he whispered, 'and draw out the pleasure till we both get positively wild with lustful frenzy. That is the only way to get the very acme of real enjoyment. A young fellow who rams in like a stallion or a rabbit and spends in a moment scarcely makes the girl feel any pleasure before he finishes and is off.

'Many married women have stupid husbands of that sort; who never fuck them properly. Is it to be wondered that women swoon over a man who introduces them to the real delights of love?'

'Yes, yes, yes, darling – but push it in faster now. Ah, I feel its head poking at every thrust. That's so delicious. Are you coming? I'm simply swimming in spend. Oh, there it is. It's lukewarm, shooting into me.

Oh, oh. Don't stop – go on a few more strokes. I'm coming again. Ah, you darling. Oh!'

After this they had a sound sleep till seven o'clock, when the housekeeper knocked to say Mr Verney had come. Thus awakened, Polly was delighted to find the young barrister's prick still encased in her tightly contracted sheath.

She wanted another stirring up, but Capias declined the retainer and promised to make up for it at night.

'You're in luck, my boy!' said Verney, as his friend Capias introduced him to Miss Polly D. 'No other fellow ever has such luck as you in the field of Venus.'

'Her action is better than her looks,' replied Capias, making Polly blush up to her eyes. 'Nothing to be ashamed of, my darling, I always tell Verney of all my love affairs. Don't you believe him – he's a devil for the girls himself, and one to please them too. Now let's have supper. She's taken all the strength out of me and I want refreshing.'

Verney's hand was now up between her thighs and his lips imprinted hot kisses on her burning cheeks. Higher and higher crept that insinuating hand, till he got fair possession of her chink, all moistened as it was with warm creamy emissions. She sobbed on his shoulder as her legs slightly parted, whilst a perceptible shudder of suppressed emotion told him too surely that his success would soon be complete. Withdrawing his hand for a moment from that burning spot, he lifted her naked foot till it rested on his rampant tool, which was as stiff and hard as iron. It throbbed under that caressing foot, which his hand directed so that it gently rubbed him.

From her face, his lips found their way to her bosom, and her sighs and ohs plainly spoke her feelings. Taking her boldly in his arms, he carried Polly to the sofa and stretched himself by her side, with his tremendous truncheon stiff against her belly. He placed her hand upon it, and opening her legs, she herself directed it towards her cunt. They commenced a delightful fuck, their lips glued together. This made him spend in a moment, but rolling her over on to her back, he kept up the stroke, till she also spent in an agony of delight. After resting for a few moments, he went on again. Her legs were entwined around his loins as she heaved and writhed in all the voluptuous ecstasy of her lascivious nature, spending every few minutes a perfect flood of warm spunk to the intense delight of his prick, which fairly revealed in the delicious moisture which excited him more and more every moment.

After this he promised to take care of her and gave her an address where she could get two nice rooms.

Polly drove to the address where Mrs Swipes, the landlady, said she was always glad to welcome any friend of Mr Verney's, who was such a very kind gentleman.

Her new lover called in the evening to renew his fucking, much to the ever randy Polly's delight. He left her several bawdy books to read, including *Fanny Hill*, *The Ups and Downs of Life* and *The New Ladies' Tickler*. Also, three large and especially interesting volumes, full of large coloured plates and every variety of erotic reading – including tales and songs – called *The Pearl Magazine*, which he assured her cost him thirty pounds. On taking leave after breakfast the next morning, he particularly advised her to be guided by Mrs Swipe's advice in everything.

About ten o'clock Lord Rodney was announced and shown into the drawing room, where Polly, Bessie and their landlady awaited his arrival.

'Strangers first,' said his lordship, kissing Polly in the most amorous fashion, slipping the tip of his lascivious tongue into her mouth as he did so.

'Look at the man! What a whore-monger he is! I can't have a modest girl in my house, but he takes the most impudent liberties with her!' exclaimed Mrs Swipes. 'How dare you, sir, thrust your wicked tongue into Miss Polly's mouth like that?'

'Mind your own business, you old bitch,' retorted his lordship, a fine, handsome young fellow of about eight and twenty, 'or I won't lend Bessie my dildo to fuck you with presently.'

Supper was pleasant but soon over, and his lordship, who had sat beside Polly all the while, making her caress his prick under the table, arose from his seat with a yawn.

'Who'll take the horn out of me?' he exclaimed. 'Or will you give way to Miss Polly?' he asked Bessie.

'With the greatest of pleasure,' she answered, 'only I mean to make you gallop and not let you tease her with one of your lazy fucks.'

All three helped to disrobe Polly, who was soon as naked as Eve when first presented to Adam. They opened the folding doors into a bedroom, where she was laid down on the outside of the quilt, blushing and quivering with excitement as Lord Rodney, equally reduced to a state of nudity, got between her legs and lay over her, his stiff machine throbbing against her belly.

Now Bessie, taking a huge dildo from a drawer in the dressing table, fitted it on to herself and proceeded to fuck Mrs Swipes, who threw up her clothes and took in the big india-rubber instrument with the greatest of pleasure as she reclined backwards on a sofa.

'Look, Rodney,' exclaimed Bessie, 'you can fuck me dog-fashion as I give the old bawd the pleasure she is so fond of!'

Thus challenged, his lordship withdrew his still rampant and reeking prick from Polly's quim, then, getting behind Bessie, he clasped his arms round her loins. Then his well-oiled prick slipped into her longing cunt from behind.

After this bout, his lordship was fain to confess himself quite used up, but fortunately for our heroine, whom the scene had left in a state of raging unsatisfied desire, a late visitor arrived at the house – a real prince from the west coast of Africa. They persuaded her to have him for a bedfellow for the night. He was a real prince and a champion of love between the sheets. His tremendous pego was so untiring in its exertions that the next morning at breakfast, where they all met again, the landlady asked Polly, who looked a little blasé, if she still wished for any more fucking .

'Good God, no!' ejaculated poor Polly. 'His monster of a prick hasn't a drop of spend left. He was coming again and again all night. His prick is the blackest part about him, and it did make me love him so. White men can't compare with such a prince of fuckers as he.'

Mrs Swipes expressed her desire to feel just for once such a champion in her. King Cuntaboo was only too glad to oblige her, and Bessie afterward when he saw how her eyes glistened at the sight of his coal-black battering ram.

Lord Rodney and the other gentleman very much enjoyed the scene, handling his prick and putting it in for them. His lordship made some very learned remarks on the capability of the female organ to accommodate itself to the biggest pricks, as he saw how easily the women managed to take in all King Cuntaboo could give, notwithstanding its enormous size.

Mr Verney did not appear a bit jealous, but finding our Polly so well supplied with gallants, his visits gradually became more and more rare, till at length, finding she was quite capable of taking care of herself, he kept away altogether.

She was such a favourite that in a few months she saved enough money to furnish a house for herself. She was so clever in her profession, as well as select in her circle, that she became one of the most fashionable and expensive bits about town. Noted for the extraordinary versatility of her ideas, every visitor to her cosmopolitan boudoir went away delighted.

An incident in the experience of the erst barmaid will fitly conclude this tale of her amorous adventures.

Taking a walk early one summer's morning, she entered Kensington Gardens and sat down by herself on a chair in a rather secluded spot, closing her eyes as various pleasant reveries floated before her vision.

'What a lovely leg! Alas! Get thee hence, Satan!' she heard ejaculated in low, trembling tones, and suddenly opening her eyes, fixed them on an elderly gentleman, whom she at once recognised as a particularly pious Earl.

'Excuse me, young lady, I really thought you were asleep. May I present you with a little tract? It will show what dangerous temptations we men are subject to from the attitudes or coquettish dress of the pretty girls of the present day. Do read it!'

She held out her hand and glanced her eye over its contents – which was as follows:

Young women, your dress is often the creator of your thoughts and feelings. When modesty has presided at your toilette, the looks of men have neither the boldness nor the fire of desire. Kept within the limits of discretion and respect, they do not offer to your imagination the always tempting image of pleasure – and your sensibility remains in a calm, favourable to your virtue. A dress, calculated to inflame the passions of men, produces a contrary effect. Their countenances tell you soon what you ought not to be told. Why do you blush if you do not understand their language? How could you blush if that language did not force in your heart a sentiment it is not decent for you to indulge? When you are in a dishabille, that half conceals and half discovers your charms, you generally avoid the company of men. Is it virtue or fear that makes you so cautious? It is fear! You are conscious that, in those circumstances, men have over your virtue an advantage of which all your prudence might not deprive them. Should nature happen to be silent, vanity would speak, and bring the same rapturous confusion into your heads. The transports of a lover are so flattering – his admiration is so eloquent a prize of our charms – there is such a life in his looks and actions – we are, in our hearts, so inclined to let him praise and admire. Young women, I say it again, sip not from the intoxicating cup, turn your sight from it. In your flight only you can find your safety.

Her face flushed with indignation.

'Now, sir, where are the park-keepers? I intend to charge you for an indecent assault – you whore-mongering, religious hypocrite. Come with me to my house, where for a twenty-pound note you shall have such pleasure as you seem quite unacquainted with.'

His face turned white and red, and his knees fairly shook under him as he stammered, 'The sight of your leg quite upset me. I am so sorry if that tract has offended you. You must excuse me. I wouldn't be seen in your company. My reputation would be blasted forever.'

Then, turning to go, Polly almost brought him on his marrowbones as she seized him by the arm and hissed in his ear, 'Where you go, I go. Expect no pity or respect for a hypocrite's reputation – what do I care for that after your gratuitous insult!'

The poor old man was lost. Making the best of a bad situation, he elected, as a sensible man would, to go along with the beautiful whore.

So, finding him submissive, she told him he could hold his handkerchief to his face if he was too ashamed to be seen walking arm and arm with her.

They walked out of the park and, hailing a cab, were soon driven to her pretty little house, but not before the pressures of her electrical fingers had already raised a cock-stand for the old man, who sighed and protested in vain against such wickedness.

However, Earl Goodman sensibly recovered himself as soon as the retreat of love was reached and he felt safe from observation in Polly's elegant and luxurious boudoir. It was amusing to her to watch the variations of his face as, picking up a decidedly naughty book, he eagerly scanned its contents. At first his withered face flushed a little, then his eyes fairly started from his head. She could actually see his old cock stiffening in his trousers.

'That is the kind of book to warm up your blood,' said Polly. 'You seem to relish that kind of literature, my lord.'

'Humph! Awfully disgusting! How such ideas could be evoked from the human brain I can't understand – it's ruin to body and soul to read such suggestive filth!'

'There's no filth in the Bible you pretend to love so, is there?' asked Polly. 'But how about Lot, Abraham, David and Bathsheba, Rachel or Tamar, who played the harlot with Judah, Solomon and all his wives – besides, you know as well as I do, bawdy books don't drive religious people mad or out of their minds in any way. Used properly they act as a stimulant to the natural pleasures of love!'

Here she gave a quiet double ring, and a young girl, hardly yet nineteen years of age, presently entered as naked as she was born (not even yet fledged on her fanny), carrying a bottle of fizz and glasses on a tray.

Sissey was quite naked, so she reclined on the sofa and, taking his head in her arms, presented to his eager mouth one of her lovely, small, round, plump bubbies, the firm strawberry nipple of which was indeed a morsel to tempt a hermit. She made him raise his shirt so that her warm belly pressed against his hairy bosom as he lay between her legs, which were amorously entwined round his body.

This position left her bottom a little above his cock. Ruth, kneeling down by the side of the sofa, took his cock into her mouth and titillated it with the tip of her lascivious tongue.

This lascivious attack on his virtue overcame him at once, so yielding himself up to the excitement he could not avoid, one of his hands clasped and pressed the young, firm, warm flesh of Sissey's bum, or groped a finger into her hairless slit, whilst the other pressed and stroked the head of pretty Ruth as she was giving him such exquisite pleasure with her tongue. How he sucked at Sissey's bosom, his mouth watering and his prick gradually swelling till in a few minutes it was a perfect monster to what it had looked before. Ruth showed it in triumph to her mistress as she continued softly to frig.

'Don't you think it's too big for Sissey. Shall I let him have me?' asked Ruth of Polly.

'No,' said her mistress, 'place it to her crack. She'll manage it. Then take my ivory dildo out of the warm water and fuck yourself with it.'

No sooner did Ruth present the head of his machine to Sissey's crack than the lecherous little whore slipped herself down upon it and, assisted by his lordship's eager fingers, succeeded in wriggling it all into herself. She managed to slip under him and get him fairly on top in the orthodox position.

The old man was fairly carried away by his lustful feelings. Aided by the sight of Ruth working the ivory dildo in front of him, and Polly's hands behind as they handled his buttocks and positioned his fundament, he groaned with pleasurable anguish. He had never been in such a tight, little cunt before, or felt such warm nippings on his pego, which seemed to grow larger and larger every moment under the flood of Sissey's spendings

It was too much for the old man when the final crisis came on him once more. He fainted from the excess of his enjoyment, and it almost took them all they knew to bring him round.

As a finish to this tale of Miss Polly's *amours*, it may be said that Earl Goodman, although very careful to preserve his reputation, often called to give her a check for the 'Midnight Mission', and she actually got a little spoony on his grand old prick, which she said was such a delightful fuck when once fairly got in working order.

~ 14 ~

The Autobiography of a Flea

Stanislas de Rhodes 1887

Quick, name the most lascivious Victorian novel you know, the one with the most different erotic themes running through it. What comes to mind first? *The Pearl, The Romance of Lust, The Lustful Turk, Nunnery Tales, Dolly Morton* or *'Frank' and I*? All good choices, but what if asked for one with no flagellation or sadomasochism in it? If you are really savvy in your erotic literature you will think of *The Autobiography of a Flea*.

The lack of spanking and sadomasochism is only one element that makes this book outstanding in its genre. *The Autobiography of a Flea* is a genuine erotic classic. To start with, it is over a century old, and has been in print nearly continuously since its first printing in London. It is dated in language, sentence structure, and illusion, but we continue to read it even today because it has the basic meat and potatoes of all good erotica – detailed descriptions of hot sex, and lots of them. What is different about this novel generations later is that we no longer criminally prosecute it. From its first appearance in 1887 it has shown up on just about every list of banned books. It even, in 1914, became one of the few English-language volumes to be prosecuted in France. Yet now it is freely available as an in-print paperback from adult book retailers everywhere, and also as more expensive, and often illustrated, old editions.

Does longevity alone make this a classic? The number of foreign translations (the first into French as *Les Souvenirs d'une Puce* within three years of its first edition) would indicate so. So would the fact that three pastiche 'sequels' to the novel have been written over the years! For all its notoriety, *The Autobiography of a Flea* has actually been commented on very little in the erotica bibliographies. C. R. Dawes, the great English collector and bibliographer of erotica, the twentieth century's equivalent of H. S. Ashbee, wrote in 1934 that *The Autobiography of a Flea* was a 'coarse and rather stupid book'. (The fact that Dawes was gay might have tainted his opinion of it). Yet the *Prince G**** catalogue issued the same year as the novel declared the book 'very well written by an English advocate (i.e. lawyer) well known in London'. Ashbee himself had nothing to say about this, as it appeared two years after the last volume of his expansive erotobibliography. Most writers have in fact commented solely on the bibliography of this novel.

The bibliography of *The Autobiography of a Flea* is an erotobibliophile's dream; it is almost too easy. The title page of the first edition read 'The Autobiography of a Flea, Told in a Hop, Skip, and Jump, and . . . Published by Authority of the Phlebotomical Society, Cytheria, 1789'. A hundred and fifty copies only were printed, of which ten were on handmade paper watermarked '1885', and twenty more were printed on special large paper. The date of 1789 is of course false. The book's absence from Ashbee's three massive bibliographies which listed nearly every known item of English-language erotica prior to 1885, its notice in the 1887 *Prince G**** catalogue and its watermark narrow the date of first printing. The typography (fancy title page, type faces in multiple colours and fonts) and various type elements used to decorate the pages are identical to those used by the London pornography publisher Edward Avery, who incidentally printed the Ashbee bibliographies using the same type elements! An 1887 first edition date is concurred with by such erotica authorities as Rose, Dawes and Kearney; 1890 was the first French translation, and in 1895 an English reprint (probably by Charles Carrington) appeared. The most famous American edition was dated 1901 (actually *c.*1935) and it reprinted separately pornographic illustrations issued by the original publisher.

The author of *The Autobiography of a Flea* is not too hard to divine either. As noted, the *Prince G**** catalogue identified him as a London lawyer. Apollinaire's 1913 *L'Enfer de la Bibliothèque Nationale*, an annotated shelf list of the erotica in the French National Library's restricted 'Hell' collection, notes a London lawyer named 'M. St–n–sl–s de R–des' as the author of a contemporary erotic novel, *Gynecocracy*. Pascal Pia's 1978 update of the *L'Enfer* catalogue spelled out the first name as 'Stanislas', and Patrick Kearney's research in the London Bar Directory located a lawyer named Stanislas de Rhodes who was active in the 1880s and 1890s. The author of the book was even kind enough to leave us a short autobiography. Ostensibly in the form of the background of the novel's narrator, a flea, he says of himself: 'I have heard it somewhere

THE ENCYCLOPEDIA OF EROTIC LITERATURE   157

remarked that my province was to get my living sucking blood. I am not the lowest by any means of that universal fraternity, and if I sustain precarious existence upon the bodies of those with whom I come in contact, my own experience proves that I do so in a marked and peculiar manner, with a warning of my employment which is seldom given by those in other grades of my profession. But I submit that I have other and nobler aims than the mere sustaining of my being by the contributions of the unwary. I have been conscious of this original defect, and, with a soul far above the vulgar instincts of my race, I jumped by degrees to heights of mental perception and erudition which placed me for ever upon a pinnacle of insect-grandeur.' This could well be a lawyer describing himself!

What then is *The Autobiography of a Flea* all about? Simplistically stated, it is a 'flea's eye view' of sexual shenanigans occurring in the English countryside a century or two ago, or in the words of the book's subtitle 'Recounting all [the flea's] Experiences of the Human, and Superhuman Kind, both Male and Female; with his Curious Connections, Backbitings, and Tickling Touches; the whole scratched together and arranged for the Delectation of the Delicate, and for the Information of the Inquisitive, etc., etc.'.

The novel is decidedly picaresque. Young Bella is discovered by her confessor while being deflowered by her beau. The unscrupulous Father uses this to seduce her for himself and his two local partners in religion. The attendant orgy is witnessed by her uncle, who claims a piece of the action for himself, while his wife is happily falling prey to one of the other lusty priests. Bella, now as passionate as any courtesan in history, is recruited to help seduce her best friend, Julia, for the enjoyment of the priests and her own father!

Mastery in *The Autobiography of a Flea* is in its use of words, not only its extensive polysyllabic vocabulary, but also its use of sexual slang. The scenes are as explicitly written as any in English erotica, and its socially unacceptable colloquialisms (i.e. swear words) are used not for shock effect, but because they ideally suit the activity described. The action is fast paced, heavy on the sex scenes, and with little regard for character development, plot advancement or erotic realism. Its use of a flea as a narrator is a noteworthy gimmick. How better to get the most intimate of all possible views of genital activity? (The flea as a theme in erotic literature is not unique to this book, as evidenced by a thirty-six-page bibliography, in German, of 'Flea Literature', issued in 1913 by the erotica bibliographers Hayn and Gotendorf. The use of non-human narrators and perspectives in sex stories is centuries old.

Diderot's 1798 *Bijou Indiscrète* has a magic jewel tell the erotic story, while the *c.*1750 *History of a Bank Note* lets a piece of English currency advance the amorous plot, and Marcus Van Heller's 1977 *The Ring* uses this item of jewellery to recount the sexual activities it instigates in its environs.)

Perhaps most outstanding is the thematic range of this novel. The Drs E. & P. Kronhausen, in their 1959 pioneering study of erotic literature, *Pornography and the Law*, found *The Autobiography of a Flea* to be a most amazingly remarkable erotic novel. They used it repeatedly as an example to support their thesis on the nature and structure of pornography, 'obscene literature' and erotic realism. In fact, of the eleven thematic headings they created for their analysis of erotica, this book fitted into a record nine of them (i.e. seduction, defloration, permissive authority figure (parent/clergy), incest, profanation of the sacred, 'dirty words', supersexed males, nymphomania, and the 'brute' as a sexual symbol). Had they used the categories, the Drs Kronhausen could have equally discussed the book under voyeurism, zoophilia, group sex, sodomy, and oral sex! The good doctors found *The Autobiography of a Flea* 'lacking' only under the themes of flagellation and homosexuality. (It could be argued that group sex in fact entails a latent element of homosexuality in addition to voyeurism.) What is also glaringly absent, aside from the sadomasochism that seems to pervade all Victorian erotica, is fetishes. The actors in this book have little on their mind except genitalia and fornication, and require no complex psychological stimuli to set them off.

All in all, *The Autobiography of a Flea* is a remarkable work. Through the years it has gained respectability commensurate with its antiquity. It is distinctive, if not yet distinguished (and perhaps another 100 years will accomplish that metamorphosis). Here then is an episode that occurs after the female protagonist, Bella, is caught in the act of fornication by her local priest, and is summoned to his vestry for counselling and penance.

from *The Autobiography of a Flea*

Father Ambrose was the living personification of lust. His mind was, in reality, devoted to its pursuit. His grossly animal instincts, his ardent and vigorous constitution, no less than his hard, unbending nature, made him resemble in body, as in mind, the Satyr of old. But Bella only knew him as the holy Father who had not only condoned her offence, but who had opened to her the path by which she might, as she supposed, legitimately enjoy those pleasures which had already wrought so strongly on her young imagination.

The bold priest was singularly charmed, not only at the success of his stratagem which had given into his hands so luscious a victim, but also at the extraordinary sensuality of her constitution and the evident delight with which she lent herself to his desires. Now he set himself leisurely to reap the fruits of his trickery and revel to the utmost in the enjoyment which the possession of all the delicate charms of Bella could procure to appease his frightful lust.

She was his at last. As he rose from her quivering body, his lips yet reeking with the plentiful evidence of her participation in his pleasures, his member became yet more fearfully hard and swollen. The dull, red head shone with the bursting strain of blood and muscle beneath.

No sooner did the young Bella find herself released from the attack of her confessor upon the sensitive part of her person already described and raised her head from the recumbent position into which it had fallen, than her eyes fell for the second time upon the big truncheon which the Father kept impudently exposed.

Bella noted the long and thick white shaft and the curling mass of black hair out of which it rose, stiffly inclined upwards. Protruding from its end was the egg-shaped head, skinned and ruddy and seeming to invite the contact of her hand.

Bella beheld this thickened muscular mass of stiffened flesh and, unable to resist the inclination, flew once more to seize it in her grasp.

She squeezed it, she pressed it, she drew back the folding skin and watched the broad nut as it inclined towards her. She saw with wonder the small slit-like hole at its extremity and, taking it in both her hands, she held it throbbingly close to her face.

'Oh! Father, what a beautiful thing,' exclaimed Bella. 'What an immense one too. Oh! Please, dear Father Ambrose, tell me what I must do to relieve you of those feelings which you say give our holy ministers of religion so much pain, uneasiness and frustration.'

Father Ambrose was almost too excited to reply. Taking her hand in his, he showed the innocent girl how to move her white fingers up and down upon his huge affair. His pleasure was intense, and that of Bella was hardly less.

She continued to rub his limb with her soft palms and, looking up innocently in his face, asked softly if it gave him pleasure and was nice and whether she might go on as she was doing.

Meanwhile, the reverend Father felt his big penis grow harder and even stiffer under the exciting titillation of the younger girl.

'Stay a moment. If you continue to rub it I shall spend,' softly said he. 'It will be better to defer it a little.'

'Spend, my Father?' asked Bella, eagerly. 'What is that?'

'Oh, sweet girl, charming alike in your beauty and your innocence. How divinely you fulfil your divine mission,' exclaimed Ambrose, delighted to outrage and debase the evident inexperience of his young penitent.

'To spend is to complete the act whereby the full pleasure of venery is enjoyed, and then a rich quantity of thick white fluid escapes from the thing you now hold in your hand. Rushing forth, it gives equal pleasure to him who ejects it and to the person who, in some manner or other, receives it.'

Bella remembered Charlie and his ecstasy. She knew immediately what was meant.

'Would this outpouring give you relief, my Father?'

'Undoubtedly, my daughter. It is that fervent relief I have in view – offering you the opportunity of pumping from me the blissful sacrifice of one of the humblest servants of the church.'

'How delicious,' murmured Bella. 'By my means this rich stream is to flow, and all for me the holy man proposes this end of his pleasure – how happy I am to be able to give him so much pleasure.'

As she half pondered, half uttered these thoughts, she bent her head down. A faint but exquisitely sensual perfume rose from the object of her adoration. She pressed her moist lips upon its top. She covered the little slit like hole with her lovely mouth and imprinted upon the glowing member a fervent kiss.

'What is the fluid called?' asked Bella, once more raising her pretty face.

'It has various names,' replied the holy man, 'according to the status of the person employing them. Between you and me, my daughter, we shall call it "spunk".'

'Spunk!' repeated Bella innocently, making the erotic word fall from her sweet lips with an unction which was natural under the circumstances.

'Yes, my daughter, "spunk" is the word I wish you to understand it by, and you shall presently have a plentiful bedewal of the precious essence.'

'How must I receive it?' enquired Bella, thinking of Charlie and the relatively tremendous difference between his instrument and the gigantic, swollen penis in her presence now.

'There are various ways, all of which you will have to learn. At present, we have too slight accommodation for the principal act of reverential venery, of that permitted copulation of which I have already spoken. We must therefore supply another and easier method. Instead of my discharging the essence called spunk into your body, where the extreme tightness of that little slit of yours would doubtless cause it to flow very abundantly, we will commence by the friction of your obedient fingers, until the time when I feel the approach of those spasms which accompany the emission. You shall then, at a signal from me, place as much as you can of the head of this affair between your lips and there suffer me to disgorge the trickling spunk. Once the last drop has been expended, I shall retire satisfied, at least for the time.'

Bella, whose salacious instincts led her to enjoy the description which her confessor offered and who was quite as eager as he for the completion of this outrageous programme, readily expressed her willingness to comply.

Ambrose once more placed his large penis in Bella's fair hands. Excited alike by the sight and touch of so remarkable an object which both her hands now grasped with delight, the girl set herself to work to tickle, rub and press the huge and stiff affair in a way which gave the licentious priest the keenest enjoyment.

Not content with the friction of her delicate fingers, Bella, uttering words of devotion and satisfaction, now placed the foaming head upon her rosy lips and, allowing it to slip in as far as it could, hoped by her touches, no less than by the gliding movements of her tongue, to provoke the delicious ejaculation of which she was in want.

This was almost beyond the anticipation of the holy priest, who had hardly supposed he should find so ready a disciple in the irregular attack he proposed. His feelings being roused to the utmost by the delicious titillation he was now experiencing, he prepared himself to flood the young girl's mouth and throat with the full stream of his powerful discharge.

Ambrose began to feel he could not last long without letting fly his roe, thereby ending his pleasure.

He was one of those extraordinary men the abundance of whose seminal fluid is far beyond that of ordinary beings. Not only had he the singular gift of repeatedly performing the venereal act with but very short respite, but the quantity with which he ended his pleasure was as tremendous as it was unusual. The superfluity seemed to come from him in proportion as his animal passions were aroused. As his libidinous desires were intense and large so also were the outpourings which relieved them.

It was under these circumstances that the gentle Bella undertook to release the pent-up torrents of this man's lust. It was her sweet mouth which was to be the recipient of those thick and slippery volumes of which she had had as yet no experience and, all ignorant as she was of the effect of the relief she was so anxious to administer, the beautiful girl ardently desired the consummation of her labour and the overflow of that spunk of which the good Father had told her.

Harder and hotter grew the rampant member as Bella's exciting lips pressed its large head. Her tongue played around the little opening. Her two white hands bore back the soft skin and alternately tickled the lower extremity. Twice Ambrose, unable to bear, without spending, the delicious contact, drew back the tip from her rosy lips. At length, Bella, impatient of delay and apparently bent on perfecting her task, pressed forwards with more energy than ever upon the stiff shaft.

Instantly, there was a stiffening of the limbs of the good priest. His legs spread wide on either side of his penitent. His hands grasped convulsively at the cushions. His body was thrust forwards and straightened out.

'Oh! Holy Christ! I am going to spend!' he exclaimed. With parted lips and glazing eyes, he looked his last upon his innocent victim. Then he shivered perceptibly and, with low moans and short, hysteric cries, his penis, in obedience to the provocation of the young lady, began to jet forth its volumes of thick and glutinous fluid.

Bella, sensible of the gushes which now came slopping jet after jet into her mouth and ran in streams down her throat, hearing the cries of her companion and perceiving with ready intuition that he was enjoying to the utmost the effect she had brought about, continued her rubbings and compression until gorged with the slimy discharge. Then half choked by its abundance, she was compelled to let go of this human syringe, which continued to spout out its gushes.

'Holy Mother!' exclaimed Bella, whose lips were reeking with the Father's spunk. ' – Holy Mother! What pleasure I have had – and you, my Father, have I not given you the precious relief you coveted?'

Father Ambrose, too agitated to reply, raised the gentle girl in his arms and, pressing her streaming mouth to his, sucked humid kisses of gratitude and pleasure from her warm, pink lips.

A quarter of an hour passed in tranquil repose, uninterrupted by any signs of disturbance from without. The door was fast and the holy Father had well chosen his time.

Meanwhile. Bella, whose desires had been fearfully excited by the scene we have attempted to describe, had conceived an extravagant longing to have the same operation performed upon her with the rigid member of Ambrose that she had suffered from the moderately propor-tioned weapon of Charlie. Throwing her arms round the burly neck of her confessor, she whispered low words of invitation, watching as she did so the effect on the already stiffening instrument between his legs.

'You told me that the tightness of this little slit,' and here Bella placed his large hand upon it with a gentle pressure, 'would make you discharge abundantly of the spunk you possess. What would I not give, my Father, to feel it poured into my body from the top of this red thing?'

It was evident how much the beauty of the young Bella, no less than the innocence and *naïveté* of her character, inflamed the sensual nature of the priest. The knowledge of his triumph – of her utter helplessness in his hands – of her delicacy and refinement, all conspired to work to the extreme of lecherous desire his fierce and wanton instincts. She was his. His to enjoy as he wished – his to break to every caprice of his horrid lust and to bend to the indulgence of the most outrageous and unbridled sensuality.

'Ah, by heaven! It is too much,' exclaimed Ambrose, whose lust, already rekindling, now rose violently into activity at this solicitation. 'Sweet girl, you know not what you ask. The disproportion is terrible and you would suffer much in the attempt of it.'

'I would suffer all,' replied Bella, 'so that I could feel that fierce thing in my belly and taste the gushes of its spunk up me to the quick.'

'Holy Mother of God! It is too much – you shall have it Bella, you shall know the full measure of this stiffened machine, and, sweet girl, you shall wallow in an ocean of warm spunk.'

'Oh, my Father, what heavenly bliss!'

'Strip, Bella. Remove everything that can interfere with our movements, which I promise you will be violent enough.'

Thus ordered, Bella was soon divested of her clothing and, finding her confessor charmed at the display of her beauty, his member swelled and lengthened in proportion as she exhibited her nudity, she parted with the last vestige of drapery and stood as naked as she was born.

Father Ambrose was astonished at the charms which now faced him. The full hips, the budding breasts, the skin as white as snow and soft as satin, the rounded buttocks and swelling thighs, the flat, white belly and lovely moons covered only with the finest down. And above all, the charming pink slit which now showed itself at the bottom of the mount, now hid timorously away between the plump thighs. The fierce priest saw and admired all these things and, with a snort of rampant lust, he fell upon his victim.

Ambrose clasped her in his arms. He pressed her soft and glowing form to his burly front. He covered her with his salacious kisses and, giving his lewd tongue full licence, promised the young girl all the joys of paradise by the introduction of his big machine within her slit and belly.

Bella met him with a little cry of ecstasy. As the excited ravisher bore her backwards to the couch, she felt the broad and glowing head off his gigantic penis pressing against the warm, moist lips of her almost virgin orifice.

And now the holy man, finding delight in the contact of his penis with the warm lips of Bella's slit, began pushing it in between with all his energy, until the big nut was covered with the moisture which the sensitive little sheath exuded.

Bella's passions were at fever height. The efforts of Father Ambrose to lodge the head of his member within the moist lips of her little slit, far from deterring her, spurred her to madness until, with another faint cry, she fell prone and gushed down the slippery tribute of her lascivious temperament all over him.

This was exactly what the bold priest wanted. As the sweet warm emission bedewed his fiercely distended penis, he drove resolutely in and, at one bound, sheathed half its ponderous length in the beautiful child.

No sooner did Bella feel the stiff entry of the terrible member within her tender body than she lost all the little control of herself she had. Setting aside all thought of the pain she was enduring, she wound her legs about his loins and entreated her huge assailant not to spare her.

'My sweet and delicious child,' whispered the salacious priest, 'my arms are round you, my weapon is already halfway up your tight, little belly. The joys of paradise will be yours presently.'

'Oh, I know it! I feel it! Do not draw back, give me the delicious thing as far as you can.'

'There then, I push, I press, but I am far too largely made to enter you easily. I shall burst you possibly, but it is now too late. I must have you – or die.'

Bella's parts relaxed a little and Ambrose pushed in another inch. His throbbing member lay skinned and soaking, pushed halfway into the girl's belly. His pleasure was most intense and the head of his instrument was compressed deliciously by Bella's slit.

'Go on, dear Father. I am waiting for the spunk you promised me.'

The confessor needed little stimulant to exercise his tremendous powers of copulation. He pushed frantically forwards. He plunged his hot penis still further and further at each effort and then, with one huge stroke, buried himself to the balls in Bella's tight, little person.

Ambrose cried aloud in rapture as he looked down upon the fair thing his serpent had stung. He gloated over the victim now impaled with the full rigour of his huge rammer. He felt the maddening contact with inexpressible delight. He saw her quivering with the pleasure of his entry. His brutal nature was fully aroused. Come what might, he would enjoy this girl to his utmost. He wound his arms about the beautiful girl and treated her to the full measure of his burly member.

'My beauty, you are indeed exciting, but you must also enjoy. I will give you the spunk I spoke of, but I must first work up my nature by this luscious titillation. Kiss me, Bella, then you shall have it. While the hot spunk leaves me and enters your young parts, you shall be sensible of the throbbing joys I also am experiencing. Press, Bella, let me push. My child, now it enters again. Oh! Oh!'

Ambrose raised himself a moment and noted the immense shaft round which the pretty slit of Bella was stretched.

Firmly embedded in this luscious sheath and keenly relishing the exceeding tightness of the warm folds of youthful flesh which now encased him, he pushed on, anxious to secure as much enjoyment to himself as he could. He was not a man to be deterred by any false notions of pity in such a case, and now pressed himself inwards to his utmost, while his hot lips sucked delicious kisses from the open and quivering lips of the poor Bella.

For some minutes nothing now was heard but the jerking blows with which the lascivious priest continued his enjoyment, and the 'cluck, cluck' of his huge penis as it alternately entered and retreated from the belly of the beautiful penitent.

Nature was asserting herself in the person of the young Bella. The agony of the stretching was quickly being swallowed up by the intense sensations of pleasure produced by the vigorous weapon of the holy man. It was not long before the low moans and sobs of the pretty child became mingled with expressions, half choked in the depth of her feelings, expressive of the delight she was feeling.

'Oh my Father! Oh, my dear, generous Father! Now – now push. Oh! Push! I can bear – I wish for it. I am in heaven! The blessed instrument is so hot in its head. Oh! My heart! Oh! My – Oh! Holy Mother, what is this I feel?'

Ambrose saw the effect he was producing. His own pleasure advanced apace. He drove steadily in and out, treating Bella to the long, hard shaft of his member up to the crisp hair which covered his big balls at each forward thrust.

At length, Bella broke down and treated the electrified ravisher with a warm emission which ran all over his stiff affair.

It is impossible to describe the lustful frenzy which now took possession of the young and charming Bella. She clung with desperate tenacity to the burly figure of the priest, who bestowed upon her heaving and voluptuous body the full force and vigour of his manly thrusts. She held him in her tight and slippery sheath to his balls. But, in her ecstasy, Bella never lost sight of the promised conclusion of the enjoyment. The holy man was to spend his spunk in her as Charlie had done, and the thought added fuel to her lustful fire.

It was then that Father Ambrose, throwing his arms close round her taper waist, drove up his stallion penis to the very hairs in Bella's slit and, sobbing, whispered that the spunk was coming at last.

The excited girl straightaway opened her legs to the utmost and, with positive shrieks of pleasure, let him send his pent-up fluid in showers into her very vitals. Thus he spent for a full two minutes. At each hot and forcible injection of the slippery semen, Bella gave plentiful evidence of her pleasure by her writhings and cries of ecstasy the powerful discharge was producing.

~ 15 ~

My Secret Life

'WALTER' 1888-94

More words have been written about *My Secret Life* than any other
work of erotic prose or verse. It figures prominently in every post-1900
bibliography of erotica and study of erotic literature. The Drs
Kronhausen wrote an entire volume of over five hundred pages about
this single title, and Steven Marcus devoted over half of his book on
mid-nineteenth-century English sexuality and pornography (*The Other
Victorians*, 1966) to this title alone. When *My Secret Life* was 'rediscovered' in the 1960s, with the Grove Press reprint of the entire text,
hundreds of essays, reviews and analyses of the book appeared in print.
It is safe to say that no study of erotica or Victorian sexuality is now
complete unless reference is made to *My Secret Life*. In all, few erotic
books, other than say Aretino's *Sonetti* or Musset's *Gamiani* or Cleland's
Fanny Hill, have had such a celebrated existence. What then is this
book, and why all the fuss?

My Secret Life is the longest, frankest, most fact-filled sexual autobiography ever printed. The first edition was published in eleven thick
volumes totalling over four thousand pages, nearly all of it descriptions
of sexual activity or the author's philosophy about sex. It is a first-hand,
accurate, almost photographic picture of a Victorian sexual compulsive,
a 'gentleman' who reckons that he had sex with over twelve hundred
women during his life (nearly all of whom he paid to obtain their sexual
favours). Fortunately for historians, sociologists, psychologists, and
psychiatrists, 'Walter', as the author of *My Secret Life* chose to refer to
himself in his autobiography, was a more than competent recorder of
his life and times. Details of dress, manners, social customs and
activities of daily living, as well as the myriad of sexual diversions
available to the Victorians, fell under his scrutiny, and were preserved
in ink for future generations to study.

Who then is the author, 'Walter'? Gershon Legman wrote a fifty-page bio-bibliographic introduction for the Grove Press reprint of *My Secret Life*, identifying 'Walter' as the English erotica collector and bibliographer (and merchant) Henry Spencer Ashbee. This is nearly certainly incorrect, although Ashbee may well have had a hand in the actual publication of the autobiography. The author, who ever he may actually be, has been psychoanalysed in print *ad nauseam*, most completely by Drs Phyllis and Eberhard Kronhausen, in their aptly titled study *Walter: the English Casanova* (1967). The author's true identity seems to have been established by other researchers in the United States and England, who are currently seeking final proof before publishing their results. Best evidence, as taken from 'Walter's' own words, and those of contemporaries, indicate that he was born *c*.1820 into a middle-class family that experienced financial reversals several times during his life. He established himself in business and did well enough to travel extensively and afford the services of prostitutes several times a week. He died about 1894, and other than writing *My Secret Life* seems to have done nothing else in his life of lasting consequence. Even his current descendants in England seem to know very little about his life or activities.

The printing history of the fabulous *My Secret Life* is a bibliographic nut that has been cracked. The actual first edition of this book (probably the second-most-expensive work of English-language erotica, exceeded in financial value only by a first edition of *Fanny Hill*) tells little. The title page simply states: 'Amsterdam. Not for publication'. The original introduction, written by the claimed executor of the author, states that the manuscript for *My Secret Life* was given him before 'Walter's' death, and years later recopied with identifying names removed to protect anonymity before being committed to type. Two prefaces by the author himself indicate that *My Secret Life* was started for his own amusement as a diary when he was about twenty-five, in response to what he saw as the 'truthfulness' of *Fanny Hill*, a 'woman's experience' without a male counterpart. In the text at one point there is an apology for the numerous printing errors in the volumes, due, we are told, to the printer's lack of knowledge of English. In the last volume is a note that only six sets of the eleven-volume work had been printed, and that the index was necessarily defective because of the massiveness of the original manuscript.

Additional facts about *My Secret Life* come from contemporary sources. The 1902 *Forbidden Books: Notes and Gossip on Tabooed Literature* by An Old Bibliophile (Paris, Charles Carrington) gives an apparently first-hand description of how in 1888 a Dutch bookseller and erotica publisher (later identified as Auguste Brancart, who at the time in question was operating out of Brussels) was called to London by one of his customers, a rich old Englishman (thought by some to have been Ashbee), who desired to have privately printed for his own enjoyment an enormous manuscript which he defrayed all costs of printing on the condition that no more than six copies be struck off. (The cost of publishing the first edition of *My Secret Life* was apparently £1100.) The Old Bibliophile continues that a few years later the Englishman died and copies of *My Secret Life* were publicly offered for sale at £100, leading him to believe that as many as twenty-five or so sets had actually been printed. Additional information from Carrington catalogues and other booksellers' catalogues over the years indicate that it took seven years to print the entire eleven volumes, and as many as forty sets were printed, although many sets are known to have been destroyed by fire or customs confiscation.

Whatever the number, first editions of *My Secret Life* are exceptionally rare. Decades of research have located only two complete sets in institution libraries (The British Library and the Kinsey Institute) and four sets in private hands. There is in addition known to be in the US a three-quarters-complete set and at least one complete odd volume. Despite this rarity, the text of *My Secret Life* has never really been 'lost'. As early as July 1894, the introduction, prefaces and index were published under the title *My Secret Life: Contents*, as a type of prospectus. In 1901 Carrington reprinted the first six chapters as *The Dawn of Sensuality*. A partial French translation appeared in 1923 and again in 1930. An abortive reprint of the original in the US was halted by police raids in 1933 after only three volumes had been printed; part of another volume appeared in 1934 as *Marital Frolics*. Complete typescripts of the text existed in the 1930s (rumoured to have been done for the great Philadelphia bookseller Rosenbach). Finally in 1966 the text again saw the public light of day with its complete unexpurgated publication by Grove Press (and piracies thereof).

With the text of *My Secret Life* now readily available in inexpensive soft-cover editions, and the bibliographic details solved, why the continued fascination with it? Foremost is its enormity and compass. In terms of actual sexual encounters described it surpasses even the *Memoirs of Casanova*, and remains the most extensive sexual autobiography in the world. Then there is its sociological insight into the *sub rosa* aspects of Victorian sexual life, and the author's own musings on his obsessive sexualism and sex in general. Finally there is

'Walter' himself, a Casanova complex of grandiose proportions, literally begging to be taken to the psychiatric couch by trained professionals and amateur readers alike.

Here then is an excerpt from this extraordinary sexual autobiography.

from *My Secret Life*

Again I sought Camille's society, who helped further to destroy any lingering prejudices I still had about the ways in which the sexes may use their genitals, either in giving pleasure to each other or men with men, or women with women, and she told me so many erotic incidents of which she had heard or known, that I feel certain now, that whatever men and women may say in public about this and that being immoral, dirty, abominable, and so on – that by themselves, they give free reins to their lusts and gratify their sensuality in any way which they find gives them pleasure. Who can object to this? Your body is your own, and you may use it as you like. Its usage concerns no one else but its owner.

I was much out at parties just then, which diverted me in a degree from sexual vagaries, and for perhaps a month saw Camille but twice a week, so I was in fine condition when I had her. To make sure, I used to write to say when I should call, and always found her ready awaiting me. I used to fuck her with great delight in which she participated, for she undeniably was still fond of me, and that I must have been in fine condition I am sure from the quantity of sperm I shed in her. She used to remark it. 'Ah, *mon Dieu*, what sperm, there is enough for two men.' She several times said this and I verified it by inspection of her cunt occasionally, for it pleased me to think of my strength and health.

For all that one day I frigged myself over a sheet of writing paper, to see how much sperm issued, and its quality.

A week or two after this I went to dine with a friend. He was a married man, childless, extravagant to a degree in expenditure generally, and particularly in fine food and wines (he has since ruined himself). A dozen or so of us men had everything of the choicest which money could buy, and after sitting, eating, drinking and smoking for four hours, we left him. It had turned out a pouring night, I had no carriage, his house was a quarter of an hour's walk from a cab stand, and his footman could procure me no cab. One of the guests kindly offered me a seat in his carriage for part of my way home, and at half-past one in the morning, set me down at the top of Regent Street.

The deluge of rain had just ceased, and though pitch dark, it was clearing up. Never in my life have I seen Regent Street so deserted. The rain had long driven everyone home, and I don't think I met six people on its whole length as I walked down it, pleased with the novelty of its absence of life, and glad to walk off the effects, in a degree, of my heavy gorging.

There was not even a gay woman to be seen until I got to the Haymarket. There, one or two only showed, and one asked me to pay her cab fare home, and a well-dressed woman she was, cleaned out, without a farthing, the Argyle had been empty, not a friend had she got, she must walk home if someone did not give her half a crown, and she told me where she lived at West Brompton.

A dinner such as I had had always heats my testicles in two or three hours, and as I stood looking and listening to the young woman, a wave of lust rushed through my genitals, and I began to want a cunt. Yet I had no intention of having her, indeed had an intention of not having her – for I had other views about the lodging of my penis next day. Then came on one of those bawdy inspirations I am subject to, and in spite of the evident absurdity of the offer (looking at the dress and style of the woman though she was not quite first class), jokingly I said, 'I'll give you a half-crown if you'll let me fuck you.'

I rarely accosted a female with such frank bawdiness, but I was a little elevated, though not in the least intoxicated. She seemed in a similar state, and laughing much replied, 'Oh! Lord, I haven't come to half a crown yet. You are liberal, but I'd sooner walk home if I get wet to my skin.'

I laughed about it. 'Ah, you don't want fucking.'

'That's just what I do want, for I haven't had a man for four days.'

'You've been poorly?'

'Just what I have been or I shouldn't want half a crown.' After a minute's more talk, I gave it her, and had intended to do so from the first. 'Here it is, and a shilling for a glass of wine, and now if you won't let me fuck you for half a crown, let me do it for love.'

'Thank you,' said she, not moving, but looking at me and clapping the money, with a chink, from one hand to the other and then back again. 'Did you expect I'd let you for half a crown?'

'No, my dear, but for love.'

'Well, I'll let you for love. Where shall we go?'

'What, to fuck you?'

'Yes, for love,' said she quite seriously.

Taken quite aback, I thought she was up to some trick. The empty streets and the time of night made me suddenly suspicious. 'I was joking, I'm in a hurry, let me feel your cunt, that's all.'

'Very well – and all for love, mind.' There was a narrow court leading into a wider one then (it still exists, though better lighted) which looked dark enough, and in a second we were in it, her back against a house, my finger on her cunt.

'You've got drawers on.'

'Well I can't pull them off here. Let us go to Overdon Street.' I would not, but between the loose linen I plied my fingers.

'I'll frig you.'

'No. fuck me. No one will pass. I want it – let me feel your prick.'

I wouldn't let her. I got coy, began to want her, but didn't like a strange woman in the dark. 'No, I'll frig you,' and I commenced, putting my left arm round her waist and my stick against the wall. She let me.

'Oh, fuck me do, I want it so. Oh, I shall spend – you shan't feel me unless you let me feel you,' and her hand sought my trousers. But before she could unbutton me, her bum shivered, she caught me round the head, pulled me to her, kissed me and my hat tumbled off as she murmured, 'Oh – oh – you beast – you've made me spend.' And she was silent, whilst I picked up my hat.

'You haven't spent.'

'I have though.'

'You haven't,' I said, though I felt pretty sure she had done so. Then again I put my hand on her cunt, and after a fingering under the prick receiver, I satisfied myself that she had.

'Why didn't you fuck me? I've never been frigged in a street before.'

'But you've frigged a man.'

'Only one or two. Why don't you fuck me? Come – fuck me for love, mind, let's go to Overdon Street, or come home and sleep with me. I want you.'

I had dropped her petticoats, but I was so lewd now that I could scarcely restrain myself, and when holding me she began feeling at my trousers again, my resolution gave way.

'We can't do it here.'

'Yes we can, no one will come through here. If anyone's coming we can hear them. Do it to me. Oh, what a big one.' She had got hold of my prick, and then without another word, she lifted up her petticoats. 'Damn my drawers,' said she. The next instant my prick was in her cunt and against the wall we fucked. The affair was short; and she spent with me.

'I hope you are all right,' said I when my prick had left her.

'Quite. Don't be frightened, come and see me.' And she repeated her name and address – and that every night she was at the Argyle rooms. 'Is it likely I should have made you do it to me if I was ill? Come with me to a house and see me undressed. I'm beautifully made.' She tried hard to induce me but it was all useless.

Slight rain began to fall. 'I'd best get back,' said she, and in the Haymarket she hailed a cab, and was going off.

'Stop my dear, you must have a little bit of gold.'

'I haven't asked for any. And now you won't come to see me, though you've just promised. I want you to have me for love.'

I had promised that I would go to see her, and repeated her name and address over again as she wished me, but certainly had no intention of doing so. She had a superstition that I should not after I paid her, but she took a half-sovereign which I pushed into her hand.

'I'll call on you soon.'

'No you won't.'

'Yes I will.'

'No you won't.' And the cab drove off as the 'won't' died away in the noise. I never did call on her – or see her afterwards. She was a nice, bright-looking, dark-eyed woman, of one or two and twenty years of age perhaps.

I walked then down to the colonnade of the opera house, when a smart shower came on. I intended to go to my club which had not closed, to get some soda water – but, being without an umbrella, waited two or three minutes. Just as I was about to hail a cab, a tall, full grown, portly looking woman, whom I had seen standing at the angle by Pall-mall, came up to me, addressed me with a broad Irish accent, and asked me to go with her. The accent was so broad, and it was such a novelty to hear anything like it out of Ireland, and she looked so portly, so like a respectable tradeswoman – and so unlike a Paphian – that being in a bawdy mood, far bawdier than when the other woman had asked me for a half-crown, I stopped, talked, and then chaffed her.

Yes, she was Irish, and not ashamed of that, and had not long been in London. I'd just had a woman had I, but her soul, I'd never had a woman like she was, nor seen a cunt like hers. She'd swear she'd more hair on it than was on any two women's cunts. If I'd go and see it, and she hadn't told me God's truth, I shouldn't pay her anything. She was a married woman, but the times were so bad with them that she must get her bread somehow, would I come? No, she wouldn't pull up her petticoats to show me in the street – not for five shilling (which I offered). 'Yer a big baste to be after asking me to do it. Divil a bit if I will though but you may put your hand up and feel a bit.'

I accepted the offer, put my hand between her thighs, but long before I reached her cunt, as it seemed to me, I felt long hair. Then she jerked her rump back, and pushed down my hand from beneath the clothes. She had roused my curiosity, I chaffed on, she got angry, and extolled her own charms, and said there wasn't a finer woman in London than she was. After telling her where I'd just fucked – and she refusing still to do anything in the street to satisfy my curiosity – it ended in her saying, 'Never – never in the street, I'd just sooner be dead – no – not for the half-sovereign' (which at last I offered), 'but I'll strip to ye, and ye may do what you like with me in a house, for half a sovereign, and glad I'll be to get it.' No, she was a stranger about there, and knew no houses. I took her to a convenient brothel nearby.

'Give me the half-sovereign,' said she so soon as we were in the bedroom. A bilk thought I, but not caring whether I was bilked or not, for I had only taken her out of curiosity, I got the money ready.

'Then if you haven't got such a hairy cunt as you say, I suppose you'll give it me back,' said I laughing.

'Sure God – there's no chance of your getting it back, for it's hairy as a King Charles' (dog she meant).

'Catch.' And I threw it to her. She caught it, spat upon it, and put it in her pocket.

'Sure and ye'll say ye niver seed such a pussy as moine. Ye'll be airfter giving me another bit of gould when you have seen it. Shall I take all my things off?' I nodded, and she began divesting herself of her clothing.

As she did so, she went on demanding my admiration of her charms, in a very singular manner. I have known women very proud of their form, and who have shown great vexation if I made any remark even inferentially disparaging them. I have known some who drew my attention to some particular part of their form, and which in most cases justified their self praise, but this Irish woman extolled herself from head to foot as she undressed – 'Isn't that a foine arm – look – here's breasts I needn't be ashamed of – my foot's not big for my size is it? I've a splendid leg haven't I?' – and so on, and certainly she'd a good deal to be proud of. Looking at her under the colonnade, with indifferently made, homely clothes, put on seemingly in a heap, she gave no promise of what was underneath. She looked what may be called, a homely, motherly woman, and one I should never have lusted for.

'Let me see your cunt,' said I.

'Wait a bit.' She drew off her chemise. 'There – did you ever see anything like that?' Indeed I never had, for I could not see the cunt at all, but only a long pendant mass of darkish brown hair, which, seeming to be rooted in her *mons*, hung down some inches below her cunt, and hid it entirely from view. It reminded me of a patriarchal beard, and I laughed, which much offended her.

Astonished curiosity at once made me serious, for a cunt is never a thing to be laughed at – its view is too absorbing and stimulating. Quickly I got her on to the bed. She opened her thighs quite wide, and pulling aside the shaggy covering, I saw a cunt of the usual mature type but with long hair (though not so long as that from the motte) surrounding it. The hairs everywhere had but slight signs of curling. The shorter ones at the upper part had perhaps a little curl, but the rest were long, nearly straight and in large quantity. To please her I said it was fine, but I thought it ugly. Yet the novelty stiffened me. 'I'll fuck you,' said I.

'Sure an yer may.' And she moved on to the bed.

'No, here, I want to see the hair round my prick,' and bringing her to a proper position – up it went into her. The hair mingled with mine and hid every vestige of my balls as I looked down. Then I pushed her thigh high up over my shoulder with my left hand and held her to me with it, whilst I buried my fingers in the shaggy thicket and spent very soon up her.

'You've not spent,' said I still up her.

'Sure and I haven't, and I ought wid such a poker,' she replied in the strongest brogue and we went talking till I found myself nearly out of her.

'Lift up both your legs,' said I, and she complied. I meant to do it when I asked her, and laying hold of the cunt beard (the best name for it), I drew it right across the orifice, which showed, when my prick was out of it, my semen issuing, and wiped it with the hair. 'I never saw a cunt which could be wiped with its own hair before.'

'No and I dare say never will, and it's a baste that you be adoing it.' Yet she laughed, as she washed her cunt. I felt it as she rose from the basin, and it was just like a wet mop.

She dried it and again I looked. There was hair all round the cunt and it was long and ragged. It was about the ugliest cunt I have ever seen. Straight hair on a cunt is always ugly. It usually curls, though I have seen several with straight hair, and that on one or two very nice women. But this woman was proud as a peacock of her hirsute gap.

'Lie still,' said I, as I sat contemplating it – for I now began to be curious about the woman, whom in all my midnight prowling I had never seen before.

'Sure and you'll give me a trifle more if you keep me long.' I promised that. Then I lay feeling my prick whilst I pulled her about in various ways. She had only the usual quantity of hair in her armpits and on her head. She had not a bad form, though too thick at the joints to be handsome. She, however, evidently thought herself a beauty from head to foot. She must have been between thirty-five and forty years old.

'You've had children.'

'Yes and three alive worse luck,' or she would not be at that kind of work; she'd got plenty to do with all she got, and ever would get she supposed. She had no regular friends. She wouldn't mind meeting me again. But she couldn't do it before half-past eleven – no never – she wouldn't say why – no – what did it matter to me whether she was married or not. Then I put down another half-sovereign. Then she said, 'Are you going to do me again?'

'I don't think I can.'

'Try get on the bed and on top of me properly.'

'Do you want it?'

'Maybe I shall,' and though I didn't like either her or her cunt, on to the bed and on top of her I got, had another fuck, and hard work I found it. 'Haven't I a nice pussy?' said she, as I lay up her.

That finished the business, and we left together. Should she meet me? – 'but not before half-past eleven'. I made no assignation, said I should take my chances some night of seeing her after the theatres were closed, but I never did and didn't want. Next day I wondered how I had ever tailed her, so ugly did her cunt seem to me when I thought of it.

The woman no doubt was gay – but she was for all that not much like a gay woman in manners not that she had any modesty. Ah! no – yet she seemed to show her nakedness out of conceit, not bawdiness.

* * *

Since I had finished with Camille, her sister Louise and the French *artistes*-in-lechery whom she introduced to me when I was twenty-one years old, I do not recollect having gone with a Frenchwoman excepting when abroad. My tastes ran on my own countrywomen. Now in a year of national importance, and one in which strangers came from all parts of the world to London, I was to have a Frenchwoman again.

Was it for the sake of change only, or because they were more willing, salacious, enterprising and artistic in Paphian exercises? I cannot say.

At quite the beginning of the month of June, about four o'clock in the afternoon, I saw a woman walking slowly along Pall Mall dressed in the nicest and neatest way. I could scarcely make up my mind whether she was gay or not, but at length saw the quiet invitation in her eye, and slightly nodding reply, followed her to a house. She was a French woman named Camille.

I named my fee, it was accepted, and in a quiet, even ladylike way she began undressing. With a neatness unusual in gay women, one by one each garment was folded up and placed on a chair, pins stuck in a pin-cushion, *et cetera*, with the greatest composure, and almost without speaking.

I liked her even for that, and felt she would suit my taste. As each part of her flesh came into view, I saw that her form was lovely. When in her chemise I began undressing, she sitting looking at me. When in my shirt I began those exquisite preliminaries with this well-made, pretty woman, feeling her all over and kissing her, but my pego was impatient, and I could not go on at this long. Smiling, she laid hold of my prick. 'Shall we make love?' This was in the bedroom.

'Yes.'

'Here, or in the salon?'

'I don't like a sofa.'

'*Mais ici*,' said she, pushing the door open wide, and pointing to a piece of furniture which I had not noticed, though noticeable enough. In the room was a sort of settee or divan as long and nearly as wide as a good-sized bed; so wide that two people could lie on it side by side. It had neither head nor feet but presented one level surface, covered with a red silky material, and a valance hanging down the sides. At one end were two pillows, also red, and made flat like two bed-pillows.

'There, on that,' said I at once.

I never saw any divan or piece of furniture like it in my life since, neither in brothel, nor in private house, here or on the Continent, excepting once when quite in the extreme east of Europe.

It was a blazing hot day. 'Shall I take off my chemise?'

'Yes.' Off she took it, folded it up, and took it into the bedroom.

'Take off your shirt.' Off I drew it, and we both stood naked. She laid hold of my stiff prick, gave it a gentle shake, laughed, fetched two towels, spread one on the divan for her bum, laid the other on a pillow for me, went back to the bedroom, poured out water in the basin, then laid herself down naked on the divan with her bum on the towel. I kissed her belly and thighs and she opened them wide for me to see her notch, without my having asked her to do so. To pull it open, have a moment's glance at the red, kiss and feel her rapidly over, mount her, fuck and spend, was only an affair of two or three minutes, so strongly had she stirred my lust for her.

I laid long up her, raising myself on my elbow to talk with her whilst my prick was still in her sheath. At length it slipped out. Gently she put her hand down and caught it, taking off the excess of moisture. Delicately she raised the towel and put her hand on her cunt, and saying with a smile, '*Mon Dieu, il y en a assez*,' went to the bedroom, I following her.

She wiped her cunt with the towel, half squatting to do so, then rose up quickly saying, 'Shall I wash you?' I had begun but the offer pleased me. I have no recollection as I write this of any gay woman having made such an offer since the first French Camille and one or two of her set, excepting yellow-haired Kitty, who liked doing that to me.

'Yes, wash it.'

'Hold the basin then.' Taking it up she placed it under me so that my testicles hung into it whilst I held it. She washed me.

'Soap?'

'Yes.'

'Inglis sop,' she said, laughing, the first English words I heard her speak. My prick washed, she performed a similar operation on herself. All was done so nicely, cleanly and delicately that I have never seen it excelled by any woman.

'*Causons-nous?*' said she, leading the way to the divan. Then both lying down naked, we gossiped. She was from Arles, in France, eighteen years of age, had been in London a fortnight, had been tailed six months and lived with her father most of that time. A month ago she had been persuaded to go to Lyons by an old woman who there sold her pleasures and kept her money. Another old one snapped her up there and brought her to London, where a young Frenchwoman more experienced than Camille induced her to work on her own account. That was told me lying naked with her on the divan.

She was alone in London and still exercising her occupation the other day, thirty-one years after I first had her. I have known her, and had her occasionally, during all that time, though sometimes two or three years have elapsed between my visits to her. She has been in poor circumstances for years past, and oftentimes I have gone out of my way purposely to meet her, and give her a bit of gold, out of regard for her.

We lay during her narration (which was soon told) naked. Hot as it was I felt a slight coolness, and drawing myself closer up to her, 'It's cool,' I said.

Without reply, she put one hand over me to help my embrace of her, with the other handled gently my prick, the next instant kissed me, and I felt her tongue peeping out of her pretty lips, seeking my tongue. My fingers naturally had been playing gently about her cunt all the time of our talk, and her hand rubbing gently over my naked flesh. So for a minute in silence our tongues played with each other and then without a word and with one consent, like one body we moved together gently she on to her back, I on to her belly, my prick went up her, and with slow, probing thrusts, with now and then a nestle and a pause, till the rapid clip-clip of her cunt drove me into more rapid action, to the rapid in and out and the final short thrusts and wriggle against her womb, till my prick with strong pulsations sent my sperm up her again.

'Ah! Chéri, mon Dieu, ah,' she sighed as she had spent with me. 'You fuck divinely,' said she, but in chaste words afterwards.

A wash as before, and then with chemise and shirt on, we talked about France, London, beer, wine and other topics. 'Let me look at your cunt.' I had scarcely looked at it.

Without reply she fell back, opened her thighs, and then I saw all, all, and so for two hours we went on, till it was time for me to dine, and with a parting fuck which we both enjoyed, we parted. I added another piece of gold to what I had already put on the mantelpiece before she began to undress. A custom of mine then, and always followed since, is putting down my fee – it prevents mistakes and quarrels. When paid, if a woman will not let me have her, be it so, she has some reason, perhaps a good one for me. If she be a cheat, and only uses the money to extort more, be it so – I know my woman, and have done with her henceforth.

Camille was a woman of perfect height, about five foot seven, and beautifully formed, had full, hard, exquisite breasts, and lovely legs and haunches, though not too fat or heavy. The hair on her cunt, soft and of a very dark chestnut colour, was not then large in quantity, but corresponded with her years. Her cunt was small, with small inner lips, and a pretty, nubbly clitoris like a little button. The split of her cunt lay between the thighs with scarcely any swell of outer lips, but had a good *mons*, and was altogether one of the prettiest cunts I have ever seen. I am now beginning, after having seen many hundreds of them, to appreciate beauty in cunts, to be conscious that there is a special, a superior beauty in the cunts of some women as compared with others, just as there is in other parts of their body. She had pretty hands and feet.

Her skin had the slightly brown gypsy tint found in many women in the south of Europe. I never saw a woman in whom the colour was so uniform as in her. From her face to her ankles it was the same unvarying tint without a mottle, even in any cranny. It had also the most exquisite smoothness, but it neither felt like ivory, satin or velvet; it seemed a compound of them all. I have scarcely felt the same in any other woman yet.

That smoothness attracted me at first I expect, but it was only after I had had her several times that I began to appreciate it, and to compare it with the skin of other women. She had with that a great delicacy of touch with her hands.

Her face was scarcely equal to her form. The nose was more than *retroussé*, it bordered on the snub. She had small, dark, softly twinkling eyes and dark hair; the mouth was ordinary, but with a set of very small and beautifully white, regular teeth. The general effect of her face was piquant rather than beautiful, but it pleased me. Her voice was small and soft, an excellent thing in a woman.

Such was the woman I have known for thirty-one years, but of whom there is scarcely anything to be told. No intrigue, nothing exciting is connected with her and myself. I cannot tell all the incidents of our acquaintance right off as I do those of many of my women who appeared, pleased me and disappeared, but she will be noticed from time to time as I had her, or sought her help in different erotic whims and fancies which took hold of me at various periods. I write this now finding that her name appears in my manuscript a long way further on. She was moreover a most intelligent creature, clean, sober and economical, and saving with a good purpose and object, to end, alas, for her in failure.

I never had a more voluptuous woman. Naked on that divan or on the bed when the weather was warm, I had her constantly during that summer. I know nothing more exciting than the tranquil, slow, measured way in which she lay down, exposing her charms; every attitude being natural yet exciting by its beauty and delicate salacity. She always seemed to me to be what I had heard of Orientals in copulation. She had the slowest yet most stifling embrace. There was no violent energy, no heaving up of rump as if a pin had just run into her, nor violent sighs, nor loud exclamations, but she clung to you, and sucked your mouth in a way I scarcely ever have found in English women, or in French ones; but the Austrians and Hungarians in the use of tongue with tongue and lips with lips are unrivalled in their voluptuousness.

Beyond a voluptuous grace natural to her, she had not at first the facile ways of a French courtesan, they came later on. I saw the change, and from that and other indications feel sure she had not been in gay life long before I had her. I could tell more of her history, but this is a narrative of my life, not of hers.

She soon got a good clientele, picked up English rapidly, dressed richly, but never showily, and began to save money. She made affectionate advances to me which I did not accept. After a time she used to pout at what I gave her, and got greedy. So one day I said, 'Ma chère, here is more, but adieu. I don't like you to be dissatisfied, but cannot afford to come to see you.' She slapped the gold heavily down on the table.

'Ah! Mon Dieu, don't say so, come, come, I am sorry. You shall never pay me. Come when you like. I did not want you to pay me but you would. Come, do come, that lovely prick – do me again before you go. Don't go!' And she never pouted about my compliment, till many years afterwards.

I suppose that having this charming fresh Frenchwoman made me wish for another; for despite my satisfaction and liking for her, I made acquaintance with another Frenchwoman, as unlike Camille as possible. Her name was Gabrielle, a bold-looking woman with big eyes and a handsome face, very tall and well made but with not too much flesh on her bones, and with a large, full-lipped, loud-looking cunt in a bush of hair as black as charcoal. I never told Camille about her, and think it was the great contrast between the two which made me have her. That woman also seemed later on to have taken some sort of fancy to me.

She had all the ready lechery of a well-practised French harlot, I saw it from the way she opened her thighs and lay down to receive my embraces. About the third visit she brought water and made me wash my prick, on which the exudation of healthy lust was showing whitish, before she let me poke her.

I liked her cleanliness, but to my astonishment, no sooner were we on the bed than she reversed herself, lying side by side with me, and began sucking my prick. I had no taste for that pleasure, nor since a woman in the rooms of Camille the first did it to me had my penis been so treated that I recollect, though I had made ladies take it into their mouths for a second. I objected.

'Mais si, mais si,' and she went on. My head was near her knee, one leg she lifted up, showing her thighs, which opened and showed her big-lipped cunt in its thicket of black hair.

She played with my prick thus till experience told her she could do it no longer with safety, then ceasing her suction and changing her position, I fucked her in the old-fashioned way.

The amusement seemed not to have shocked me as much as I thought it should have done, and it was repeated as a preliminary on other days without my ever suggesting it. After I had had my first poke, the delicate titillation of the mouth seemed vastly pleasant, my prick then being temporarily fatigued by exercise in its natural channel; but I felt annoyed with myself for relishing it at all.

I had not overcome prejudices then though evidently my philosophy was gradually undermining them. Why, if it gives pleasure to the man to have his prick sucked by a woman, who likes operating that way on the male, should they be abused for enjoying themselves in such manner? A woman may rub it up to stiffen it, the man always does so if needful – that is quite natural and proper. What wrong then in a woman using her mouth for the same purpose, and giving still higher, more delicate and refined pleasure? All animals lick each other's privates, why not we? In copulation and its consequences, we are mainly animals, but with our intelligence, we should seek all possible forms of pleasure in copulation and everything else.

With these two women I was satisfied till towards the end of August, both of them trying to make me see them much. Gabrielle for some fancy of her own took to calling me Monsieur Gabrielle. I did not see her nearly so often as Camille, but one or other I saw almost daily, Camille generally between luncheon and dinner, Gabrielle after dinner. I have seen both on the same day, and then both were fucked, but I usually copulated but once daily. I was in good health, and one daily emission of semen kept me so and seemed as needful to me as sleep. I had much lewd pleasure in comparing mentally their two cunts, there being a most striking difference in the look of the two.

Near September I wanted to be by the seaside, and without delay took myself off to a healthy, but vulgarish town. It was a place where I expected a little fun, a few kisses from healthy lips and a little intrigue perhaps, and the chance of getting some young, healthy, unfucked cunt.

I know pretty well now that with townwomen out for a brief holiday, idleness, better air, more and better food than they are accustomed to, heats the cunts, and makes many a modest one long for a male, and discontented with her middle finger.

I had not been at my hotel a day before I met an intimate friend with his wife and eldest daughter, a girl of eighteen. He had taken the upper part of a house over a shop, being a man of but moderate means, and intended to have brought two other children and a maid, but something prevented that. I liked both him and his wife, and at his suggestion went to occupy one of his rooms and live with them (paying my share). I found the rooms were over a greengrocers, which I didn't like, and think I should have cried off had I not seen that the servant was a healthy, full-fleshed bitch, and I thought there might be a chance of prodding her, like Sally on a previous autumn.

The shop seemed flourishing. Anyone going in at the private door could not fail to see the whole of the shop, down to a small parlour having a window on to the garden. The first thing I noticed was a strong, healthy, red-cheeked, saucy looking girl about eighteen years of age, with a curly but dishevelled head of deep-red-coloured hair, a very unusual and peculiar deep-red, and but rarely seen. The girl standing at the shop-front stared hard at me when I arrived, and nudged a big boy about seventeen years old who was half sitting close by the girl upon a sack of potatoes. The girl called the woman of the house Aunt. She attended to the shop, I found, when the aunt was away (cooking chiefly when so). The boy took home the goods purchased and left nightly after closing the shutters. Red-Head slept in the attics over me, and took off her boots at times as she went upstairs, so as not to make a noise over the lodgers' heads. The aunt slept there also. The two ate in the kitchen or the shop-parlour.

I was at once cheery with the servant but it did not promise much. The red-haired one (another Louisa, and called Loo) pleased me, though I did not like her hair. She spoke so loud, laughed so heartily with customers, took chaffing, lifted such heavy weights, and then flung her short petticoats about so much in moving her haunches, that I longed to pinch her. She looked so hard at me (and also my friend) when we passed the shop, for she was generally at the door, and often outside it, goods being placed there, that I made up my mind she was pretty strongly in want of a man.

In a day or two I was buying fruit two or three times daily. 'Keep the change, Loo, it will buy you some ribbon.'

'Oh! Thankee, sir.' She put it quickly into her pocket without hesitation. Emboldened, I gave her half a crown.

'Keep the change, and you shall give me a kiss for it.' Into her pocket it went. She looked quickly towards the back of the shop: there was the boy. She slightly shook her head.

'I can't,' said she in a low voice, taking the change out of her pocket and tendering it to me. I winked, pushed out my lips as if kissing and left the shop, leaving her the change. The boy was out of sight somewhere when I was buying the fruit.

Between eleven and one o'clock she was mostly alone, her aunt in the kitchen the boy out, and the same for an hour or two in the afternoon.

Unfortunately, those were the bathing and promenading hours so there was difficulty in getting at the girl unobserved, but nothing stood in my way when cunt hunting, and never had. From always thinking how and where, I all my life have got my opportunities with women. I also found that of an evening her aunt just at dusk went out at times to get, I heard her say, a mouthful of fresh air. Then the girl was alone with the boy till he left.

About the fourth night, the boy had left, Loo was alone in the shop's parlour, my friends upstairs. I went out (as I said) to have a cigar and a stroll, but when just at the bottom of the stairs the shop door in the partition opened and Loo appeared. She stopped, I caught hold of her, and then I kissed her as I pleased.

'Oh! Don't, Mary [the servant] is in the kitchen.' I kissed again. 'Oh! don't.'

'You owe me a kiss.'

'Oh! Not here, go to the front door,' said she. I did. She came there and just outside the door, but up against it, she kissed me and went rapidly back.

'I'll wait for you as you go to bed,' I said, and did so with slippers off. About half-past ten she passed my bedroom. I heard movement in the room opposite me, but on the landing I pinched Loo's bum hard, very hard, as she passed. She winced and passed on very quickly, shaking her head and smiling, candle in hand. I put my head down, shamming to look up her clothes.

We were intimate already. I had begun *double entendres* which she took and I began to think that the fresh-looking saucy one knew a prick from a cucumber. Then I found that the servant went home each night to sleep.

It wasn't a week before I wanted female assistance. Picking up a casual and thinking of my intention, I gave her five shillings to show me a bawdy house or two, which she did. One, a very quiet one, was in the part of the town over a china shop.

Parting with the woman I strolled on to the beach and met her there again, and felt her cunt, I sitting on a seat, she standing by the side of me. My cock stood and I gave her money for a poke. It was not a dark night. 'There is sand low down,' said she, 'no one will notice us when we are lying down.' But a fear came over me and I told her so.

'Well, I've got your money and if there was anything the matter with me, I'd hardly ask you to have me. I'm here every night and live with my mother.' Then, near to the waves, she lay on her back on the soft dry sands and I fucked her, and enjoyed her very much.

'How do you wash your cunt?'

'I piddle now, and wipe it with my handkerchief, down there (nodding her head). There are rocks and pools of water. I'm going to wash it there, I always do after gents,' and she went off to do it.

Next day buying something, 'Come Loo, and kiss me in the passage.'

'I can't. He'll be going out at half-past eleven.' Excusing myself from accompanying my friends, I was at the lodgings at that hour. The servant above had then all the beds to make and the aunt was cooking. It was risky yet I had a brief talk with Loo in whispers in the passage, and kissed and hugged her, and told her I had fallen deeply in love with her. I had not begun smut, but her bold manner made me wonder why I had not. That afternoon I overheard a quarrel between her and her aunt, and saw Loo wiping her eyes. Loo said to me, when I told her what I had heard, that she wished she'd never come and would sooner go to service.

I noticed also, for I was dodging in and out all day and listening in the passage where I could hear much said in shop and parlour, what seemed to me a very familiar manner between the girl and the boy. One day he took her round the waist. She, seeing me enter the shop, pushed his hand away and boxed his ears. He stooped, pulled her petticoats a little way up, and then suddenly appeared very busy. Evidently she had given him a hint. It annoyed me, and I wondered if the boy had felt her.

I did not quite give up hopes of the maid, who looked five and twenty. I kissed her and gave her a little present for cleaning my boots nicely. She took that fairly well. Then I felt for her notch outside her clothes. She repulsed me violently, and with a look which I didn't like. So for a time I desisted, but recommenced, and at length kissed her every time I got her alone. My friend's daughter caught me at it, and her father spoke to me. He didn't mind, but his wife did. I must take care, it wouldn't do to let a young girl see that game going on. Nothing more was said, but I noticed that he and his wife looked after me.

One night when we were walking alone, he said, 'You want that woman and a damned nice woman she looks. If my wife wasn't here I'd try to get her myself, but for God's sake don't let either of the ladies catch you. It won't do.'

The young lady's room was opposite to mine, and such was my

insatiable desire to see females in *déshabillé* or nude, that it passed through my mind to bore a hole (which I had done at foreign hotels) through her door, to spy her. I could have done so, but I did not, though I could not restrain myself from listening to hear when she piddled, and a few times succeeded. I felt quite a liking for the girl, but not sexually, and brought her presents which pleased both her and her parents.

In a fortnight I had often kissed Loo, and pinched her bum till she said it was blue. I told her I should like to sleep with her, for I loved her. This was on the first night she got out for a walk at dusk. I had heard her aunt say she'd keep a tight hand on her, and I found Loo was fast almost to a gallop. We walked and sat down on a beach seat. 'How can you love me? You're married.'

'I never said I wasn't, but I hate her and do nothing to her, and love you.'

'Oh, gammon!' she replied. I had now a little changed my opinion about the girl. She wanted to know the meaning of my 'doing nothing', was free in manner, and any delicate smut which I began using she answered frankly to. 'Oh! I knows what you means well enough, but don't you go on like that.' I concluded she had been brought up with coarse people who spoke of all their wants and acts openly, so that the girl saw no harm in such things. She had only been with her aunt that summer. She told me of her relatives, and where they lived in Northumberland. There was a large family, but that was all I could get out of her. 'Yer don't want to call on 'em,' said she laughing.

All was soon finished with the servant. One morning I waited indoors in hopes of getting at Loo, and spied the servant as she brought a slop pail to the closet close to the bedroom.

When she came out I asked her into that room, which I had never entered before. 'Come here, I've something particular to tell you.'

Reluctantly she came in, then I kissed, and gradually getting to the unchaste, got my hand on her cunt. 'Be quiet, Mrs Jones will be up to see if all's right.'

'No, she's out. Oh! What lovely thighs.'

'Oh, leave off, I'll tell Mrs Jones, I will.'

I desisted for a moment, but only to pull out my prick. I pushed her against the bedside, and got my fingers on to her cunt again. 'Let me have you.' I fucked her standing.

After, she took the money without a word, and pushed me off when I tried to kiss her, and I never got at her again.

16

Parisian Frolics

ADOLPHE BELOT 1889–94

La Belle Epoque (The Beautiful Time) – The Grand Age – The Gay Nineties. All names for the period of human history at the end of the nineteenth century, when Paris was the centre of fashion and society. It was an age when appearance counted for everything, and substance counted for nothing. Artifice and venial pleasures motivated both the established leisure class and the newly emerging working class. It was a world of cabarets and Can-Can, 'houses of pleasure' and high-priced society courtesans. This constant pursuit of hedonism, however, was not easy. Rich men bankrupted themselves and their businesses attempting to keep mistresses in luxuries beyond their financial means. Their wives prostituted themselves to the family creditors if they felt any honour for their family name, or engaged in casual sexual *liaisons* if they did not. After all, society at large was just as corrupt, politically and morally.

The hypocrisy, decadence and moral decay of this period has been brilliantly portrayed in the 'establishment' novels of Feydeau, Octave Mirbeau and Emile Zola, though often with legal repercussions for the authors and publishers. It is no wonder that such times became fertile grounds for *sub rosa* writers as well. One had only to observe daily life carefully, and give an accurate, unblushing, uncensored account of what was to be seen. Anonymous and clandestinely published erotic novels abounded, and *Parisian Frolics* was one.

Unlike with most erotica that has been published, we know the author of this book. *Parisian Frolics*, originally written in French, is a collection of short stories by Adolphe Belot (1829–90). The individual episodes were published separately over the years 1889–94, and first issued together in 1906 under the title *Les Heures Galantes Modernes*. This volume was translated into English perhaps as late as 1912, and appeared as the present work. The translator of *Parisian Frolics* is unknown; the title page of the first English edition credits the anonymous author of *The Way of a Man with a Maid*, a book very similar in style and language to this work. The very British prose and argot in this rendering indicate the translator to be perhaps a journalist, such as George Reginald Bacchus, the author of *Nemesis Hunt* and the *Pleasure Bound* novels. Bacchus incidentally also translated erotica for a 'Gerard N—', a turn-of-the-century London pornography publisher identified in an autobiography, *The Early Life and Vicissitudes of Jack Smithers*, which was written by the son of the celebrated publisher Leonard Smithers (whose own *sub rosa* dabblings are well documented). Alternately the translator may have been any other clandestine English author of erotica, e.g. J. P. Kirkwood, who wrote *Sadopaideia*. It has even been suggested that John S. Farmer, the lexicography expert and author (with the poet W. E. Henley) of several dictionaries of French and English sex slang, may have been responsible for the appearance of Belot's book in English. Whoever was responsible, the first edition of *Parisian Frolics* was printed in continental Europe, as evidenced by the style of the typography. The book was well enough known that the British Library received a copy for their secret and restricted Private Case Collection, where the copy still resides at pressmark P.C.14.g.56.

Little is actually known of the original author Adolphe Belot. The bibliographies credit him with nearly a dozen erotic novels. He was known for his brutally realistic portrayal of the sex lives of his contemporaries. In fiction his repeated themes included lesbianism, group sex orgies, incest, secret assignations, super virile amoral 'gentlemen', and sexually liberated and nymphomaniacal women. For Belot, copulation was an intricate technical art to be practised in all its conceivable variations. The question faced by his characters was not whether they wanted a sexual *liaison*, but rather when their next opportunity would present itself. Pleasure was pursued without thoughts as to morality. Participants did not expand as human beings through their encounters, they simply chalked up conquests.

Parisian Frolics contains four erotic stories that are representative of the licentious and debauched behaviour of 'sophisticated' turn-of-the-century French society. The reader is shown episodes in the life of a typical *roué* of the period. The language is explicitly clear. Henri R. is a wealthy man of leisure who regularly spends afternoons in an exclusive *maison à plaisirs*, enjoying the sexual charms of various women selected for him by the very discrete Madame in charge. Here Henri can expect to share intimacies not with common prostitutes, but with women of his own social station, women who are usually married, bored with their legal mates or simply seeking some new erotic adventures. So it is one day that he is introduced to a sensual, well-bred lady who turns out to be his own cousin Gilberte – long the object of his secret and suppressed erotic fantasies. After a moment of embarrassment, the two abandon themselves to the sports of love they had expected to enjoy that day. Their libidinous *liaison* is enriched with the arrival of their mutual friend, Mme Valencay, whose nymphomaniacal temperament stimulates a *ménage-à-trois* of orgiastic proportion.

The second episode details Henri's affair with Mme Liancourt, the hedonistic wife of a friend, who maintains a secret apartment for her extramarital pleasures. For sexual variation, the woman decides to seduce the shy and naïve Martha, while her lover secretly looks on. The scene played out is so erotic that Henri cannot help but leave his hiding place and join in the action. Henri is next seen spying on Mme Baisieux, a young married woman who must resort to masturbation to assuage her sexual fires. Always the gallant, Henri literally steps into the breach to aid the lady, much to the delight of both participants. The final chapter details the seduction of a Viennese beauty who has caught the fancy of Henri. By skilful manipulation of unforeseeable circumstances during a society riding party, the aloof, reserved, and cultured lady is undone.

Here is an episode from these delightful and stimulating tales of French lust. They recall a past time when sex was both everything and the only thing. From the Paphian *maisons* of Paris, to the sybaritic lodgings of the countryside, erotic pleasure was the grand pursuit and failure was unthinkable.

from *Parisian Frolics*

Mme de Liancourt accompanied me one day when I had arranged to meet Martha; she went forwards by herself to meet her as from me, while I slipped off to her chambers. She told Martha the latter's husband was suspicious and was endeavouring to have a watch kept on her, and this was why I had asked her to come instead – to explain and to bring her to where I was awaiting her. After a little hesitation, Martha consented to accompany her to the Rue de Suresnes. I saw them come in and pass into the bedroom.

'You're quite safe here! You're in my own rooms! Here you can bill and coo as much as you please with your lover!'

Martha coloured to the tips of her little ears. 'But Madame, Monsieur R. isn't my lover! We have never . . . '

'Really? My child, you have done well to tell me this. You need fear no indiscretion on my part, for I also have a lover! The danger you were running has made me take an interest in you, and this is why I gladly brought you here at the request of Monsieur R. Really, it was almost heroic of me to do so, for there are not many women who would go out of their way to bring to a mutual male friend another woman younger and prettier than herself! But it is so, dear, for you are certainly prettier than me!'

She kissed Martha. Then she invited her to take off her wraps and to make herself at home. But when she observed that Martha remained fully dressed with the exception of her mantle, she said to her: 'Don't be afraid, dear! Make yourself at home and do as I do! You mustn't remain as you are and receive your lover so – for men like to see their sweethearts in some dishabille when they come to visit them. Besides this, I have to change my dress for my evening's engagements. It will be pleasant to take advantage of this and see how some of my dresses will look on you – an excellent idea – for should anyone have followed us here and finds us so engaged, it will completely throw them off the scent!'

Mme de Liancourt rapidly divested herself of her dress, corset and petticoats till she had on her chemise only. Then she proceeded to reduce Martha to a similar condition of undress, in spite of the latter's hesitation, especially as to removing her corset, as she alleged that she should keep this on if she was to try on any dresses! This, Mme de Liancourt would not agree to.

'I do not know whether my dress will fit you dear,' she continued. 'I think I am bigger than you are in the bust!'

Under this pretext she threw open her chemise and exhibited her breasts, which she set to work to compare with those of Martha, after having first unfastened and opened the latter's chemise.

'What deliciously white and firm little bubbies you have, dear! I expect you have often been complimented on them! A very fortunate man is your lover.'

'Suppose he should suddenly turn up and catch us as we are?'

'I should rush off into any corner that I could!' replied Mme de Liancourt with a smile she tried vainly to repress. But at a ball, we women show quite as much of ourselves as you and I are now doing! I, at all events, have my dresses cut low enough to let my nipples be seen! Besides, it is only a woman with a bad figure that objects to being found naked or practically so! I'm not one of that lot – see!'

With a touch, she caused her chemise to fall to her feet and stepped forwards out of it in all her glorious nudity, the effect being heightened by the contrast caused by the triangular patch of tawny golden hair at the junction of her belly and thighs and her black, silk stockings with their rose-tinted garters worn above the knees!

'This is how I meet my lover!' she said.

Martha became scarlet.

'How you are blushing, dear! Is it because of the sight of me standing naked? If so, you remind me of one of my girlfriends who declares that the sight of me naked excites her much more than the sight of a naked man would do! Every time she comes to see me, she insists on my undressing myself completely in front of her! – and then you should see how she kisses and embraces me just as if she was playing with a naked man! Then she will go and do a thousand things to me which at first used to make me feel horribly ashamed, but which now I really like – even to the length of paying her back in the same coin! Oh! It's lovely! And mind you, we're not deceiving our husbands! Strange but true, isn't it, eh?'

She kissed the blushing Martha. 'Even since I have had lovers and . . . enjoyed them, I still recollect those delicious hours with my girlfriend! We used to caress and kiss each other's breasts like this . . .'

'Oh! you're biting me!'

'Doesn't your lover do this to you? . . . Oh! see how the pretty little nipples are stiffening and standing out!'

'Oh! Madame, you're tickling me . . . Oh! take away your hand! Oh! what are you doing! No . . . no! I don't want it!'

Mme de Liancourt had seized Martha and was passionately clasping her against herself, holding her tightly with one arm around her waist while she slipped her other hand between Martha's thighs.

'Oh! But Madame, what . . . are you going . . . to do . . . to me?'

'Make love with you, darling! Don't you know how two women can mutually prove their love for each other? At school, didn't one of the bigger girls take charge of you, and teach you . . . this? Ah, you're blushing now. You little humbug!'

'That was so long ago! I quite forget it all . . .'

'Really? Well, I know. Come, you'd like to do it again, wouldn't you . . . with me?'

'No – no! Suppose . . . he came in . . .'

'He can't without our hearing him. Come, you pretty little coward, come! Place yourself against me. Take off your chemise. You can have a dressing gown if you like!'

She gave Martha one.

'No, don't fasten it . . . leave it quite open! . . . I want to have a good look at you! . . . your breasts . . . your belly . . . your hairs . . . how they curl and cluster!'

Suddenly she knelt and applied her lips to the dark triangular patch that luxuriated at the end of Martha's stomach, the latter still offering a shamefaced resistance.

'No, no!' she cried, squeezing her legs closely together.

Martha, now half-willing and still half-reluctant, passively allowed herself to be placed on the sofa. Mme de Liancourt seated herself at Martha's side, passed one arm round her and slipped her other hand between Martha's thighs while she passionately kissed her, darting her tongue into Martha's mouth! Her finger, directed by both art and passion, soon produced the desired result! Martha's breath began to come brokenly, her eyes half closed, her bosom and breasts heaved agitatedly! At this moment Mme de Liancourt, no longer content to play only the part of the communicator of pleasure, caught hold of one of Martha's hands and gently conducted it to her own cunt with a mute demand for reciprocity! And Martha did not draw it back – she recognised the silent request, and her gentle little hand began to do its untutored best!

'Martha! Oh darling . . . keep on . . . oh . . . keep on! You're . . . doing it . . . beautifully! Oh! Oh . . . I'm coming . . . Oh, I'm spending! Ah . . . ah!'

A moment of silence followed this ecstatic crisis, Mme de Liancourt still keeping her hand on Martha's slit!

'Oh, how wet you are! You've also spent, you naughty thing! Darling, we've done it together! Wipe yourself.' She gave Martha a handkerchief. 'Now, wasn't it good?'

'Yes,' replied Martha timidly.

'Then let's do it together!'

'If you like!'

Immediately, our two lascivious heroines recommenced their lubricious caresses! Martha extended herself flat on her back on the sofa, and while her seducer, bending over her, looked her all over and felt and handled her as spirit willed her, and freshly aroused in her new lust (as was manifest from the agitation of her bosom and breasts),

Martha's hand without invitation stole to Mme de Liancourt's cunt and resumed its loving ministration. She had caught the fancy – she, so timid with me!

Nevertheless, she began to protest when, after having tenderly sucked her breasts, her mistress in lesbian pleasures carried her lips lower down!

'No, no – not there!' she panted, trying to raise herself.

'Yes, yes! I wish it! Let me kiss your sweet cunny with its pretty hair! I'll do it just as well as your lover can!'

'But he has never . . . kissed me there!'

'Then he doesn't know his duties as your lover! So much the better for me! I shall now be the first to do it to you! You'll see how delicious it is! I used to be just like you at first, but now I simply adore this way! And you'll always do it this way in the future whenever you get a chance. So, open wider these pretty thighs . . . '

For response, she was dragged down to the foot of the sofa and her thighs widely pulled apart, as Mme de Liancourt, falling on her knees between them, murmured almost unconsciously: 'Oh, what a lovely sweet fresh little cunny! Oh, the beauty!' Then, like the swoop of a hawk on a chicken, her mouth attacked it and remained there as if glued to it! Completely defeated, Martha fell on her back again and resigned herself as best she could to abandon herself to the voluptuous sensations that now were thrilling through her, induced by the ardent tongue of her passionate friend! Some minutes thus passed! At last Mme de Liancourt raised herself, red, flushed, panting, almost delirious!

'Together . . . together? Will you . . . '

'What?' gasped Martha.

'This! Let's do it together. Will you?'

'If you wish it. But how?'

'I'll show you, darling. Now watch . . . '

She got on the sofa, turned her bottom towards Martha's head, straddled across Martha, then placed herself astride of her face, her belly resting on Martha's breasts and her cunt seeking the same lingual caress which she was recommencing on Martha's one now lying below her lips. Her thighs hid half the face of my sweet little mistress, and I could only see a bit of her forehead and her pretty hair emerge from between Mme de Liancourt's buttocks. As the latter wriggled and waggled her charming globes of flesh in lascivious undulations, I noted that Martha had accommodated herself to her position and that her mouth, as docilely as her hand, comprehended and daintily executed the delicate function demanded from it! As for Mme de Liancourt, she was simply mad with passionate lust! What a strange thing it is that a woman can thus procure for herself such keen and ecstatic enjoyment in thus caressing another woman! I was splendidly placed for contemplating her and the object of her delirious worship! I saw her face in profile, her chin resting on the hairs, her mouth poised on the lips of Martha's slit between which her tongue was playing! These secret charms of Martha, hitherto unknown to me, made me envy Mme de Liancourt – both her place and the game she was playing! Time after time, I was on the point of bursting out of my hiding place and planting my mouth on the sweet spot she was attacking (our convention would have authorised the act) but I refrained. The charm of the spectacle fascinated me!

Sometimes Mme de Liancourt seemed as if she wanted to get the whole of Martha's cunt into her mouth! Sometimes she amused herself by administering little touches to the clitoris with her tongue! Then she would pass her tongue right along the tender slit from top to bottom. Sometimes she would, with her fingers, separate the sensitive lips and thrust her tongue between them as deeply as she possibly could!

How Martha must have revelled in bliss! I would have liked to have been able to watch her face. She evidently was most satisfactorily reciprocating Mme de Liancourt's attentions, if one might judge by the plunging and jogging of the latter's body as she brokenly ejaculated, 'Oh, oh, you do it well! I can feel your tongue! Now, do you feel mine? Wait . . . I'm going to shove it right inside this sweet cunt . . . as far in . . . as . . . it will go . . . '

The ecstatic crisis was fast approaching. The breathing became more and more broken.

'Martha . . . Martha! Oh! Darling . . . I'm coming! Ah! Ah! I'm spending . . . are you . . . spend . . . together . . . wait a moment . . . Now! Now! Oh! I'm spending . . . again! Spend also . . . spend!'

Their bodies stiffened, constricted. I heard a deep sigh of unspeakable pleasures. They had finished.

Mme de Liancourt slowly slipped off her position and then gave her pupil kiss after kiss of approbation and satisfaction.

'Darling! Your face is all wet with what you have drawn out of me! And I've drunk you. Use my handkerchief. How flushed and red you are! Now, wasn't that good?'

'Oh, yes. Much better than I could have believed!'

Was it not now time for me to put in an appearance? But what could I do with two women whose lust had been thus satiated! Nevertheless, I

THE ENCYCLOPEDIA OF EROTIC LITERATURE

decided to show myself and opened the door, regretting that I had delayed so long!

Two piercing cries saluted me! Martha leaped on her piled-up garments and covered herself as best she could with the first she could snatch, then hid herself behind the bed curtains. Mme de Liancourt caught up a velvet mantle trimmed with fur and threw it hastily around her, but it reached only to her fleshy buttocks and did not even cover the fur of her belly.

'What do you mean, sir,' she exclaimed with a fine pretence of anger and outraged modesty. 'What do you mean by thus rushing into a lady's room without first knocking? It is a piece of the greatest impertinence! You are a mannerless brute!

'Madame, I humbly and earnestly beg your pardon for having surprised you in this way,' I replied, suppressing as best I could the desire to laugh. 'But I came in trusting in your promise to give the kind refuge to this lady and myself!'

'Yes – but Madame has been waiting for you for some time now; Is this your idea of the proper way of keeping an appointment? But I will abide by my promise; you can have my room and my bed. Only be prudent! I know your secrets now and if I choose I can be nasty!' She winked at me out of the corner of her eye as if to qualify her menace, then walked past me towards her dressing-room.

'Take care about the sheets!' she added with a meaningfully wicked smile.

I watched as she walked, her lovely plump and round bottom quivering and waggling with every step. I would dearly have liked to have put myself into her! But I went and dragged Martha out of her hiding place.

'What makes you so red, dear?'

'I've been laughing! Madame has been telling me the funniest stories . . .'

'You look simply charming in that dressing gown – but don't fasten it up, it's quite unnecessary!'

'Oh . . . very well. But wait a minute. Don't look!'

She disappeared into the lavatory, and while she was engaged in clearing away all traces of her recent pranks, I undressed myself, then when she reappeared, I took her in my arms and carried her to the bed on which I gently laid her. Her desires, which I had feared were by now dormant, were quickly restored to life again, having another promise of satisfaction in a different way! Her modesty after so rude an experience had become less troublesome and I did not meet with any marked resistance on her part, when after bestowing a thousand kisses all over her body, I did to her what Mme de Liancourt had so sweetly inaugurated – the deliciousness of which she now fully appreciated as with her two little hands she pressed my face against her slit so as not to lose a single movement of my tongue!

I thought of Mme de Liancourt and wished she could see us now! But she did even better than that; she stood stark naked by the side of the bed, and while I was busy between Martha's thighs, she kissed her lips and squeezed her breasts – while the former, having within her reach her friend's thighs, slipped her hand between them and let it disappear under the plentiful cluster of curling hairs without interrupting my ministrations.

Excited, inflamed, burning with hot desire, I rose to throw myself on Martha and quench in her the fire that was raging in my veins! But at that moment Mme de Liancourt carried her hand to the lowest point of my belly and seized the object she found there in a state of furious erection!

'Look, Martha!' she exclaimed. 'Have you ever seen it before? Isn't it splendid? See, how stiff it is – that's in honour of you, my dear! Oh, I must . . . I can't help it . . . '

I was then kneeling on the bed. With a single quick movement she seated herself with her head at the required height, then covered with hot kisses my member which she found just on a level with her lips. She kissed and rekissed the glans, the hairs, the testicles, murmuring endearments; then she took my prick into her mouth and sucked it madly in front of Martha, who was watching her in utter astonishment!

'Now, Martha, you take it – it's your turn. Suck it. Do as I did!'

'I don't know how to! It's so big!'

Now redder than fire, she approached it, kissed the tip and tried for some time in vain to take it into her mouth – when all of a sudden it slipped in, as if in spite of her, completely filling her mouth. And she then proceeded to suck me. Oh, my raptures! It was Martha! Martha herself that was sucking me! It was not with the lascivious skill of Mme de Liancourt, but her inexperience itself gave to her caress a special and indescribable spice of pleasure.

Finally I put Martha flat on her back. I let myself fall between her arms and legs and shoved my prick into her burning cunt – tasting delights hitherto unknown – divine, delirious! Already I could see Martha's eyes slowly turning upwards and half closing, indicating her approaching ecstasy – when Mme de Liancourt, no doubt jealous of our transports, put herself astride across Martha's face, blindly seeking for her cunt a further caress which it was impossible to refuse to her! Being thus suddenly driven away from Martha's lips and tongue, I transferred my kisses to the two luscious globes of flesh which I had at my mouth's command, kissing, nibbling and playfully biting them in spite of their squirming and constant agitation!

But everything must end. We three spent simultaneously! The blissful ejaculations of sperm calmed us! One by one, we came to our senses and rose to purify and refresh ourselves.

'My gracious, I've got it all over me!' cried Martha in pretty confusion. 'Even on my stockings . . . they're quite wet!'

'Well, dear,' said Mme de Liancourt to her, 'you've done very well for one time. You must be very tired! By the time you get home, your eyes will have dark rings round them – and then what will your husband think, eh?'

'Ah! I'll risk that! That won't stop me from . . . doing it again.'

17

The Simple Tale of Susan Aked

c.1892

The Simple Tale of Susan Aked, or Innocence Awakened, Ignorance Dispelled
is the type of erotic book that severely challenges erotobibliographers.
The first copy of the text seen by this writer was a stout volume of 208
pages. Despite the imprint of '1898, Printed for the Erotica Biblion
Society. London & New York', the book was clearly American *c.*1935
based on its physical construction and the fashions shown in its
illustrations. Yet the writing style, plot, and particulars mentioned (such
as garments) were of at least three decades before! Reference to the
standard bibliographies of erotica to discover the first printing was of
limited assistance. None listed editions that seemed early enough, and it
wasn't even mentioned in Ashbee's exhaustive three-volume bibliography of nearly all English erotica prior to 1885. The necessary clues
finally came from the last resort of any bibliographer – old catalogues
and book advertisements. An ad at the end of an 1892 edition of *The
Bagnio Miscellany*, published in Amsterdam by Auguste Brancart, offered
for sale, 'By the same publisher . . . , *Susan Aked or Innocence Awakened,
Ignorance Dispelled*. That this title was the same book as the *c.*1935 *The
Simple Tale of Susan Aked* . . . was confirmed when this writer discovered
the identical text in an undated edition of *Susan Aked* . . . with the
imprint 'Rotterdam–London', and the title-page information, 'By the
Author of *Venus in India*' (known to have been published in 1889). This
newly discovered book is a first edition, and examination of it showed
the printing style to be *c.*1890 and Belgian (i.e. inverted quotation marks
at the beginning of each line of quoted text, exclamation points treated
typographically as letters rather than punctuation marks, catch words
facing the signature marks, etc.). This book also had printed chapter-
head devices, identical to those known to have been used by Brancart,
who incidentally often had his English-language erotica typeset in
Brussels to avoid police action. That the devices were very worn

indicated the printing to have been done near the end of Brancart's career, which seems to have been about 1892–4.

One mystery solved, but the author's identity still unknown. We can make some educated guesses as to what type of person must have written this by examining the content of the book. The style of *Susan Aked* is extremely formal – 'starched Victorian' one might say. Even in matters of impropriety the characters never fully relax. There is a 'proper way' to do even improper things! Though within a decade of the actual end of the Victorian age (Queen Victoria died in 1901), *Susan Aked* does not display any of the frivolity that had already entered English life in the 1890s. *La Belle Epoque* and the moral excesses of the Third Empire in France had already eroded the strict formality of Victorian England. Restrictive social order (in employment, fashion, and even married life) had slowly given way to less ceremonial and pedantic human interaction. Language reflected this in the increased use of colloquialisms and a less structured syntax. People in short became more familiar with each other, but this is not evident in *Susan Aked*. Here the language is baroque, classical illusions abound and the plot structure is anything but 'modern'. Accepting the author to have also written *Venus in India*, we could guess him to have been born c.1810–20, to have been a 'gentleman' of good family and education, interested in science and Far East travel, and irreversibly steeped in Victorian mannerisms.

The tag line 'An Instructive Story' appended to the book's title in the 1898 and subsequent editions is most apt. The book is, in fact, a quasi-autobiographical novel that can double as a sex manual. The narrator of the story, a young woman named Susan Aked, loses both her parents suddenly, and invites her cousin Lucia Lovette to live with her while the estate is being settled. Lucia, finding Susan to be a sexually ignorant virgin, proceeds to educate her, with word and action. Special attention is given to matters of sexual anatomy, technique, hygiene and contraception. Susan learns that her libidinous cousin secretly operates a house where assignations can be carried out most discreetly, and it is there that her education is completed, with the assistance of her distant cousin Charles, a stud of the first order.

Aficionados of erotica will recognise many of this novel's elements. The self-told story of an orphaned young woman has been met with in *Fanny Hill*. The style of long quotes and plot advanced through letters is typical of eighteenth-century English novels in general, and erotica in particular. Sexual education of one young woman by another is at least as old as *The Dialogues of Luisa Sigea* (c.1660). Printed erotica as sex

instruction goes back farther, to 1527, when Aretino's *Sonetti Lussuriosi*
first appeared in Italy, with erotic verse elucidating the sexual activity
explicitly illustrated in a series of engravings. Even before printing,
prehistoric drawings, Egyptian papyri, Greek and Roman art and
artifacts, and Oriental pillow books all served multiple purposes as
aphrodisiacs, erotic entertainment and repositories of sexual knowledge.

Susan Aked is not just a sex manual like its contemporary erotic works
The Horn Book and *Love and Safety*. It is first and foremost an erotic
novel, mixing reality with fantasy. The author had an obvious interest in
sexual science. Here is, perhaps, the first writer to incorporate a
microscope into his erotic narrative! As a nineteenth-century man his
interests and observations were in the realm of the then new areas of sex
anatomy, as opposed to a twentieth-century counterpart who would
more likely show interest in the then 'new' psychological factors of sex.

Susan Aked is perhaps unusual in that while being a heterosexually-
oriented work, it has several protracted scenes of lesbian activity. In
fact, over half the book describes female homosexual conduct although
neither of the main actresses are presented as stereotypic 'dykes'. Both
are very feminine and prefer the sexual company of men and it is
doubtful that this book was written for a lesbian or even female
audience. It is not known how many women have read such descriptions for their own erotic stimulation, but it is most likely that they
would have found them sadly unsatisfying, especially when compared
to the more delicate and sensitive erotic depictions of such female
authors as Anaïs Nin or the great Sappho herself. Observing lesbian
activity is a common male fantasy, and it appears with great frequency
in erotica written for men by men, but usually as isolated episodes only.
Only relatively recently have women openly written erotic lesbian
literature; past works with extended lesbian themes were usually male
authored, such as Pierre Louÿs's *Songs of Bilitis* or Gautier's *Mademoiselle de Maupin* or Verlaine's *Les Femmes*. Even as late as the 1960s a
great amount of 'lesbian fiction' was penned by men, such as Paul
Little (aka 'Sylvia Sharon'), and predominantly for a male audience.
Prior to the twentieth century only a very small amount of all erotica
had been authored by women, and an even smaller amount by
homosexual women. Hence genuine scenes of lesbian love from past
epochs are extremely rare, though not for lack of actual female
homosexual activity. Religious exhortations aside, the fear of venereal
disease (poorly treatable even with mercury compounds until the
present century) and unwanted pregnancy (with its risks of social
ostracism and puerperal mortality) should have been enough to induce

Victorian women into celibacy or relations with their own sex. Legal suppression of lesbianism was not a great problem for the Victorian woman. It is said that Queen Victoria exempted females from the English sodomy laws enacted to deter and punish male homosexual behaviour because she herself could not imagine how women possibly had sex with each other! Obviously a reading of *Susan Aked* would have cured that ignorance.

Here then is an excerpt from *The Simple Tale of Susan Aked*, in which the narrator receives lessons in the ways of physical love from the less than pure hand of her female cousin.

from *The Simple Tale of Susan Aked*

As she had promised, Lucia came to my bedroom after Martha and the servants had gone to bed. She sprang into my bed and clasped me in her arms and then began kissing me repeatedly.

'Oh, Susan, we will have such a night of it! I'll tell you all you want to know, and I will show you more, and I will prove to you that it is downright folly to lose years of youth, which can be so well turned to profit by using the charms and senses nature has given you. But let me put my hand between your legs, darling. That's it! Now I'll just slip my finger in this delicious little cunt. You do the same to me. Now, am I not nice and hot and soft inside?'

'Indeed you are, Lucia, like velvet warmed before the fire.'

'And so are you, darling. But now we won't have any tickling yet. Now I will tell you, my dear, everything about men.'

'Ah, do. I am dying with curiosity, Lucia!'

'Well now, just here,' said she, pressing her thumb on a spot above my cunnie, 'a man's thing grows out from him. That thing is called his prick or his yard or his tool or his Johnnie – or half a hundred other names. When it is not standing it is about two or three inches long, all small and soft and flabby and wrinkled, but when it stands, it is seven or eight inches long, as big round as my wrist and hard as iron. A most formidable weapon to thrust into the poor little belly of a girl!'

'But what makes it stand, Lucia?' I asked, breathless with unaccountable emotion and feeling a strange shiver pass through me at the notion of such a monstrous thing being thrust into my belly!

202 THE ENCYCLOPEDIA OF EROTIC LITERATURE

'Oh, there are physical reasons for that which I won't go into now, but the actual cause of its standing is desire. When a man thinks of a girl and wants to have her, up goes his prick; it lifts itself up, fills and swells out with pride and power, and becomes just like a bar of iron covered from end to end with a thick, soft, velvety skin. If you were to take a good hold of one in that condition you could move your hand up and down without the skin slipping from under your fingers, just like you can move the skin of a cat on its body!'

'Really! How curious!'

'Yes, well, there it stands. But it is not exactly round. It is slightly broader than it is deep, so to say, and it has the most curious-looking head imaginable. It is something like a cherry at the end, and in the tip is a little hole, out of which comes the dangerous stuff which makes babies!'

'Oh, my!'

'Well, the head is shaped there like a bell. It is bluish purple round the lower rim, which rim forms a regular shoulder. You can slip the movable skin right off the head and behind the shoulder, and there it will stay unless it is forcibly put back again. Underneath the nose, as I will take it, of the prick, the movable skin is fastened not far behind the point, and when the stand or stiffness is gone out of the prick, this fastening pulls the cap over its head again.'

'How very curious. How convenient.'

'Well, now, under the prick, nearly as far back, but not quite, as the place where it springs from, is a very curious, very wrinkled bag, in which the balls are. Balls are something like small eggs and far nicer both to feel and see. I dearly love feeling a man's balls, and does not he like it, too! They feel slippery and hard, but you must take care not to squeeze them tight, as that hurts a man very much; but gently handling them, lifting them up with the tips of the fingers and gently rolling them about in their bag is most pleasing to every man, and if his prick has gone down, such treatment will quickly bring it back grand and stiff and big and ready for work again.'

'And what are his balls for, Lucia?' said I.

'His balls hold the stuff he spends when he fucks us, darling. A white creamy-looking stuff like milk, only thicker, which spouts out in jets. I have seen Charlie Althair spout it three feet high!'

'Charlie Althair!' I exclaimed.

'Yes, darling. Charlie was my first love, and it was he who took my maidenhead. He is a grand fellow, and no girl could have him in her bed without going half mad over him. He is able to give extraordinary pleasure, and I ought to know for I have had plenty of experience.'

'Then there is a difference between men that way, Lucia?'

'There is indeed! Sometimes one gets hold of a fellow, well made in every respect but an indifferent bedfellow, not simply because he does not, or cannot, give one enough but because he does not know how to do it properly.'

'And how should it be done properly, Lucia?'

'I'll tell you, darling. Oh, if I only were a man, if instead of this cunt I had a rattling, fine, big, long prick, as stiff as a poker, and a well-furnished pair of balls, I would show you, my Susan. I would show you what a real, good, unmistakable fuck is. I am one who knows how it should be done!'

'Lucia, though you have no prick and no balls, can't you tell me all the same? I am dying to know.'

'Ah, my sweet Susan is growing randy. I know she is. I think a little bit of a spend would do her good. I tell you what,' she said, her voice growing thick and hurried as though emotion were choking her, 'I will show you how a man gets on to you and how he moves, and I will make you spend a dozen times. For, darling, I must either spend myself or burst!'

So saying, she pulled my chemise above my boobies and rolled it on my neck, and, pulling up her own and holding its end under her chin and on her bosom, she got between my knees.

'Open your thighs wide, darling!' she cried in a most excited manner. 'Open your thighs, draw up your knees. That is it. Oh, I'd forsake a kingdom to have a prick now.' She sank on to my belly. She put one hand under my hips to raise them. The other she put round my neck. Her boobies coincided with mine. I could feel their hard little nipples pressing into my breasts, whilst mine, equally hard, met her harder and more elastic globes. She pressed her bushy motte to mine, lifted me a little with her hand and brought the two hot lips of her burning cunnie on to mine. Then she, as it were, sank her hips. The top of her cunt touched the bottom of mine, and then, with a pressing upward sweep, she brought her cunnie all over mine from end to end of the slit. Down she swept again. Then up. Then down, until I thrilled through and through with extraordinary and untold pleasure. I felt her grasp growing tighter and tighter. Her breathing became more and more hurried, her breasts crushed mine. They seemed to swell and become harder and harder. Then, when she had come to the end of one of her long upward sweeps, she suddenly spent all over my motte. I could feel the hair there inundated. At the same moment she received my offering full on her cunnie, as she swept down mine. This excited her immensely, and she redoubled her efforts to make the spasms come again. I clasped her to me. I returned the rain of furnace-like kisses she showered all over my face. I felt wild. Again and again we spent all over one another's cunt and bush, I can't tell you how many times, until at length drenched, breathless and tired, Lucia lay heavily on me, and for a moment we were motionless. Then, lifting her head, she kissed me in the most loving manner.

'My little darling! My own sweetest darling Susan, how did you like that?'

'Oh, Lucia, it was heavenly. Do it again, darling!' I cried, clasping her between my thighs and pressing my glowing cunt to hers.

'Not just yet, dearest. No, Susan, I have come at least fifteen times, and you are as wet as a drowned rat. Indeed, so am I. You naughty little girl, how you do spend!'

'You taught me,' said I.

'Ah, yes, you are a darling and splendid pupil, my Susan, and a perfect mine of these pearls,' said she, pointing to a drop depending from her bush, and which, when it dropped on to my thigh as she got off me, felt cold.

'Now,' she continued, 'come, get up. We must wash.'

We both got out of bed. Lucia dropped her chemise and stood naked and beautiful before me. I did the same. She again exclaimed at what she called the extraordinary gracefulness of my figure, and again wished she were a man.

We washed one another's cunnie, and then, naked as we were, again got into bed, and with arms round one another's waist, and thighs locked in thighs, we pressed our bosoms together, and Lucia continued her instructions.

'Well, Susanna *mia*, that little bit of initiation was a nice little interlude, and imperfect as it was, it has shown you at least how you will have to lie when you are had, *à la* Adam and Eve, by a man, for you must not imagine for a moment that a man has only one way of fucking a girl. There are heaps of ways, all more or less nice, but to my simple mind the Adam and Eve is the best of all, because it is the most natural and the most perfect.'

'But, Lucia darling,' said I, 'I have not a notion of what you mean by "Adam and Eve" as compared with other ways. You said you would tell me how a man should well do it with a girl so as to be perfect in his action.'

'Oh, my modest little mouse, now, Susan, say fuck.'

'I was not quite sure of the term, Lucia dearest. I did not mean to be over particular. Well, tell me exactly how a man should fuck a girl so as to give her the most complete pleasure. For my part, not knowing what it is like, I should imagine that the mere sensation of having so big a thing – as you say a man's prick is – inside one's cunt would be rather disagreeable than otherwise! Why even you, who have, you tell me, been fucked, have quite a tight little cunt. How on earth can such a small, little slit like this take in a thing as big as one's wrist? I can hardly believe it, or, if I do believe it, I can hardly fancy its being pleasant.'

Lucia listened to me with a smiling face. She kissed me and put her hand on my motte, slipping her finger up to her knuckles into my still-throbbing cunnie.

'Yes, my Susan, our cunts are, luckily for us and our lovers, small and tight. If they were not, neither they nor we would have half the pleasure we do. I say we, because it won't be long now before you know what a delicious, deliriously rapturous and excessively delightful thing it is to be well and often fucked. Oh, dear, why have I not a prick? How easy it would be to show you, darling. Far more easy than to explain!'

'Oh! Lucia! Do go on! Tell me! You keep me actually on thorns of expectation!'

Lucia laughed, passed her finger deliciously two or three times up and down my cunnie, then took it out and grasped my left breast in her hand, pressing it gently, as though she loved doing so. 'Well, Susan, here it goes. Now I'll do my best to describe what a man should do to give you the acme of pleasure. First of all, he should put his prick into your hand. It is a most thrilling thing to feel. Oh, it is delightful! You feel it from end to end. Its hardness like iron, its soft velvety skin, its soft cushion-like head and its shifting hood, his grand balls in their wrinkled, silky, soft bag, and the thick, rough bush out of which this galaxy of manly charms grows – all form objects of delight to the hand that knows how to caress them and to the cunt that expects so soon to feel their powerful action.

'Whilst you hand is enjoying itself and giving your lover the greatest delight also, his hand will be stirring up the very depths of pleasure in you. By the way, before I forget it, let me warn you that when handling a man's prick in this way, do not caress its head too much. It is excessively sensitive, and too much rubbing produces spasms, very delicious for him but destructive of your pleasure, for you might make it too excited and cause him to be too ready to spend. The longer a man takes during the fuck, the more your pleasure, for he does not spend over and over again during a fuck, but once only. That done, he is done, too, for the time. So confine your caresses to the shaft of his prick, to his balls, his groins and his bush, but leave the head of his prick alone if you are wise.

'Whilst you are thus caressing him, he will be kissing you. He will be squeezing your dear little boobies. He will be toying with your tongue with the tip of his. Presently his mouth will kiss you along your neck until it reaches your bosom. He will kiss your breasts with rapture, and nibble each little hard rosebud. Whilst sending you wild in this manner, his hand will glide over your smooth body and seek your motte. You will feel his hand press between your thighs. Then he will stroke your cunnie, so.' She did it to me. 'He will gently press the lips of your cunt together and tickle your clitoris, this little kind of tongue – a veritable imitation of his own prick, but much smaller – then he will slip his big middle finger deep into your cunnie and tickle you here.' She slipped hers in and found the narrow, tight, inner entrance, which she set on fire immediately with her caressing, making me involuntarily spend.

'You quick little darling!' she exclaimed. 'How you do spend! Won't you just like being fucked? Well, now, I must not use you up in that way. Keep your spend for by and by, when we will have another bout of rub-cunnie.

'Now, Susan,' she continued, again taking possession of my glowing boobies, 'you can feel, even from my poor, little, feminine hand, how very sensitive your cunt is all about the entrance. It is sensitive all along its whole depth, but the sensitive portion *par excellence* is about the entrance. The difference between a good fucker and an indifferent one is in the fact that the really good fucker knows this and does his best to produce the most ecstatic pleasure in you by cultivating this extra sensitiveness of the entrance to your sweet cunnie.

'Suppose your man now has his two knees between yours. He leans over, but not upon you. He supports himself on his elbow. You take his prick and plant its head justly and neatly between the lips of your cunnie. Then you put your arms round his waist and, with a little pressure on his part, in goes his prick, quite over the shoulder of its head. Its hood slips back, and you feel the sweet thing filling the outer vestibule of your cunt. Then he draws back until he is almost out, and again smoothly and gently pushes in. This time, with an indescribable thrill, you feel that big head force its way sweetly past the inner, narrow entrance. That thrill is worth a fortune, it is so delicious. Then he draws back until he is almost out again; with a more decided sweep, he thrusts his powerful, swelling prick in, passes the narrows and buries it halfway in your throbbing and beating cunnie. These movements he continues, always drawing almost out, always gaining – by gentle but smoothly repeated thrusts – ground in your cunt. Presently, and all too quickly, you feel his pendant balls touch you beneath your cunnie. Then they beat more firmly against you, and, last of all, his belly, which has been touching yours all along, presses yours; his hairy motte mingles its brush with yours; your cushion feels his, and his last thrust brings your bodies into the most intimate and close contact.

'Now the real delight begins! Every stroke, every thrust he gives, is from head to heel of his prick. He gives you long, smooth, deliberate thrusts; every line of those long seven or eight inches tells upon you. You come! You spend, time after time, yet not a drop goes outside. His prick, so to say, closes your cunnie tightly, and your spend only makes its movements more easy. As your pleasure increases, so does his. Presently his agonies of delight begin. All his nerves seem concentrated in the head of his prick until his sensations are so vivid as almost to take his senses away. Then begin the all-too-short, as far as time is concerned, short digs. He shortens his strokes but quickens them, banging his balls against you with great force. Then, suddenly, he spends; he pours out the fullest riches of his manly strength. You feel it in you like a torrent, like a powerful artery shooting its blood into you. He presses you as though he would crush you into pulp. He forces his prick in even farther than you would think possible. Your motte is flattened by his and all Heaven and its glories seem open to you! It is over! You have been fucked – and well fucked. Then comes a delightful interval of repose.

'He lets his body lie all along yours, and he kisses you and pets you and calls you all the pretty things he thinks of. His manly bosom rests on your heaving boobies; your cunnie, if it has the nutcrackers, tightens and loosens on his prick, giving him further delight. Your motte throbs against his until you become conscious that his prick does not fill you quite so much as it did, and you feel it gradually slipping out. His stand has come to an end. Your lover gets from between your thighs and lies at your side, clasping you with his arms and locking his thighs with yours, as mine do now. The fuck is at an end and cannot be repeated until his prick stands again.'

'What are the nutcrackers, Lucia?' said I, gasping for breath. My heart was in my throat with the emotion her description had raised.

'The nutcrackers, darling, are when your cunnie grasps his prick, as it were, like this,' she said, taking my wrist in her hand and clasping it at intervals of time with her forefinger and thumb. 'It must be the muscles about the narrow entrance that do it, for my lovers always tell me that they feel the tightening of my cunt about two inches up from their balls, and only there.'

'I say, Lucia!'

'What, darling?'

'Do you know by what geographical expression our cunts ought to be called?'

'No! What do you mean?' said Lucia, laughing.

'Why, the Red Sea to be sure! Just inside the lips should be the Gulf of Aden, where it is pretty wild. The narrows should be Bab-el-Mandeb Straits, and the rest the Red Sea!'

'Capital, darling! I'll tell Gladys, who will laugh, I know! Now,' she continued, stroking my cunnie in a lively manner, 'open your thighs again, my own sweetest darling, deary Susan, and let me have you again!'

Nothing loath, I did so, and soon Lucia was thrilling both herself and me with the pleasure her up and down strokes gave to each of us. At last she made me so tremendously excited that I could lie quiet no longer. I clasped her to my belly with all my might, and, as her cunnie swept down over mine, I gave a vigorous push up with mine. The result was delicious! Both Lucia and I gave vent to a little cry of pleasure, for it so happened that her stiff little clitoris had just reached mine, and my push up made these delicate and charmingly sensitive little organs penetrate – slightly, indeed, but still penetrate – our respective cunnies. The immediate consequence was copious spending on either side. Lucia kissed me frantically, gave up the sweeping movement and pushed her cunt straight at mine. Our clitorises rubbed one another in a most ravishing manner. We writhed and thrust and thrust and writhed, and spent time after time, until fairly exhausted, and, with perspiration standing in little pearls on our foreheads, we relaxed our hold on one another, and Lucia, resuming her place by my side, lay panting but quiet. At length, she said: 'How nature does teach, Susan.'

'Yes, dear,' said I, still struggling for breath, 'but how?'

'But how!' she cried. 'Why, what made you give such a delicious buck, darling? It had not entered my head to tell you. I never did it with any girl myself and would not have believed it could have been of any use had it been proposed. What made you do it?'

'Do you mean why I did push up?'

'Yes! Why did you buck?'

'Buck rhymes with fuck, does it not, Lucia?'

'Of course, and cunt with hunt, prick with lick, balls with halls, bush with push, and so on, but what has that to do with your bucking, Susan?'

'I can't tell you, darling,' said I, kissing her. 'I only know I could not lie quiet any longer, and so I gave a buck up, like a horse does when his rider spurs him too much.'

'Well, Susan, I can only say that if ever a girl was created for the purpose of fucking, you are she! You seem to take to it like a babe does to its mother's breast. Ah! I do envy the fellows who will have you! I know right well they will think your cunt is heaven!'

'I don't know, Lucia. They may not like it at all.'

'Oh, won't they? A man likes a girl to show that he gives her pleasure. They don't like bucking horses, but they do love a good bucking girl – and you do it as if you had been trained to it!'

'No one trained me, Lucia, as you know, for I did not imagine any pleasure such as you have given me was ever to be extracted from my cunnie. But do you buck when a man is fucking you?'

'Oh, yes! But there is an art in it.'

'How?'

'Well, you see, the object of bucking is to get in the very last quarter inch of the fellow's prick, which would probably remain outside if you did not buck, to get a good strain on to his balls, to get a good squeeze together of your two mottes. All that adds to the pleasure of both of you. The time to buck is when you feel his balls begin to touch you, then begin a gentle upward stroke, or perhaps a kind of circular stroke, ending with a good bump against his motte. If you begin too soon, you hurry his stroke, a thing to be avoided because it makes him spend too soon. The buck should, as I say, be so scientifically done as to complete the entire swallowing up of his prick in your cunnie!'

'I see. Now tell me, Lucia, if I have learned the lesson right. When a man fucks you, he ought to get his prick in little by little?'

'Just so!'

'Then, after he has once got it in the whole way, he should draw it all but out, and then, with one long, sweeping stroke, bring it again right up to his balls?'

'Right up to his motte, darling, for his balls touch you first.'

'Ah, yes, right up to his motte. Then he should go on so until he begins to feel that he can no longer withhold his spend, and then he is to fuck like fury!'

'Just so – like fury!' repeated Lucia, laughing and kissing me.

'Well, then, should I fuck like fury, too?'

'No, because unless you kept exact time, you might throw him off his stroke. The best way is to raise your hips as much as possible and, so to say, give him your cunt more freely than ever. When you feel him spending, clasp your thighs round him. Press him to your boobies and belly, bite and kiss him, and let him feel that you are as much in heaven as he is, transported to spheres of pleasure.

'There is another thing you might do that is not bad. When you feel him spending, shake him well by alternately and quickly drawing up each foot and thrusting it out straight again. Get on me and I will show you how, darling.'

I got between Lucia's thighs. I pressed my cunnie to hers. I could not resist giving her some strokes with mine. Our mutual fury recommenced, but the roles were altered. At first, Lucia responded to my thrusts by vigorous pushes; at last, she held me tight so that our cunts exactly covered one another and our clitorises were side by side, and then, drawing up one knee, she suddenly straightened it, at the same time drawing up the other and again straightening it.

Then Lucia said, 'Now, Susan darling! Put one leg over each of my shoulders! Ah! That is it! Now I have this sweet little cunt of yours in full view! Lie still, darling, whilst I examine it to my entire satisfaction in all its beautiful detail!'

I lay quiet as a mouse. I felt her arms encircle my thighs, and her hands approach my motte, of which she stroked the long curling bush, and then her fingers, separating and parting the hairs which crossed the soft entrance to my cunnie. It seemed as though Lucia delighted in giving me fresh experience, and each experience brought me fresh pleasure. Presently I felt her thumbs pressing gently so as to open the top of my cunt.

'Oh! The sweet, sweet, little ruby clitoris!' she cried. 'Oh, Susan! You have such a pretty, pretty little tongue here! I really must kiss it!'

I cried out: 'Ah! Lucia! Don't do that, darling! That is not nice!'

'Not nice!' cried she, raising her head, 'do you mean, Susan dearest, that I hurt you, that my kisses there are unpleasant?'

'No, darling, but surely it is not a nice thing to put one's lips on that.'

'Oh,' said she, 'is that all! Darling, I like to do it to you, and I like it done to me, and I strongly suspect when you have had a little more of it you will like it extremely!'

Down went her lascivious mouth on to my cunt again. Really and truly I had liked it there the moment I felt what the sensation was like – I had only cried out because I felt the small stock of modesty I had left repugnant to such an action. However, as Lucia said she liked doing it I did not mind, and lay still.

But only for a moment, for Lucia, having seized my stiff little clitoris between her lips, began to mouth and touch it smartly with her tongue in so ravishing a manner that I could not help crying out with the excessive pleasure she gave me! I did not resist, but I could not lie still! I moved under her devouring mouth, driven half frantic with the sensations of exquisite, almost painful delight she gave me. Lucia seemed prepared for this, for she followed all my movements with skill and patience, whilst her fingers tickled my motte or gently plucked at my curling bush.

Presently she left my clitoris and ran down the line of my cunt with the tip of her tongue. I felt her face press my motte, her hands smoothly passing up my belly until they reached my boobies. They took possession of them; my nipples were sweetly squeezed between her fingers, whilst she felt my breasts with her caressing palms. Her cheeks felt so hot against my thighs they seemed to burn them. But oh! How to express my astonished sensations when I felt her tongue, gathered as it were into a rod, penetrate deep within my cunnie's lips and touch the exquisitely sensitive Straits of Bab-el-Mandeb.

'Lucia! Lucia! For God's sake, don't do it any more! You are killing me with pleasure,' I cried. 'Oh! I'm going to spend! I'm going to spend!' and I felt a flood leave me. It must have inundated Lucia's face, but she only continued her actions, until at last, having spent several times, I actually managed, by drawing my foot up and planting my toes on a delicious elastic breast, to push her away.

Lucia rose with fire flushing from her eyes, her cheeks red with passion, her bosom shining from the moist offerings I had ejected, and seizing me by the thighs, placed me full length on the bed. With her knees she opened mine, spread out my thighs and then commenced a passionate amorous combat, for which in truth I was nothing loath! Our cunts seemed to fit, our clitorises clashed, and seemed to penetrate deeper than they had yet done! I twisted, I wriggled, I fought valiantly, for I was maddened with the almost supernatural excess of voluptuous feelings. At length, prolonged until nature seemed to become exhausted, Lucia lay motionless but panting on my belly, until we had both somewhat recovered our breath. Then, still lying between my thighs, Lucia raised her head and with a look of inexpressible love, kissed me with rapture, gently rubbing her cunt with mine and said: 'There, Susan! I have no more to teach you of the pleasure one girl can take with another!'

18

Teleny

OSCAR WILDE *et al.* 1893

There is a special glee in discovering that an erotic, obscene or pornographic book has been written by or is attributed to an otherwise famous personality. This pleasure goes beyond that found in the tabloid headlines and 'inside journalism' TV shows that daily entertain us with marital infidelities, illegitimate offspring, current bedmates and the sexual peculiarities of our favourite celebrities. Gossip, based on the amount of time people spend reading and listening and talking about it, seems to be the world's favourite pastime. Tell-all autobiographies and scandal-mucking biographies are the order of the day; the public feels somehow cheated if there isn't some illicit sex to be confessed, even in television personality interviews.

Uncovering secret authorship of erotica is in a league different from all this gossip type of intrigue. Its more akin to finding sexy and obscene photos or movies or videos of current celebrities, e.g. the Sylvester Stallone skin-flick, the porno shots of Barbara Payton with Franchot Tone and Tom Neal, the explicit photos of a former Miss America, or the *sans culottes* snaps of Carmen Miranda. Even the unsubstantiated attribution of participation in pornography garners interest. People still wonder if Chuck Connors and Marilyn Monroe really did star in stag films in the 1950s. Gossip entails the thrill of knowing something we shouldn't; this activity is more voyeuristic.

Time was, such secret discoveries were the stuff of scandal, blackmail and social ostracism. Ken Anger's *Hollywood Babylon* documented just this in pre-sexual-revolution America. There is however today a totally different attitude. Many authors freely admit they write sexually explicit material, either by writing it under their real names, or identifying their pseudonyms, as with Anne Rice, who authored the fantasy *S/M Beauty* trilogy under the name of A. N. Roquelaure.

Where once individuals and families and estates would sue for libel in response to the 'accusation' of authorship of an erotic piece, now instead they sue for the royalties! The Henry Miller estate was happy to accept payment to allow in print the Miller attribution to *Opus Pistorum* (a rumour denied by Miller during his lifetime), and currently in Europe the estate of the author of *Bambi* is trying to collect money for editions of *Josefine Mutzenbacher*, a pornographic novel long attributed to Felix Salten.

Which finally brings us to *Teleny*, and its famous supposed author, Oscar Wilde. Since its first publication in 1893 the book has been attributed to this flamboyant *fin-de-siècle* dandy and bon vivant. Famous for his wit, *bon mots*, novels, plays and other writings (e.g. *Salome*, *The Importance of Being Earnest* and *The Portrait of Dorian Gray*), he was equally infamous as the convicted catamite in the Lord Alfred Douglas scandal, which, with his imprisonment in 1895 for homosexual practices, destroyed his health and brilliant career. For all Wilde's acknowledged fame and infamy, there has persisted for nearly a hundred years the secret aside that he wrote the erotic novel *Teleny*.

Teleny, or the Reverse of the Medal: A Phychological Romance of Today is a haunting, disturbing novel of male homosexual love and yearnings. Resident in Paris, the narrator, Camille Des Grieux, the cultured, romantic, neurotic and effete scion of an upper-crust family, falls madly in love with René Teleny, a handsome pianist, currently the rage of the town. The story unfolds in the form of a psychosexual clinical history, elicited by an anonymous, almost phantom, 'over narrator', who, as if a hired psychiatrist, induces Des Grieux to tell his tale, sparing none of the thoughts, emotions and fantasies that attended and fuelled his ill-fated affair. In the course of the novel Des Grieux recalls his formative sexual development – his deep love for his mother, his confused distaste for women, and his early fumbling and failed heterosexual attempts. He recounts the intense lust that seized him on first seeing Teleny, and the emotions that controlled him as he voyeuristically spied on the bisexual artist and finally led him into in a tragic physical relationship that transgressed contemporary Victorian morality.

The writing in *Teleny* is decidedly uneven. Classical, biblical and literary allusions are jumbled together. Parts display a delicate temperament with an almost Beardsleyesque use of language and imagery. Other parts are strong narrative descriptions of heterosexual activity, while others empathetically portray the anguish and repressed yearnings of a tortured homosexual soul screaming for release. Finally there are poignant and violent scenes of homosexual sex. There is an overall air of smothering depression, a florid *ennui* with life. *Teleny* reads very little in the style and language of vintage Oscar Wilde. Why then the persistent attribution?

The true story of *Teleny* and Wilde's participation in its creation has been known in print since 1934, the year there appeared in Paris a French translation of the book, with an introduction by Charles Hirsch. Hirsch was a bookseller in London in the 1890s. Among his customers was Oscar Wilde, who brought around his circle of friends, and also had the bookseller obtain pornographic novels for him from France. One day Wilde left a tied bundle with Hirsch, with instructions that it be given to a man who asked for it and presented Wilde's card. This form of exchange occurred several times, and finally Hirsch examined the contents of the parcel. He discovered a manuscript, written in several different hands, with many corrections and editings, that concerned homosexual love, set in London's artistic circles. The manuscript was picked up one last time, and Hirsch thought nothing more of it until its 1893 publication. What Hirsch found was a text greatly changed from what he remembered. The prologue was missing, and the characters' names and backgrounds were altered, as was the locale from London to Paris! (Years later, one of the secret publishers of the first edition, Leonard Smithers, confessed to making the changes to avoid scandalising his British customers. The co-publisher, H. S. Nichols reissued the same text in 1906 , and it was not until the 1934 French edition, made directly from the still extant original manuscript, that the world could read the story of *Teleny* as the author(s) meant it to be.)

Hirsch, who had visited Wilde's house, wrote that he found several settings in *Teleny* closely matched Wilde's own personal living quarters. Did then Wilde write any of *Teleny*? We know for sure that at least he was the catalyst for its round-robin production, and he may have acted as overall editor to tie together and structure the various episodes into a single novel. Wilde is clearly the model for the character of Teleny. Both were narcissistic artists, Wilde an author, and Teleny (perhaps as a pun) a pianist; both were flamboyant bisexual toasts of society, and both were the objects of mad desire by a confused, younger man. Des Grieux seems based on Wilde's lover Lord Alfred Douglas, who may have written parts of *Teleny* as a declaration of his affections, or as a psychological catharsis, perhaps at the urging of the likes of Havelock Ellis, the great turn-of-the-century sex psychologist (and himself accused of writing *Suburban Souls*, an erotic novel of male masochistic inclination).

Teleny is neither greater nor lesser literature for its author's true identity. It is a genuine testament to human emotion and homosexuality in Victorian England. Here then is a scene in which Des Grieux espies his beloved in the company of a lady and hallucinates about what passes between them.

～ from *Teleny*

'I suffered. My thoughts, night and day, were with him. My brain was always aglow; my blood was overheated; my body ever shivering with excitement. I daily read all the newspapers to see what they said about him; and whenever his name met my eyes, the paper shook in my trembling hands. If anybody mentioned his name, I blushed and then grew pale.

'I remember what a shock of pleasure, not unmingled with jealousy, I felt when for the first time I saw his likeness in a window amongst those of other celebrities. I went and bought it at once, not simply to treasure and dote upon it, but also that other people might not look at it.'

'What! You were so very jealous?'

'Foolishly so. Unseen and at a distance, I used to follow him about after every concert he played.

'Usually he was alone. Once, however, I saw him enter a cab waiting at the back door of the theatre. It had seemed to me as if someone else was within the vehicle – a woman, if I had not been mistaken. I hailed another cab and followed them. Their carriage stopped at Teleny's house. I at once bade my Jehu do the same.

'I saw Teleny alight and offer his hand to a lady, thickly veiled, who tripped out of the carriage and darted into the open doorway. The cab then went off.

'I bade my driver wait there the whole night. At dawn, the carriage of the evening before came and stopped. My driver looked up. A few minutes afterwards the door was again opened. The lady hurried out and was handed into her carriage by her lover. I followed her and stopped where she alighted.

'A few days afterwards I knew who she was.'

'And who was she?'

'She was a lady of an unblemished reputation with whom Teleny had played some duets.

'In the cab that night, my mind was so intently fixed upon Teleny that my inward self seemed to disintegrate itself from my body and to follow like his own shadow the man I loved. I unconsciously threw myself into a kind of trance, and I had a most vivid hallucination, which, strange as it might appear, coincided with all that my friend did and felt.

'For instance, as soon as the door was shut behind them, the lady caught Teleny in her arms and gave him a long kiss. Their entrance would have lasted several seconds more, had Teleny not lost his breath. You smile. Yes, I suppose you yourself are aware how easily people lose their breath in kissing, when the lips do not feel that blissful intoxicating lust in all its intensity. She would have given him another kiss, but Teleny whispered to her: "Let us go up to my room. There we shall be far safer than here."

'Soon they were in his apartment.

'She looked timidly around, and seeing herself in that young man's room alone with him, she blushed ashamedly.

' "Oh! René," said she. "What must you think of me?"

' "That you love me dearly," quoth he. "Do you not?"

' "Yes, indeed. Not wisely, but too well."

'Thereupon, taking off her wrappers, she clasped her lover in her arms, showering her warm kisses on his head, his eyes, his cheeks and then upon his mouth. That mouth I so longed to kiss!

'With lips pressed together, she remained for some time inhaling his breath, and – almost frightened at her boldness – she touched his lips with the tip of her tongue. Then, taking courage, soon afterwards she slipped it in his mouth, and then, after a while, she thrust it in and out, as if she were enticing him to try the act of nature by it. She was so convulsed with lust by this kiss that she had to clasp herself to him in order not to fall, for her knees were almost giving way beneath her. At last, taking his right hand, after squeezing it hesitatingly for a moment, she placed it upon her breasts, giving him her nipple to pinch, and, as he did so, the pleasure she felt was so great that she was swooning away for joy.

' "Oh, Teleny!" said she. "I can't! I can't any more."

'And she rubbed herself against him, protruding her middle parts against his.'

'And Teleny?'

'Well, jealous as I was, I could not help feeling how different his manner was now from the rapturous way with which he had clung to me that evening, when he had taken the bunch of heliotrope from his buttonhole and had put it in mine.

'He accepted rather than returned her caresses. Anyhow, she seemed pleased for she thought him shy.

'She was now hanging on him. Her dainty, bejewelled fingers were playing with his curly hair and patting his neck.

'He was squeezing her breasts and lightly fingering her nipples.

'She gazed deep into his eyes, and then sighed.

' "You do not love me," at last she said. "I can see it in your eyes. You are not thinking of me, but of somebody else."

'And it was true. At that moment he was thinking of me – fondly, longingly. And then, as he did so, he got more excited, and he caught her in his arms and hugged and kissed her with far more eagerness than he had hitherto done – nay, he began to suck her tongue as if it had been mine, and to thrust his own into her mouth.

'After a few moments of rapture, she stopped to take breath. "Yes, I am wrong. You love me. I see it now. You do not despise me because I am here, do you?

' "Ah! If you could only read in my heart and see how madly I love you, darling!"

'And she looked at him with longing, passionate eyes. "Still you think me light, don't you? I am an adulteress!"

'And thereupon she shuddered and hid her face in her hands.

'He looked at her for a moment pitifully; then he took down her hands gently and kissed her.

' "You do not know how I have tried to resist you, but I could not. I am on fire. I cannot help myself" said she, lifting up her head defiantly as if she were facing the whole world. "Here I am. Do with me what you like, only tell me that you love no other woman but me. Swear it!"

' "I swear," said he, languidly, "that I love no other woman."

'She did not understand the meaning of his words.

' "But tell it to me again. Say it often. It is so sweet to hear it repeated," said she with passionate eagerness.

' "I assure you that I have never cared for any woman so much as I do for you."

' "Cared?" said she, disappointed.

' "Loved, I mean."

' "And you can swear it?"

' "On the cross, if you like," added he, smiling.

' "And you do not think badly of me because I am here? Well, you are the only one for whom I have ever been unfaithful to my husband, though God knows if he be faithful to me. Still, my love does not atone for my sin, does it?"

'Teleny did not give her any answer for an instant. He looked at her with dreamy eyes, then shuddered as if awaking from a trance.

' "Sin," he said, "is the only thing worth living for."

'She looked at him, rather astonished, but then she answered: "Well, yes, you are perhaps right. It is so the fruit of the forbidden tree was pleasant to the sight, to the taste and to the smell."

'They sat down on a divan. When they were clasped again in each other's arms, he slipped his hand somewhat timidly and almost unwillingly under her skirt.

'She caught hold of his hand.

' "No, René, I beg of you! Could we not love each other with a platonic love? Is that not enough?"

' "Is it enough for you?" said he, almost superciliously.

'She pressed her lips again upon his and almost relinquished her grasp. The hand went stealthily up but the legs closely pressed together prevented it from slipping between them and thus reaching the higher storey. It crept slowly up, nevertheless, caressing the thighs through the fine linen underclothing and thus, by stolen marches, it reached its aim. The hand then slipped between the opening of the drawers and began to feel the soft skin. She tried to stop him.

' "No, no!" said she "Please, don't! You are tickling me!"

'He then took courage and plunged his fingers boldly into the fine curly locks of the fleece that covered all her middle parts.

'She continued to hold her thighs tightly closed together, especially when the naughty fingers began to graze the edge of the moist lips. At that touch, however, her strength gave way The nerves relaxed and allowed the tip of a finger to worm its way within the slit – nay, the tiny berry protruded out to welcome it.

'After a few moments she breathed more strongly. She encircled his breast with her arms, kissed him and then hid her head on his shoulder. "Oh, what a rapture I feel!" she cried. "What a magnetic fluid you possess to make me feel as I do!"

'He did not give her any answer. Unbuttoning his trousers, he took hold of her dainty little hand, introducing it within the gap. She soon boldly caught hold of his phallus, now stiff and hard, moving lustily by its own inward strength.

'After a few moments of pleasant manipulation, their lips pressed together, he lightly pressed her down on the couch and pulled up her skirt, without for a moment taking his tongue out of her mouth or stopping his tickling of her tingling clitoris, already wet with its own tears. Then he got his legs between her thighs. That her excitement

THE ENCYCLOPEDIA OF EROTIC LITERATURE

increased could be plainly seen by the shivering of the lips, which parted of themselves to give entrance to the little blind god of love.

'With one thrust he introduced himself within the precincts of love's temple; with another, the rod was halfway in; with the third, he reached the very bottom of the den of pleasure. Her flesh was not only firm but she was so tight that he was fairly clasped and sucked by those pulpy lips.

'After a few seconds of this, he began to breathe strongly – to pant. The milky fluid that had for days accumulated itself now rushed out in thick jets, coursing into her very womb. She showed her hysteric enjoyment by her screams, her tears, her sighs. Finally, all strength gave way; arms and legs stiffened themselves; she fell lifeless on the couch.

'He soon recovered his strength and rose. She was then recalled to her senses but only to melt into a flood of tears.

'A bumper of champagne brought them both, however, to a less gloomy sense of life. A few partridge sandwiches, some lobster patties, a caviar salad with a few more glasses of champagne, together with many marrons glacés and a punch made of maraschino, pineapple juice and whisky, drunk out of the same goblet, soon dispelled their gloominess.

' "Why should we not put ourselves at our ease, my dear?" said he. "I'll set you the example, shall I?"

' "By all means."

'Thereupon Teleny took off his white tie, that uncomfortable useless appendage invented to torture mankind, and then his coat and waist-coat, and he remained only in his shirt and trousers.

' "Now, my dear, allow me to act as your maid."

'The beautiful woman at first refused, but yielded after some kisses, and, little by little, nothing was left of all her clothing but an almost transparent *crêpe de Chine* chemise, dark steel-blue silk stockings, and satin slippers.

'Teleny covered her bare neck and arms with kisses. This little titillation was felt all over her body, and the slit between her legs opened again in such a way that the delicate little clitoris, like a red hawthorn berry, peeped out as if to see what was going on. He held her for a moment crushed against his chest, and his *merle* – as the Italians call it – flying out of his cage, he thrust it into the opening ready to receive it. He stretched her out on the panther rug at his feet, without unclasping her.

'All sense of shyness was now overcome. He pulled off his clothes and pressed down with all his strength. She – to receive his instrument far deep in her sheath – clasped him with her legs so that he could hardly move. He was, therefore, only able to rub himself against her, but that was more than enough, for after a few violent shakes of their buttocks, legs pressed and breasts crushed, the burning liquid which he injected within her body gave her a spasmodic pleasure, and she fell senseless on the panther skin whilst he rolled off of her and lay motionless by her side.

'Till then, I felt that my image had always been present before his eyes although he was enjoying this handsome woman, but now the pleasure she had given him had made him quite forget me. I therefore hated him.

'What right had he to love anybody but myself? Did I love a single being in this world as I loved him? Could I feel pleasure with anyone else?

'No, my love was not a maudlin sentimentality. It was the maddening passion that overpowers the body and shatters the brain! If he could love women, why did he then make love to me, obliging me to love him, making me a contemptible being in my own eyes?

'In the paroxysm of my excitement I writhed. I dug my nails into my flesh; I cried out with jealousy and shame.

'This state of things lasted for a few moments, and then I began to wonder what he was doing, and the fit of hallucination came over me again. I saw him awakening from the slumber into which he had fallen when overpowered by enjoyment.

'As he awoke, he looked at her. Now I was able to see her plainly, for I believe that she was only visible to me through his medium.'

'But you fell asleep and dreamt all this whilst you were in the cab, did you not?'

'Oh, no! All happened as I am telling you. I related my whole vision to him some time afterwards, and he acknowledged that everything had occurred exactly as I had seen it.'

'But how could this be?'

'There was, as I told you before, a strong transmission of thoughts between us. This is by no means a remarkable coincidence. You smile and look incredulous. Well, follow the doings of the Psychical Society, and this vision will certainly not astonish you any more.'

'Well, never mind. Go on.'

'As Teleny awoke, he looked at his mistress lying at his side.

'She was as sound asleep as anyone would be after a banquet, intoxicated by strong drink. It was the heavy sleep of lusty life.

'The breasts – as if swollen with milk – stood up, and the erect nipples seemed to be asking for those caresses she was so fond of, over all her body there was a shivering of insatiable desire.

'Her thighs were bare, and the thick curly hair that covered her middle parts, as black as jet, was sprinkled over with pearly drops of milky dew.

'Such a sight would have awakened an eager, irrepressible desire in Joseph himself, the only chaste Israelite of whom we have ever heard, and yet Teleny, leaning on his elbow, was gazing at her with all the loathing we feel when we look at a kitchen table covered with the offal of the meat, the hashed scraps, the dregs of the wines which have supplied the banquet that has just glutted us.

'I felt again that he did not love her, but me, though she had made him for a few moments forget me.

'She seemed to feel his cold glances upon her, for she shivered and thinking she was asleep in bed, she tried to cover herself up, and her hand, fumbling for the sheet, pulled up her chemise, only uncovering herself more by that action. She woke as she did so, and caught Teleny's reproachful glances.

'She looked around, frightened. She tried to cover herself as much as she could and then, entwining one of her arms round the young man's neck –

' "Do not look at me like that," she said. "Am I so loathsome to you? Oh! I see it. You despise me." And her eyes filled with tears. "You are right. Why did I yield? Why did I not resist the love that was torturing me? Alas! It was I who sought you, who made love to you, and now you feel for me nothing but disgust. Tell me, is it so? You love another woman! No! Tell me you don't!"

' "I don't," said Teleny, earnestly.

' "Yes, but swear."

' "I have already sworn before, or at least offered to do so. What is the use of swearing if you don't believe me?"

'Though all lust was gone, Teleny felt a heartfelt pity for that handsome young woman, who, maddened by love for him, had put into jeopardy her whole existence to throw herself into his arms.

'Who is the man that is not flattered by the love he inspires in a high-born, wealthy and handsome young woman who forgets her marriage to enjoy a few moments' bliss in his arms? But then, why do women love men who care so little for them?

'Teleny did his best to comfort her, to tell her over and over again that he cared for no other woman, to assure her that he would be eternally faithful to her for her sacrifice, but pity is not love, nor is affection the eagerness of desire.

'Nature was more than satisfied; her beauty had lost all its attraction. They kissed again and again. He languidly passed his hands all over her body, from the nape of the neck to the deep dent between those round hills that seemed covered with fallen snow, giving her a most delightful sensation as he did so. He caressed her breasts, suckled and bit the tiny protruding nipples, whilst his fingers were often thrust far within the warm flesh hidden under that mass of jet-black hair. She glowed, she breathed, she shivered with pleasure, but Teleny, though performing his work with masterly skill, remained cold at her side.

' "No, I see that you don't love me, for it is not possible that you – a young man . . . "

'She did not finish. Teleny felt the sting of her reproaches but remained passive, for the phallus is not stiffened by taunts.

'She took the lifeless object in her delicate fingers. She rubbed and manipulated it She even rolled it between her two soft hands. It remained like a piece of dough. She sighed as piteously as Ovid's mistress must have done on a like occasion. She did like this woman did some hundreds of years before. She bent down and took the tip of that inert piece of flesh between her lips – the pulpy lips which looked like a tiny apricot, so round, sappy and luscious. Soon it was all in her mouth, and she sucked it with much evident pleasure. As it went in and out, she tickled the prepuce with her expert tongue.

'The phallus though somewhat harder, remained limp and nerveless.

'You know, our ignorant forefathers believed in the practice called *nouer les aiguillettes* – that is, rendering the male incapable of performing the pleasant work for which nature has destined him. We, the enlightened generation, have discarded such gross superstitions, and still our ignorant forefathers were sometimes right.'

'What! You do not mean to say that you believe in such tomfoolery?'

'It might be tomfoolery, as you say, but still it is a fact. Hypnotise a person and then you will see if you can get the mastery over him or not.'

'Still, you had not hypnotised Teleny?'

'No, but our natures seemed to be bound to one another by a secret affinity.

'At that moment I felt a secret shame for Teleny. Not being able to understand the working of his brain, she seemed to regard him in the light of a young cock that, having crowed lustily once or twice at early dawn, has strained his neck to such a pitch that he can only emit hoarse, feeble, gurgling sounds out of it after that.

'Moreover I almost felt sorry for that woman, and I thought if I were only in her place, how disappointed I should be. And I sighed, repeating almost audibly: "Were I but in her stead."

'The image which had formed itself within my mind so vividly was all at once reverberated within René's brain, and he thought if instead of this lady's mouth, those lips were my lips. And his phallus at once stiffened and awoke into life. The glands swelled with blood. Not only an erection took place, but it almost ejaculated. The countess – for she was a countess – was herself surprised at this sudden change, and stopped, for she had now obtained what she wanted.

'Teleny, however, began to fear that if he had his mistress's face before his eyes my image might entirely vanish and that – beautiful as she was – he would never be able to accomplish his work to the end. So he began by covering her with kisses; then deftly turned her over. She yielded without understanding what was required of her. He bent her pliant body on her knees, so that she presented a most beautiful sight to his view.

'This splendid sight ravished him to such an extent that his hitherto limp tool acquired its full size and stiffness and in its lusty vigour leapt in such a way that it knocked against his navel. Placing himself between her legs, he tried to introduce the glans within the aperture of her two lips, now thick and swollen by dint of much rubbing.

'Wide apart as her legs were he first had to open the lips with his fingers on account of the mass of bushy hair that grew all around them, for now the tiny curls had entangled themselves together like tendrils, as if to bar the entrance. Therefore, when he had brushed the hair aside, he pressed his tool in it but the turgid dry flesh arrested him. The clitoris thus pressed, danced with delight so that he took it in his hand and rubbed and shook it softly and gently on the top part of her lips.

'She began to shake and to rub herself with delight. She groaned she sobbed hysterically and when he felt himself bathed with delicious tears he thrust his instrument far within her body clasping her tightly around the neck. So after a few bold strokes, he managed to get in the whole of the rod down to the very root of the column, crushing his hair against hers, so that far in the utmost recesses of the vagina it gave her a pleasurable pain as it touched the neck of the womb.

'For about ten minutes – which to her felt like an eternity – she continued panting, throbbing, gasping, groaning, shrieking, roaring, laughing, and crying in the vehemence of her delight.

' "Oh! Oh! I am feeling it again! In – in – quick – quicker! There! There! – Enough! – Stop!"

'But he did not listen to her and he went on plunging and replunging with increasing vigour. Having vainly begged for a truce she began to move again with renewed life.

'Having her from behind, his whole thoughts were thus concentrated upon me, and the tightness of the orifice in which the penis was sheathed added to the titillation produced by the lips of the womb, which gave him such an overpowering sensation that he redoubled his strength and shoved his instrument with such mighty strokes that the frail woman shook under the repeated thumps. Her knees were almost giving way under the force he displayed, when again, all at once, the floodgates of the seminal ducts were opened, and he squirted a jet of molten liquid into the innermost recesses of her womb.

'A moment of delirium followed. The contraction of her muscles gripped him and sucked him up eagerly, greedily, and after a short spasmodic convulsion, they both fell senseless side by side, still tightly wedged together.

'And so it ended.'

19

Lascivious Scenes in the Convent
1898

Lascivious Scenes in the Convent is one of the most competently written volumes of Victorian erotica. It is also one of the most sophisticated and sexually stimulating books ever to appear. It would certainly have been hailed a classic, in the ranks of *The Romance of Lust*, *The Pearl*, *My Secret Life*, *The Autobiography of a Flea* and *Pauline*, were it not for one detail. From the time of its first publication, this book has been almost entirely unknown. It is listed in none of the major bibliographies, and no copy is known to exist in any library open to the public. It is certainly one of the rarest of all volumes of erotica, even more so than the fantastic *My Secret Life* (two sets being in public collections). The reason for this rarity is itself a product of the Victorian–Edwardian era that saw the first appearance of this novel in 1898.

At the turn of the century, popular literature had already come into its own with the advent of cheap methods of printing. The penny magazines hawked on the street corners in the first half of the nineteenth century had given way to popularly priced editions of classic and contemporary works in all genres. All genres that is except erotica, which was still seventy years away from such democratic availability. The suppression of sexually explicit literature caused it to be produced only in secret, clandestine and very limited editions. Perhaps a few hundred copies of a work could be printed. The costs of such a small print run drove the price of erotica beyond the reach of the general public. A single volume might cost more than an average worker's monthly wages! Only the wealthy and politically powerful could afford such books, and also not fear censorship or legal action against themselves.

Lascivious Scenes in the Convent was published in an even more restricted fashion than other erotic works of the time. The title page of the book indicates it to be the product of an exclusive organisation in Brussels, the Société des Beaux Esprits (the Society of Fine Senses). English-language erotica was often printed in non-English-speaking countries to lessen the chances of the police understanding the text and arresting the publishers and printers. This particular novel was printed in only thirty-five copies, exclusively for members of the society. No expense was spared in its production. The edition was deluxe, printed from hand-set type, on large handmade paper, in two colours of ink throughout. Who the members of the society were, or where the few copies of the book went, are unknown. It was only by good fortune that a single copy of the work (to that time never reprinted) was found to exist in a private library, overlooked and lost to the world for decades.

What then is the nature of this *rara avis*? The plot is direct. Tasso, a handsome young gardener, seeks employment. The only available job, though, is in a Catholic convent populated by an attractive Mother Abbess and several beautiful and impressionable novices. Realising that his good looks would ordinarily disqualify him from such employ, Tasso pretends to be deaf and mute, and by so doing gains the job. Once within the confines of the cloister, he is unable to conceal his virile disposition, and soon becomes the object of the novices' admiration and lustful thoughts. He is seduced – without any difficulty! – by two of the young nuns, who enjoy his manhood first separately and then together. The three are discovered in the sexual act by the other sisters, who wishing the same carnal delights, volunteer their bodies and souls to this pursuit. During one bout of intercourse Tasso shouts out at the moment of climax, and the young nuns believe they have witnessed a miraculous restoration of the gardener's long lost faculties. This news is brought to the attention of the Mother Abbess, a notorious lesbian and female libertine, who is not so naïve as her charges. She organises a suitable celebration for this 'miracle', an orgy! Fearing that the sexual demands being made upon his body will soon kill him, the exhausted gardener takes his leave of the convent, and deprived of their new found ecstasies, the sisters follow suit.

Many readers will recognise this plot as coming from *The Decameron* of Boccaccio, written in Italian in the fourteenth century. (The exact story is 'Masetto and the Nuns', told in Novel One of Day Three.) *Lascivious Scenes in the Convent* is not simply an academic English translation of this classic ribald tale. Boccaccio's original was a few short pages, and while free in nature, was delicate in language. Not so this present work. Here is a full-length novel, distinguished by its masterful use of Victorian sexual slang, as well as its explicit erotic descriptions, and strong anti-clerical feelings.

The latter is hardly unique in English literature, or the works of other European countries. Since the founding of the Church, anti-clerical diatribes and treatises have been common. (One need only think of Chaucer's fourteenth-century *Canterbury Tales*, where the clergy is enjoined to maintain their vows of morality, for if gold – the clergy – were to rust, then what would iron – the common folk – do?)Real or supposed scandals, as well as religious sexual misconduct, have often been the grist of popular pulp reading. Perhaps the most successful of these was the 1836 *Awful Disclosures of Maria Monk*, by the Reverend Slocum. Erotic literature abounds with this anti-clerical theme also. A few examples from the past centuries include: *Thérèse Philosophe* (French, c.1748, recounting the 1731 scandal involving Father Girard), *The Autobiography of a Flea* (English 1887), *Nunnery Tales* (translated from the French c.1866), *Schwester Monika* (German c.1815), and *The Adventures of Father Silas* (English translation c.1890 of the c.1748 French original). All these used clerical immorality as a focus for erotic stimulation.

Lascivious Scenes in the Convent is more than a simple religious attack. It is a well-written erotic novel. The language is frank to the fullest; the entire gamut of four-letter Anglo-Saxonisms is employed, but not as a string of increasingly boring obscenities. The author is a craftsman. The narrative is brisk. The sexual action develops, builds and climaxes. The sexual activities evolve and permutate as the naïve characters gain experience, and exercise previously unused libidinous facets of their nature.

The anti-clerical aspects of this book are not easy to dismiss. They are present for a specific purpose. The author uses the respites between the acts of intercourse to allow the novices to tell their individual tales of sexual development, initiation and abuse at the hands of their religious leaders. Here are innocents who have been seduced by confessors and lecherous older nuns who have used the authority of the Church to subject impressionable girls to their own perverse sexual pleasures. If the novel is shocking, it is so in the revelation of the sexual exploitation of the naïve by morally corrupt clergy. (It is no wonder that in the insulated world of a convent, the atmosphere of suppressed natural desires tends to lead to epidemic outbreaks of sexual perversion, such as lesbianism, voyeurism, flagellation, rape, and sodomy. One of the most infamous such examples was the French nuns of Loudon case of 1634, vividly brought to the cinema screen in 1971 by Ken Russell as *The Devils*.)

Our author though is a humanist and, despite all, an optimist. For him it is not the Church that is held to blame, but rather the humans who misuse its cloak of piety. *Lascivious Scenes in the Convent* uses its anti-clericism in an attempt to educate and enlighten, literally and symbolically. After all, in juxtaposition, the entire Victorian Age was a secular attempt to suppress the free expression of mind and body. The saving grace against the totalitarianism, then as now, was sexual curiosity, one of the strongest and most basic of all the natural human instincts. This then is the catalyst and insurance that even those oppressed by their accepted and elected leaders will still have the opportunity to exercise the full capacities of their psychology and physiology. George Orwell wrote of this same condition in his classic novel *Nineteen Eighty-Four*. What could be more heartening for this or any time, than the realisation that sexual ecstasy may be the best safeguard for liberty, democracy and freedom?

◁◁◁ from *Lascivious Scenes in the Convent*

Tasso's great hope was that the two sisters would return to their seats and favour him a little more by their delightful conversation. Nor was he disappointed. The sisters quickly reappeared and, bringing with them their embroidery, sat down in the seats they had occupied before.

Tasso was conscious that they now regarded him with peculiar interest, and that their eyes looked as if they were trying to penetrate that portion of his attire just below the belt. He therefore pushed it out and made it as prominent as he could.

Lucia was speaking: 'Well, Robina, you certainly had a grand success! How I envy you! It must have been delightful to watch him, when he thought he was all alone, first piddling and then actually playing with his thing! But tell me, like a good dear, exactly what it was like: its size, its colour and, above all, tell me its shape.'

'You must try and see it yourself, my dear,' replied Robina, 'for it is not an easy thing to describe. It seemed about eight inches long and nearly as thick as your wrist, but quite round. It was covered with a soft, white skin which slipped easily up and down. When he pulled this skin back, the top stood up like a large, round head, shelving to a point. But it was its purplish-red colour that attracted me most. My dear, it had a most wonderful effect on myself. My hairy slit began to thrill and throb in such a way that, for the life of me, I could not help pulling up my dress and rubbing it with my hand. And it grew hotter and hotter, until a warm flow came and gave me relief.'

'What a delightful time you must have had, Robina,' commented Lucia. 'Do you know, your telling me all this has made mine frightfully hot too?' And she twisted about, rubbing her bottom on the seat. 'How I wish Tasso were not watching us. I would ask you to put your kind hand on my slit and afford me a little of the same pleasure.'

Robina laughed. 'I fancy he's not thinking of us at all. He is too dull to have any notions of that kind. Stand up, dear, as if you were pulling some buds from the branch overhanging us, and I will slip my hand up from behind so that he can see nothing. Now, do you like that, dear?'

'Oh! Your fingers are giving me great pleasure!' replied the excited Lucia. 'There! That's the place! Push it up! Oh! Wouldn't it be nice to have Tasso's delightful thing poking me there! You said, Robina, that that was nature's intention, and that the mutual touch of our differently formed parts gives the greatest satisfaction. What fools we were to give it up!'

'What a child you are, Lucia! The holy fathers will teach you that you may enjoy it now more than ever, and without doing anything wrong either. Only, they will tell you it must be done with them alone.'

'Now! Oh! Now, Robina! Push your finger up! As far as you can! How I long for Tasso's dear thing! . . . Oh! . . . Oh! That will do!'

She sat down and leaned her head against Robina for support.

It will be easily understood what an overpowering effect this scene had on poor Tasso. His sturdy prick, glowing with youthful vigour, seemed to be trying to break its covering and burst into open view.

The unsuspecting talk of the two sisters almost maddened him. He felt that if he could only present his 'dear thing', as they called it, openly before them, he might obtain from one or the other, or perhaps from both, the sweet favour he desired.

In this mood he gradually moved closer to them, and slyly unbuttoned his clothes down the front.

He restrained himself, however, so that he might learn something more from the sisters, who went on talking.

'But Robina, what shall we do about confessing this touching of ourselves and one another to the priests? If we conceal it, our confession is incomplete and sinful, as they tell us we ought to make a full avowal of all our shortcomings and faults. You know how they are always urging this upon us as a sacred duty. And if we give him the slightest hint, Father Joachim will be sure to worm out from us all about Tasso, and that might cause him to be sent away. We too may be separated, and not allowed to walk with one another.'

'Quite true, Lucia. We must do all we can to guard against these two evils. And there really is no way but to keep the whole matter a secret between ourselves. I, for my part, won't let that press upon my conscience, as I now know that there is so much humbug and deceit about the confessional that I have no faith in it as a religious duty at all.'

'I am with you again, Robina,' replied Lucia. 'It would be an awful wrong to injure poor Tasso, who is quite innocent; and if you and I were separated . . . why I should die.'

Tasso was greatly pleased at hearing this, for his mind was now satisfied that so far as these two sisters were concerned, he had no cause to dread exposure and its certain consequences.

'Well, Lucia dear, we'll try to prevent that, at all cost. We shall have to go to the priest, but we must carefully avoid all reference to anyone but ourselves. It will be great fun, I am sure, to confess our looking at and petting our own slits. We can tell him our dreams also. That will sufficiently please him, and perhaps draw him on to commit himself with us, and then he will have to keep quiet for his own sake.'

At this thought they both laughed.

Just then, a little accident happened to Tasso which gave a sudden turn to their conversation. As he was bending at his work, his foot slipped, and he rolled over on his back. This motion, in the most natural way, set his prick free, and it started out, very stiff and inflamed.

He quickly jumped up and, looking at his naked prick with stupid amazement, began to utter uncouth sounds, like an ordinary donkey: 'Hoo! Awe!' And he made some ineffectual attempts to push it back into its place.

'There, Lucia!' cried Robina. 'Your wish is granted. This poor, simple fellow has accidentally given you the view for which you were longing. Don't you admire it?'

'Yes! But what should we do, Robina, if any of the sisters were to come by? What a hubbub there would be! But see! I declare, he can't get it back in.'

'Well, go and help him, Lucia. Make haste, and I will keep a lookout.'

Lucia's eyes were intently fastened on the interesting object. Her face flushed, and she looked extremely excited. She had no time, however, for reflection. So she jumped up, as her friend advised, went to Tasso, and tried to help to get his rebellious tool back into its hiding place.

Taking advantage of his apparent simplicity, and wishing to expedite matters, she took hold of his prick with her hand.

How the touch of that piece of animated flesh thrilled her! It felt so warm and soft, yet so firm and strong! She could neither bend it nor push it back.

'Oh, dear! Oh, dear! What shall I do, Robina? It won't go back for me!'

Robina laughed until the tears ran down her cheeks.

'Bring him into the summerhouse,' she replied.

This happened to be conveniently near, and was well screened by bushes. With a smile Lucia pointed it out to Tasso and, still holding his prick, gently drew him on.

Tasso, putting on a most innocent look, went readily with her, and Robina followed in the rear.

As they entered the leafy shade, she said: 'Now, Lucia, you have him all to yourself. If you don't succeed in getting him to do everything you want, you are a less clever girl than I take you to be. If all else fails, just show him your mossy nest, and that will draw him as surely as a magnet attracts iron. Meantime I'll keep a sharp lookout here at the door.'

But in very truth, Tasso did not need much drawing. His prick was throbbing with desire. It was fairly burning to get into the folds of her soft recess.

She led him on until she backed against the inner seat. Then she sat down, and he remained standing before her. In this position his prick was now close to her face. She rubbed it softly between her hands, and then kissed its glowing head. She moved it over her nose and cheeks, sniffing with delight the peculiar odour which it exhaled.

Every time she brought it to her lips, Tasso pushed it gently against her mouth. Her lips gradually opened, and the prick seemed to pop in of its own accord. He felt her pliant tongue playing over its head, and twining round its indented neck. The sensation was so delicious that he could not help uttering a deep guttural 'Ugh!' and pressing up against her.

Bending over her, he quickly drew up her robes and lifted her legs in such a way as to expose the whole of her beautiful bottom, and give him a full view of her delicious love chink, surrounded with luxuriant hair. Oh, how it seemed to pout out with a most unspeakable delight! He took his prick in his hand and rubbed its glowing head between the soft, moist lips.

This action proved just as pleasant to her as it was to him. She pushed upwards to meet him, and called to her friend: 'Look, Robina! There has been no failure – he's just going to do it. Pity you could not come and watch it going in! Oh! It does feel nice! Oh! So nice!'

'Ha! Ha! My dear,' laughed Robina, 'you will have to suffer a little before you know how really nice it is!'

Tasso now began to push in earnest, and Lucia winced not a little as she felt the sharp pain, caused by the head of his huge prick forcing its way through the tight embrace of her vagina, for she was a true virgin, and her hymen had never been ruptured. However, she bore it bravely, especially as she knew her friend was watching.

'Robina,' she called, to show her indifference to the pain, 'I wish you would go behind and give him a shove, to make him push harder.'

But just as she spoke, the obstructing hymen suddenly gave way, and his fine prick rushed up and filled all the inside of her cunt, and his hard balls flapped up against her bottom.

'Ah!' she cried, as she felt the inward rush of the vigorous tool. 'Now it's all over! He's got it all in! Well, it wasn't so bad after all. And now it feels delicious! How nicely he makes it move in and out. Can you see it, Robina?' she asked, as she noticed her friend stooping behind Tasso and looking up between his legs.

'Yes, dear Lucia. I see your pretty slit sucking in his big tool, and I feel his two balls gathered up tightly in their bag. He certainly is no fool at this kind of work. I am sure he is just going to spurt his seed into you . . . There! Tell me, do you like it?'

'Oh! Yes! It feels grand! He's shedding such a lot into me! And more is coming too! It is the nicest thing I have ever felt!'

And throwing her arms about him, she hugged him with all her might.

Presently he drew his prick out of her warm sheath. It was slightly tinged with blood – the token of his victory. Robina carefully wiped it with her handkerchief and coaxed him to sit down between them on the seat. Then they made signs to him to produce his slate.

Lucia wrote: 'Dear Tasso. I greatly enjoyed what you did to me. Have you any name for it, that I may know what to ask for when I want it again?'

He smiled when he read the question, and then wrote a reply: 'It is called fucking.'

Then he handed her the slate.

'Doing this is called fucking,' she said to Robina.

Then pointing to his prick, which was beginning to stand again, in all the pride of youthful vigour, she wrote: 'What is the name of this?'

'It is called a prick and yours is a cunt,' he wrote, 'and they are made for one another.'

Lucia laughed when she read it.

'Why, Robina,' she cried, 'we are getting a grand lesson. His thing is a prick and our slits are cunts; but he need not have told us that they are made for one another, for all the world knows that. What a pity he can't talk! I would so much like to hear him speak of his prick and our cunts. But it is well that he can write about them.'

Then she took the slate and wrote: 'Your prick is getting quite large and stiff again. Would you like to fuck Sister Robina?'

Tasso grinned.

'Do you know what I have just written?' said Lucia, turning to Robina. 'I have asked him if he would like to fuck you.'

'Oh, you horrid girl!' retorted Robina.

'Of course he will say he would. Men always love a change of cunts. I suppose we must use that word now when talking to each other.'

Tasso's delight was almost uncontrollable. He longed to use his tongue and to give audible expression to his joy, but that would have spoiled everything. So he resolved to persevere with his role, and wrote: 'If Sister Robina will follow your kind example, and grant me the same favour, it will call forth the everlasting gratitude of poor, dumb Tasso.'

'Why, he has written quite a nice little speech, Robina,' said Lucia, handing her the slate.

'He writes a fairly good hand too,' Robina remarked with a smile; and then, handing back the slate, said, 'Tell him to stand up and let me kiss his prick as you did.'

Lucia wrote accordingly: 'Stand up, Tasso, and let her kiss your prick first, and then you can fuck her cunt just as much as you like.' She handed over the slate.

Tasso at once complied. He stood before Robina and pushed between her knees so as to place his prick more conveniently for her eager inspection and caresses.

Taking it tenderly in her hands, she felt it all over, as if measuring its size and ability to give pleasure. Then she turned her attention to the heavy bags which held his large stones, and pushed her fingers back even as far as the aperture behind.

Tasso repaid the caresses she gave him by bending to one side and thrusting his hand up between her warm thighs. He grasped the fat lips of her cunt and rubbed the hot clitoris which jutted out between them. Then, as they both became eager for the sweet consummation to which these thrilling touches invariably led, he gently pushed her back. She yielded readily enough, for her cunt was already moist with the expectation of taking in the delicious morsel she held in her hands. She allowed him to uncover all her hidden charms, and spread her thighs to their utmost extent. But just as she felt him inserting his fiery tool, she called to Lucia, who, though standing at the door, was intently watching Tasso's interesting operation.

'Dear Lucia, keep a strict watch! It would be an awful thing if anyone caught us here!'

'Don't be afraid,' replied Lucia, 'I'll keep a good lookout. There's no one about now, and I only take a peep now and then to see how you and Tasso are enjoying yourselves. I love to watch you. I was just thinking that next to being fucked oneself, there is nothing like watching another going through it.'

She hungrily watched the action inside and then continued her banter. 'I never saw your cunt look so well as it did just now, when Tasso opened the lips and rubbed the head of his prick inside the rosy folds. And now he has got it all in. It is most delightful to watch it slipping in and out. But how is it that he does not seem to hurt you as he did me? For I notice that he got in quite easily, and you kept hugging him closely all the time! Oh, how nice it must have felt!'

As she said this Lucia pressed her hands between her own legs, and jerked her bottom backwards and forwards.

'My, how you talk, Lucia! But anyway, keep a good lookout, and you may watch me between times. I don't mind your seeing how much we are enjoying ourselves. Poor Tasso can't hear me, or I would tell him how well pleased I am. I am sure the squeezing of my cunt is making him feel that already.'

She breathed heavily and heaved her bottom up convulsively to meet his rapid thrusts.

'You might put your hand on us now, Lucia, if you like. He's just finishing. Oh, it's grand!'

All her muscles relaxed as she reclined back, and Tasso lay panting on her belly.

Lucia sat down by them and leaned over Tasso, squeezing her thighs together, for she felt her own fount of pleasure in flow.

After a moment's rest, Tasso got up, shook himself and, having arranged his clothes, wrote on his slate: 'Dear kind ladies: You have made poor, dumb Tasso very happy. Let me now thank you and return to my work, lest any harm should happen.'

He then bowed himself out, and disappeared among the laurels.

The two young nuns succeeded in having a pleasant meeting with

Tasso not only that evening, but on some of the following days as well. They several times enjoyed with him their favourite sport.

As they had done their utmost to avoid attracting observation, they thought that their friendly intercourse with Tasso had escaped the notice of everyone. But as is usually the case in such matters, they were very much mistaken.

The sisters were not permitted to form special friendships; yet when they enjoyed any freedom together, they naturally fell into pairs or sets.

Two other nuns, named Aminda and Pampinea, had similar tastes and usually walked together.

They observed the intimacy which had sprung up between Sisters Lucia and Robina and the gardener; and feeling certain that there was something in the wind, they watched him closely.

So it was arranged that Pampinea was to hide among the thick bushes by the side of the summerhouse one evening, to watch and report to her friend all that she could find out.

At their next meeting, Aminda at once asked: 'Well, Pampinea dear, what news have you?'

'Most wonderful, beyond our wildest imagination. Frightful in one sense, delightful in another. I must begin at the very beginning.'

'Yes, dear, do.'

'I found a capital hiding place, where I was quite concealed, and yet, by drawing aside a branch, I could see right into the summerhouse. Shortly afterwards, the two sisters, looking as innocent as a pair of doves, came and sat down. And as soon as all the others had left the garden, Tasso marched in with a broad grin upon his face. They smiled at him and let him place them as he liked. Without losing a moment, he had them both kneeling on the seat with their ends turned out. Then he whipped up their petticoats and uncovered to view their large, white bottoms.

'Then, my dear, he took out his big, red . . . "what-you-call-it".

'I was horrified at first, and felt ready to sink into the ground with shame, but it is odd how soon one gets accustomed to these things!

'I could not keep my eyes off it. I wondered at its size and its great, red head. Well, my dear, he pushed it first up against the bottom of one, and then of the other.

'They had no feeling of modesty at all, for they poked themselves out and spread their legs apart, so as to let him see all they had – their cute little bottom holes, hairy slits and everything.

'He rubbed their bottoms with his tool, and then pushed it all into Lucia's slit. She seemed to like it well, for she laughed as she felt it going in. But she did not hold it long, for he quickly pulled it out and shoved it into Robina in the same way.

'Then when he had given her a similar prod, he went back to Lucia, and so on from one to the other.

'All the time they were thus engaged, they continued laughing and talking to one another; and, my dear, you would hardly credit the words they used. They said that Tasso had fucked them that way before, but they thought it very pleasant. They said they liked to feel his hairy belly rubbing against their bottoms and that his prick seemed to get even further into their cunts than ever before. Tell me, did you ever hear such words?'

'I did. I remember hearing them when I was a girl at school. They are coarse words, and perhaps for that very reason all the more exciting. So go on, and use them as much as you please. Your description is very amusing – and, do you know, it is causing me a peculiarly pleasant feeling in my cunt? You see, I use those words too. Would you mind putting your hand on it, dear, while you are describing what followed?'

'Not in the least. I shall quite enjoy it, and you can do the same for me, for my cunt too is burning with heat. And I have had to pet it. Twice I witnessed the wonderful enjoyment which both Lucia and Robina showed, when they had Tasso's prick poking their cunts.'

Then the two nuns, in very un-nunlike fashion, managed to get their hands on the other's cunt as Pampinea went on: 'After changing several times, I noticed that Tasso's prick looked larger and redder each time it came out. He plunged it with great force into Sister Lucia; his belly smacked against her bottom. Robina stood up and, pushing her hands between them, began fiddling with his stones and Lucia's arse.

'After a couple of minutes or so he drew out his prick, now all soft and hanging down, and some kind of white stuff dripping from it. Lucia then turned about and sat down, and had Tasso sit on the seat beside her, while Robina knelt on the ground before them, between Tasso's legs.

'Lucia put her hand on his balls and Robina took hold of his prick. And, my dear, she put it into her mouth, wet as it was.

'Lucia laughed: "Ah, Robina, you are like me – I love to taste the flavour of your cunt and now I hope you won't find that the flavour of mine is disagreeable."

'Robina lifted her head, and said: "Not in the least. I like the salty taste, and the smell is delicious."

'Then she recommenced her sucking, while Lucia's fingers played about the root of the prick, occasionally touching the chin and lips of her friend.

'Tasso's prick grew stronger, until its head seemed too large for Robina's mouth to take it all in. Lucia remarked its size and said: "I think, Robina, that you have sucked Tasso's prick into working order again. What would you think of getting him to lie down there on his back, and then for you to straddle over him, place his prick in your cunt with your own hand? I will help you if you like."

' "Capital notion! Let us at once put it into execution, for our time is nearly up."

'They both stood up and soon had Tasso on his back on the ground. Then Robina, tucking up her skirts all around, straddled him and made her cunt descend upon his standing prick.

'Lucia fixed it aright and kept it steady as a candlestick with her hand, while Robina, with a downward push, caused it to rush up into her to the very hilt.

'Lucia then laid herself down by Tasso's side and rested her cheek on his belly, so close to his prick that she was able to touch it with her tongue while also tasting the fleshy little knot of Robina's cunt. All the while she allayed her own excitement by working a finger between the hairy lips of her own affair.

'Altogether it was a most voluptuous scene. What with their lustful motions, their wanton cries and the sweet visible union of prick and cunt, nothing could have been more exciting. I envied them with all my heart, and I am sure, Aminda, you would have done so too.'

'I am quite certain I should. What's more, I know of no reason why we may not share in their sports.'

20

Wide Open
JEM 1899

Paris, the city of love – and love there was in the French capitol at the turn of the century. Love in the air, in the parks, on the benches, in the bushes, in the cafés , in the alleyways, everywhere one looked there was love (or at least sex). Paris was a veritable hooker haven and paradise for liberated men and women seeking a lascivious dalliance. Such is the setting for *Wide Open*, a 1935 English translation of the 1899 French novel *En Plein Air: Mystères Nocturnes des Champs-Elysées* by 'Jem' (Paris, Imprimé au Temple de Cythère au Paphos).

The narrator is a young man in Paris for the summer. A keen observer of daily life, he soon discovers a cornucopia of erotic adventures available to him. The women are pretty and easily accessible, the society is *laissez-faire* towards impromptu acts of an overtly sexual nature, and the erotic opportunities are limitless.

This novel is, however, more than a cold recitation of sexual escapades and encounters with street prostitutes. The reader gets a genuine feel for the city and the times – the sights and sounds and smells and carefree attitudes. In addition there is an unparalleled first-hand account of Parisian prostitution at the time. Along with the episodes of sex there are 'navel eye' views of how the working girls plied their trade on a daily basis, with such psychological insight and careful descriptions of what was done, and how, and where, and for how much, that the book could have been a textbook for one wishing to join the trade, or a primary reference source for one interested in this social phenomenon. Other books of the same era, such as *The Shuttered Houses of Paris*, discussed prostitution in a non-fiction manner, but none have spoken so well of the street walkers and women who worked the parks and cafés and public thoroughfares.

Rarely has such civility been brought to the writing of an erotic novel. A social document and at the same time tantalising reading, this book once again proves that time changes little in the ways of professional love.

〜〜〜 from *Wide Open*

The pretty Parc Monçeau, located in an aristocratic quarter, also has its professional masturbatrixes, and not only that but it appears professional male masturbators as well. In this connection, here is what I saw one evening on the circular walk near the Baths of Diana.

I had been accosted by a young woman whom I had already met several days before and to whom I had paid the customary coin to be shown her very attractive titties at my leisure. The regular exhibition of voluptuous white breasts was staged for the price, then I tranquilly seated myself on one of the benches along the walk.

Some moments after, another bench, placed closer to the road, gave refuge to a couple whose manner was ever so slightly mysterious. The girl of the pretty bubbies went over at once to offer her services. They must have been accepted, no doubt, for I saw her raise her skirts and remain standing before the man, showing him everything from her knees to her belly, while the lady on the bench was agitating her escort's cock. At this moment, a tall young man, fashionably attired, passed in front of the group. Mademoiselle Pretty-Tits at once let fall her skirts and hastened over to the young man, who was just then passing within earshot of me.

'Come on over,' says she to him. 'He won't mind. His prick is large enough for the two of us.'

The young man, apparently irritated at the indiscretion of the young woman, for he guessed correctly that I had overheard, replied in the negative. But the siren wouldn't take no for an answer and followed after him, making further propositions – very seductive ones, no doubt, for she finally succeeded in bringing back the recalcitrant.

The group was formed again, the young lady resumed her job of masturbating the man at her side, and the girl with the voluptuous tits once more hoisted her clothes to have her charms admired. But where that ended, to my surprise, was when I saw the strange young man put himself in the place of the masturbatrix to complete her task. His technique was, without doubt, more subtle or better handled, for the result was not long delayed, and I could see the silhouette of the one jerked-off slightly lowering the head of his cock and spreading his knees to avoid the gobs of sperm.

It is thus everywhere: at the Palais Royal, at the Trocadero, in the Parc Montsouris, on the quays of the Tuileries, on the esplanade of the Champ de Mars, on the avenue of the Bois de Boulogne as well as at the Place de la Caroussel – everywhere, in brief, where there are shadowy nooks to be found, women are continually on the hustle.

But this joy-peddling assumes a more attractive exterior when it is practised by the higher-class and more attractively dressed ladies that frequent such and such a walk or neighbourhood. Thus I have seen again and again along the Champs-Elysées, in the little gardens that border the Palais de l'Industrie, seated on the benches or on the grass under the trees, scarcely a stone's throw from the police station, luxurious ladies on the lookout for customers, generally clad in the lightest and flimsiest of dresses, outrageously low-cut in the bosom to give maximum display to the wares they offer for hire.

I was strolling one evening in this particular part of town with a friend of mine, at whose house I had just dined. My friend was a married man, but he was thoroughly familiar with the nocturnal mysteries of the beautiful avenue, while I, a bachelor, was still at this time totally ignorant of these interesting facts of life.

Arriving in the vicinity of the gardens in question, my friend called my attention to the suspicious bearing of certain persons. They were crowded together as if holding a heated political discussion; nevertheless, they were actually doing very little talking.

As we approached the group, two unengaged wenches gave us the eye, then favoured us with their most gracious smiles. Drawing near to them, we were not a little astonished to see that they had their luscious breasts completely outside the bounds of their clothes. Gallantry imposed upon us the not unpleasant duty of saluting these pretty globes, so white and round, with a caress. Seating ourselves alongside these lovely belles of the evening, we discussed the terms for a few rounds of lovemaking, each of us all the while titillating the pretty rosy nipples which offered themselves to our touch and communicated to our senses a warmth that soon we were going to extinguish between their bountiful thighs in one of the nearby hotels.

Everything agreed upon, we engaged two adjoining rooms connected by an open door and gave ourselves up, each respectively to the most complete explorations possible upon the charming persons of our new friends. Everything came off to perfection, including myself, and after a separate fuck apiece, we rejoined each other in the larger of the two rooms and there, in the same costume that Adam and Eve wore in their terrestrial paradise, we set to telling each other scores of dirty stories.

Lustful desires having once more been aroused in us, and our companions evincing great willingness for further action, we resumed our amorous play. The most voluptuous and lascivious caresses conceivable were exchanged without hesitation by all four of us in the presence of each other. We topped it off with an exchange of women, acting on the adage 'fresh cunt, fresh courage'. Just for the sake of variety, I took my friend's companion dog-fashion, while he fucked mine face-to-face.

That was my first completely enjoyable encounter with the ladies of the Champs-Elysées. It was not going to be my last. Many people find that it increases their sexual pleasures tenfold to experience them with third persons – preferably strangers – looking on, gathered together by a similarity in taste.

The women generally serve as the go-betweens, and as they make additional profit thereby, they do all they can to incite their clients to this practice.

For that purpose they generally work in pairs. When one of them has picked up a customer who is in the mood to get laid, she grants him at first only the meagrest caresses to excite him further, and to save the more serious business till her sidekick has found herself a hot-nutted man, too, or at least a voyeur, or watcher, who will pay for the privilege of being present at the sport.

The party is generally made up of even more than two couples, and it is this which makes it interesting. You might pass near a circle of men and women seated in a dark corner, chatting and laughing, without dreaming for a moment, if you're not one of the initiated, of the delightful things that are going on and of the lustful caresses that are being discreetly exchanged.

The ladies raise their skirts up to their bellies, opening their waists to expose their titties, and the men, all or nearly all of them, have their pricks outside their trousers. Men and women finger and stroke each other mutually, and it sometimes happens that the caresses bestowed on one man are coming from another male, or, reciprocally, that a juicy cunt is being manipulated by the darling hand of a creature in petticoats.

The lack of privacy does not prevent amateurs of this pastime from glimpsing or exhibiting a plenitude of bare flesh, and voyeurs can fill their eyes with tableaux of the highest suggestiveness and realism. Certain hussies I knew, young and attractive ones, too, would come to the places where these games were practised dressed only in a chemise or a petticoat, over which they would wear a sort of cape or coat that they could easily remove. Sometimes they would be wearing under their capes nothing more than a silk chemisette or brassière to add allure to their breasts. The siren so lightly accoutred had only to raise her petticoat or flimsy chemise, or merely remove her cape, to show us the smooth skin of her thighs, her brace of dainty knees and the dark silky fleece nestled under her white belly. By turning around, she could disclose the charming rotundities of her inviting behind, the two darling cheeks of her buttocks – in all, a heap of lovely things.

If, during this time, she had occasion to open her cape and raise her chemise, holding it up under her chin, we would be regaled by the vision of the startled quivering softness of her bubbies, crowned by tiny pink nipples that would stiffen with excitement and the coolness of the evening air.

It is then that a mere man would feel himself impelled to kiss and suck these pretty titties (they are always pretty when seen under these circumstances), whose rosy tips would always stand up under the tongue's excitation, and who could resist the temptation to squeeze her polished thighs at the same time, or perhaps insert a finger between the lips of her vulva to titillate her clitoris?

One may well imagine that a woman, no matter how frigid and *blasée* she may be at the outset, cannot remain entirely insensible to all these caresses. They are soon aroused, and it is then that the party becomes interesting. When, in addition to these circumstances, the heated female finds in the crowd a cavalier who is especially pleasing to her, she yields her body completely to him, their happiness attains its greatest intensity and the assistants or onlookers are treated to an erotic tableau of no mean proportions.

As already explained, the voyeurs are persons, male or female, who do not care to be active participants in the party, but are content, and willing to pay, to assist passively at the spectacle offered by the real fucksters.

The men generally remain mere spectators. The women, on the other hand, rarely do. Their senses are more quickly and thoroughly excited and, once this has happened, they abandon themselves to conduct of unrestrained lustfulness. They not only forget all the curbs of modesty, but divest themselves at the same time of the last vestige of both their clothes and their dignity. And since it is not always possible to achieve a completely satisfying orgasm in the open, it is plausible to predict that the party will wind up in a neighbouring hotel or in the back room of some café.

The voyeurs I describe are quite numerous in these parts, and almost all of them are members of high society, too jaded by past excesses, perhaps, to find pleasurable success in more active roles.

A single instance will suffice to show to what extremes the desire to spy on others' pleasures may bring a person – in this case a woman, probably quite respectable in the ordinary acts of her life, but who, under the sway of this strange desire, loses all restraint and gives herself over to the deeds which she has perhaps never sunk to in private.

Taking my usual stroll one autumn evening, I noticed an elegant, stately woman who had the unmistakable manner of seeking for a dark place to satisfy a natural need. In order not to frighten her, I slipped back into the shadows and followed her only with my eyes. I saw her raise her dress and squat alongside a tree. Pretending not to be noticing her very personal procedure, I directed my steps towards her and reached her just as, her little business completed, the woman was rising to her feet once more and readjusting her clothing.

'Ah!' said I. 'I come just in time to miss a pretty eyeful.'

Far from being offended at my audacity, the woman smiled at me and replied: 'No, I assure you, you didn't miss a thing.'

'Allow me, madame, to disagree with you,' I continued. 'It is always gratifying to see a woman with her skirts trussed up a bit, especially when she has as shapely a behind as yours seems to be. And then there is always the exciting hope of seeing something even further . . . '

'Do you want to very badly?' she asked coyly.

'Certainly, my dear lady, and I would indeed be very grateful to you if you were to do the whole thing over again for me.'

'But I do not even know you!'

'The pleasure will, therefore, be all the keener. And for that matter, if it is agreeable to you, I will reciprocate by showing you what I have on me and which differentiates us – the finger which even now is ready to adjust itself to your thimble.'

'Oh! I'm curious to see if you really have the nerve to show it to me!'

'Well – there it is, madame,' said I, taking out that part of me in question, which unhappily was not at the moment in a condition of which to be proud.

'Ah! But how little it is! It's not a bit interesting, that thing of yours!'

'Just give me a glimpse of yours, my dear, and you will see it take on importance under your very eyes – especially if you will deign to fondle it a bit with your pretty hand.'

Grasping her skirts in her hands, she raised them up to her very breasts, disclosing to my excited gaze two dainty knees and thighs, imprisoned in elegant tight-fitting panties that were just open enough in their texture to permit me to catch a little glimpse of her vermilion crack, shaded by dainty shrubbery of a pretty black. I put my hand upon the irresistible spot, and through the thin silk of her panties I began to titillate the little joy button hidden in the folds of the juicy lips, when suddenly the woman pushed down her dress and, recoiling from me, whispered: 'Be careful! Someone's coming!'

'It is nothing,' said I. 'Probably some other lovers like ourselves.'

And sure enough, those approaching were a young couple, both light-haired, the young man with a rather weary demeanour, the young lady short and dainty, nicely dressed in a handsome princess gown of pearl-gray silk. They passed alongside us and stared straight at us, audaciously enough.

'I'll wager,' said I to my new friend, 'that these lovers would like to watch us play with each other. They're certainly acting as if they're waiting for us to put on a free show for them – which is probably just what they've come out here for.'

'But,' said she, 'I, too, came here tonight to see some goings-on, and not to be seen. But since you've got me started, let's go to a place where we can be alone.'

'In that case,' I rejoined, 'you won't see anything.'

'You're not much taking into consideration the darling instrument that you just put into my hand a moment ago, and which I wouldn't have seen if I hadn't come here,' said she laughingly.

'Then come along,' said I, offering her my arm.

We strolled down by the park menagerie, which was now closed and deserted, and there we were able to devote ourselves to such agreeable manipulations of our most sensitive parts, respectively, as soon sent us soaring to the seventh heaven of lustful bliss.

Scarcely had we both spilt the sweet tears of pleasure, all aquiver still with the voluptuous climax, than we saw advancing towards us a person well known to the amateurs of open-air love frolics. He was a member of this Society of Joy, famous for his total lack of bashfulness in offering to the girls of the Champs-Elysées his insatiable prick, for the amusement of the onlookers as well as for his own. He was especially well liked, too, for the reason that he knew all the plainclothes policemen by sight and was always willing to warn couples when the detectives were in the vicinity. We called him Jesus Christ because of his pretty blond beard.

When he drew near, I introduced him to my lady friend and told him of her wish to see some action in the park. I also told him of the couple that had passed us.

'You were wrong then to let the opportunity slip,' said he. He added that he thought there was still a chance to find the other pair and stir up a little excitement.

Being myself contented with the events of the evening, I turned my companion over to him and bade them good-night – not without having gallantly kissed the pretty fingers which had so recently entwined my cock.

I had intended going straight home, but once outside the Champs-Elysées, I regretted my decision and suddenly resolved to turn back.

On the walk where I had left them, I noticed a group of six people seated on two sides of a double bench.

Drawing close, I saw J. C. on one side and with him a young telegraph operator I knew. They were on watch for the cops, and were casting furtive glances now and then at the persons seated on the other side of the bench – among whom I recognised my charming female companion of before and the blond couple whose curiosity had first attracted our attention.

'As you can see for yourself,' J. C. addressed me, 'I found them, and everything is working fine.' And sure enough, I could plainly see that the dainty little blonde lady was being fondled at the same time both by her fiancé or husband on the one hand and by her elegant female neighbour, the one I had picked up before, on the other, while her shapely young tits were being intermittently patted and squeezed by a handsome dark-haired girl of distinguished bearing.

'You gay dog!' said I to J. C. 'You certainly have fixed things up!'

'One does the best one can,' replied he modestly. 'But, I say, since you've already been pulled off, what do you say to keeping watch for me while I go over to get taken care of myself by one of them?' He uncovered his javelin and offered it to the little blonde, who immediately abandoned her escort's cock to caress that of the newcomer.

The telegraph operator, randy as a Carmelite monk, following his example, took out his own, which, on my word, was of unusually high calibre, and presented it to the strange brunette.

'Ah! This is fine!' she cried, and forsaking the female charms she had just been fondling, she set to agitating the monstrous morsel with her soft hands while she devoured it with her eyes. Soon she could feel the premonitory stiffening of his part as it prepared to go off, and fearing the tempestuous deluge that she had every right to expect, she said to the young fellow, 'Stop me before you come. I don't want to get my new dress all mussed up.'

'Have no fear, madame,' replied the man, and he took out his handkerchief and held it in readiness to catch the prolific discharge when it should come.

Leaning over the bench towards the woman's ear, I whispered, 'It's always risky for your clothes when you do it that way, any unlucky jet may get out of control and get all over your clothes. Better take it in your mouth. It will be much safer.'

'You're a devil,' she laughed, 'but your advice is good.' And she lowered her pretty mouth over the huge delicacy and set to earnestly sucking the spongy head of the gland.

Scarcely was the great jewel thus honoured than it begun to spit. The lustful beauty held the morsel in her mouth during the entire discharge; but thereafter, no doubt but little accustomed to swallowing the smoke of such fleshly cigars, she went away a little distance and spat the results of his enjoyment at the foot of a tree.

Meanwhile, J. C. had crouched down before her and, with his hand up between her soft thighs, was rubbing her clitty with a vengeance. As all this handling had uncovered a good deal of her lovely white buttocks, I could not resist the temptation to slip an arm over the back of the bench and in my turn pass a caressing palm over the cushioned eminences of this darling creature.

After having relieved her mouth of the load of sperm that she had nursed up, our pretty cock-sucker came back to the bench and was greeted with the congratulations of her companions.

'Oh, keep quiet!' she exclaimed good-naturedly. 'I'm so ashamed of myself, I've never done such a thing before.'

'Do you think you'll ever do it again?' I asked her.

'I don't know,' she replied, 'but it's quite likely – when once the first fatal step has been!'

'And then,' I added, 'one doesn't make babies by that route.' The pretty blonde once more had J. C.'s member in her hand, and he was beginning to be very much moved by her skilful manipulations.

'Why don't you blow me, too?' he begged, breathing heavily.

The passionate darling was undoubtedly willing and anxious; but she didn't dare to do it in the presence of her lord and master; she looked at the latter questioningly. Whereupon he leaned towards the ear of his better half and whispered his authorisation. The charming little woman at once proceeded to take out J. C.'s massive balls, squeezed them lovingly with both her dainty hands, and then, lowering her shapely head towards the good man's prick, she engulfed it in her mouth, timidly, it was true, but with an air of greediness and enjoyment.

Soon we saw J. C. trembling with tight shut eyes – then, finally, he withdrew his instrument, shooting gobs of sperm.

The little blonde did not spit. She had no doubt swallowed the good human cream of asparagus before.

The other woman, astonished at her complete daring, and not a little envious, kissed her heartily, darting her tongue hungrily between her lips.

'Oh, give me a little of it, you darling!' she gasped, herself strangely overcome by passion. 'I would like to kiss you all over!'

The husband, a little dazed and disturbed by this scene, and by the undreamt-of prurience his wife had exhibited, cried in chagrin, 'God damn! To think that I never dared ask her to do as much for me!'

'Ah! No need to worry yourself about that any more,' I put in consolingly. 'You know she'll satisfy you now.'

It was time for me to go home. I therefore paid my respects to the pretty brunette and her companion and we all went our separate ways.

~~~ 21 ~~~

The Initiation of Aurora Trill

1903

The great literature of all cultures, the classics, have one thing in common. They all present characters and circumstances that are symbolic and representative of all people, throughout history, struggling with the timeless and universal fabric that is the human condition. While any work of fiction can be read into deeply enough to appear to be symbolic, the majority of fiction presents specific individuals in specific situations in a dramatic conflict that is an end unto itself. Any greater 'truths' are accidental or mundane, and of future interest only in so far as they portray time and place with historical accuracy. The genius of great writing, whether it be the ancient Greek anti-war play *Lysistrata* of Aristophanes, the medieval morality play *Everyman*, or Beckett's masterpiece *Waiting for Godot*, is that it is intentionally crafted to portray anyone at any time confronting the ever recurring problems that plague day-to-day existence.

The Initiation of Aurora Trill has a claim to this same universality, albeit unintentionally. By plan or accident, here is a novel in which an unnamed man, of unknown profession, with unknown mission or destination, sitting on a train, in an unspecified geographic locale, at an undetermined time in history, encounters an equally anonymous woman, with whom he spontaneously proceeds to copulate! An eighth of the book lapses before the characters (or the readers for that matter) learn anything about each other beyond their anatomies! And not until the very end of the book are the place (England) or the year (the turn of the twentieth century) even hinted at.

All this ambiguity detracts not a wit from this erotic novel. What could be more general – Man, Woman, Sex! Here is any man, with any woman, engaged in the greatest wish fulfilment on earth. No great moral or lesson to be learned, just a story of two people who happen to get really lucky on a train ride.

We need not be quite so cavalier with the merits of this book. While no masterpiece of prose, it still reads as surprisingly 'modern'. We have here a novel in which there is unparalleled equality of the sexes. Women and men are all gainfully employed and economically self-sufficient. They have sexual interests, curiosities, randiness and lusts of comparable intensities. 'Kinkiness' is not reserved for one sex over the other (pardon the pun). Fetishes – particularly for the buttocks, coprolalia, exhibitionism, voyeurism, and the urge for group sex are initiated and engaged in by male and female alike. Despite the obviously English sexual slang ('quim', 'teat', 'spunk', 'arse', 'bollocks', 'wc', 'get his greens', etc.), the lack of specified time and place could easily allow one to think that this novel was the modern product of a Britisher living in the United States.

This would, however, be a very wrong, although completely understandable assumption. The truth behind this novel is startling to say the least, and demonstrates it to be a surprising and remarkable example of the erotic genre. The genesis of the book can be discovered, although with some difficulty, as its bibliography is ignored in all the English-language erotica references. It is from the French bibliographies we learn that the novel was actually written by an Englishman from New Zealand who, in 1903, while travelling through the French capitol, sold the manuscript of this and several other similar works to the publisher Elias Gaucher. The book was printed by the London expatriate Charles Hirsch, who sold the book from his shop, apparently until it was condemned by the Paris courts in December 1914. The subsequent reprint, from which this current text is taken, indicates itself to be 'London, 1932, For Private Circulation Only', although it is clearly of New York origin.

Perhaps it is the New Zealand background of the author which makes *Aurora Trill* so distinct from other Edwardian erotica, and as fresh and vital today to the American reader as when it was composed nearly ninety years ago. This is a novel that literally speaks best for itself. Here are two episodes from *Aurora Trill* when Harry Temple and Aurora Trill (the names are puns on the characters' occupations), having just seduced each other during a short train ride, pose as man and wife and check into a railside hotel to continue their lubricious encounter.

from *The Initiation of Aurora Trill*

Mrs Dallas was delighted to see us. She introduced us to her sister, Lettice, an engaging, pink-faced girl who looked as if she would later develop into as fine a woman as her sister. The latter, I may mention, was no prude, for though I had never fucked her, I had taken lesser liberties which were by no means resented. I don't suppose she would have been troubled if she had known Aurora was merely my mistress. In fact, I caught more than one expressive look, as much as to say she thought I was in luck with such a mate.

It was pretty late when we arrived, and after a meal Aurora made no secret of her desire to retire as soon as possible. Once in the comfortable bedroom, she flung her arms round my neck, kissed me passionately and, feeling for my cock, asked, 'Is it up, dear? Are you ready to fuck me all night, naked? Naked as two babies, mind?'

I modestly expressed my intention of doing my best, and hinted that perhaps she, on her side, would find 'all night' too long. We were very quickly in a state of nature, and could admire one another's proportions at ease. I took special note of her voluptuous bubbies, and told her so. Aurora blushed with pleasure at the praise for her beautifully swelling breasts, and held up the teats to my mouth.

'They are all for you, dear,' she said tenderly, 'and all that I have.'

'Even this?' I asked, referring to her bottom. She blushed again and hid her face upon my shoulder without replying, but playing freely with my balls and prick.

'Harry, dear, will you do something for me?' she whispered. 'Will you let me see your juice flow out of this dear prick? I have felt it gushing into me, and I am curious to see what it is like and how much there is of it when it comes flying out with such force.'

'You want to frig me till I spend?'

She nodded.

'Well, I will on one condition, that you lie on your back, open your crack as widely and indecently as possible, and frig yourself till you spend too.'

'Oh Harry, what an idea! I don't think I could do that, frig myself before a man.'

'It would be delightfully obscene, and I think that's just what both of us want and what we are here for. Remember, you vowed you would do all sorts of things.'

'Yes, well, I suppose I must . . . But you first.'

I sat down and told her to kneel in front of me. I put my jock between the salient bubbies – warm and elastic they were and pointed out that by bending her head slightly she could take the crown into her mouth. 'Then, my dear, with my bollocks pressing on your chest if you hold my prick in this warm nook while sucking at the nut, you will soon get the desired result. I will tell you when I am coming, and you can watch the jets leap out. If you'd like to hold your mouth open, the cream won't be wasted. Otherwise, it will run over these adorable titties.'

It did not take much frigging, as may be imagined, to bring about a discharge which was quite thick enough to satisfy my lady. She had the pleasure of gazing at half a dozen ropy jets shooting into her mouth. Only she was so intent on inspecting the operation that she received a good portion on her lips and chin, whence it dropped slowly on to the bulging bosoms, and shone in the candlelight like pearls. I took her face in my hands, gazed at the still virginal-looking countenance and pined my tongue to hers, stirring up the contents of her mouth. Finally she swallowed the broth. I enquired if she was satisfied.

'It is funny to see a sticky, white stream coming out where you would expect another colour. With what force it spurts up! No wonder I felt it so distinctly in my cunt. And so hot. It was almost steaming. But I never told you, sir, to fire it into my mouth.'

'Well, my darling, you couldn't expect me to allow my noble spunk, my most precious fluid, to fall unheeded to the ground. I had to get it into your belly some way.'

Picking the dear girl up in my arms, cuddling her like a baby and depositing her upon the bed, I gently pulled apart her thick thighs and guided her hand to the pink gash, now tight again. What a charming sight! There lay stretched before me the naked, well-matured form of a modest-faced lady, her features blushing and handsome, full of love, fire and desire. Her expansive bosoms now flowed backwards, swelling out towards the neck and shoulders. Her broad, white stomach, lily-white thighs and shapely buttocks accentuated the delicious rosebud glowing in the centre. Her jewelled hand, sparkling with gems, played nervously and timidly, uncertain still as to its task. I bade her open wide the folds and then the frailer inner lips. As she warmed to her novel employment, the hand flew in and out, her mouth opened, her bosom heaved and the broad bottom began to jump a little. To quicken the motion I gently applied my finger, and when Aurora called out that she was coming, I stooped down, applying my mouth to the nervously-contracting quim, receiving her spend in my face.

'Dear, what a naughty boy you are to make me fuck myself. Come and let me love you.' She hugged me fondly to her bosom and, finding myself in a convenient posture, I slipped a pillow under her bottom and proceeded to fuck her in orthodox fashion.

'Ah, that makes you jump, does it, my dear? I am going to split you in two. Do you feel that, and that,' I asked, drawing out my prick to the end and then jamming it in the full length.

My weapon had arrived at its goal and was jolting against her tender womb. Aurora was intent on sucking in every drop she could get.

'Every inch, darling. Fuck me for all you are worth. Rattle your bollocks on my bottom. Pound away dear, and flood me with your scalding cream.'

Putting my hands under her bottom, I clutched the cheeks and told her to throw her thighs over mine. She did so eagerly. I drove my cock in to its full length, and shouted, 'Fuck like hell!' The bed rattled and creaked, and must have been heard all over the house. But what did we care? We melted into one another, I holding my prick right against her womb. With the intense satisfaction of a deed well done, I poured a continuous stream of nature's lava upon the greedy matrix that I felt sure was sucking it all in.

* * *

Next day, after breakfast, when the hostess returned to remove the remains of the meal, Aurora accompanied her outside the door, and there held an earnest conversation in which I caught a tone of wonderment and what seemed to me a rather feeble expostulation on Mrs Dallas's part. Presently, back came my mischievous singer, pulling the woman with her.

'Now, my dear woman, you needn't be so bashful. If Harry hasn't already seen what you've got to show, and if he hasn't poked you, as he has been doing to me all night, I'm sure it isn't because you aren't willing. You do as I want and you shan't lose by it. You see, Harry, I want her to pose in the same position as you put me yesterday. Then I will sketch you and, having got Mrs Dallas's position, I will fill in myself afterwards by sitting in front of a mirror in the same posture.'

'But, Mrs Temple, do you want to undress me, strip me before your husband? And he nearly naked too? Oh, I couldn't, I couldn't. He has never seen me so, and I should be so ashamed.'

'You won't be naked. At least, only a part of you will, though I'm afraid a very important one. And Harry will have to take some liberties with your person. You see, to be an exact reproduction, this awkward thing' – tapping my cock, which was standing out stiffly under my shirt – 'must be in your cunt. And if he treats you as he did me, it will not be the tip only that will be in. Come, now, there's a good woman. Don't make any more fuss. You know quite well you are secretly pleased with the idea of getting this fine weapon between your thighs.'

Aurora meanwhile was busily unfastening the corsage, and baring a pair of fine bosoms. Putting her hands under the dress, she hunted for the strings of Mrs Dallas' drawers. Having loosened them, she rather impertinently fumbled the good lady's bottom and thighs, remarking, 'I don't think you will have any need to be ashamed of what Harry may see.' She pushed her down upon the edge of the sofa, and to the poor woman's astonishment made her put her feet up, exposing a brace of stout thighs and rounded hams, with a well-favoured slit peeping from between.

'What a posture!' she murmured, looking at me imploringly, 'and how uncomfortable it must have been. How you must love your husband to let him take you like that.'

By this time I had got out of my clothes and, kneeling down, Aurora put my cock into the widow's cruise herself.

'Oh my, Harry. It's taking all her skin with it. And look how it makes the lips bulge on each side. Why, Mrs Dallas, your quim is all curving inwards. And what a big thing you have!'

'I've had three children, and I dare say you won't be so proud of your own cunt when you've had it cracked a few times by a bouncing kid. It may have been small enough yesterday, but what will it be like when Mr Harry has done you over a few hundred times?'

'Oh, it has stretched already, it has. I can take his dear prick easily now.'

She saw my cock being pushed well home and, lifting my shirt, told me to hold it up myself so that she could see my bare bottom.

'I must have that horrid part of you in my picture, or it wouldn't be rude enough.' She sketched rapidly while I gently poked Mrs Dallas, so as not to disarrange the tableau, occasionally kissing lips and bubbies. When Aurora signified she had finished, I gave several energetic thrusts.

'That's right,' cried my pseudowife, 'she deserves a little encouragement. Fuck her as hard as you like, my dear. Splendid! What a beautiful expression she wears. Do I look like that, Harry, when you make me spend?'

With this she finished me off and I sent my spunk flying into the widow's waiting cunt. Mrs Dallas was too overcome to move for a moment, and the juice trickled from her quim on to the floor. She wiped herself, impulsively kissed Aurora and me, and was about to hurry rather shamefacedly from the room when I caught hold of her.

'Now, tell me, Mrs Dallas, what you think of my sweetheart.' I stripped off Aurora's nightdress and revealed her wealth of nakedness. 'Isn't she a beauty? What you farmers call a good, roomy mare, eh? There's an elastic belly to spend on, and I can assure you it has a most engaging entrance to it – feels like velvet, and clutches like India rubber.'

'Yes,' cried Aurora delightedly, 'and he must like it, for I've had his prick in it about fifteen times already, and I've stood up, or rather, lain down to it well, haven't I, dear?'

'Fifteen times!' sighed Mrs Dallas. 'And my husband only covered me four times all told on our wedding night. But indeed, Mr Harry, you have a lovely companion. She would make any man's prick stiffen. Yes, she's broad in the barrel and I expect you've done the trick already with that long pin. I felt it in me twice as far as my old man used to go. But I must go now.'

'Take your drawers with you,' Aurora said maliciously.

Aurora's eye fell on my shrivelled penis and, kneeling down between my thighs, the lustful beauty began sipping at it with her lips, running her tongue under the skin, savouring the mingled juices she found still there.

'How soft it's gone, like a piece of putty. Quite shrunken up. However, if it isn't stiff enough to get into my quim, I can always take it into my mouth, can't I? This is the first time I have ever sucked a prick that's just been soaked in another woman's belly. Tastes of cunt. Rather salty, Harry. But there, I won't tease it any longer. It has done splendidly, and to tell the truth, I am beginning to feel a little sore myself. I am sure my pussy must be swollen a bit. So I will have a bath. No, you are not to come. I am going to get Lettice to help, on pretence of massaging me, and then . . . you shall see. I shall bring her back with me. You are to hide behind the bed as soon as you hear us coming, and you can amuse yourself watching. And then, young gentleman, I think I shall find this piece of shrivelled skin' – flicking my prick contemptuously – 'in a more courteous state than it is now.'

I waited and in due time heard steps in the hall. I slipped under the bed, quite resolved to have a good deal more to say in the coming interlude than was in Aurora's programme. Aurora entered with Lettice, both in wrappers and both much flushed, the girl, it would seem, rather bashful.

'Oh, Mr Temple is not here, so I want you to give me a good rubbing.'

Aurora dropped everything and stood up robustly, glowingly naked. The sofa received her, and Lettice began her task to which she was clearly quite unaccustomed. The giddy singer made the girl put her hand between her thighs, saying 'that part particularly wants attention after the exercise my terrible husband has given it,' and then complained of Letty's garment irritating her. 'Take it off, my dear. I am sure I shall enjoy the process better if you are undressed like myself.'

Lettice demurred a little, but Aurora generally got her way, and the young woman was soon reduced to nudity. I watched the disappearance of such clothes as she had with much interest, and was charmed with the resultant display of creamy flesh and well moulded limbs. Less developed than the other two, she was still a fine, healthy specimen. Aurora vowed she must have a look at the girl's virgin quim.

'Just think. Yesterday mine was like yours, and today I'm a woman and you're still a girl. I'm sure you have a pretty little pussy here. I want to see if it is like mine was.'

Lettice blushed and said it was very rude, but in the end Aurora got her down, opened her thighs and examined the slender cunt at will. She exclaimed with pretended enthusiasm, 'What a dear little crack. I must kiss it,' and did so despite the maiden's murmurs. Next, she frigged it gently, and when the girl had been worked to spending point, the would-be lesbian laid aside all further pretence and, gluing her lips to the quivering slit, sucked and tongued it with a fury. The result was Lettice discharging, though not a great deal, before she quite knew what was happening. Her gammahucher seemed disappointed at the small quantity of spunk she had extracted from the girl.

'You don't spend very freely, my dear. If you don't do better than that when your husband gets up your little twat, he won't be pleased. Why, I let out twice as much when Mr Temple sucks me.'

Letty's modesty was greatly shocked, and underwent further alarm when her tormentor insinuatingly suggested that they should try again, and proposed to do it together.

'What!' Letty, almost shrieked, 'do you mean I should put my mouth there!' pointing to my mistress's dark motte.

'Yes, my dear. Haven't I just done it for you? I think you would come more freely if you had my cunny on your lips.'

'Oh, never, never. Mrs Temple, you are most immodest. I let you take such indecent liberties with me to please you. But to think of sucking another girl there, why that's disgusting! Besides, your husband may come in at any moment.'

'Not disgusting at all when you're used to it,' replied the amorous frigger, putting her arm round the naked waist, and kissing the girl's titties and lips. Her eye fell on the rings on her hand.

'See here, wouldn't you like this pretty ring? Now you suck my cunt nicely, and in return for the ring of flesh I put on you mouth, I'll put this ring on your finger.'

Lettice still showed some distaste for the task, but Aurora's persuasions and the thought of the ring overcame her scruples, and she laid her mistress back on the sofa, diving on her quim and plumping her own capacious pussy on her lover's face.

'Now, my dear,' Aurora implored, 'let me feel your tongue well in, and see if you can make me spend like my Harry does. That's right, open it well and lick the side up and down, and especially the knob at the top. That's the sensitive part. Delightful. I am sure you'll make a splendid cunt-sucker with practice. What a dear little cunt – narrower than mine is now, but it will expand when you get a nice, handsome cock stroking it. You'd be surprised how easily my husband gets into me now, though he only opened me yesterday.'

I thought I might join in at this stage. Crawling out, I flung off my shirt and, rising suddenly, opened the door as though just coming in.

'Well, Aurora, I've had my bath,' I cried. 'Hello, Mrs Dallas. What, at it again? Can't you let my wife's quim alone? Shocking, Aurora, to show so much bottom. The very sight of that noble arse makes my prick spring out again. I must have another fuck.'

Poor Lettice in a fright tried to disengage herself, but the artful Aurora clasped her head tight between her powerful thighs, and smothered all remonstrances. Looking round, she pointed to her quim and said, 'It isn't Mrs Dallas, but Lettice, my love. Put it in and show the dear girl what a thorough, loving fuck is like. I must spend or I shall burst, and I am afraid her inexperienced tongue won't make me come.'

I knelt behind the attractive arse and with my bollocks dangling over Letty's face, quietly shoved my cock into the cunt, already yawning to receive it. The girl said something about 'disgusting', especially when she saw my hairy arse above her face, with the brown hole in dangerous proximity to her mouth. But feminine curiosity was too much for her, and she resigned herself to watch the performance, impelled a good deal by the pleasurable titillation her own cunt was undergoing beneath Aurora's soft tongue.

When I gently asked her to help me by squeezing my balls, she did not demur and, taking them in her hand, moulded them softly, even shifting herself to get a better view. We weren't long in coming, and Aurora had much ado keeping her erotic ejaculations within reasonably decent bounds.

The withdrawal of my cock was followed by the appearance of the creamy injection from the agitated quim, and great was Letty's surprise to see that, whereas it went in like a raging lion, it came out humble and despondent. She wonderingly asked Aurora how the insertion of that terrible thing could give her so much pleasure, and what she had done to it to make it so limp.

We kissed and cuddled the shamefaced girl who could not keep her eyes off my prick and balls, and even ventured to touch them timidly. In her interest she forgot her naked state. Aurora told her she was responsible for the white juice because she had squeezed it out of 'those bollocks you were handling so tenderly, my dear. My quim couldn't have pumped so much out without your help, for which I thank you. The more spunk a woman can extract from her sweetheart's prick, the more enjoyable her fuck is, you know. You wait till some handsome boy fills your little quim with it, scorching hot, and see how it will make you whinny with pleasure. Won't she be a nice armful, Harry, when her time comes?'

Privately I thought it was likely to come very soon, and so, I fancy, did Aurora, for she winked knowingly at me as much as to say, 'Here's a nice new crib for you to crack, my lord.'

I took Lettice across my knees and, while Aurora sucked her titties and rubbed her bubbies up, I frigged her unresisted till her head fell back and she saturated my hand with come.

'Heavens!' she murmured, 'I am so ashamed. What will my sister say?' But the sparkle in her eye showed that the episode was not altogether displeasing, and that though her modesty had undergone a severe strain, it was not likely to suffer so very much.

I was moved to whisper, 'If you don't like Aurora's great bottom on your mouth, would you prefer to try this?' placing her hand on my doodle.

'Oh, no,' blushing furiously. 'That would be too indecent.'

'Well,' said Aurora, 'if you don't care for it, I do,' and there and then she plumped down on her knees and crammed my penis in *holus-bolus*, stretching it to its full elastic length and letting it go, playing such other antics that Letty's eyes opened very wide indeed.

'Oh, it's just lovely to be stark naked with an adorable, fucksome sweetheart, even if he is cuddling another pretty, naked miss and trying to get his finger in her naughty hole. I'm going to stay naked and fuck all day,' Aurora cried ecstatically.

Letty started, for in her excitement she had scarcely noticed that I was frigging her. Getting up, she grabbed her clothes and bolted precipitately, as though fearing something further might be extracted from her weakness.

~ 22 ~

The Confessions of Marie Carey

GEORGE REGINALD BACCHUS 1902

'No actor need apply.' Not many people today can remember when this type of notice was common in front of apartment buildings and rooming houses. The sad fact was that in America and around most of the world, up until the twentieth century, professional actors, entertainers, 'show folk', and all others of the same ilk who 'tripped the boards' were, for the most part, regarded with extreme suspicion, and held in very low esteem, a far cry from the attitude today, when the public insatiably craves entertainment idols (democratic America's substitute for the royalty of other countries), and turns them into multimillionaires overnight, doting on every move they make and every word they say (assiduously reported in the regular news media as well as the specialised gossip publications that have sprung up like weeds), and forgiving them even the most outrageous crimes and moral lapses.

Not so though in previous times. Entertainers, men and women, and especially those associated with travelling circuses and carnivals, were equated with con artists (at times with justification). Female 'actresses' were placed on a par with prostitutes (which some incidentally were between, after, or instead of shows and theatrical engagements; it also did not help that many actual 'working girls', then and now, would refer to themselves as actresses when asked for their occupation).

Entertainers were certainly different from common folk, especially before the electronic media of phonograph, radio, television, cinema and video allowed them to be brought directly into our homes as friends. In the days of exclusively live, in-person performances, the professionals who provided entertainment were not the modest, anonymous members of the community flock. They were instead self-promoting, 'famous', travelling troubadours, outgoing, socialising and

without apparent roots or stable family life. They had no responsibility
to the community they happened to be temporarily playing in, nor to
any of its churches. They were outside the pale of conventional
morality; e.g. entertainment 'marriages' were often mock, a convenience
for rooming accommodations on the road, or a euphemism for
temporary *liaisons*. Such renowned nineteenth-century actresses as
Lola Montez and Sarah Bernhardt were equally known as the mistresses
and intimate companions of royalty, politicians, business moguls and
society doyens. In short, entertainers were bad examples for young and
old alike.

No wonder then that entertainers have been the subject of so many
well-known erotic books. *The Loves of a Musical Student*, *Pauline the
Prima Donna*, *Crissie: A Music-Hall Sketch* and *Aurora Trill* are just
a few examples which 'justify' the moral prejudice against actors and
singers. To these we can add *The Confessions of Marie Carey*, a turn-
of-the-century Edwardian 'autobiography' of a 'schoolgirl, actress and
entretenue', in the author's own words.

The Confessions of Marie Carey is actually part of a trilogy entitled *The
Confessions of Nemesis Hunt*, but more about that later. Here then is one
episode from the life of the retired actress 'Nemesis Hunt', now using
her real name of Marie Carey as she dictates her memoirs to her typist
Gladys.

from *The Confessions of Marie Carey*

'I yearned to go to see my lover again, but I was frightened. I was
always feeling those queer yet delightful sensations, and I was possessed
with a great longing to know more about the secrets of life.

'At last, at the end of the term, I felt that I must see him. In another
day school would have broken up, and for all I knew he might be
leaving. I had an excellent opportunity as I had to go to his house to see
my music master. It was the day of the annual football match between
the school and the old boys, and my boyfriend had been chosen for the
first time to play in the school fifteen. I knew he would be awfully
proud and I felt proud of him. It was a great honour at his age, and if he
distinguished himself he would get his cap. I slipped into his room just
as I had been used to doing and found him sitting in his football

clothes; his white knees were bare, and his arms uncovered below the elbow . . . '

Lord, it's funny for me, the Marie Carey of today, to look back on those days when I was innocent. I feel I must have a little rest in the dictation.

'Gladys,' I say to my typewriter, 'how do you think the story's going?'

'Beautifully, you dear,' she answers. 'I'm fully interested. I feel that you're going to tell something dreadful now. Do go on.'

'Wait a minute, you're getting the privilege of hearing the story first-hand – and without having to pay for the book. Likewise, you're getting paid for your work – happy Gladys.'

'It makes me feel so naughty, dear,' she said plaintively.

Then a knock comes at the door. Gladys starts. 'Shall we see anyone?' she asks.

My confidential maid enters and gives me a card. 'Oh, it's only the Baron,' I say, tossing the card into her lap. 'We'll see him, Edwards.'

The old Baron comes in and gives a little start of pleasure as he sees that neither of us, and Gladys in particular, is at all fully dressed.

'This is indeed a pleasure,' he says, kissing my hand and then Gladys's. 'And what are you two doing?'

I tell him that I am writing the story of my life – quite fully. 'You'll figure in it, Baron,' I say.

He starts again and lifts the hands that had been resting on Gladys's naked shoulders. 'Oh dear! Heaven forbid!' he says.

I reassure him and we chat over whiskys and sodas. I notice that the Baron drops a little tablet into his drink. 'What's that for?' I ask.

'Oh, a wonderful preparation, dear,' he answers, a wrinkled grin coming over his old face. 'It makes me feel thirty years younger,' he continues, putting down the empty glass.

'And what do you want to feel thirty for?' I ask. Then I notice him looking amorously at Gladys. 'Well, do you want me to leave the room?'

'Oh no,' says Gladys quickly.

'I've brought you each a little present,' says the old man, fumbling with his pockets. He produces two cases and there, on their plush beds, glitter two beautiful diamond brooches.

'It's good of you, Baron,' I say, 'but understand I'm not going to do anything for it. I've given that up. Besides, I'm in the middle of a literary work. Still, I think Gladys ought to. I'll take myself off.'

'Oh no, don't,' says the old man pleadingly.

'No, don't go, Marie,' says Gladys. 'Your story made me feel so wicked. I don't care what I do.'

'Very well, then,' I say, settling myself into an armchair. 'Give me a cigarette and I'll play a very up-to-date gooseberry.'

Little Gladys jumps up from her chair at the typewriter and whips the tulle from her shoulders. She is naked to the waist now. Below that, a pair of Parisian drawers, large and full, with beautiful lacework at their nether extremities. Below these again, silk, openwork stockings encase a pair of perfectly shaped legs.

Gladys has a beautiful figure. Her skin is white as ivory, and her arms, neck and shoulders are perfectly rounded. Dark chestnut hair falls round her oval face. Her eyes are wide open and gleaming, and her lips are half-parted.

'Now, let's see what your medicine will do for you, Baron,' she says. 'Do you want me to take anything more off?'

'Oh no,' says the old man. 'I love those pretty drawers.' And dropping to his knees he kisses the lace hem. Then he quickly begins to unfasten the fly of his trousers.

Alas! The thing that comes forth does not look at all like the cock of a man of thirty. It is wrinkled and it droops. Gladys looks disappointed, and I laugh aloud.

'But I feel awfully wicked,' says the Baron, plaintively.

'Yes, but you'll never get that wrinkle in,' I say. 'Gladys, you must work him up.'

Gladys fingers the incompetent penis daintily, touching it dexterously, and it brightens up a little. 'I think I can manage now,' says the old man.

But the moment her fingers leave his cock, it relapses. She drops on her knees and, raising it to her lips, begins to kiss it. I call to the Baron to turn round so that I can see when the veins swell. 'You'll have to jump on him quickly and ride him,' I say to Gladys while the Baron edges backwards till he is sitting on the chair.

She takes me at my word, but the instant she takes her lips from the swollen bulb, the penis becomes flaccid again. The skin wrinkles up towards the top, and the Baron looks the picture of despair.

'I did my best, Marie,' says Gladys.

'Oh, I see I shall have to look to this,' I say with a laugh. 'Get up on the table, Gladys, so that the Baron can have you standing up. I'll bring him up to the scratch.'

Gladys puts a great soft cushion on the table, climbs upon it and lies down, opening her legs wide and drawing her knees up till the red lips of her cunt can be plainly seen through the opening of her drawers. The Baron looks at the dear woman's little cunt – longingly, but despairingly.

I make him stand quite close to her, then go down on my knees before him and lick his penis with my lips and tongue as only I, Marie, know how. I run my tongue over the string which holds up his foreskin, and sweep it round beneath the bulb. I let my teeth press ever so daintily upon his cock, and I feel it swelling in my mouth. I push my mouth over it till the end touches my uvula, and all the time I stroke his balls gently. I feel his thighs wriggling against my head, and then I hear him say, 'That'll do, Marie. That'll do!'

As I withdraw my lips from the cock, which is now a cock for a man of any age to be proud of, Gladys's waiting fingers clutch it and guide it into her cunt. When I get up I see the old Baron working into her like a much younger man.

After a few thrusts he begins to scream, a sort of falsetto neigh, like a horse, and I know the longed-for end is near. His feet are doing a sort of double shuffle as he pushes feverishly. With a sigh, he falls on to her breast and I can see his shoulders heave as he comes.

'Oh, Baron,' murmurs Gladys, 'you are spending!'

I see his tongue darting into her mouth, his fingers clutching at her shoulders; and, as I realise how the old man is enjoying himself, I feel quite proud of my share in his action.

He pulls it out at last, all dripping, and sinks back into a chair. I give him the whisky and soda which I had prepared in readiness.

I throw Gladys a handkerchief. She stands up and wipes her cunt. Well, you see what sort of interruptions I am liable to get during the telling of my tale. I have written in the foregoing account of the doings of Gladys and the Baron while she has been lying exhausted in a chair. 'God, Marie, I am tired,' she says, throwing her cigarette end into the fire. 'The old man fucks like a young one.'

So we split a bottle of champagne and sit on the sofa with our arms around each other, sipping it, leaving the scene with my lover in his study till the next chapter. We're going out to dinner at Princess —'s and I know I shall come home in a gay mood.

Gladys and your humble servant, the authoress, slip out of our dinner gowns and get out of our corsets. It's quite early in the evening but, though the dinner was genial, we wanted to get home to our work. My little boudoir is delightfully warm and cosy. The firelight glitters on the cut-glass decanters, and the bubbles sparkle in the syphons. Gladys pushes her typewriting table up close to the fire and waits for the dictation:

Well, I am in my lover's study, bending over him with my lips on his, so pleased to be with him again. Attention readers!

He fondled me lovingly and pulled me on to his knee. 'Why haven't you been to see me?' he asked.

'Because of what you did before.'

'It wasn't anything serious,' he said, and I felt his hand slipping up my legs again. This time I didn't resist. He got it up till his fingers were tickling my pussy – I wore open drawers even then (it was economy – old ones of my mother). 'Isn't it nice?' he whispered in my ear.

'Yes, it is nice, but I don't understand why it is!' I answered.

'This is real love, Marie – what people do when they're married.'

I don't know how the impulse came to me, but I was impelled to put my hand between his thighs. I felt something hard under his thin football trousers, and instantly the remembrance of the great piece of flesh that had come out of another's trousers when he lay on top of the maidservant came back to me. I felt a burning desire to see if he had the same thing too. He had both hands up my clothes now. One was feeling the cheeks of my bottom, and the other finger had entered, ever so little, into my pussy. I felt a sudden thrill, and then I felt that I was all wet down there. How I remember that day! It was the thirteenth of December (never mind the year) and it was the first time that I had come. I didn't know what it was then. How many times have I come since then, I wonder?

Convulsively I gripped the hard flesh that I felt within his trousers.

'Oh, Marie,' he said suddenly. 'I mustn't get naughty today. I've got to play football.'

I gripped it all the tighter. I hadn't any idea what he meant by getting naughty – and how was I to know that such a feeling would hurt his football playing? At the same time I pressed my lips on his and kissed him again and again.

As I kissed, I shifted my position till I was sitting astride his knees, and then worked myself forwards till the upper part of my body was quite close to his. I wore very short skirts, only just to my knees, so of course they came up easily, leaving my thin drawers next to his football pants. But the opening at the head of the drawers let the bare flesh of my pussy press against him, and it touched exactly that spot where he had swollen so. I clutched him round the neck and wriggled delightedly.

Charley – that was his name – did not know very much about the arts of wickedness at that time. I don't think it ever occurred to him that he could have a woman, or make an attempt to do so, in the position that I was in then, sitting astride him. At any rate he never attempted to take his member out of his trousers.

'What is it, Charley, that's swelling up in your trousers?' I asked.

He seemed to hesitate, and then said, rather shyly, 'It's what men have and women haven't. It's the difference between men and women.' I am reminded as I write this of the women's rights meetings, when an austere old crow from Girton announced: 'After all the difference between men and women is only a little one,' upon which a rude man shouted out, 'Three cheers for the little difference!' But I digress.

'What do you call it, dear?' I asked. It was funny that although he seemed rather timid, it never occurred to me to be shy. Of course I hardly realised the enormity of what we were doing.

'We call it a cock,' he said in an attempt to be blunt.

I was possessed with a longing to see the thing. I slipped off Charley's lap and stood looking down at him. There was a blush on his handsome face.

'Charley,' I said, 'Have you much time before the match?'

'Yes, about half an hour.'

'And no one's likely to come in here?'

'Oh no, everyone's at "call over". I've got leave off.'

'Then – take your clothes off, will you? I – I – want to see you – naked.'

'My word, Marie,' breaks in Gladys. 'You had a pretty fair cheek when you were younger.'

'Well, you see, I hardly knew it was wrong,' I answered. 'I had been brought up entirely by men, and had had no one to tell me anything.'

'Then go on dear,' says Gladys. 'Only I know that for myself I always thought that a man had a fig leaf between his thighs – till I was nineteen.'

The boy seemed to hesitate. 'I'll – take off mine too, if you will,' I said. 'I want to see the difference!'

Without another word the dear fellow stood upright and, running his fingers down the front of his football trousers, undid the buttons and let the trousers slip down to his knees. Another little shuffle and they were at his ankles. A couple of kicks and they lay tumbled and discarded upon the floor. He stood upright now in only his boots, stockings and his jersey, which reached barely to the middle of his stomach. Another quick motion disembarrassed him of the striped jersey, and he was upright before me, stark naked save for the yellow football boots and the thick woollen stockings.

He was blushing furiously, but he stood manfully up to my curious gaze. My eyes stared straight at his cock, as he called it, which started out from the pit of his stomach. It was not very large – not nearly so large as the one I had seen put into the maidservant – but it was of a delicious ivory whiteness and oh, so stiff! It was about as big around as an ordinary school ruler and four inches or so long. At its base grew great little tufts of curly brown hair, and below the delightful thing hung a little round bag of tight skin, pinky-white in colour. I reached my hand out and touched it. It was very hot to the touch and quivered under my fingers.

Charley started as my hand lay on his cock. 'It's your turn now,' he cried. 'Off with your clothes. You promised you would.'

I did not hesitate – it was curious that I had not the slightest feeling of modest hesitation – and tore off my little jacket. I wore no corsets, and the undoing of a few strings set all my things loose. To jump out of my petticoat and drawers and get my chemise over my head was the work of a moment. Then, save for my shoes and stockings, I stood as naked as he. I stood straight up, my legs a little apart, and let him look at me. My long, dark hair hung down over my shoulders, but that was my only garment. Not a blush came into my face.

We stood for a moment, staring at each other. A goodly couple we made. My figure was as nearly perfect as might be, and Charley – well, he was as perfectly modelled as a statue. The muscles swelled up on his arms and legs, and upon his shoulders and chest, and above them that delicious white skin was stretching as tight as the parchment covering of a drum.

Then he rushed forwards and pulled me into his arms, pressing my hot and palpitating belly to his. All my veins seemed full of a coursing blood that was charged with a madly delicious sensation. I was supremely unconscious of what the legitimate conclusion of our embrace should be. I only felt certain there must be something more – some entrancing culmination.

His swelling cock thrust against my stomach, burning like a bar of heated iron, and both his hands were kneading the soft flesh of my bottom. My arms were round his shoulders, and my fingers played with the curly hair that fell on the nape of his neck. We kissed once, but he shyly drew his lips away and I felt his hot breath in my ear.

He pulled me down to sit beside him on the big armchair. He bent down so that his arm was underneath me. I could feel the two cheeks of my bottom closing upon his wrist, and his hand between my thighs. Charley's finger – his middle finger this time – worked in between the lips of my pussy and began to push in and out. The sensation was glorious when I got used to it.

'Will you put your hand on my cock,' he asked, taking my fingers and twining them around the swollen piece of flesh, 'and rub it up and down?'

I obeyed him without hesitation and we two sat silent, each one working at the other. I was in a dream of bliss, and I could see from the expression in his eyes, whenever I looked into his face, that he was as happy as I.

I remember that I was noticing a coincidence in the action of our knees. They were both opening and shutting quickly – in time with the movement of our hands. And then I heard the door open and looked up – to find someone else in the room.

A big – enormous, it seemed to me then – figure in football clothes stood with his back to the closed door. I recognised him at once. It was Benger, the captain of the school fifteen – quite the biggest – and the most important boy in the school. He was a monitor, and had about the same authority in his own house as a master.

Instinctively I ducked my head and turned it so that my hair shook over my face. I felt Charley's finger slip from my cunt, and I could hear him shuffling his feet.

'Good God!' came in brutal tones.

'Oh, get out, Benger,' I heard Charley saying. 'Please, get out of here.'

A sort of desperate courage came into my heart, and I held my head up to look him in the face. A hot flush surged up into my cheeks, and my whole body tingled as if on fire. But I still looked him straight in the face.

I could see his eyes flaming as mine stared into them. Then he slipped his hand under my arm and lifted me to my feet. I could feel his great fingers quivering on my soft flesh, and the pleasant sensation which it produced partially took away joy, fear and shame.

'Well, what have you been doing to her?' he said, speaking to Charley but still keeping his eyes on me.

'Nothing really, Benger. Nothing, I swear. Oh, do clear out and leave the poor woman alone. You can do what you like to me afterwards.'

But the great lout of a boy took no heed. He drew me close to him till my naked body pressed against his jacket. 'My word, you're a well-formed woman,' he said with a coarse chuckle. His fingers had slipped down till they were touching my breasts.

'I suppose you know this is an expulsion job, Tremlett?' the monitor said, rubbing me against him all the time. Somehow I did not feel inclined to struggle, but as I turned to look at poor Charley I was surprised to see that his little cock had lost all its stiffness and now simply hung there, limp.

'Surely you wouldn't make a scandal of it. You can lick me afterwards, but leave her . . . and why don't you take your hands off her yourself? I swear I haven't done anything serious to her. We were only playing about.

'Well, perhaps I won't make a scandal about it. But – ' He let go of me, walked back to the door, turned the key in the lock and put it in his pocket – 'But you aren't going to have all the picnic to yourself.' He ran his finger down the front of his football trousers, as Charley had done, and in a moment an enormous cock was displayed before my startled eyes. It seemed about a foot long and as big around as my wrist. In a minute he had hold of me in his strong arms, on the floor beneath him. With one hand he pushed my legs apart and then I felt his tremendous cock pressing between my thighs.

'Oh, stop it, Benger!' I heard Charley say. 'She could never take that enormous cock of yours.'

'We'll see about that,' the big boy grunted. 'And don't try to interfere. Also, I'll kick you out of the football team. I won't hurt her.'

He got the end of his cock a tiny way within the lips of my cunt, and gave a push.

'It's no good, I told you,' said Charley in a hushed voice, and I felt Benger pulled from me.

He made no resistance and got up. 'I don't want to hurt you,' he said breathing heavily. 'Don't make a noise.'

'You'll never get that great thing into me,' I said. 'Do leave me alone.'

'Well, what did Tremlett do?' he said very gruffly.

'He only – only – put his finger – a little way in.'

Benger looked around at Charley and my eyes followed his. I noticed that the boy's cock was stiff again now.

'I must work it off somehow,' he said roughly.

'No, no. Think of the football, Benger,' said Charley. 'Leave her alone. The big boy had his fingers upon the tip of his cock and was agitating the end of his great thing.

All this time I experienced a delicious sense of physical pleasure from looking at the great swollen thing. I had risen to my feet and, acting on impulse, I took it in my hand and began to work it as I had worked Charley's. He clutched one arm round me. 'That's right, dear, go on!' he said. He kissed me hotly upon the lips, and then did a thing that surprised me – at that time.

Charley was standing quite close to us. Benger stretched out his free arm and pulled the boy up to him, so that their bodies touched. 'You put your hand on it, too,' he said to Charley. 'I want you both to toss me off together.'

Then he kissed Charley on the lips, just as he had kissed mine. It astounded me that two boys should kiss each other, but I was too excited to think. And the feeling of Charley's hand by mine, working on the great cock, excited me more and more.

Benger had an arm round each of us now, pressing us to his sides. Between us was that great cock, with both our hands working in unison on it.

It seemed a long time (but I do not suppose that it was, in all, more than a couple of minutes) before the palpitating, fleshy thing gave several tremendous throbs. It stiffened till it seemed like a red-hot rod of steel in my hand and then, from the little mouth in the middle of its end, a jet of liquid stuff shot out.

'Oh, he's spent at last, has he?' says Gladys, leaning back in her chair. 'Marie, my dear, if you're going to deal with all your amatory experiences in the same lengthy style, the *Encyclopedia Britannica* won't have anything over *The Confessions of Marie Carey.*'

'Dear,' I answered, a little vexed – for the telling of this first experience of anything really sensual in my life had excited me and I disliked the interruption – 'everything must have its beginning. Which do you consider the most important event in a woman's life: her first fuck or her last?'

'I'm not at all sure,' she answers, 'nor shall I be able to tell you till I come to my last – which I sincerely trust will not be for a deal of years to come yet. Besides, begging your pardon, there hasn't been much fuck about this charming episode in the study up to now. Am I to infer that . . . ?' she bent over the machine again.

'Certainly not,' I said. 'There was no fuck, as you coarsely put it, on this occasion. It's a sentimental memory.'

'Sentimental – funny name isn't it, you and a boy frigging a great lout for all you were worth!'

'Haven't you ever tossed a man off?'

'Of course,' answered Gladys. 'But only when I was unwell and he couldn't do anything better to me. I'd have had one of those footballers in me if I'd died for it, Marie.'

'Well,' I continued, severely ignoring the interruption, 'Benger's cock flung fluid all over the place.'

'Fluid, surely to goodness you know what it's called?'

'Naturally I do now; please remember, Gladys, I'm telling this story as it happened to me. I was a younger girl then.'

'What a dear little girl; stark naked in a boy's nice room, helping another stark naked being of the opposite sex to – '

'That's enough! To continue. This fluid shot out of Benger till there was a great pool on the floor. His body worked convulsively all the time. But at last his cock shrank under my grasp; he pulled himself from us and began buttoning up his trousers hastily. In a minute he was gone from the room.

'I got my clothes quickly; somehow I felt ashamed then, and I'm sure Charley did. As soon as I was dressed I left the room also.'

~ 23 ~

The Romances of Blanche la Mare

GEORGE REGINALD BACCHUS 1903

The Romances of Blanche la Mare is the second volume of the previously discussed trilogy *The Confessions of Nemesis Hunt*, which can safely be considered the semi-fictionalised erotic biography of an Edwardian actress. Although the book's three-volume format mimicked the Victorian triple-decker structure for novels (which was still popular from the 1880s), this was certainly not Charles Dickens. The language is sexually explicit, the scenes anatomically intimate and the details erotic, but in the service of erotic realism. The lifestyles and *amours* are portrayed from life in an authentic and naturalistic manner. It is oddly, and fortunately, also written in a somewhat naïve fashion. Simple details and tasks of daily living and the objects used in their performance, as well as fashion and social conduct, are reported, even when an antithesis to the eroticism of the narrative. (As an odd aside, this is the first erotic novel to mention the use of a typewriter to compose erotica. Likewise it is one of the first works in this genre to have mention of telephones, Vaseline and the etymology of the then new term 'flapper'.) Additionally, there is a great amount of exegesis on the physical and sexual maturation of a woman growing up in late-Victorian times, and the traumas attendant. The reader is presented the lust to be sure, but the more mundane as well: the sweat, the smells, the distresses, etc.

Those familiar with turn-of-the-century London will discover many of the characters in the *Nemisis Hunt* series to seem oddly familiar, as if they were caricatures of well-known people in the theatre, arts and publishing worlds. This is very likely the case. *Cognoscenti* of the early-twentieth-century English erotica trade (the authors, publishers, printers, translators, artists, etc.) are struck with the names and details of the characters throughout the trilogy, especially in a scene set in the office of the *Dial* magazine. Here are apparent descriptions of the publishing partners H. S. Nichols (assiduous printer) and Leonard Smithers (wealthy, dapper lawyer) both from Manchester and responsible for the famous art and literary magazines *The Yellow Book* and *The Savoy*, as well as the sexual fare of the Erotica Biblion Society. Additionally there appear certain of their friends and circle: Ernest Dowson (the unkempt poet and translator), Aubrey Beardsley (famous *fin-de-siècle* art-nouveau illustrator), and the journalists Cyril Ranger Gull, John Poole Kirkwood and George Reginald Bacchus.

Though not up to the literary standards of now classic nineteenth-century authors, the work is eminently readable, and delightfully so. Its episodic construction allows for perusing over several leisurely sessions without fear that forgotten facts will disrupt the understanding or enjoyment of further reading. It has charm and humour, even if somewhat sluttish. Though probably never intended to be used as a first-hand account and primary reference for sexual and social life at the time, it should be, for it is truly a novel that imitates life, rather than fictionalising it.

Here then is an excerpt in which the author, having assumed the stage-name Blanche la Mare, recounts an episode that demonstrates why entertainers had such an unsavoury reputation at the time.

~~~ from *The Romances of Blanche la Mare*

Theatrical folks, one of whom I now proposed to be, inhabited principally, I had heard, strange and unknown lands across the water, called Kennington and Camberwell and Brixton. I had never been on the Surrey side of the Thames in my life, and had no intention of going there now. So, possibly very extravagantly, I determined to set myself up in the West End. My little *costumière*, Eloise's friend, who had so kindly given me credit, lived close by in Jermyn Street, and it occurred to me that I might get a room there.

I will skip all further details of my life in London till the Herbert Restall Company got away on tour. We were to open at Oxford and the 'train call' was for Paddington, eleven-thirty one Sunday morning. I turned up early, unaccompanied, for Madame Karl had gone out to supper the night before, and had not returned – perhaps as a little revenge for my absences.

Still, I was not the first on the platform, and I soon got to learn that the habit of theatrical companies was to arrive very early at the station, and exhibit their best frocks. I had my best frock on, and I'm certain it was the best in the company. Herbert Restall cast an admiring glance at me when he arrived. He did not speak to me, and I noted the reason: his wife, an angular lady past fifty, and of forbidding and nonconformist type of countenance, followed him everywhere.

Annesley found me the train, and he found me also the acting manager, who was engaged in gumming labels on the carriage windows – labels indicative of the compartments to be occupied by various members of the company. I was not put to travel with the chorus ladies, but with the two 'Sisters Knock', the dancers, to whom also Annesley introduced me. We all repaired to the bar together, in which pleasant spot were assembled the majority of the company, some seventy all told.

When we arrived at Oxford I was undecided where to stay. Being quite in ignorance of theatrical tours and living arrangements, I had intended to go to a hotel. Certainly my salary was only thirty-five shillings a week, but I had a little spare cash. The genial sisters Knock, however, quickly disabused me of that. 'Come and stop with us, old dear,' they said, 'don't go putting up at hotels and making folks think you're a tart before they can prove it.' And so I went.

The rooms were rather a shock, small and meanly furnished. The mural decorations consisted of a religious tract and lithographs, and the landlady was as dirty as she was familiar. But the sisters seemed to think they were in clover. 'Old Ma Osborne's a bit of all right,' explained one of them. 'Doesn't mind who we have in, or what we do, and that's saying something in a place like Oxford.'

When the question of dinner was mooted, old Ma Osborne grinned. 'Well, me dears,' she said, 'I haven't worried about getting you any dinners, because, knowing your likes and your habits, I've took the liberty of telling Lord Hingley of the House, which is Christ Church, me dear, that he might be at liberty to call. And Lord Hingley, me dears, will see as how you have a better dinner than I might be able to offer to you here.'

I was inclined to be annoyed, but held my peace.

Maude Knock (the one with the mole) became businesslike at once.

'Many thanks, Mrs Osborne,' she said, 'but who is Lord Hingley? He's not on my visiting list.'

'Is he all right?' chipped in the moleless sister. 'None of your courtesy title paupers, eh, what?'

'All right; that I would say he is. Ten thousand a year he has, as I should know, dearies, my husband being his scout for nigh on two years in college, and as generous a gentleman as ever was.'

The sisters Knock nodded assent, and Ma Osborne retired, beaming.

The highly recommended Lord Hingley presently made his appearance, accompanied by his friend, Mr Charles Latimer; apparently they had only reckoned on two, and I saw breakers ahead, for, without conceit, I knew well enough that neither of the sisters could hold a candle to me in looks, or in any sort of attraction.

We were conveyed in cabs to Mr Latimer's room. Mr Latimer was a rich young gentleman, son of the famous brewer of that name, and he occupied the most elegant apartments. He was plain but well groomed, and very well dressed. Despite his origin he was a gentleman. Lord Hingley was nice looking, if rather stupid, and obviously rather too fond of drink. They were both scrupulously polite to us girls. We had a most admirable dinner, cooked and served in a style which would not have disgraced a smart West End restaurant, and we all of us drank rather too much champagne, to say nothing of subsequent liqueurs. Still nothing happened, and the men made no attempt at lovemaking. The sisters obliged at the piano, and so did I, and after I had done so, Lord Hingley contrived to get me alone in a corner.

'I say,' he stammered, 'you're a lady, aren't you?'

'I'm certainly not a man.'

'But don't joke; you aren't like the others. How did you come to be living with Maude and Mabel?'

'Because they are my friends.'

The poor boy became very nervous, so I explained.

'I am a lady by birth, but who I am and how I came to be here, I don't care to have anybody know. If I told you my father's name, you would probably know.'

But he squeezed my hand, not as a man would squeeze the hand of a chorus girl tart, and I knew that he was in love, the first young man of title who had loved me. He likewise made an appointment for the following day, to meet at the Queen's Restaurant for lunch, a drive, and a hasty little dinner at his own rooms to follow (he lived out of college).

I went down to the theatre on the following morning – the first time I had entered a theatre as a member of a theatrical company. Early as I was, several of the girls were there before me, and the best places in the dressing room, which was to contain six of us, were taken.

There were the twin sisters Knock; Lily Legrand, a show lady of more or less mature age, but undeniable charm of figure; and little

Bertha Vere, Restall's mistress, who was not, however, allowed any special privileges in the company because of her relationship to the 'Guvnor'. I had to hang my clothes up in the middle of the room and do without a looking glass. My brand-new make-up box occasioned great joy among the other girls, who all appeared to have come with the tiniest remnants of the necessary powders and pigments.

My first day in Oxford – also my first day on tour – was fairly uneventful. I went out to lunch with my lordling friend, but he treated me with extreme courtesy, to say nothing of a very good lunch. I found out afterwards that Oxford boys, while always delighted to get to know any actress on the road, expect little in return for their hospitality. My young man did not even attempt to kiss me, though we sat for a long time in his rooms after lunch – I think that he was even rather shocked that I smoked.

When I got back to my lodging I found the sisters Knock there, back also from a luncheon party. They had brought on my letters from the theatre. One of them was from the poet, and of a distinctly improper nature. Its pretty indelicate imagery, and a most sensual drawing by an artist friend which was enclosed, brought so much moisture on my legs that I had to get upstairs and wash before I dared face the semi-public undressing of the theatre dressing room.

As the majority of the company had appeared in *The Drum Major* before, we had no dress rehearsal, and I had not even seen my costumes till I got to the theatre that night. *The Drum Major* was a 'tights play', and all the girls in our room wore those fascinating garments. I was rather anxious to see how the legs of the other girls looked. Mine, I knew, were all right, a little on the small side perhaps, but quite perfectly modelled. I could submit to the difficult task of inserting a threepenny piece between my naked thighs when placed together, and keeping it there. I had also silk tights, a present from Mr Annesley, who had informed me that the management considered cotton good enough for the chorus. He had found out the colour of my dresses, and had these made for me.

The girls in the room displayed little delicacy. Maude undressed stark naked, and walked about the room rubbing herself down with a towel. Her figure was good. Shapely legs, if perhaps a little too muscular to satisfy the artist who takes his ideal from the ancient Greek statues, but that was the fault of her dancing training. A firm, rather brownish skin, but without wrinkles, and round breasts with scarlet nipples. Her arms were also muscular, and she had the hair under her armpits shaved off, though a great abundance of dark luxurious hair curled round the lips of her cunt and blossomed up on to her stomach.

Lilly Legrand kept her vest on while putting on her tights, not omitting, however, to show the hair on the lower portion of her body, and the sexual organ underneath. Mabel Knock stripped boldly to the buff, and displayed a figure which was almost an exact counterpart of her sister's, but she was more modest, and turned her back on us while she hurriedly slipped into her tights. Little Bertha, Restall's mistress, was far more discreet, and got into her leg attire under cover of other garments. The reason for that was, I afterwards discovered, that she padded. I was also as modest as might be, and immediately aroused the suspicion of the elder Knock girl that I had come to the theatre with my pads on, a common enough practice with some chorus girls who are ashamed of letting their companion tarts know that nature had not been altogether kind to them. She took me by surprise, and ran her hand all over my legs. 'Genuine,' she pronounced, with a laugh, and Bertha looked envious.

I was one of the officers. It was a military play, and I had to open the show with five others, headed by our captain, a very dapper little lady who was the principal boy of the play. When I first walked on to the stage, I could hardly see for fear (luckily I was placed last). I felt practically naked as the music surged in my ears, and it was only when I heard the other girls break into the surging melody of the song that I regained enough self-possession to join them. However, in half an hour I was all right, and got the brace of lines allotted to me off swimmingly.

The piece went well; Restall was in great form, and was ably backed up by his leading lady, a well-known exponent of soubrette parts. In the third act he was at his very best, but I had an awkward moment when he selected me as the other half of an impromptu gag scene. To his great surprise, I answered him back and got a big laugh for myself. When the show was over, and he had taken numerous calls, he stopped me on the stage. 'Clever little girl,' was the comment. 'We'll do that again tomorrow. Come up to my room when you're dressed, and we'll have a little drink and a little rehearsal.'

I was naturally elated, but the other girls laughed and more than hinted that I was wanted for something very different from a business chat.

However, he began in a businesslike enough manner, complimented me on the way I had made his gag go, and in his quiet, incisive, clever way, suggested the necessary outlines of working it up.

Then he asked me to sit down and gave me a whisky and soda. I noticed that his eye was devouring my charms with a hungry gleam. He began to let his conversation get rather frisky, and then boldly praised various portions of my body, my legs, my waist, and my breasts even. I finished my drink quickly and got up to go, but as I rose he followed me and clasped me in his arms before I had moved a step. I felt a passionate kiss on my throat, and his hand pressed roughly against the lower part of my stomach.

I protested and struggled, for I had no wish to make myself cheap in his eyes by an easy surrender. However, nothing was of any avail. He did not prolong the struggle, but calmly locked the door and proceeded to talk the matter over.

His arguments were pretty matter of fact. He was altogether carried away by my beauty, he said, and was mad to enjoy me. 'What harm was done?' he argued, and he added that he could be a very good friend to me.

Of course, in the end I surrendered, and then came a very improper piece of business. Restall's costume necessitated skin-tights, without any trunks, and, in case of any untoward swelling, he had his penis bound to his stomach. So, when he had slipped off his tights, this curious arrangement met my astonished eyes – and he made me undo the wrapping till a fine stalwart member sprang from its bounds. I was surprised at its size and condition, for Restall was a man of over fifty who had lived every day of his life. His position had brought him into contact with thousands of girls who were only too ready to submit to overtures, and, if rumour was to be trusted, he had availed himself of every opportunity. Also he was a drunkard; I don't suppose he had gone to bed sober any night for the last twenty-five years.

When once we got to business I was randy enough. There was no sofa, and the floor looked rather dirty, so he had me straddlewise across his knees, easing me down on to him till I had his penis within me right up to its hairy hilt. He grabbed me frightfully tight to him and fucked me quite fiercely, but there was something in his savagery which delighted me. When it was over he drained a tremendously stiff whisky and soda and then sat back in the only big chair in the room. 'Well, you'd better be back to your room,' he said after a minute. 'The girls will be suspicious.'

'I thought as much,' I answered rather angrily. 'You've had all you want from me, and want to get rid of me.'

He became quite tender on the instant, and assured me that he meant nothing of the kind, only he was nervous lest I should be suspected of over familiarity with him. In fact he became so tenderly solicitous that he took me in his arms and kissed me. He became naughty again, and the dirty beast fucked me again.

Nothing much of great interest happened during our three-day stay at Oxford – we were only allowed half a week by the university authorities, in accordance with the wise regulation that more than three days of the society of any particular set of musical comedy sirens is bad for the peace of mind of the undergraduates. I went out to all meals, some with my lordling, and some with the friends of Miss Sarel, the leading lady, who had graciously deigned to take me up. She was a bright, pretty little thing, quite passably clever, of a naughty temperament, and very much on the make, as the theatrical saying goes; she came out of Oxford with one or two valuable presents in the jewellery line.

I was always stared at in the street, but the stare was not the sensual glance of the man-about-town, who feels his cock raised at the appearance of an attractive female, but the simple admiration of a healthy young mind. Not that everything of a sensual nature was absent from our little stay – to say nothing of that already recounted scene in Restall's dressing room – for I experienced the beginning of a love affair.

One night the sisters Knock brought home the tenor of the company to supper. Jean Messel was a strikingly handsome man, about thirty-five or so, I supposed, whose dark features betrayed a foreign origin. He had often eyed me at the theatre, but we had never spoken till this party. On this occasion, however, he found courage to press my hand, and, later, to snatch a kiss. That kiss set me on fire. I had known well enough before the delights of a sensual feeling, but never a sensual feeling coupled with love. I dreamed of him all night, and the next morning when we met at the station, and exchanged some common-place greeting, I experienced the sensation known as blushing all over.

I did not continue in lodgings with the sisters Knock. Some little unpleasantness over my intimacy with the young Lord had arisen, to say nothing of my obvious attraction for Jean Messel, so at our next stop, which was Manchester, I chummed with a Miss Letty Ross, who played the third principal part. Miss Ross had many acquaintances among the wealthy manufacturers of the north: fat, jolly, middle-aged men, with any amount of money, which they enjoyed spending, and a great deal of which found its way into the pockets of the pretty little tarts of the various wandering companies. They wanted very little for their money, and I was glad for it, for my passion for the tenor produced a longing in my heart to remain quite chaste. Still one cannot exactly accept a diamond bangle for nothing, and more than once little Blanche suffered herself to be extended on the sofa of a private hotel room, her dainty clothes elevated till the exposure of her naked charms caused some great Lancashire cock to crow lustily with anticipation. How hard they fucked, those north-country merchants, and what quantities of sperm they spent, but they spent quantities of money, too, bless their enlarged hearts. At the time I grew very frightened of getting in the family way; those lusty devils were just the sort of men to get me caught, and I could not help a reciprocal spend when they came.

At Edinburgh, we boldly went to one of the best hotels, trusting to our fortune to find a mug to settle our bills, and sure enough we did find one, in the guise of a well-known whisky distiller. He was staying in the same hotel and took on the two of us, first Letty and then myself. I was not jealous, for it gave me a rest, and I was really sweet to him on my nights. He swore his cock had never, never felt such pleasure. He was nearly sixty, but he had never been sucked off, so I cleaned his cock up one night, and taught him that. He nearly went off his head with joy.

On the Saturday night after an uncommonly good supper, and too many liqueurs, the old man falteringly asked if we two would mind his coming to bed with both of us. He had done so well during the week that we had not the heart to say no. We arranged for him to come to our bedroom in half an hour, when we should be undressed, but our door was barely closed behind us when in he slipped blushing like a schoolboy detected in a fault, begging to undress us himself.

He went for me first; I was wearing a three-quarter-length frock that night, and the dear old gentleman got excited over it. I didn't raise a hand to help him, and he stripped me right to the buff. After he got me out of my bodice, his frenzied cock was nearly bursting his trousers, and when he had got me down to my drawers and vest, the poor panting thing had to be released. I gave it just one pat with my hand and the spend flew all over me, covering my body right up to my neck. He was disconsolate, and Letty was angry and said it was unfair to start so soon. But Blanche was equal to the occasion. I sponged myself clean, did the same to his cock, told Letty to tongue his mouth, and we very soon had him stiff. Then he finished my undressing, till I sat in all my naked beauty on the bed before him.

He was so randy that he would have liked to fuck me again, then and there, but Letty naturally interfered. There was such a beautiful fire in the room that we both lay naked on the bed while our old friend tore off his clothes as if he was undressing for a swimming race against time. Funnily enough, though I often slept with Letty, not till that moment had I the least physical desire for her, but the filthiness of the whole scene overpowered me. I rolled over on the top of her, feverishly fingered her pretty body and covered her lips with hot kisses, which she returned in no halfhearted spirit. In a trice I had a finger up her cunt, so that ingress was barred to the old man. Next moment, however, he was up me from behind, his arms gripping both our bodies, and he came in me while my lips were glued to Letty's and all my lust was for her. Still, he must have had a good fuck, for I was wriggling my stomach against hers like a fury. Even when he had finished I was filthily randy. I drew my finger, all covered with spend from Letty's cunt, and made him lick it clean, an innovation in sin which he thoroughly enjoyed.

Subsequently he fucked Letty and myself once more, and that finished him. He shambled back to his bedroom, while Letty and I, after a hot bath together, had one delicious bout of mutual cunt-sucking, then fell asleep in each other's arms.

Next morning when the bill was presented, our old friend had something of a shock, but he could not, after the events of the previous night, make any complaint. I fancy the one hundred and two whiskies and sodas worried him. Of course, we didn't give it away that we had had all our friends in during the daytime, while he was at his business, and he thoroughly believed we had slipped all that intolerable deal of liquor down our own fairy throats. He paid us the compliment of remarking that there wasn't a bonnie lass from Maidenkierk to John o' Groats that could have done the like.

All this time I barely had an opportunity of seeing my dark-eyed Jean Messel. His wife, who figured in the bills as Miss Henden, became suspicious and never let him out of her sight. She wasn't a bad little woman, and on the stage she looked very nice, but what a fake. To begin with, she wore lifters to give her an added inch in height. When she went on the stage her legs were entirely encased in shapes, and even in ordinary walking dress she sported hip pads. Her bust – well, one night I got wet coming to the theatre and wanted a change of stockings, and every available stocking that woman had stuffed into her bodice. She even padded her arms, for she wore tightly-fitting, transparent sleeves, and the flesh-coloured pads that showed through had the appearance of the most fascinating rounded arms. She wore a yard of false hair, and what she had of her own was dyed. Her teeth, I need scarcely add, were removable at desire. Some of the girls used to question whether she had a false cunt or not.

One night Jean and I got a chance to walk home from the theatre together, while she was at home ill. We came by a short-cut through a mean street, lit only by an occasional lamp, and towered over by gaunt, stark walls. We were quite alone, for it was late and very dark, and the neighbourhood had a dangerous reputation. There was no noise save a faint flip-flop of water, and presently we came to a place where the river was lazily licking a flight of stone steps. It was an eerie place, and I started nervously, brushing my shoulder against my companion. The next moment his arms were gripping me to him, and my lips had sought his. I was willing enough to have let him have me, there and then, but presently he pushed me from him.

'Little Darling,' he said, 'next week my wife will not be with us. Shall we live in the same house?'

I said, 'Yes,' with a kiss; he saw me to my hotel door, and we parted.

The Story of Nemesis Hunt

GEORGE REGINALD BACCHUS 1906

As noted, *The Story of Nemesis Hunt* is a genuine showbusiness memoir, of sorts. The entire *Nemesis Hunt* story was first published in three volumes, appearing in 1902, 1903 and 1906; *Blanche la Mare* was the middle volume and *The Story of Nemesis Hunt* the last. The books emanated from a secret press in London, operated by a 'Gerald N—', according to the autobiography of Jack Smithers, son of a famous Victorian publisher of 'lewd' books. The original printings are genuinely rare, and known more by reputation and legend than from actual reading. There are no sets in any of the great libraries of Europe, and to date there has been only one complete reprint, that a now scarce three-volume illustrated version done in America (NY?) about 1935, but issued with unrelated titles for each of the volumes. There have additionally been a number of incomplete and partial reprints by several erotica publishers over the last eighty years.

C. R. Dawes, in his 1943 unpublished history of English erotica, notes the publisher of *Nemesis Hunt* to state: 'This book marks a new departure in English erotic literature. It has a definite and interesting plot, and is told in able and easy language, with a distinct literary style, and whilst being free from the banalities of the ordinary English erotic book it possesses a raciness and an intensely amusing chatty manner, which places it far above the level of any modern work of that kind in our language.' As Kearney points out in his *History of Erotic Literature*, although these are the sentiments of someone trying to sell copies of the novel, they are quite astute, the novel being both light and amusing.

The author of the entire *Nemesis Hunt* series was most likely George Reginald Bacchus (1873–1945), an Oxford-educated journalist, who also translated foreign erotica at the same time he wrote pieces for religious weeklies. The initial background for *Nemesis Hunt* could well have come from his wife, the actress Isa Bowman, one of the famous Bowman Sisters of English stage fame, whom he married in 1899. His own personal experiences in the worlds of the English theatre and *sub-rosa* publishing would have contributed the balance. This theory is bolstered by manuscript notes made in an unpublished erotica catalogue by Lawrence Forster and from title-page information that Bacchus was also responsible for three other Edwardian erotic classics: *Pleasure Bound, Pleasure Bound Ashore* and *Maudie*.

Of added interest to the erotobibliophile is the fact that this volume contains a scene set in a publisher's office which covertly describes several of the actual participants responsible for this book's publication. Thus it contributes to its own bibliography and is also important corroboration for other accounts of the workings of erotica and *sub-rosa* figures of the period.

Here is an excerpt from the last volume of *Nemesis Hunt*, recounting some of the further 'adventures in love and lust of a pleasurable woman on the English Stage', who has now taken the professional name of Nemesis Hunt, as a star of Restall's Travelling Players.

✎ from *The Story of Nemesis Hunt*

We were playing at Liverpool and in the audience was a very august personage who, of course, must be nameless. The party came to the theatre late. As luck would have it, I was playing a principal part that night and I was rattling through in particularly good form. The theatre was crammed. Everything merry and bright, and everyone complimented me on my appearance.

I noticed that I came in for a lot of attention from the box whose occupants were supposed to be incognito – it was quite a fusillade of opera glasses – and when the curtain fell for the last time I saw two of the said occupants standing in the wings. Restall touched my shoulder as I was leaving the stage.

'I want you to come out to supper with me tonight, child,' he said, 'with . . . ' and he whispered, 'but of course you must forget it afterwards.'

I was a little doubtful and told Jean. 'Go! I should think you ought to go,' was his decision, 'you don't get a chance of hobnobbing with folk like that every day. Put on your nicest things, I'll wait up.'

Restall fetched me from my room. 'You haven't told any of the girls?' he queried.

'Not one.'

'That's a good little girl. Now this is a great compliment. He thinks a lot of you, and has sent some very complimentary messages.'

The august party occupied a suite of rooms in a big hotel, entrance to which was gained through a private door in a side street. Restall and I were met in an anteroom by two young-old men, who were civil with Restall, and very polite to me.

We had sherry and in a moment or two a door opened and the august personage appeared, and made himself promptly very pleasant. He spoke English with a great deal of difficulty and seemed very pleased that I spoke French. I was very nervous and frankly glad when a lady joined us.

Who she was, I did not know, but she was English and pleasant and pretty, though obviously verging on middle age. Her complexion was still fresh and the extreme *décolletage* of her dress showed to their fullest advantage a pair of breasts, firm, round and upstanding. The nipples were barely concealed, and she wore no shoulder straps. It was one of those dresses which was kept up with 'tact and luck', and necessitated shaving under the armpits. She soon made me feel at home.

Supper was bright and decorous; Restall was amusing and I content to look nice. I suppose I succeeded, for the Hereditary Grand Duke of — (you see, readers, it was quite whom you expected) never took his eyes off me, and if I know anything about glances, those eyes were telegraphic communication of a stiffly standing prick underneath the tablecloth.

Supper over, Madame took me into an adjoining room, a cosy sort of room with subdued lights and delicate perfumes. She sank with a swish of her skirts into the corner of a luxurious divan, and lay there, showing her stockings to the garters, while she lazily lit a cigarette. I tumbled to the game in a minute when she began to pump me about my morals.

From 'I suppose actresses have a great many admirers?' came a delicately graded series of questions, and more than one hint that there was expensive jewellery in the air of this particular room for any pretty, if improper, little girl who chose to go the right way about earning it. At last I surprised her by my bluntness.

'I quite understand,' I said. 'His Highness wants me, and your job is to find out whether I'll let him . . . well . . . I will.'

'You are a little angel, to save me so much trouble,' she cooed, delightedly rising to her feet and crossing to me. 'His Highness is mad for you and my life has been a burden, I can tell you. Thank Heaven, this party is arranged at last. No one will ever know, and his Highness, you may be sure, will not be mean.'

'It isn't that . . . ' I began.

'No, no, I dare say not, my dear; but valuable presents of jewellery are always acceptable to the most moral of us, and especially when they come from Royal Dukes – '

'But I mustn't say – ' I interrupted.

'Oh, yes, you may . . . If I know Henri, you will find some little inscription about your art that will make the display of your present quite all right. Henri is no novice . . . but seriously, he is a great deal in love with you and – stop me if I anger you – if I were you, I would let him get me with child. If the result is anything like its royal father, you may find yourself mother of a duke. Things like that still happen in south-eastern Europe.'

I laughed and blushed but the idea commended itself to me.

'Well, dear, don't think of me only as procuress,' whispered Madame, kissing me lovingly. 'You won't regret this, and Henri is no mean performer either – I can vouch for that. You'll find the bedroom through these curtains.' And with a laugh, she slipped from the room.

In the bedroom I found everything the most fastidious woman might want. I came into the sitting room. Whether I was expected to undress and wait in bed, I do not know, but at any rate I did not. Royal Highness or not, he must make some kind of a bluff at lovemaking before he got me.

A huge mirror confronted the corner of the divan that Madame had just vacated, and there I arranged myself; not too suggestively but with an air of comfortable naughtiness which should tell a man that his evening was not going to be wasted.

The divan was covered with an immense bear skin and my flesh showed very white against the dead black of the fur. I drank two glasses of *crème de menthe* and lit a perfumed cigarette. When in the bedroom I had withdrawn most of the pins from my head, so that very little disarrangement would allow my hair to fall in all its glory. Thus I waited.

He was a long time and my cunt moistened with anticipation. That I did not wish and I had only just finished wiping it dry again, when the door opened to admit his Highness.

'At last I may tell you, adorable little English girl, how I have admired your acting at the theatre,' he murmured, his lips almost touching my ear and his hot breath causing a delicious excitement to my naked throat.

'Your praise is – '

I was interrupted again. His Highness put his arm around my waist while his other hand began to toy with my breasts. I made no resistance and his lips pursued mine, which were instantly joined in a long, luscious kiss. I slipped further and further on my back and was almost in a horizontal position when the kiss came to an end.

My legs were opened wide and I was ready to be fucked, but he pulled me back in a sitting posture, knelt by my side and for the first time I had a sight of the royal prick, and a very decent-size one it was. He guided my hands to it, throwing back his head with a faraway look in his eyes, and as my fingers played with it, his whole body quivered. Then, with a touch of his hand, he bent my head down. I took the hint, and my lips and tongue were soon busy with the throbbing gland.

He seemed to go mad with pleasure; his fingers feverishly toyed with my hair; his body twisted in every direction. He moaned, almost screamed. His prick stiffened till it seemed like cast iron.

'Suck it!' he cried.

I did.

'Harder! Harder!'

I sucked it as hard as I could, never for a moment relaxing the lightning movements of my tongue. His fingers left my hair and played with my ears, my cheeks, the corners of my lips, even as they quivered round his burning penis. At last they caught my breasts and each little hard, standing nipple was caressed by his fingers. His prick stiffened to such an alarming extent that I knew the end was near. A violent convulsion of the body, an upward jerk of the prick and my mouth was filled with spurt after spurt of semen.

As for me, I wanted to be fucked, willing enough as I was to play the gamahuche game, but my cunt actually ached for relief. I had no thought whatever for Jean during the evening. Anybody could have fucked me at that moment, but particularly did I want the royal member – now, alas, dangling rather weakly against his trousers.

His Highness crossed to a little table, filled two brimming glasses of champagne from an open bottle, which I had not perceived. Was it possible that someone, Madame for instance, had entered while I was sucking him?

We talked very little. I fondled his hair and face while his hands wandered nervously over my calves. Occasionally I let my fingers fall on his inert cock and a little flicker rewarded me.

But I was too hot for dalliance. I flung my body over his, thrust my tongue into his mouth, and at the same time violently frigged his shrunken prick. It had the desired result. He stiffened and thrust me from him.

'Undress, my adorable little darling!' he whispered.

Standing before him, I did so, slowly and deliberately, allowing his lustful eyes to gloat severally over the varied charms that came to view.

I showed my breasts first; as I flung wide the corsets and stood with only a transparent chemise around me, and as that slipped to my feet, he stood up, his cock rampant, and pressed my naked body to him.

I pulled his tie undone and jerked the collar from its studs. Presently I felt his trousers slipping and I pulled them eagerly to his ankles, lifted his feet and got rid of the tiresome things. To ease him of the rest of his things did not take long, and there we were, both naked.

In a moment he was fucking me in the usual way, flat on my back, with my legs twisted around his calves, his arms around my back, mine around his, his cock banged in up to the hilt, his tongue in my mouth, working for all he knew.

It was a short, sharp fuck, a strong animal feeling pervading it from start to finish; no brain excitement; purely pleasure, the fuck that means children as a rule. We both spent together and, remembering Madame's injunction about getting in the family way, I was anxious lest he carry me into the bedroom and introduce me to the syringe, so I feigned faintness and fell back helplessly on the couch.

My exalted lover was most concerned; he bathed my forehead with brandy, and began to get nervous, so I judged it best to recover, lest he summon Madame to his aid. With a sigh and a nicely spoken, 'Where am I?' I gently came to.

After that we went to bed. His Highness assured me that no one would know of my staying there for the night, which meant, I suppose, that everyone would know, but no one would dare say anything. There was no more fucking. The room was deliciously warmed and we slept naked, clasped in each other's arms, but barring a prolonged kissing of my body, which included a short journey of his tongue up my cunt, there was no more sexual familiarity.

When I awoke, a stray beam of light through the shutter illumined the clock face and showed that it was midday. I sat up with a start, disengaging myself from the bare arms that were still around me. My royal lover came to his senses with a grunt.

'I must go!' I said.

'But you must have breakfast . . . ' as I seemed to be about to leave the bed. I was really rather scared of Jean, now that I had come to my proper senses, and wanted to be back and explaining. 'No, no, my dearest precious one; you shall not go till it is full time for the theatre to begin once more. No, it is useless to protest.'

I let myself be pulled back on his naked hairy breast and kissed lovingly. I suffered his vagrant hand to play with my cunt, which did not feel particularly saucy; it wasn't awake at present, but I suffered him to draw my hand to his prick, which was swollen to a considerably greater extent than the night before. I resigned myself to the morning fuck but nothing more happened.

'We must have tea and things,' he said, 'but I cannot summon my man.'

'I'll get up and go,' I volunteered.

'No, no, darling,' he answered, 'I have not begun to enjoy you yet.'

'Well, I will hide in the bathroom, while you ring for your man.'

'No, no,' he pressed me to him and his prick seemed so stiff that I thought it would stab into my stomach. 'Would you mind, darling, if Madame Kahn . . . she suspects, you may guess; if Madame were to come?'

'Of course, I know she knows,' I laughed. 'Madame has to find you all your little delights, is it not so?'

'Ah, Madame, she collects for me the spectacle of young ladies who cuddle each other, till I spend at the sight. young ladies who toy with each other's naked bodies . . . but enough, I excite myself too much. If you wish, Madame shall find a spectacle which you shall see also.'

I was possessed of a feeling of lazy naughtiness by this time. I thought it would be very nice to see the spectacle, but kept my modesty. 'Oh, no,' I whispered, breathing hotly into his ear, 'but I don't mind if she comes in here.'

There was a little telephone at the side of the bed and a momentary conversation elicited the fact that Madame Kahn would be with us in a moment.

His Highness would not allow me to put anything on and we were both stark naked when she came in. We sipped and nibbled. At last he finished, and to my surprise, got up from the bed and walked naked, his penis rampant, across to the table where the champagne bottle was.

'Serge,' cried Madame, 'but you are marvellously fit this morning.'

'It is what you have brought me that has done it,' he answered, and coming to the bedside he flung off the clothes and, showing me all bare, pressed a hot kiss to my cunt.

As I lay there quivering, all on fire for filth, Madame toyed with me, her dexterous fingers running all over my body.

His Highness pulled her from me, and dragged off her bodice from her, exposing too her naked breasts, not such a good sight as mine but very tempting. She flung herself on the bed by my side and grappled me; the contact of her warm flesh sent flames of desire all through me. The Prince came back to the bed and between them rolled me from side to side, kissing me everywhere, licking my flesh. I think that Madame thrust her tongue further down my cunt than anyone ever had before.

It was glorious; I panted for lust; my hands flew over their bodies, now gripping his throbbing cock; now dipping into her sweltering cunt. His Highness pressed two of my fingers together and pushed them into her cunt, then licked the moisture from it. Occasionally a drop appeared at the end of his penis, which I kissed away, but he would delay the fuck. For myself, I could scarcely count the number of times I had spent; the moisture was streaming down my legs, and Madame was in a like plight.

At last he freed himself from me.

'Put the cushions under her!' he said huskily to Madame.

She waited while she undressed altogether, and then lifted my willing body and piled the cushions beneath me till my arse was lifted high above my head.

Then she sat herself behind me and I felt her warm body supporting mine, her knees around my waist, her arms clutched about me, her wet cunt oozing against a cheek of my bottom. It was a delicious position. She was herself backed up with pillows so that she half reclined with my body resting on her stomach, and his Highness, his cock almost at bursting point, stood and surveyed us.

It could not last long. I put my hands behind me and drove two fingers into her cunt for very wickedness. My legs were opened wide and I felt as if my whole body were one great gasping cunt.

His Highness lit a cigar; even in my anger at further delay, I could not help noticing the wonderful aroma. He blew the perfumed smoke over our bodies, while his hands slowly caressed me. He straddled over my expectant body, pressing his taut cock against my belly while he kissed the face of the woman behind me. Her hands were now messing with my cunt, and the smell of the escaping semen mingled with that of the cigar, and the delicate breath of the perfumes with which Madame's body was covered. Would he never come to the point, I thought. I would not ask, but all my quivering body begged for fucking, and he knew it!

He then lay upon me his legs between mine and discussed with Madame the many beauties of my body, and – well, at last he had me. We spent mutually. Madame then took me to the bathroom and bathed my tired body in scented water till new life glowed in it.

In another hour I was dressed. A caviare sandwich and a cocktail and Madam espirited me to the coach. His Highness, she said, would meet us at the LNWR Hotel presently.

His Highness picked me up and we had a bracing drive, only just returning in time for me to go straight to the theatre. I met Jean in the passage.

'Well,' he said, 'what happened? You didn't come home – I waited up.'

'I wasn't well,' I answered, 'and thought it better to stop over for the night.'

'That means that you slept with the Prince?'

'It doesn't.'

'Come into my room.'

When we were alone, he pulled me on his knee and slid his hand up my clothes suddenly. 'Those are not your drawers,' and he drew my skirt up.

I had forgotten, they were some that Madame Kahn had given me and what was worse – they had a coronet embroidered on them.

'You did sleep with him?'

'Oh, well, if you must know: Yes, I did! One doesn't get the chance of sleeping with royal princes every day – and it doesn't make any difference to my love for you, Jean.'

'Oh, I don't mind, it's all in the business; what did he give you?'

'Nothing.'

'You damned little fool; do you mean to say you slept with a prince and got nothing – nothing?'

That nettled me and I left in a temper; I was beginning to find Jean out.

I had no chance to speak to Restall during the first act but he glanced quizzically at me. Going to my room in the interval, the hall keeper said there was a *commissaire* to see me. The man wore the livery of a London hotel. 'I've come from London to bring you this, Miss,' he said. 'Will you give me a receipt, Miss?'

I gave him a receipt, and opened the parcel and found a velvet case which I opened. A collar of pearls; black and white intermixed and obviously of enormous value. The clasp was a medallion of blue enamel, heavily set with diamonds and inscribed in small but very white diamonds: 'To N. H. in remembrance of her delightful performance.' It was a magnificent present and the *double entendre* of the inscription pleased me.

Halfway through act two, I changed to a prince's costume. With that I could wear the collar. The prince, Madame Kahn and a young man were in the box, and I longed to wear it. There was a general gasp of astonishment in the dressing room when I put it on.

'Wherever did you get that? Why, it must be worth thousands.'

I said an old admirer had sent if from London. As I was waiting in the wings for my cue. Restall bustled up to me. 'Well, dear,' he whispered, 'how did it go?' I pointed to my collar and at that instant a shaft of light from the opposite side illuminated the beautiful jewels. 'Good God, child, it is worth a fortune; whatever did you do to him?'

'If I show you, will you take it as payment of a commission?'

'Rather! Tonight?'

'No, wait till Sunday night, when we are not tired,' and I pinched his thigh.

Presently a little note came from His Highness.

DEAR CHILD, The trifle becomes you well. I leave tonight for London. Send your permanent address to the Legation. We must not lose sight of each other.

When I next went on the stage, the box was empty. As the curtain fell, Restall stopped me. 'You mustn't take that thing home, child; it's dangerous. Meet me in the bar and we'll put it in the theatre safe till you are back in London.'

From Liverpool we were to cross to Douglas, another sea voyage.

'Going to be a dirty night, I'm afraid,' said one of our comedians.

'Speak for yourself,' was the answer: 'I'm going to sleep alone.'

~ 25 ~

Josefine Mutzenbacher

FELIX SALTEN 1906

Have you ever wondered what would happen if the author of *Bambi* tried to write a book for adults? Well, image no longer, for Felix Salten (1869–1945), the author of the world-famous children's story wrote such a novel, and it is a triple-X-rated eye-opener! Appearing in 1906 under the title *Josefine Mutzenbacher*, in a limited edition of 1000 copies only, this book described itself as 'the story of a Viennese prostitute, told in her own words', and was in fact the sexual memoirs of the said woman's early years. The volume was an instant success, and was reprinted numerous times in the original German, as well as in various translations. Early critics of the work declared it one of the best written German sotadic novels of any time, and praised its realistic, naturalistic and psychologically adroit picture of daily sexual life, captured in the rough vulgar argot of the Viennese lower classes. Readers of the book soon found it to be one of the most erotic, raucous, orgiastic, good-natured, and honest sexual accounts ever authored, and humorous as well.

Josefine Mutzenbacher is certainly a classic of erotic literature. Its frankness, insight and universal popularity have placed it in league with *The Memoirs of Fanny Hill*. The following excerpt recounts an early voyeuristic experience of Josefine's, that turned into a participatory adventure with a neighbourhood woman and her beer-salesman lover.

∾ from *Josefine Mutzenbacher*

One day on my return from work I saw Mrs Rhinelander and Mr Horak talking together. She was wearing a loose, red blouse, and no corsets, so that her whole titties, even the nipples were plainly visible. He leaned close to her, both of them laughing. When he reached for her titties, she pushed him away, and when he made a movement to put his hand under her clothes, she jumped back, but all in fun. Soon they were talking earnestly in low tones, then he disappeared into the house, immediately followed by Mrs Rhinelander who went down to the cellar.

Mr Horak and Mrs Rhinelander were in the centre of the cellar hugging and kissing. He had unbuttoned her blouse and was playing with her boobies. They were milk white, large and firm. I noticed as Mr Horak played with them that the nipples seemed to grow stiff. While he was kissing her she was feeling around the front of his trousers; then she opened the flap, and pulled out a cock reaching away up to his watch charm.

As she stroked it, she began to shiver, getting much excited. It was so long that her hand seemed small beside it as she worked it up and down. I was astonished at its great length and thinness.

Mr Horak, breathing so hard that I could hear him plainly where I stood, now pushed her towards a large barrel, on which she sat down with her back against the wall. She whispered: 'Come quick. I can't stand this any longer!'

He then took her legs in his arms, and thus held her while she inserted his cock. He shoved it into her as far as he could, and she whispered hoarsely: 'For goodness' sake . . . you are pushing my stomach out of place!'

As I had never seen it done in this way before, I watched closely, missing nothing. He had his hand down between her titties, she constantly kissing him, grunting and moaning:

'Oh! I can't stand this any longer . . . I am going. Now! . . . now . . . don't squirt yet . . . I am coming . . . my goodness . . . I am coming again . . . Oh Lord! . . . hold back . . . don't squirt, I beg you . . . this is heavenly . . . I . . . Jesus . . . Mary . . . if my old man could only fuck me as you do . . . I am going again . . . that cock feels so big in me . . . shove it clear in . . . Oh! God! I have never had anyone as good as you are! I can feel it clear up in my throat. If I had only known this, you could have had it long ago! A person must be a fool to deny herself such a great pleasure. Oh! Oh! Lord! Faster, faster! My God! Oh, my! but that feels good!'

He, however, did not answer, but kept right on fucking. She was now writhing and twisting around on the barrel, her arse extending away out in front. He grabbed her arse-cheeks and with one final push, forced his cock away in, and said: 'Now, now,' while she was moaning with pleasure.

His head then sank exhausted. He withdrew his cock and she jumped down, arranged her clothing, and threw herself around his neck, kissing him, and exclaimed: 'Not one man in ten can do it like that!'

He began playing with her again, then lit a cigarette, asking: 'How many times did you come?'

'Oh, I don't know . . . at least five times.'

Then, while he played with her titties and slit, she apparently getting great pleasure as he did so, he asked: 'How many times do you come when your husband fucks you?'

She replied in a disgusted tone: 'Not at all . . . He no sooner puts it in . . . Then he squirts, just teasing me, leaving me so excited, that I have to satisfy myself with my fingers!'

'But why don't you tell him to treat you better?'

'I do, but he says that all men fuck alike . . . that there is no different way . . . but I know different! He does not dream that I get myself a little booty on the side now and then. A piece of real tail! I often think that I can make him do it a second time . . . it would take longer and perhaps I could go off . . . but . . . of no use. He can't raise another hard-on; often I try very hard, by taking it in my mouth . . . but no success. You can't imagine how far such a man can drive a woman . . . insanely mad for want of it. Then after taking it into my mouth and making it stiff, I quickly put him in my pussy when, with one push . . . off he goes . . . all the work for nothing, leaving me worse off than before. He nearly drives me crazy . . . He simply won't fuck me properly.'

Horak stepped up a little closer to her, saying: 'You must show me that . . . That's a new one on me. I never had it done that way to me.'

He was still holding her white titties, which looked very good to me.

'I don't believe that, Mr Horak,' said she. 'I am sure that you could have any woman you wanted . . . They will all be only too glad to do that for you.'

In my hiding place I thought the same and would be glad to do anything for him.

'No,' he remarked, 'I want it done that way to me. Come on . . . show me!' He pushed her back on the barrel, still holding her titties, and stood very close to her.

'But that is not necessary with you,' she said. 'You will get a hard-on without that.'

At which he pulled out his cock, which now hung down soft and limber, saying: 'See, he will not get stiff again!'

She took hold of it, saying: 'You are getting me all excited again, and I haven't got any time . . . I must go . . . ' But he kept on caressing her, playing with her titties.

Suddenly she stopped and took it in her mouth! It was now his turn to cry: 'Mother . . . Mary . . . and Joseph!'

At that moment I heard someone descending the cellar stairs, which they seemed to be too engrossed to notice. Unthinkingly I called out: 'Someone is coming!' and darted out of my hiding place.

Thunderstruck, they stared at me, unable to move. Mr Horak put his 'engine' back in his trousers and buttoned them hurriedly. He then helped Mrs Rhinelander button up her blouse again. I stepped up beside them, also afraid of who might be coming. We stood there staring at each other . . . they looking very much ashamed, but saying nothing. It happened to be the landlord of the building, however, and he passed, nodding to us, and seemed to notice nothing unusual in our appearance. He got a broom from the corner and went back upstairs.

Mr Horak stood staring at the wall, not daring to look at me; Mrs Rhinelander seeing that he would not talk, caught my hands, crying: 'Wait a little, young woman!'

She whispered something in Mr Horak's ear; he turned quite red. As she continued to hold me, they looked at each other helplessly. Mr Horak put his hand in his pocket and took out a silver coin, a gulden, which he handed to me. I was much pleased at this turn of affairs. I laughed, starting to go, but she said: 'Come here, pretty one! Now tell us . . . what did you see?'

'I saw you take his thing in your mouth.'

As she hugged me tightly in her arms she asked: 'And do you know what that is called?'

Mr Horak came closer to us; she winked at him as she again asked me. Anxious to show I was not so green, I answered: 'Yes, Mrs Rhinelander.'

'Come, my young woman; then tell me what it is?'

I snuggled close to her, refusing to tell. She reached over, took Mr Horak's cock, which was again stiff and straight, and as I watched closely, she said, as she stroked its head: 'Now, won't you tell?'

As I was still silent, she put my hand on his cock, to which I did not object, but slowly worked the foreskin back and forth, smiling up at him at the same time. His knees began to quiver. Mrs Rhinelander pushed my head down until my mouth was close to it . . . I could not resist, but took it in my mouth and . . . began to suck on it myself!

'Don't squirt; I want some too!' Mrs Rhinelander said.

She gently pushed me away and at once buried his cock in her cunt as far as she could take it; turning to me, she said: 'Now . . . oh, you know what it is called!'

'Fuck!'

Now Mr Horak reached under my dress and began playing with my pussy, putting in one finger after the other; he finally forced his little finger in. My legs shook with pleasure . . . I seemed to be burning up . . . !! In this manner we all three went off together.

Having finished, Mr Horak, while buttoning his trousers, remarked: 'The young woman is an artist.'

Mrs Rhinelander smilingly said: 'I saw that at once; she is a wench, a natural whore!'

She asked me: 'Have you fucked much before?'

I naturally denied it, but she insisted: 'I don't believe it . . . Don't lie; how often have you done it?'

But I insisted: 'Never! Only I have seen it done at home.' She and I then went upstairs, Mr Horak remaining in the cellar. She seemed now like a partner; and I was very proud of this community of interest with an older women. I thought of Ferdl having fucked her, up in the garret, and as he had often fucked me too, it seemed as if there was a bond between us; as we got upstairs, I confessed I had not told her the truth before and I now owned up that I had done it before She wanted to know all about it; how often and with whom. I said possibly ten times or more.

I now played my trump card and said: 'With several boys . . . one of them Ferdl, the big chap, Anna's brother; you know him!'

She still denied it, but I kept on saying: 'You surely remember him, he helped you to carry the washing to the attic.'

She said: 'Oh, yes, I remember him now.'

Leaning close to her, I whispered: 'You know . . . he told me all about it!'

She cut me short, saying: 'Shut your mouth!'

That settled that.

A few days later I saw Mr Horak going into the cellar. I called hello to him, and spying me, and making sure that no one was in sight, he called to me: 'Come along to the cellar.'

I was only too glad to go. As we reached the dark passageway, he turned, and catching my head, pressed my face to the front of his trousers. I immediately put my hand into his trousers and took out his cock, which I held in both of my hands, rubbing it gently.

He remarked: 'How nicely you do that.'

After such praise, I tried to please him . . . I reached into his trousers and began to play with his testicles, with the other hand continually rubbing his foreskin back and forth!

'Take it in your mouth!' he begged.

I refused. I don't know why, but I wanted to do it somewhere else.

'I will give you another gulden if you will take it in your mouth!' he said.

But I still declined, saying to him: 'Do it to me like you did it to Mrs Rhinelander!'

In great astonishment, he said: 'You want me to fuck you . . . ?'

I nodded.

I kept on playing with his cock, rubbing my cunt against it and trying to put it into my hole, saying: 'I want to get fucked!'

'Have you ever done it?'

As I nodded, he said: 'How often?'

I said: 'Several times.'

He lifted me up and held me astride one of his hips, as one would carry a child, holding me with one hand while I put my arms around his neck. With his other hand, he lifted my clothes up and opened my slit with his fingers . . . and then started to put in his cock! I could feel the head going into me . . . I jumped up and down trying to help! It would not go, however. After trying for some time, he put me down, saying: 'No! It won't go in like this!'

I noticed how red his cock had become from the rubbing against my body. He sat down on a small keg and rolling a smaller one in front of him, he turned to me and then drew me to him with my back to him, standing on the small keg. This pleased me greatly, as I realised that he was going to do it from behind as Robert had done to me in bed. He ordered me to bend forwards. I did so, bracing my elbows on another keg, my bottom up in the air. I turned my head and saw him wetting his cock with saliva. He said that that would make it go in easier. Then, raising my dress up over my arse, he got up, leaned over me in the same position that I was in. He then started boring his cock into my pussy hole, saying: 'If it hurts, tell me.' He then pushed further into my snatch! 'Does it hurt?' he asked.

Although it did hurt a little, his finger on my clit and a wonderful sensation that tickled my whole body were so delightful that I answered: 'No!'

He then pushed further until I thought that his cock must be all the way into me. (He told me, later, that he could only get about half of it in.) I became calmer and it felt so good that I began to moan with pleasure.

He immediately asked if it hurt me. I could hardly answer . . . so excited was I!

He then withdrew his prick, anxiously asking whether it had hurt me. This was an unpleasant interruption to a wonderful sensation, and I said: 'No, no! It doesn't hurt . . . ! Please put it in and keep on fucking.'

He put it in again and I whispered: 'Just keep it there . . . there . . . Oh! But that feels so grand and good!'

He was very gentle about it, and kept playing with my clitoris all the time. Finally he was all in. I could not help thinking of the ragged boy who had fucked me in the bushes and who was the first one to get my maidenhead . . . of the soldier who tried so hard but could not make it; of Robert who had succeeded in getting it part way in, and of Mr Eckhard; the thoughts made me so excited that I was almost beside myself. Mr Horak, clutching me to him tightly and working violently, whispered: 'You darling . . . that's right . . . kiss some more . . . you sweet little whore . . . you must let me fuck you thoroughly every day. I'll meet you right here tomorrow and every day!'

'Every day?' I asked.

'Yes, every damned day, you darling whore! Every day I want to fuck you!'

This conversation wrought me up to a still greater pitch of excitement.

'You want to fuck me every day . . . but that will be impossible! Don't you think so?'

'Why will it?' he asked, pushing still harder.

'But what if Mrs Rhinelander should come?'

'Nonsense!' he whispered. 'I like you a great deal better, with your darling pussy!'

'I don't believe it!'

'But, I tell you!'

He was now in me so far that I could feel his balls bumping against my legs.

'But,' I reminded him, 'Mrs Rhinelander has big titties.'

'I don't care . . . you have lovely ones too!'

I was so pleased at this that I squeezed him several times . . . He stopped talking and breathed very hard.

Suddenly he said: 'Now! Now! Oh, my goodness!'

I felt something warm inside of me and knew he was going off, his cock jerking furiously . . . deep within my cunt. I felt one hot wave after another go through my body . . . as though I were being tickled all over by being licked with a red-hot tongue! I was breathing hard and moaning!

When I finally got up, the hot juice was running down my legs . . . I was all wet. It seemed as though I could feel his big sword still inside me . . . I was so dizzy I could hardly stand . . . My back ached. He was standing as though drunk, his long cock hanging down nearly to his knees, limber, dripping and wet. He took out his handkerchief; I took it from his hand and wiped his cock dry.

'See here,' he said. 'You are an expert whore! Has this ever happened to you before? You seem to have had much experience.'

Without answering his query, I again started to talk of Mrs Rhinelander's big titties.

He remarked: 'But I like you much better!'

That made me feel very proud, and I asked: 'What if she happened to come down? Whom would you fuck, her or me?'

'Why . . . you! Beyond a doubt!'

'But what would Mrs Rhinelander say?'

'Well, what could she say?'

I was a true woman and loved flattery and admiration. I started for the stairs, but he held me back.

'Stay a while,' he said. Sitting down on the beer keg, holding me between his knees, he asked: 'Well, now, tell me the truth. Have you ever fucked before like this?'

'Never like today!' I answered.

'Well, then how?'

'Never!'

'Don't lie now. You told me so yourself.'

'Well . . . yes . . . then.'

'And with whom?'

'With a strange man.'

'Who was he?"

'A soldier.'

'Where?'

'In the forest field.'

'Perhaps you enjoyed it with him?'

'Oh, no.'

'But with me you like to do it?'

I put my face against his, threw my arms around his neck, and I kissed him with great passion.

When I left him he called out: '*Auf Wiedersehen*, sweetheart!'

Sadopaideia

J. P. KIRKWOOD 1907

Sadopaideia is a true erotic classic of the twentieth century, and one of the most famous English-language sexual novels of all time. Its theme is elucidated by its subtitle: 'Being the Experiences of Cecil Prendergast, undergraduate of the University of Oxford, showing how he was led through the pleasant paths of Masochism to the supreme joys of Sadism.' The novel first appeared in 1907, in two volumes, with the imprint 'Edimburg: G. Ashantee & Co.'. The place of publication was more likely Paris, and the authorship has been reliably attributed in Lawrence Forster's unpublished *c*.1913–23 *Catalogus Librorum Prohibitorum* to John Poole Kirkwood, an Oxford-educated English provincial actor. It should be noted that authorship of this work had been ascribed also, in print, to the poet Algernon Swinburne and the psychologist Havelock Ellis, based no doubt on the personal interest both of these men had for the particular *psychopathia sexualis* of this novel.

This book has been equally praised and condemned because it is the ultimate distillation of the Victorian/Edwardian mania for flagellation and sadomasochism by both men *and* women, the latter a fact that is often forgotten by those censuring it. In fact, it is a young woman, a widow, who introduces the protagonist to the world of s/m, and together they demonstrate that pain and pleasure are irrevocably bound in the human species, with all people possessing the capacity to derive erotic stimulation and sexual pleasure from either end of the rod, even being able to switch roles for their mutual pleasure.

This is not to say that *Sadopaideia* is a scientifically accurate treatise on the conscious and unconscious aspects of flagellation, nor a factual historical record of the practice of flogging in the British Isles. The fact is that flagellation has been an integral part of Britannic society for hundreds of years. Corporal punishments in the school, military and penal system are well documented. Flogging for pleasure was re-counted in novels, including the 1748 *Fanny Hill*. Continental Europe even referred to flagellation as the 'English Vice'. The passion English gentlemen had for this activity was no more acutely demonstrated than in the life of the Victorian author and poet Algernon Swinburne, whose latently erotic works (e.g. *Lesbia Brandon*) were parallelled by more sexually explicit ones (e.g. 'Charlie Collingwood's Flogging' and *The Whippingham Papers*). Uncensored biographies of his life also recount his frequent visits to private whipping parlours that prospered in England at the time (and still do). Whatever the aetiology of this passion of the British, the rod and birch have long been utilised to rejuvenate their flagging libidos and sexual potency.

Many stories have been written with flagellation and sadomasochistic themes. The reason for *Sadopaideia*'s repeated reprinting and continued enjoyment is that it is not only well written, but concentrates on the ecstatic pleasure that this practice is capable of producing in all participants. The twentieth-century erotica bibliographer C. R. Dawes even described the book as 'brightly written, in a lively style, and the flagellations, though frequent, are not so exaggerated and repellent as is only too often the case in such books. As a flagellation book of the milder kind, it is better than most and some parts are not unamusing.'

While a long excerpt of 'heavy' sadomasochism would limit the commercial distribution of this work, it is possible to give the reader a taste for the erotic power of this novel by reprinting its opening scene, an episode which starts as a completely normal heterosexual seduction.

~~~ from *Sadopaideia*

I first met Mrs Harcourt at my college ball, my last term at Oxford. She had come up to chaperone the cousin of one of my chums. Only the blessed ceremony of marriage gave her this right, for she was still well under thirty. I learned from Harry that she was a widow, having married an elderly and somewhat used-up brewer who most consider-ately died quite soon after marriage having, I have every reason to believe, decidedly shortened his life by vain, though praiseworthy, attempts to satisfy his wife's insatiable appetite.

She was a little woman, beautifully made, with magnificent red-brown hair, the fairest possible skin, a bust that was abundant without being aggressively large, a neat waist with splendidly curved hips, and in a ball dress – discreetly yet alluringly cut – she fired my passion at once.

Harry was very *épris* with his cousin and so was only too glad for me to take Mrs Harcourt off his hands. We danced one or two dances together. She had the most delightful trick in the Boston of getting her left leg in between mine now and then. At first I thought it was an accident, but it happened so repeatedly that I began to suspect, and my old man began to suggest, that more might be intended. At last I felt what seemed a deliberate pressure of her thigh against my left trouser. John Thomas responded at once, and I, looking down at my partner, caught her eye. There was no mistaking the expression. She gave a little self-conscious laugh and suggested that we should sit out the rest of the dance.

Now, I had helped to superintend the sitting-out arrangement and knew where the cosiest nooks were to be found. After one or two unsuccessful attempts, when we were driven back by varying coughs or the sight of couples already installed (in one case, a glimpse of white drawers showed that one couple had come to quite a good understanding), I succeeded in finding an unoccupied chesterfield in a very quiet corner of the cloisters. Here we ensconced ourselves, and without further delay I slipped my arm round my partner's back, along the top of the couch and, bending down, kissed the bare white shoulder.

'You silly boy,' she murmured.

'Why silly?' said I, putting my other arm round her in front so that my hand rested on her left breast.

She turned towards me to answer but before she could speak, my lips met hers in a long kiss.

'That's why,' she said, with a smile, when I drew back. 'Kisses were meant for lips. It is silly to waste them on shoulders.'

I needed no further invitation. I pressed her close in my arms and, finding her lips slightly parted, ventured to explore them just a little with my tongue. To my great joy and delight, her tongue met mine. My hand, naturally, was not idle. I stroked and squeezed her breast, outside her frock first, and then tried to slip it inside, but she would not allow that. 'You'll tumble me too much,' she murmured as she gently pushed it away. 'I can't have my frock rumpled. People would notice. Take that naughty hand away.'

As I didn't obey, she took it away herself and placed it with a dainty little pat on my own leg, above the knee. 'There it can't do any harm,' she added with an adorable smile. She was going to take her own hand away, but I held it tight. I drew her still closer to me and kissed her again and again, my tongue this time boldly caressing her own. She gave a little sigh and let herself sink quite freely into my arms.

By this time the old proverb that 'a standing prick has no conscience' proved its truth. My right hand released hers and I took her in my arms – my right arm this time encircling her below the waist, with the hand clasping the left cheek of her bottom. Modern dresses do not allow for much underclothing and I could distinctly feel the edge of her drawers through the soft silk of her frock. 'Oh, you darling,' I murmured as I kissed her. By taking her close to me, she naturally had to move the hand which had gently held mine. It slid up my leg and at last met John Thomas, for whom my thin evening-dress trousers proved an altogether inadequate disguise. She gave a little gasp, and then her fingers convulsively encircled him and she squeezed him fondly.

That was enough for me. My hand slid down her frock and up again – but this time inside. It found a beautifully moulded leg ensheathed in silk, dainty lace, the smooth skin of her thigh and, at last, soft curls and the most delightfully pouting lips possible to imagine. My mouth remained glued to hers. Her hand grasped my eager weapon and I was just about to slip down between her knees and consummate my delight, when the lips that I was fondling pouted and contracted. I felt my hand and fingers soaked with her love, and I realised that her imagination had proved too much for her and that, while I was still unsatisfied, she had reached at least a certain height of bliss.

She pulled herself together at once, and just as I was unbuttoning my trousers she stopped me. 'No, not here,' she said. 'It's too dangerous, and besides, it would be much too hurried and uncomfortable. Come and see me in town, there's a darling boy. Now we must go back and dance. This naughty fellow,' she added, playfully patting my trousers, 'must wait'. She then got up, arranged her dress and, giving me a lovely kiss with her tongue, led the way back to the ballroom. I followed, but do the best I might, John Thomas took his revenge on me by weeping with disappointment, which made me extremely sticky and uncomfortable. But for Mrs Harcourt's invitation to see her in town, my evening would have been spoiled.

I went down the next day, and on my arrival in town lost no time in calling on Mrs Harcourt at her little house on South Molton Street. When I rang at the door, it was opened by a very neat, I thought, though not particularly pretty, maid. She had, however, an alluring little figure and a perky naughtiness in her face which was, perhaps, even more fascinating than mere beauty.

'Is Mrs Harcourt at home?'

'I will see, sir. Will you come this way? What name shall I say?' She showed me into a delightfully little morning room, very tastefully furnished, and disappeared.

She did not keep me waiting long, but returned and said, 'Will you come this way, sir? Madame is in her boudoir. Shall I take your hat and stick?'

She took them from me and turned to hang the hat on the stand. The pegs were rather high, and in reaching up she showed the delightful line of her breasts and hips and just a glimpse of a white petticoat underneath the skirt.

'Is it too high for you? Let me help,' I said.

'Thank you, sir,' she said, smiling up at me.

I took the hat over her shoulder and hung it up. She was between me and the hat stand and could not move until I did. I lowered my arm and drew her towards me. She looked up at me with a provoking smile. I bent down and kissed her lips, while my hand fondled the delightfully plump breast.

'You mustn't,' she murmured. 'What would my mistress say if she knew?'

'But she won't know,' I answered as my hand went further down to the bottom, which her tight skirt made very apparent.

'She will if I tell her,' she smiled, 'you naughty boy,' and playfully patted my trouser leg as she passed me.

'Which, of course, you won't,' I said lightly as I followed her. She laughed rather maliciously, I thought, though I didn't pay much attention at the time. I had reason later, though, to remember it.

We went upstairs and I was shown into a lovely room where a log fire was burning, although it was no colder than most June days in this country. There was a splendid, deep, low couch – or rather divan, for it had no back – facing the fire, covered with cushions, which took my eye at once, and I mentally promised myself what should happen on it. My expectations fell far short of the reality, as will be seen.

Mrs Harcourt was sitting on a low chair near the couch. She was in a delightfully fitting tea gown, cut fairly low at the neck, with very loose sleeves. It clung to her figure as she rose to greet me, and being made of chiffon with a foundation of pink silk, it gave one the idea at first that she was practically naked.

'Bring up tea please, Juliette,' she said to the maid, who disappeared.

'So you have found your way here,' she said, coming towards me with outstretched hand.

The room was heavily scented with perfume, which I learned came from burning pastilles, and she herself always used a mixture of sandalwood and attar of roses. As she approached me her perfume intoxicated me, and without saying a word I clasped her in my arms and pressed long, hot kisses on her lips. To my intense delight I found she had no corset on, and her supple body bent close to mine so that I could feel every line of it. My hands slipped down and grasped the cheeks of her bottom as I pressed her stomach close against my trousers.

'You rough, impetuous bear,' she smiled at me. 'Wait till the tea comes up.'

And she disengaged herself from me, playfully touching, as she did so, John Thomas, who was naturally quite ready by this time for anything. 'Oh, already!' she said as she felt his condition. 'I told this naughty fellow at Oxford that he would have to be patient, and he must learn to obey.'

Tea appeared most daintily served, and on the tray I noticed a delicate Bohemian glass liqueur carafe and two liqueur glasses.

'Do you know *crème de cacao*?' asked Mrs Harcourt. 'It's rather nice.'

She poured out tea and then filled each liqueur glass half-full of the dark liqueur and poured cream on top.

'*À votre santé*,' she said, touching my glass with hers. Our fingers met and a thrill ran right through me. I drank the liqueur off at a gulp and leaned towards her.

'You greedy thing,' she laughed. 'That's not the way to drink it. No, no, wait till we've had tea.'

As I tried to get her in my arms: 'Naughty boys must not be impatient,' pushing John Thomas away once again.

I sat back on the couch and drank tea rather gloomily, Mrs Harcourt watching me teasingly. At last she put her cup down and, reaching for her cigarette box, took one herself and offered me one, and leaned back in her chair looking at me with a smile.

'It's a shame to tantalise him so, isn't it?' she said at last.

I did not answer, but jumped up and threw my arms around her, kneeling in front of her and covering her face and neck with kisses. She tossed her cigarette into the grate and undid the silk tie of her gown. It fell back and showed all she had on was a dainty chemise of the finest lawn, and a petticoat. My right hand immediately sought her left breast and, pulling it out, I kissed and sucked the dainty nipple, which responded at once to my caress, stiffening most delightfully. My left hand then reached down to the hem of her petticoat and began to raise it.

I felt her right arm around my waist, and her left hand began to unbutton my fly from the top. Before she had time to undo the last button, John Thomas leapt forth, ready and eager, but she pushed it in again, undid the last button, fumbled for my balls and gently drew them out. I drew back a little from her and lifted her petticoat right up, disclosing the daintiest of black silk, openwork stockings with pale green satin garters, and above them, filmy lawn drawers with beautiful lace and insertion, through which the fair, satin skin of her thighs gleamed most provokingly. At the top there appeared, just between the opening of the drawers, the most fascinating brown curls imaginable.

I feasted my eyes on this lovely sight, undoing my braces and slipping my trousers down. Her hand immediately left my balls and began to fondle my bottom, stroking and pinching the cheeks while she murmured, 'You darling boy. Oh, what a lovely bottom.'

I was eager to be in her, but the brown curls fascinated me so much that I could not resist the temptation to stoop down and kiss them. I was rather shy of doing this, as I had never done it before, and though I knew it was usual with tarts, I was not sure if it would be welcome here. Judge my surprise, then, when I felt Mrs Harcourt's hand on my head, gently pressing it down, and heard her saying, 'How did you guess I wanted that?'

She opened her legs wider, disclosing the most adorable pussy, with pouting lips just slightly opening and showing the bright coral inner lips, which seemed to ask for my kisses. I buried my head in the soft curls, and with eager tongue explored every part of her mossy grot. She squirmed and wriggled with pleasure, opening her legs quite wide and twisting them around me.

I followed all her movements, backing away on my knees as she slipped off the chair until, at last, when she drenched my lips with love, she slipped on the hearth rug. Then, as I could scarcely reach her with my tongue in that position and didn't wish to lose a drop of the maddening juice, I disengaged my legs from hers and knelt down to one side so that my head could dive right between her legs. This naturally presented my naked bottom and thighs to her gaze.

'You rude, naughty boy,' she said, gently, 'to show me this bare bottom. I'm shocked at you.'

Her hands again fondled my balls and bottom, and I had all I could do to prevent John Thomas from showing conclusively what he had in store for her.

I had no intention of wasting good material, however, and was just about to change my position so that I could arrive at the desired summit of joy when I felt her trying to pull my right leg towards her. I let myself go, and she eventually succeeded in lifting it right over so that I was straddling right across her and we were in the position, which I knew quite well from photographs, known as sixty-nine.

My heart beat high. Was it possible I was to experience this supreme pleasure of which I had heard so much? I buried my head between her thighs. My tongue redoubled its efforts, searching out every corner and nook it could find. And just as it was rewarded by another flow of warm life I felt round my own weapon, not the fondling of her hand, but something softer, more clinging, and then unmistakably the tip of a velvet tongue from the top right down to the balls and back again. And then I felt the lips close round it and the gentle nip of teeth. This was too much.

John Thomas could restrain himself no longer, and as I seized her bottom with both hands and sucked the whole of her pussy into my mouth, he spurted forth with convulsive jerks his hidden treasure. When the spasm was over I collapsed limply on her, my lips still straining her life.

I was aroused quite soon by her pushing me off her chest. 'Get up,' she said, 'you are crushing me.' We both got up and stood for a moment looking at each other. Then she felt for her handkerchief and wiped her lips. I tried to take her in my arms.

To my surprise she pushed me away. 'Go away,' she said harshly. 'I don't like you.'

'Why, what's the matter?' I asked.

'Matter!' she replied, and she seemed to be working herself up into a temper. 'Matter! You horrid, beastly boy, how dare you come in my mouth?'

'I'm sorry,' I said. 'It happened so quickly and I – I – I thought you wanted it.'

'Wanted it? How dare you!'

I tried again to put my arms round her, but she wouldn't allow it.

'No, get away, pull your trousers up and go.' And she turned to ring the bell.

I sprang to her. 'Don't send me away,' I said. 'I'm sorry and I won't do it again. Forgive me. Let me stay a little and forgive me.'

'Let you stay!' she laughed. 'What's the use of your staying? Just look at yourself.'

And she pointed to poor John Thomas, very limp and drained dry, and looking very ashamed of himself.

'Oh, he'll be all right again in a little time,' I said. 'Come, darling, let me stay and show you how much I love you.'

I managed to get one arm around her and drew her to me. She let me kiss her but kept her lips quite shut, so that I couldn't get my tongue into her mouth. Her body was quite stiff, instead of yielding as it had been before. I grew bolder and caressed her breasts and began to pull up her petticoat again. She seemed to take no notice for a minute or so. And then, just as I had uncovered her thighs and was feeling for the soft curls of her mound, she quietly pushed my hand away, detached herself from my arms and said quite calmly, 'Well, if I let you stay, you must be punished for your rudeness. Will you do exactly as I tell you and submit to any punishment I may choose to inflict?'

Now, I knew nothing at that time of flagellation. I had heard of old men needing the birch to excite them, but beyond that I knew nothing. So I said, 'Punish me in any way you like, only let me stay and prove to you how sorry I am and how I love you.'

'Very well. Get behind that screen,' she said, pointing to a large Chinese screen that stood in the corner. I obeyed and she rang the bell.

Juliette appeared. 'Take the tea things away and bring me my leather case.'

I thought I heard a chuckle from Juliette but was not sure. After a little while I heard her come in again and whisper something to her mistress. 'Yes, very,' replied the latter. Then came more whisperings, and I heard Mrs Harcourt say, 'Oh, did he? Well, we shall see.'

She then told me to come out and I obeyed. I must have made rather a ridiculous figure, as my trousers were still down. Mrs Harcourt, however, did not seem to show any disposition to laugh. In fact she looked very angry indeed. I went towards her, but she stopped me with a gesture and said, 'You promised to do everything I tell you.'

'Anything,' I said.

'Very well. Turn your back to me and put your hands behind you.'

I obeyed.

She opened the case and took something out – I could not see what – and then she came to me. I felt something cold touch my wrists and heard a snap. I tried to move my arms and to my surprise found I could not. She had, in a moment, very deftly handcuffed me. I was too surprised to speak. 'Now kneel down,' she said.

'What for?' said I.

'You promised to do everything I told you,' she repeated.

I knelt down awkwardly enough with my hands fastened behind, just in front of the big couch. Then Mrs Harcourt took a large handkerchief and blindfolded me. I didn't like the look of things at all, but said nothing.

'Now,' said Mrs Harcourt to me as I knelt there helpless, 'you have been a very rude and dirty boy and you must be punished. Are you sorry?'

I was just about to answer when something whistled through the air and I felt as if a hundred needles were pricking my bottom. I could not help an involuntary cry.

I heard a sigh of pleasure, and felt a hand on my neck, pressing me forwards on to the couch.

'Are you sorry, eh?' she repeated, and again – whish! – the sharp pain cut across my raw bottom.

I had never been birched in my life. At school a tanning cane was used, but I could easily guess what weapon she was using.

'Will you speak? Are you sorry?' she repeated, and again the rod descended. I tried to escape, but my tied hands hampered me. Although I could and did kick lustily, her hand on my neck managed to prevent me from escaping altogether.

'Keep still,' she said, 'or I shall get Juliette to help me. Are you sorry?' At that moment, in one of my struggles, the birch just caught my balls, causing excruciating pain.

'Yes, oh yes!' I shouted.

'Will you ever do it again?' Whish!

'No.'

'What was it you did? Confess your fault.'

Silence on my part. I felt too angry and ashamed to say.

'Will you confess?' Whish! Whish! Whish!

'Oh yes, I will.'

'Well, what was it?'

'I came in your mouth.'

'And what else?' Whish! 'What else?'

'I don't know.'

'Didn't you say you thought I wanted it?'

'Yes.'

'Well, confess then.'

'I said I thought you wanted it.'

'Ah!' And again the blows fell all over my bottom.

The burning pain got worse and I struggled and wriggled and kicked so that I at last got away from her. I managed to rub the handkerchief away from my eyes and swung around and looked at her.

I never saw such a change in any woman. If she was pretty before, she was lovely now. Her eyes were shining, her cheeks were flushed. The exertion of plying the rod had caused one shoulder strap of her chemise to break, and one breast was just exposed.

I looked at her with adoring eyes. I couldn't help it. As angry and hurt as I was in my dignity and elsewhere, I could not but feel admiration and, yes, even affection for Mrs Harcourt. She met my eyes.

'Well,' she said, 'why have you turned around? I haven't finished yet.'

'Isn't that enough?' I said. 'I've said I'm sorry and confessed my fault.'

'Well now, haven't you any other faults to confess?' she asked.

'No!'

She rang the bell.

I exclaimed, 'You're surely not going to let anyone see me like this!'

She made no reply, and the door opened and Juliette appeared.

'Juliette, come here,' she said. 'You see this gentleman here. Now repeat before him the accusation you whispered to me just now.'

Juliette looked at me with a malicious smile (I remembered that smile) and said, 'When I was hanging the gentleman's hat up in the hall, he offered to help me, and then he kissed me and felt my breast and tried to feel my pussy through my skirt.'

'You little cat,' I said.

'Is that true?' asked Mrs Harcourt. 'Answer me!' and the birch fell across my thighs as I lay twisted on the couch. It flicked up my shirt-tail and exposed John Thomas to the salacious gaze of Juliette. I was too ashamed to speak.

'Will you answer me?' And again and again came the cutting strokes, one of them just catching poor John Thomas nicely.

'Well, if I did, she did as much to me,' I muttered.

'Oh, indeed,' said Mrs Harcourt as Juliette darted a vicious look at me. 'Well, we can investigate that later. Get the bands, Juliette.'

Juliette went to the case and produced a long band of webbing in a loop and, before I knew what she was about, had slipped it round my ankles and drawn it tight. Now I was indeed helpless.

'Now, Juliette,' said her mistress, 'as it was you who were insulted, it is only fair for you to punish him.'

They turned me over, face downwards, and turned up my shirt.

'Oh, he's had some already, I see,' said the maid.

'Yes, a little,' said the mistress. 'He can do with some more.'

'How many?' asked Juliette, taking up the birch.

'We'll see.'

Then the pain began again, blow after blow, cut after cut, until my poor bottom felt as if it was on fire. I wriggled as much as I could; but couldn't do much. My motions, however, must have pleased Mrs

Harcourt, for she said, 'Wait a moment, Juliette. We mustn't be too hard. He shall have some pleasure as well as pain.'

She got round to the other side of the couch, raised my head, which was buried in the cushions, and, bending down, whispered to me, 'He's a naughty boy, but I love him, so he can kiss me if he likes.'

She then pulled up her clothes and presented her pussy backwards to me which I could just reach with my tongue.

'Now Juliette,' she said, 'not too hard, and cleverly.' I did not feel at all anxious to justify her 'whishes', but to my surprise the birch fell now in quite a different way. Instead of the slashing cuts which had made me writhe and smart, the blows simply warmed my bottom. Of course now and then it touched an extra sore place and made me flinch, but for the most part the twigs seemed to caress, and the tips of them, curling in between the cheeks, gave me a delightful sensation.

I felt John Thomas answering in a way that surprised me. I forgot my resentment against Mrs Harcourt and my tongue roamed about her lovely pussy. I went even higher and caressed the other 'fair demesnes that there adjacent lay,' and which presented themselves to my eyes – a proceeding which evidently pleased her, for she opened and shut the cheeks of her bottom and, at last, with a quick side twist and a final plunge, she forced her pussy right against my mouth and murmured, 'That will do, Juliette.' She smothered my mouth and chin with her delicious cream.

She then got up and, with Juliette's aid, undid my bonds. I lay still, too excited to move. I felt her arm around my neck, while her other caressed my bottom. 'Poor boy,' she said. 'Did it hurt very much?'

I turned round and kissed her. I couldn't help it. All my rage and feeling of insult seemed to have disappeared. 'That's right,' she said, nestling close to me. 'So the whipping did him good! It didn't go on too long though, I hope,' she added, quickly pulling up my shirt and looking at my John Thomas, who by this time, after the last part of the birching, was nearly bursting. 'No, that's all right. Come to me, darling.'

'But Juliette . . . ' I said.

'Oh, never mind her. Still, perhaps she had better go,' she added with a peculiar look. 'Juliette, you can go. I shall want you in a quarter of an hour.' Juliette looked very disappointed, but had to go.

'Now, darling,' said her mistress, 'come to me and love me, and say you forgive your cruel mistress for hurting you.' She unfastened the band of her petticoat and let it fall to the floor.

~ 27 ~

James Grunnert
WERNER VON BLEICHRÖDER (?) 1908

We are all aware that fantasy plays a large roll in erotica. No wonder Drs Phyllis and Eberhard Kronhausen authored a book of nearly four hundred and fifty pages entitled simply *Erotic Fantasies* (1969). This book documents 'the sexual imagination' in classic erotica with ninety-eight excerpts, each demonstrating sexual wish fulfilment under one of eleven different subject headings (e.g. homosexuality, transsexualism, bondage, sadomasochism, incest, juveniles, animals, fetishes, etc.). Equally, we are aware that sexual literature is strongly rooted in reality. After all it is always easier to remember and synthesise, than to create any art *de novo*. It was in fact the Marquis de Sade who placed on the title page of one edition of his *Justine* the motto, 'Literature imitates Nature'. To classify this latter phenomenon, the same Drs Kronhausen in 1959 coined the term 'erotic realism' for their pioneering book *Pornography and the Law*, a book which single-handedly legitimised on psychological grounds the serious and academic study of 'pornographic' literature. It is fair to say that all erotic literature mixes fantasy with reality to some degree. Even sexual autobiographies are given to episodes of hyperbole. Authors are only human, have egos that appreciate stroking, and have subjective memory when it comes to themselves. Autobiographies are all self-promoting in general and erotic autobiographies equally serve and self-serve on many levels. There is the usual attempt to record a human life and its achievements and effects on society and history. There is also the attempt to 'educate' the reader on matters sexual, and there is the temptation to brag just a bit about one's sexual conquests. Intentional sex histories are for the most part upbeat, entertaining, and shy of depressing aspects that would cause a reader to put away the book (and deny authors part of their potential readership). Authors frequently interject

314 THE ENCYCLOPEDIA OF EROTIC LITERATURE

their philosophies and opinions on the sex they describe, and even try to psychoanalyse what they do and why.

Many genuine erotic autobiographies are easy to identify. Sellon's *The Ups and Downs of Life*, Harris's *My Life and Loves*, 'Walter's' *My Secret Life*, and Casanova's *Memoires* are just a few. Other books, like *Altars of Venus* and *Suburban Souls* are more problematic. Rarely, though, does a work of erotica read like a psychiatric document. *James Grunnert: A Novel from Berlin* is one. Whether this is really a novel or an autobiography can only be guessed at, but it is a unique piece of erotica; it is in fact one of the few original German erotic novels ever to be translated into English. It portrays the darker side of the human libido – sexual pathology in the form of the inability to establish normal sexual bonds.

James Grunnert tells his sexual memoir in the form of a flashback that reads much like a patient's psychoanalytic diary. He first introduces himself and describes his obsessive preoccupation with the female sex. Having been shot in a duel over a woman, Grunnert is in Italy recuperating from four weeks' stay in a hospital. He philosophises on 'Woman' as his passion and addiction – his grail and his downfall. He can't live with the female sex, nor without it. He tries to solve the inherent conflict of simultaneous adoration and lust, and fails. Grunnert is clearly unsettled, morose and depressed. 'If matters go on, I will certainly do something to myself.' This is the book's opening line.

The root of the narrator's problem is obvious, he is psychologically 'blocked'. He has no impulse control. His emotional development is arrested; his libido, even as an adult, retains its primitive infantile urgencies. He is gripped by obsessive lusts, and refuses to resist. Unlike Des Grieux in *Teleny*, here there is no altruistic masochism. James Grunnert is egocentric and narcissistic to the hilt. This, however, is no social impediment for him. He is the only son of a wealthy banker at the turn of the century. He is terribly spoiled, and he knows and relishes it. He is brought up in a world of privilege; royalty are his peers, the working classes are his chattel. His inability to form close emotional attachments is of no concern to his parents. As a German this is to be expected; as a future businessman this is a necessity.

Grunnert's world is a non-stop party, much as the world is for the jet-set of today. The ease and frequency of his sexual conquests would make most people envious. There is a huge emotional price to pay for this, though. What can be prized or cherished when no effort, commitment or emotional expenditure is necessary to possess it? Love affairs are acts of impulse and become not satisfying releases but acts of desperation offering temporary solace only. The inability truly to love and share simply compounds already overwhelming frustration and dissatisfaction. Grunnert is a stereotype, and a metaphor for his age, just as James Bellamy is in the English television drama *Upstairs, Downstairs*. Both act in accordance with the Edwardian male view of woman as either baby-maker or whore, and they suffer for it.

The style of *James Grunnert* mirrors the psyche of the protagonist. The lack of sustained emotional commitment precludes finely detailed, protracted sexual descriptions. We get form, but no deep substance. Sex scenes are a series of outbursts, without the rich tableaux of description and foreplay so frequently encountered in erotica. Grunnert's narration, like his emotional world, is devoid of the sensations (sights, sounds, smells, textures, etc.) that make things erotic, rather than just sexual. Copulation is not love making, but he can't realise this. He focuses his attention on body parts and fetishes, to the exclusion of the whole human being. If the Germans, stereotyped as cold, clinical, unfeeling, and devoid of expressive emotion, are truly such, then James Grunnert is a faithful subject of a sad race.

Grunnert is not a unique literary character. The anguished, self-frustrating soul has been portrayed many times, but perhaps never so well as in the German author Goethe's eighteenth-century creation, Werther. This quintessential tortured Romantic soul, who ultimately takes his own life to end his numerous 'sorrows' (*Leiden*), even spawned a massive student cult which imitated his style of dress (blue and yellow) and his suicide. Grunnert is a true heir to Werther's mantle of woes.

Is then *James Grunnert* really a psychiatric case study, a novel, an autobiography, or a combination of all these? German bibliographies of erotica tell us the book was first published privately in 1908, and reprinted many times in the German-speaking world. In 1929 the author was identified by Dr Paul Englisch (the H. S. Ashbee of pre-World-War-II Germany) as the recently deceased son of the famous Berlin banker Hans von Bleichröder. Suicide is implied, but not stated. If true, the autobiographical elements in *James Grunnert* are over-whelming. Alternately, the author has been named as the Berlin-based Viennese journalist and novelist Ernst Klein, who for years wrote under the pseudonym of Richard Werther! If this is true, then psyche more than chronology would be the autobiographical elements. Reality . . . Fantasy . . . who can tell? Is the book an exercise in self-analysis, a whining plea for emotional rescue, or a sadly prophetic story? Every age has its Werther/Grunnert. Our own is no exception. How many 'Yuppies' can all too well empathise with him?

Here then are episodes from the obsessed sex life of *James Grunnert* – first with his mother's nurse, then with a woman he meets at the opera and, finally, with the two sisters of a friend.

∼ from *James Grunnert*

The next few days were the most miserable of my life. I was dying with shame and remorse. I avoided her at meals where I had to meet her. I did not dare look at her, but I could not resist a stolen glance when I saw a look of deep sorrow in her tear-stained eyes. I wanted to die, but before I did she must forgive me. To ask her I did not have the courage, so I wrote her a letter of twenty pages. I told her everything, how I was driven to the shameful deed, told her the agonies I went through at night. Every word was a cry of great love for her. On my knees I begged for pardon if she would forgive me. If not I would shoot myself – and I was in earnest about that.

I put the letter on her dresser when I knew she was busy, stole back to my room, threw myself on the couch to think of how I could possess myself of a revolver, when suddenly my door opened softly. I wanted to cry out with happiness. She motioned me to keep quiet. Carefully locking the door, she came over and sat beside me.

'You wild untameable man,' she said. 'I am not angry with you, much as I should be, I can't, I love you so much myself. I was only so terribly ashamed – to think you could do such a thing.'

All my sickness, my weakness, disappeared at those words. My strength, my vigour was back. Before she realised it I had pulled her over and covered her face with kisses and she kissed me in return. When she finally tore herself free, she sat up laughing.

I eagerly drew her to me and told her of my manhood, and that all my sickness was on that account. I would surely die if I could not possess all of her.

'You are so grand, so beautiful Mathilda, there is not another woman like you on earth. I appreciate your angelic beauty. In my damnable night I have seen you naked, how you outshone Venus. If you were not so beautiful my suffering would not be so great, but I will die on account of it. You said you could make a man happy; let me be that man. You are so good, so noble. If not for love, then have pity, look how I am suffering. I can't stand it any longer, I am going mad. Be good, have pity.' My words, my excitement seemed to affect her.

Motionless she lay on the couch, her feet on the floor, her breast heaving. Eagerly my hands fumbled around her body but the heavy deaconess dress kept me from reaching that goal. Slowly I sought her lips with mine. She did not draw back but kissed me as eagerly as I did her, her arms wrapped around me and she hugged me tight.

'Do you really love me so much?' she whispered.

'Yes, yes – more than life, Oh Mathilda let me, let me, have pity – let me, just like this on top of you.' My excitement was beyond all bounds as I pushed up and down on top of her belly.

'What are you doing, James – don't, I beg of you,' she whispered, frightened. I couldn't hold myself, my body shook as with a chill.

'Let me – just this once – then I want to die – just let me once.'

In my madness I slid off her. 'You are in an awkward position, move up a little more – way up – there, that is heavenly.'

She saw my maddening excitement and she forgot her chastity.

'James what are you doing to me,' she moaned as she moved up. I was completely on top and began to push like mad.

'Are you angry with me, you angel you beloved?'

'No – no – if you are only happy.'

I bit her lips, my hand under those beautiful hips.

'Please raise up – help, I implore you.' Obediently she began to work up and down. That glorious feeling had taken hold of her also. She breathed and gasped and held me tight to her breast.

'Be happy – be happy,' she whispered in my ear.

'I am more than happy – I am crazed with bliss.' I soon felt that glorious moment approaching. It would be soon.

'Now – now.' She raised her belly as high as possible. She murmured, 'I love you.' I sank down in a faint. As I came to myself she was sitting with my head in her lap, covering me with kisses.

'Are you angry with me?'

'Would I be sitting here?'

I took her in my arms and kissed her. Reaching down with my hand I said: 'May I?'

'No, no, I beg of you, James – my lover – no man has ever touched me before. I implore you.'

'My dearest sweetheart, didn't you say you loved me? Then make my happiness complete.' She resisted, but only in a half-hearted way. I kept on slowly working up between her legs, until finally they opened and my fingers reached that paradise. She again got excited. Her belly, trembling, began to move up and down.

'What are you doing, James – what are you doing to me – not there –

ah, ah.' I parted her thighs and as a last effort she covered herself with her hands. I quickly overcame that. She was helpless, she belonged to me body and soul. She was as excited as I. I got on top and slowly pushed at her portal with my penis; once, twice and then I was in part way

'Oh – you are big!' she cried. Nothing could stop me now. I waited a moment and then slowly pressed further; one more strong push and I was in. She cried out as the last obstacle was removed. Her maidenhead gone, she lay quiet. I, too, cried out – and came. But I did not want to stop long. I kissed her furiously, I put my hand under her and fondled her, then slowly started to work again.

This time she felt the pleasure of love. She began to throw herself about like one possessed. Drawing her knees way up, she put them over my shoulders. She strained and worked! 'Oh this is heavenly,' I thought, 'so different from the baroness, no vulgar actions, just love – love!' Suddenly she went off for the first time.

'Oh, this is glorious,' she murmured. 'I can't stand it – I will die – oh push harder sweetheart – take me – take me – now – now – I am burning up!' I bit her tongue and clawed with my hands. What was all the joy I had known compared to this minute? I had conquered this maiden, who had defended herself against men. I had made her a woman – now she was my sweetheart. I was her lover.

Fate gave me only three days of this happiness, but I wanted more. I wanted to feast my eyes on that wonderful body. 'You gave me all your loveliness, why not let me gaze on your beauty?' I asked.

'I can't, I can't, I would sink into the earth with shame,' she said.

In the afternoon we sat in our room as usual. I was wondering how I could succeed in seeing her naked. I knew sooner or later she must succumb, but now I could not wait. She did not wear the uniform any more, but had on a plain linen dress, a black belt around her waist, and white collar and cuffs.

I was in sole possession of that loveliness but still I was not satisfied. She had allowed me to enter that paradise three times; still I was never allowed to gaze at her lovely body.

I got an idea, which I immediately began to carry out. But, frightened, she stopped me saying, 'James, aren't you ashamed with your mother dying in the next room?'

I must admit I was not.

'Are you angry because I cannot sit quietly with you?' I asked.

'No – but yes – you know in your room you may. James, I beg of you stop – James – James!' With one hand I fondled her leg, and with one quick move I had the other in that paradise between her legs.

'Oh lover – Oh God, how glorious! What if your mother should call, you little devil?'

Before she realised it, I was on my knees and had my tongue into her. She tried to push me away but I held on. Her resistance became weaker and weaker.

'You are getting me crazy,' she stammered, but every time she neared that glorious point I stopped for a while. I wanted to get her helpless. Carefully I unbuttoned her drawers so that at the first step they would drop. At last the moment arrived. I thought she was going to faint. I got up and sat beside her saying, 'Tillie, do you want to do me a favour?'

'What is it, darling?'

'I would like to see your legs at a distance, then I can appreciate your beauty. Do this, love, stand in the middle of the room and show me from there.'

'But darling, what are you asking me, that I should raise my dress?'

'Yes, love, just a little . . . to the knees, I won't ask any more.' My kisses and fingers won. Slowly she took one step . . .

Her face turned purple. Her eyes pleaded, but I was without mercy.

'If you don't do it I will use force.' I threatened. Slowly she lifted her dress.

'Higher – you promised to your knees.' Suddenly, with a wild look, she dropped it. I knew the reason. I jumped up.

'No, no,' she cried. 'I swear I will never forgive you.' Her threat did not stop me. With one jerk I had her dress above her hips. She stood with tears in her eyes, while I gazed at the wonders. She was beautiful, had skin like satin and thighs and belly firm and white as purest marble. With trembling hands I caressed those beautiful blonde curls, and with my kisses and caresses she began to tremble as I pushed her to the bed.

'Not here – your mama . . . ' But this only spurred me on. Slowly she sank on the bed. I lifted her naked legs, parted them as far as possible. Now I had a wonderful position. I could see that beautiful belly rise and fall, and I buried my face as far as I could. When we finished she swore she would come to my room that night stark naked.

She never fulfilled her oath though, for my mother died that night, and she had to leave soon thereafter.

Later I received a letter saying that she was to be married soon.

[After James Grunnert moved to Berlin, he began to lead the life of a young gentleman. It is there that his philandering started in earnest.

The following scene is just one of many affairs. The romance described here began at the opera.]

A few minutes past four there was a timid bell. It was she, heavily veiled. She slipped in and dropped into a chair. After a short rest I led her into my sitting room, quietly removed her veil and hat, helped her off with her coat and laid them on a settee. 'Now we will have a cup of tea.'

After looking in the mirror and arranging a few stray locks, she turned and said, 'And now, how do you like me?'

'You are beautiful.' I drew her to me and taking her glowing face in my hands, asked, 'May I – may I?'

'Yes,' she breathed. I kissed her rosy lips for the first time. She threw her arms around my neck and sank her teeth into my lip, sought my tongue. We were wild; we almost sank to the floor, but we soon separated and she, laughing, said, 'How about the tea, or were you only fooling?'

I led her to the next room, where tea and sandwiches were served. As we sat there I awkwardly put down my cup, fell on my knees, and began caressing her feet.

'What do you want?' she asked.

'You have such lovely feet.'

'If you keep on flattering me, it will become tiresome.'

'Let me kiss them.'

'What, my shoes?'

'No, the stockings above them.' I raised her dress and pressed my lips to that beautifully shaped leg.

'Please don't – let me drink my tea in peace.'

'I know of only one more beautiful spot than your knees.'

'And that is?'

'I will tell you later.' Slowly I moved my hand up, when I reached her knee she stopped me. I laid my head in her lap, saying, 'The road to paradise.'

'You must think me crazy, or absolutely depraved,' she whispered. 'Only yesterday I saw you for the first time and I am in your quarters, like this. It's awful, monstrous really and I can't imagine what you take me for.'

'I take you for what you are, a young hot-blooded woman, who must have those passions satisfied. A woman who wants to, and must, be loved. A woman who is not understood by her husband. But I will teach you what real love is, you angel, you wonderful woman. I am going to open the gates to that new world for you.' As I spoke I became more passionate. The effects showed on her, she was all a-tremble. She stooped and our lips met for the second time in a long voluptuous kiss.

'I am crazy – crazy – ' she whispered. I was not quite ready. I wanted to enjoy every step. I raised her dress for a look at that hidden paradise.

'No, no – not like that.' She jumped up. 'Please let me rest a minute, I shall go mad.' I waited, and presently she turned to me, a glorious creature full of love and passion, who was ready to give up all.

'Isn't it strange that I never met you before – you belong to the society circle of Berlin.'

'My husband owns two factories in Hamburg, and only a short time ago established headquarters here.'

'This time real good came from a business transaction.'

'How can you talk like that? You whose father is one of the foremost bankers in Germany.'

'How do you know?'

'Who does not know the name Grunnert? Your father is one of our largest stockholders.'

'Indeed, I was not aware of the fact.'

'My husband told me. He loves to tell me of his business matters.'

'Then I shall not. I hate business and money matters.'

'But you don't mind spending it.'

'That is what it is for.'

'I can see that from your surroundings. Won't you show me around your apartment? I have never seen a bachelor's quarters before. You love the beautiful,' she said, pointing to a statue of Venus.

'You are just as beautiful. Do you know what I would like? To undress you naked and prove that you are a thousand times more beautiful.'

'No, no, not that,' she whispered. Her face flushed, not from embarrassment, but from the realisation that she would do exactly as I said. I could see her passion was overpowering her reason. Soon I would have her.

'Come, my beloved angel.' At that I picked her up and carried her to the divan.

'How strong you are.' I kissed her and she returned kiss for kiss. With trembling fingers I opened her blouse, disclosing a breast white as marble.

'You are making me crazy.'

'Do you know the spot more beautiful than your knees – it is between them.'

'Do with me what you will,' she said at last. 'I am yours.' I knelt before her and began to undo her drawers.

'Oh James, not that, not now, I am so ashamed.'

'Please – I beg of you – you promised.' The drawers came off; I saw that beautiful dark apron. She covered it with her hand as a last stand. I pushed it away, throwing myself before her I kissed her all over – belly, hair, legs, between them, wherever chance offered – like a madman. She sighed with joy.

'Come, please come,' she sighed. I was between her legs. As I entered I saw she was not used often; she was tight like a young girl.

'Not so wild – you might hurt me – go slow. Oh, that burns like fire ah, oh, take me, there – oh – you.' I was never so excited. With every push I seemed to strike bottom, causing her to utter a little cry.

'Not so deep. Oh God I will die – oh sweetheart, now, now – ah – ah!' One little cry and she fell back like dead. She opened her eyes. saying, 'I love you – I love you.'

'Might I make a suggestion?'

'What is it?'

'Next to my room is a cosy little bath; you might take a warm douche, it will do you good.'

'You think of everything, I think you are an ideal lover. I shall fall in love with you.'

'You think you will – I have fallen in love with you already.'

That first evening she did not stay long. She had to attend a business supper with her husband.

It was always my delight to see her naked beauty as she stepped from the bathtub, and she never refused me this pleasure. On one of these occasions she complained of being cold. I sprang up, wrapped her in a bathrobe and carried her into the next room.

'You are my ideal of a man such as I always wished for myself when I was a girl.'

'I would gladly put my hands under your feet. I am a beggar beside you. I am your slave, your dog.'

'I am vain enough as it is. You don't want to turn my head completely.'

'I cannot begin to tell you how beautiful you are.'

'It is because you love me.'

When I finally kissed her goodbye, I asked. 'Now sweetheart, when will I see you again?'

'I will come tomorrow.'

'When?'

'After church, at three.'

'And you will stay?'

'Until ten.' While kissing her, my hand again clutched that hidden paradise.

'Oh, James – please don't. You make me crazy.'

'You are not angry with me?'

'No, no, I am so happy. Now one more kiss.' From then on she came almost daily. She lived only for me, and I for her.

My one great hobby was taking snapshots of her. My favourite was with her dresses raised above her knees – suggestive but not vulgar. I took pictures of her undressing and nude – but they always wound up with one of our orgies.

One day she rushed into my flat all excited and flustered.

'Jay! An impudent fellow followed me right to the door!' In a rage I opened the door, and sure enough, there stood a large well-dressed man, about to beat a retreat, but I stopped him.

'What do you want here?'

'I want to know who lives here.'

'In order that you may be able to see better I will enlighten you. At that I punched his face, then picked him up bodily and threw him downstairs.

After we watched him pick himself up and enter a cab, she threw her arms around me crying. 'My hero, I am proud of you, you are the only one.' I threw her on the lounge, and at the height of our bliss she exclaimed: 'I have a confession to make. Since first we met I have not had intercourse with my husband. I am yours for all eternity.'

We finally decided to tell her husband, relying on his honour to release her, but God intervened, for she contracted pneumonia and died in a few days.

I mourned for her for days – my love, my true love – but it was a dream – a dream I must forget.

[Young Grunnert was never at a loss for playmates. He was an opportunist, always willing to exploit an advantage for a little sexual play. In the following scene, James is in top form.]

Going back ten years, I well remember the day I surprised two sisters of a pal of mine, looking at some obscene pictures, which were so interesting they did not notice my entrance. The younger, a girl of eighteen, was so interested she was playing with herself. I quietly tiptoed in, grabbed the pictures and saw they were actually vulgar – disgusting even to me.

I could see how excited the pictures had made them. They were flushed beyond description. I felt I must put out my hand and pluck this delicious fruit I knew was ripe.

'Nice things you are looking at.' They were on the verge of crying. 'What if your mother knew?'

'For God's sake, dear Jay, do not betray us.'

'Why shouldn't I? You two are hardly out of school – what if your brother came across these pictures?' I paused for effect and to contemplate the two lovelies sitting before me. The colour of their cheeks had risen to a high crimson shade and they looked at me with imploring eyes. 'No,' I said finally, 'I can't do that.'

'You surely won't.'

'Surely not.' I drew them both on my lap and kissed them. They returned my kisses and our friendship was sealed. As Berta was sitting on that mark of manhood which was now asserting its rights, I slowly put her hand on it. It was as stiff as a poker and she clasped it for dear life.

'If you will come to my house tomorrow I will show you some real pictures, not miserable stuff like this.' I finally persuaded them.

Driven by their curiosity, they arrived on the minute and as I showed them the pictures they grew bolder and wanted to look at them alone.

'But you must not look.'

'All right.' I seated myself at the window, where I could watch their every movement.

Thinking that I had stepped into the adjoining room, they let their hands wander. Berta's went south, to the nest between her legs. For Wilhelma's part, she loosened the buttons of her blouse and sought the full breasts that perched at the top of her corset.

I was mad with passion. The stiffness in my trousers was growing unbearable. I quietly crept up behind them, placing one arm around each. They were too interested to resist. Slowly I raised Berta's dress from behind, parted her drawers in front, and reached that goal. She became more excited, but did not seem to realise what was happening. Now I began on Wilhelma. At first she jumped, but her interest in the pictures was too great. So now I enjoyed playing with both, but I had to have more. I took out old trusty, bent Berta forwards on the table, and started to bore into her.

'Jay, don't, I implore you – you are . . . I can't stand it . . . I won't . . . I won't . . . ' But her voice dissolved in a little squeal of joy and her hips began to move back and forth, trying to get more of old Rodger into her. She would have to learn to be patient. I threw her skirts up over her waist and grabbed her hips firmly. In this manner, I held her at the end of my shaft. Poor Berta was becoming quite insane. Strangely.

Minnie sat stock still, the photos forgotten by her side, watching her sister struggling to get my shaft into her quim.

'Please Jay – let me up,' Berta said. 'We shouldn't do this!' But she made no move to get up, in fact, she was wiggling her little bottom like a fish on a line.

'No, Jay, oh you . . . ah.' I was in, I worked like mad, but I was wise enough to withdraw when I went off. I got up, making all kinds of promises to my sweet girls and they smiled as I drew them on my lap.

The other now became excited, and we were soon all on the sofa in a heap, kissing and hugging. In an instant I was again between those legs. And this time she did not complain.

'Oh, that is good – that is glorious – so sweet.' Although I again withdrew as I came, she went off for the first time, and we both sank down, half-conscious. She was now my sweetheart. Poor Minnie sat beside us, her dress up high, trying to get a little satisfaction with her fingers. I took pity on her, buried my tongue in her opening and in a few minutes she cried: 'Dear sweet Berta – oh, I am coming – he is so wonderful – now – now!' She was off. We were all happy.

From then on I had the two of them to take care of, for they always came together. This lasted about four months, until they were both sent to a girls' school in Switzerland.

When they returned I was in Paris. I did not see them until some time later. Berta was the wife of a rich artist, while Minnie had become the bride of the man from whom I got the bullet that sent me here.

～ 28 ～

The Way of a Man with a Maid

1908

The Way of a Man with a Maid is the quintessential Edwardian sadomasochistic novel. It is a classic of such proportions that it is one of the books (others being Reage's *The Story of O* and Sade's *Justine and Juliette*) to which all other works in the genre must be compared.

This plot is a simple narrative of pure libidinal fantasy. The protagonist, Jack, a well-to-do Edwardian bachelor in London, decides to exact vengeance on the woman who has just jilted him, Alice. Luring her like a fly into a spider's web (in this case his secret sound-proof boudoir), he turns her into a willing convert to the sexual pleasures of algolagnia. Alice decides to take equal measures with her own impudent maid, Fanny, who once indoctrinated, joins in the 'conversion' of their mutual friend, the widow Connie Blount. Jack and his three lady confederates then turn their attentions to evening the score with a pompous, supercilious matron, and her even more obnoxious daughter.

The bibliography of *The Way of a Man with a Maid* is surprisingly difficult. So classic a book should have been reported in all the twentieth-century erotica references, but this is not the case. When mention of it in print is made, no author nor date of first publication is given. Though currently available in many editions, it seems to have been genuinely scarce until the 1960s. The restricted collections of the British Library and Bibliothèque Nationale, as well as the Rose *Register of Erotic Books*, all list the same single edition: two volumes in one, 276 pages, no date, and the imprint of 'The Erotica Biblion Society of London–New York'. Kearney's annotations in *The Private Case: An Annotated Bibliography* date this edition as *c.*1935, along with a note that the original edition should be about 1895 since the title page of a supposedly '1896' novel (*Parisian Frolics*) indicates itself to be from the same pen as the author of *The Way of a Man with a Maid* (which was first prosecuted in France in December 1914). However, the real first English-language edition of *Parisian Frolics* was *c.*1912. A 1920s short-title catalogue of a private American erotica library lists a 315-page edition of *The Way of a Man with a Maid* with no further information. Fortunately one other collector left behind a private note that his own copy of the book had printed on the cover 'H. W. Pickle and Co., Publishers, Upper River Street, Liverpool, 1908', was two volumes of 119 and 196 pages (a total of 315!), and was 'printed in Paris'. These facts would place the novel contemporary with very similar turn-of-the-century flagellation and s/m novels, such as *'Frank' and I* and *Sadopaideia*, and one could deduce that it emanated from the same circle of H. S. Nichols and his English 'pornographers' responsible for the bulk of the sadomasochistically oriented books of the day, which also included *Maudie*, *Pleasure Bound* and the *Mr Howard* series.

When we think of the sadomasochistic novel we frequently conjure up visions of whips and chains, stocks, restraints, metal-studded leather garments, jack boots, fetish implements, paddles, and equipment straight out of a torture chamber or dungeon. We think of spanking, flagellation, bondage and other forms of subjugation and corporal punishment. We expect scenes filled with screams and pleadings, pain and brutality, torn flesh and gore. What a surprise then for the genteel readers of this novel, for this book recognises that sadomasochism is first and foremost a psychological and not a physical sexual phenomenon, though its expression is replete with acted-out manifestations and rituals. Reduced to its most anecdotal simplicity, one can recall the humorous definitions that the masochist is the one who says 'Beat me, Beat me', to which the sadist responds 'No'.

Sadism (the deriving of sexual pleasure from inflicting real or imagined discomfort on another) and its counterpart masochism (the deriving of sexual pleasure from receiving or perceiving physical or psychological discomfort) are inseparably entwined in the entire ritual of love and reproduction.

Like most human activity, sadomasochism ranges the gamut from selfish altruism to criminal misconduct. Philosophically and physiologically, genital intercourse embodies 'violence' in the form of capture and penetration. The ancient Eastern religions present the principals of Yin and Yang, the female and male elements of the universe, which are pictured as in a balance of domination and submission (i.e. the penetrating male is simultaneously engulfed and neutralised by the female). As a Western philosophical concept, the correlation of pain and even death with sensuality and eroticism has been written about extensively by such writers as Guillaume Apollinaire and George Bataille.

Humans have problems with sadomasochism because they try to attach a morality to it. This is not the case in nature. The unconscious reflexes elicited by coition bespeak a violence. Certain animals engage in mating rituals that appear to be nothing less than rape or life-endangering assaults. The infliction of a painful stimulus (biting the neck for instance) is the trigger for ovulation in some species, and hence necessary for the procreation of the species. The digging of fingernails into flesh (which sometimes draws blood) is a remnant of the carpal and tarsal spasms necessary for other animals to cling together while copulating. (Unconscious reflexes at the time of orgasm cause the fingers and toes to curl). But that is nature, and nature is amoral. Who are humans then to pass moral judgement on such action?

Human beings are no different from other members of the animal kingdom. With their higher cerebral functions they have turned these instinctive reactions into a highly sophisticated and intellectualised form of erotic foreplay. Sadomasochism (which is simply these physical stimuli brought to a particular level of perceived intensity) or any of its more symbolic representations such as domination and submission are universal and intrinsic to sexual excitement and mating, and are not learned behaviours. What is individualistic is the strength of the stimulus needed to achieve the sexual arousal. For some, the mere thought of control or being controlled is sufficient aphrodisiac. Others require actual physical encounter and response, while others need only symbolic representations of the physical stimuli.

The Way of a Man with a Maid has many elements we would expect from a sadomasochistic story. There is the soundproofed room for captivity (the 'Snuggery' as it is so charmingly called) replete with cords and pulleys, flagellation implements, limb binders and the mechanical 'Chair of Treachery' for restraint. But, uncharacteristically, there are also feathers and soft ropes of silk! We soon see that implied threats and embarrassments predominate in the place of physical punishment. The psychological aspects of apprehension are exercised more than physical castigation. Maidenly shyness and reserve and multitudinous entreaties for mercy are juxtaposed with the threat of cruelty rather than the exercise of it.

Despite its basic sexual theme, close examination shows that this plot requires little physical brutality. There is charm and almost a gentleness and levity to its proceedings, with sensibilities rather than bodies being bruised. The motivation of the characters is revenge, not hate, hence embarrassment and private humiliation better serve their purpose than any torture or true physical pain. The action is slow, methodical, well structured, and builds upon itself, with raw emotional fear and trepidation evolving into psychological distress concomitant with physical pleasure. Sexual ecstasy follows, along with newly found appreciation for the erotic effects of physical stimulation coupled with subjugation. 'Victims' become willing participants and active instigators themselves. Additionally, 'victims' soon realise that this activity is an aphrodisiac, and that s/m is literally a game that all participants, male and female, dominant or submissive can enjoy. If there ever was a charmingly 'playful' sadomasochism novel, this is it.

The novel is also quite inventive and creative. The author introduces a dazzling array of equipment for sexual gymnastics, erotic applications for then recent technologies (such as electricity), and also gentle variations on old themes that are positively new and refreshing even today. No wonder the book served as a model for three pastiche sequels, a feature 'porno' movie, *The Wicked Victorians*, and parts of the play *Oh! Calcutta*. Anyone who has read the book's feather tickling scene will never forget it!

Here then is a scene from *The Way of a Man with a Maid*, where Jack finally receives into his arms the previously shy, demure, maidenly, and now suitably humbled Alice.

from *The Way of a Man with a Maid*

Thus, at last, Alice and I found ourselves together naked on the couch! Side by side on our backs, we lay in silence, my left hand clasping her right, till she had regained her composure a little.

As soon as I saw she had become calmer, I slipped my arms round her and, turning on my side towards her, I drew her tenderly to me, but still keeping her flat on her back. I kissed her lips again and again ardently, murmuring lovingly between my kisses, 'My little wifie! My wee wifie!' – noting delightedly how her downcast face brightened at my adoption of her fantasy, and feeling her respond almost fondly to my kisses.

'May I learn something about my wifie?' I whispered as I placed my right hand on Alice's maiden breasts and began feeling them as if she was indeed my bride! Alice smiled tenderly, yielding herself to my caprice and quivering anew under the voluptuous sensations communicated to her by my inquisitive fingers! 'Oh! What little beauties! Oh! What darling bubbies!' I murmured amidst fresh kisses! Alice was now beginning to look quite pleased at my using her own pet name for her treasures and commenced to enter almost heartily into my game. I continued to fondle and squeeze her luscious breasts for a little longer, then carried my hand lower down her, but suddenly arrested it, then whispered: 'May I?'

At this absurd travesty of a bridegroom's chivalrous respect to his bride, Alice fairly laughed (poor girl! Her first laugh in that room that day!), then gaily nodded, putting up her lips for more kisses! Overjoyed to see her thus forgetting her woes, I pressed my lips on hers and kept them there, punctuating with kisses the feignedly timid advance of my hand over her belly, till it invaded the precincts of her cunt! 'Oh! My darling! Oh! My sweetheart! . . . Oh! My wifie! . . . ' I murmured passionately as my fingers roved wantonly all over Alice's cunt, playing with her hairs, feeling and pressing insidiously its fleshiness, toying with her slit but not penetrating it! Alice was all the while abandoning herself freely to the lascivious sensations induced by my fingerings, jogging her buttocks upwards, wiggling her hips, ejaculating 'Ah!' and 'Oh!' in spite of my lips being glued to hers and nearly suffocating her with kisses!

After a few minutes of this delicious exploration of the most private part of Alice's body, I stopped my finger at her orifice! 'Pardon me, sweet!' I whispered, then gently inserted it into Alice's cunt as far as I could, as if to assure myself as to her condition, all the time smothering her with kisses. Keenly appreciating the comicality of my proceedings in spite of the serious lover-like air I was assuming, Alice laughed out heartily, unconsciously heaving herself up so as to meet my finger, slightly opening her thighs to allow it freer access to her cunt. My tongue took advantage of her laughter to dart through her parted lips in search of her tongue, which she then sweetly resigned to my ardent homage! 'Oh, wifie! . . . My wifie! . . . ' I murmured, as if enchanted to find her a maid! 'Oh! What a delicious cunny you have! So fat! So soft! So juicy! Wifie! . . . Oh, wifie!' I breathed passionately into her ear as I agitated my finger inside her cunt, half frigging her and stopping her protests with my kisses till I saw how I was exciting her! 'Little wifie,' I whispered with a grin I could not for the life of me control – 'Little wifie! Shall I . . . make you come?'

In spite of her almost uncontrollable and self-absorbing sexual irritation, Alice laughed out, then nodded, closing her eyes as if in anticipation of her now fast approaching ecstasy! A little more subtle titillation and Alice spent blissfully on my ministering finger, jerking herself about lasciviously and evidently experiencing the most voluptuous raptures and transports ever!

I waited till her sexual spasm had ceased. 'Wifie,' I whispered, rousing her with my kisses, 'Little wifie! Oh, you naughty girl! How you seemed to enjoy it! . . . Tell me, wifie, was it good?' She opened her eyes and they met mine, brimming with merriment. She blushed rosy red, then clasped me in her soft arms and kissed me passionately, murmuring, 'Darling! Oh, darling!' – then burst out laughing at our ridiculousness! And so we lay for a few delicious moments, clasped in each other's arms.

Alice, now rosy red with suppressed excitement and lust, quickly raised herself to a sitting position at my side. I took her dainty hands in mine, she yielding them rather coyly, turned on my back and opened my legs. I guided her right, hand on to my prick and her left to my testicles, then left her to indulge and satisfy in any manner she saw fit her senses of sight and touch, wondering whether it would occur to her that the fire she was about to excite in me would have to be extinguished in her self, as before long it would be!

For certainly half a minute, Alice intently inspected my organs of generation, leaning over me and supporting herself by placing her right hand on my stomach and her left on my thigh.

Presently she steadied herself on her left hand, then timidly, with her right hand, she took hold of my prick gently, glancing curiously at me as if to note the effect of the touch of her soft hand on so excitable a part of my person, then smiling wickedly and almost triumphantly as she saw me quiver with pleasure! Oh, the exquisite sensations that accompanied her touch! Growing bolder, she held my prick erect and gently touched my balls with her slender forefinger, as if to test their substance, then took them in her hand, watching me eagerly out of the corners of her eyes to note the effect on me! I was simply thrilled with the pleasure! For a few minutes she lovingly played with my organs, generally devoting a hand to each, but sometimes she would hold my prick between one finger and thumb while with her other hand she would amuse herself by working the loose folds of skin off and on the knob! At another time she would place my prick between her soft palms and pretend to roll it. Another time she seized a testicle in each hand, oh, so gently, and sweetly caressed them! As it was, I had to exercise every ounce of my self-control to prevent an outbreak!

Presently I said quietly but significantly, 'Little wifie, may I tell you that between husband and wife kissing not only is sanctioned but is considered even laudable!' Alice laughed nervously, glanced quickly at me, then with heightened colour looked intently at my prick, which she happened at that moment to be grasping tightly in her right hand, its head protruding above her thumb and fingers, while with her left forefinger she was delicately stroking and tickling my balls! After a moment's hesitation, she bent down, squeezed my prick tightly (as if to prevent anything from issuing out of it), then softly kissed its head! Oh, the delicious sensations as her lips touched my prick! Emboldened by the success of her experiment, Alice set to work kissing my balls sweetly, then passed her lips over the whole of my organs of genera-tion, showering kisses on them, but favouring especially my balls, which had for her a wonderful attraction, burying her lips in my scrotum and (I really believe) tonguing them! Such attentions could only end in one way! Inflamed almost beyond endurance by the play of her sweetly irritating lips, my prick became so stiff and stark that Alice, in alarm, thought she had better cease her ministrations, and with blushing cheeks and a certain amount of trepidation, she lay herself down alongside of me.

By this time I was so mad with lust I could hardly control myself, and as soon as Alice lay down I seized her in my arms, drew her to me, showered kisses on her lips, then with an abrupt movement, I rolled her over on to her back, slipping on top of her!

Gripping her tightly, I got my stiff and excited prick against the lips of her cunt, then pushing steadily, I drove it into Alice, burying its head in her! Despite the rapid movements of her buttocks and hips, I made another thrust, entering still further into her cunt. Suddenly I felt something give way inside her and my prick slid well up her cunt.

Oh! My exultation! At last I had Alice. I lay still for some seconds so as to allow the interior of her cunt to stretch a bit, but I was too wrought up and mad with lust to remain inactive long in such sweet surroundings.

With a final thrust, I sent my prick well home, Alice's hairs and mine interweaving. She shrieked again! Then, agitating myself gently on her, I began to fuck her, first with steady strokes of my buttocks, then with more rapid and uneven shoves and thrusts, she quivering under me, overwhelmed by her emotions and by the strangely delicious pleasure that the movements of my prick inside her cunt were arousing in her! Alice no longer struggled, but lay passive in my arms, unconsciously accommodating herself to my movements on her and involuntarily working her hips and bottom, instinctively yielding to the promptings of her now fast increasing sexual cravings by jogging herself up as if to meet my down thrusts!

Shall I ever forget my sensations at that moment? Alice, the long-desired Alice, the girl of all girls, the unconscious object of my concupiscence – Alice lay underneath me, tightly clasped in my arms, naked, quivering, her warm flesh throbbing against mine, my prick lodged in her cunt, her face in full sight, her breasts palpitating and her bosom heaving in her agitation, unconsciously longing to have her sexual desires satisfied. I could no longer control myself! Clasping her yielding figure still more closely against me, I let myself go – thrusting, ramming, shoving and agitating my prick spasmodically in her, I frenziedly set to work fucking her! A storm of rapid tumultuous jogs, a half-strangled 'Oh! . . . Oh! . . . Oh! . . . ' from Alice, and I spent deliriously into her, deluging her with my hot discharge, at the same moment feeling the head of my prick christened by the warm gush that burst from Alice as she also frantically spent, punctuating the pulsations of her discharge by voluptuous upheavings of her wildly agitated bottom!

I remained master of myself notwithstanding my ecstatic delirium, but Alice fainted from the sexual eruption for the first time legitimately induced within her! My warm kisses on her upturned face, however, soon revived her. When she came to herself, still lying naked in my arms and harbouring my prick in the freshly opened asylum of her cunt, she begged me to set her free! But she had not yet extinguished the flames of lust and desire which her provocative personality and appetising nakedness had kindled, and which she had stimulated to white heat by the tender manipulations and kisses she had bestowed on my testicles and prick! The latter still remained rampant and stiff and burned to riot again within the deliciously warm and moist recess of Alice's cunt – while I longed to make her expire again in the sweet agonies of satisfied sexual desire, and to witness and share her involuntary transports and wondrous ecstasies as she passed from sexual spasm while being sweetly fucked!

So I whispered amidst my kisses: 'Not yet, Alice, not yet! Once more, Alice, you'll enjoy it this time!' – then began gently to fuck her again.

I had thrown my arms over hers. I whispered, 'Hug me tightly. You'll be more comfy now, Alice!' She did so. 'That's much better, isn't it?' I murmured. She tearfully smiled, then nodded affirmatively, putting up her lips to be kissed.

'Now just lie quietly and enjoy yourself,' I whispered, then began to fuck her like a piston, with slow and steady thrusts of my prick up and down her cunt! At once Alice's bosom and breasts commenced to palpitate under me, fluttering deliciously against my chest. Exercising the fullest control I possibly could bring to bear on my seminal reserves so as to prolong to the utmost extent my voluptuous occupation and that Alice should have every opportunity of indulging and satisfying her sexual appetites and cravings and of fully tasting the delights of copulation, I continued to fuck her steadily, watching her blushing upturned face and learning from her telltale eyes how she was getting on. Presently she began to agitate her hips and jog herself upwards, then her breath came and went quickly, her eyes turned upwards and half closed, a spasm convulsed her – she spent! I stopped for a moment. After a few seconds, Alice opened her eyes, blushing rosy red as she met mine. I kissed her lips tenderly, whispering, 'Good?' She nodded and smiled. I resumed. Soon she was again quivering and wriggling under me, as a fresh wave of lust seized her. Again her eyes closed and again Alice spent blissfully! I saw that I had now thoroughly roused her sexual desires and that she had surrendered herself to their domination and that they were imperiously demanding satisfaction! I clasped her closely to me, whispered quickly, 'Now, Alice, let yourself go!' And set to work in real earnest, thrusting rapidly and ramming myself well into her!

Alice simply abandoned herself to her sensations of the moment! Hugging me to her, she agitated herself wildly under me, plunging madly, heaving herself furiously upwards, tossing her head from side to side. She seemed as if overcome and carried away by a torrent of lust and madly endeavouring to satisfy it! I could hardly hold her still. How many times she spent I do not know, but her eyes were constantly half closing and opening again as spasm after spasm convulsed her! Suddenly she ejaculated frenziedly: 'Now! . . . Now! Let me have it! . . . Let me have it all! . . . ' Immediately I responded! A few furious shoves and I poured my boiling essence into Alice, spending frantically in blissful ecstasy! 'Ah! . . . Ah! . . . ' she cried, quivering rapturous transports as she felt herself inundated by my warm discharge! Then a paroxysm swept through her, her head fell back, her eyes closed, her lips opened and she spent convulsively.

She fainted right away! It had been too much for her! I tried to bring her to herself by kisses and endearments, but did not succeed. So I drew my prick cautiously out of Alice's cunt and sprinkled her face with water when she soon came to. I assisted her to rise, as she seemed half-dazed, and supported her as she tottered to her alcove, where she half fell into a low chair. I brought her a glass of wine which she drank gratefully and which greatly revived her. Then I saw that she had everything she could want: water, soap, syringe and towels. She asked me to leave her, adding she was now all right. Before doing so, I stooped down to receive a kiss. Alice threw her arms round my neck, drew my face to hers, then kissed me passionately, quite unable to speak because of her emotion! I returned her kisses with interest.

Presently Alice whispered, 'May I dress now?' I had intended to have fucked her again, but I saw how overwrought she was. Besides that, the afternoon was late and there was just enough time left for her to catch her first train home. So I replied, 'Yes, dear, if you like. Shall I bring your clothes here?' She nodded gratefully. I carefully collected her garments and took them to her, then left her to herself to dress.

In about a quarter of an hour Alice appeared, fully dressed, hatted and gloved. I threw open the doors and she passed out without a word, casting a long, comprehensive glance round the room in which she had passed so memorable an afternoon. I called a hansom, placed her in it and took her to her station in comfortable time for her train. She was very silent during the drive but made no opposition when I took her hand in mine and gently stroked it. As the train started, I raised my hat with the customary salute.

One evening, Alice and I met at the house of a lady hostess who placed us together at the dinner table. I naturally devoted myself to Alice afterwards in the drawing room. When the guests began to depart, our hostess asked me if I would mind seeing Alice home in my taxicab, which of course I was delighted to do. Strangely enough the possibilities of a *tête-à-tête* did not occur to me; and it was only when Alice returned to the hall cloaked and veiled and our hostess had told her that I had very kindly offered to take her home in my taxi that the opportunity of testing her real feelings was suggested to me by the vivid blush which, for a moment, suffused her face and elicited a sympathetic but significant smile from our hostess, who evidently thought she had done us both a good turn. And so she had, but not in the direction she fondly thought!

The taxi had hardly begun to move when we both simultaneously seemed to remember that we were alone together for the first time that afternoon. Overcome by some sudden inspiration, our eyes sought each other. In the dim light, I saw Alice's face working under the rush of her emotion, but she was looking at me with eyes full of love and not of anger; she began to cuddle up against me, perhaps unconsciously, at the same time turning her face up as if seeking a kiss. I could not resist the mute invitation. Quickly I slipped my left arm round her, drew her to me (she yielding to me without a struggle), pressed my lips on hers and fondly rained kisses on her mouth. 'Jack!' she murmured lovingly. I felt her thrill under my kisses, then catch her breath and quiver again! I recognised the symptoms. Promptly I slipped my right hand under her clothes and touched the sweet junction of her belly and thighs. My fingers began to attack the folds of her chemise through the opening of her drawers in their feverish impatience to get at her cunt! 'Jack! Oh, Jack!' Alice again murmured as she pressed herself against me as closely as she could, while at the same time, she began to open her thighs slightly as to facilitate the operations of my ardent fingers which, just at that moment, succeeded in displacing the last obstacle and were now resting on her cunt itself!

Alice quivered deliciously at the touch of my hand on her bare flesh as I gently and tenderly stroked her cunt, playing lovingly on its moist, palpitating lips and twining her hairs round my fingers. But as soon as she felt me tickle her clitoris (time was short and we were quickly nearing her room, besides which it would have been cruel to have aroused her sexual passions without satisfying them), she threw all restraint to the winds and madly agitated her cunt against my hand, wriggling divinely as I set to work to frig her. Soon came the first blissful ecstasy. A delicious spasm thrilled through her as she spent deliriously on my fingers, then another, and another, and yet another – till, unable to spend any more, she gasped brokenly, 'Stop, Jack! . . . I can't . . . go on!' She was utterly absorbed in the overpoweringly exquisite sensations of the moment and the delicious satisfying of the longings and cravings which had been tormenting her. It was full time that we stopped, for the taxi was now turning into the street in which she lived.

Quickly (but reluctantly) I withdrew my hand from Alice's cunt, now moist with her repeated spendings, and I just managed to get her clothes into some sort of order when the cab stopped at her door. I sprang out first and assisted Alice.

'I'll see you right into your rooms so that I may be able truly to report that I have faithfully executed the orders,' I said laughingly, more for the benefit of my chauffeur than of Alice.

'Thanks very much!' she replied quietly, and having collected her wraps, I followed her into the house and up the staircase to her apartment on the first floor, carefully closing the door after me.

Alice threw herself into my arms in an ecstasy of delight. I rather think that she expected me to take the opportunity to fuck her – and gladly would I have done so, as I was in a terrible state of lust; but I always hated 'snatch-fucking', and if I stayed with her long enough for her to undress and be properly fucked, it might arouse suspicions that would damage her reputation.

So after a passionate embrace, I whispered, 'I must not stop here, darling; when will you come to lunch?'

Alice blushed deliciously, instantly comprehending the significance of my invitation. 'Tomorrow!' she murmured, hiding her face on my shoulder.

'Thanks, sweetheart. Then tomorrow! Now get to bed and have a good night's rest. Good-night, my darling!' After a few more passionate kisses, I left her and rejoined my taxi.

29

Life on Board a Yacht
1908

Life on Board a Yacht, 'London, James Kennedy, 40 Fenchurch Street, 1908', was issued anonymously and clandestinely. Of all the information on the novel's title page perhaps only the title can actually be believed! The publication date of 1908 is most likely false, as predating of erotica was a common ploy at the time to allay police action. It is known, however, that in 1913 the book was the subject of an obscenity prosecution in Paris. This and the style of typesetting indicate the place of publication to be not London, but rather France, Holland or Belgium, all countries employed to print English-language books when it was thought best not to have the local constabulary able to read the text being printed! A clue to the true publisher might be found in the last printed line of the novel. At the bottom of the final page appears 'Imperial Press, London', a reference to a publishing venture once run by H. S. Nichols, the rogue English bookseller and erotica publisher who frequently fled across Europe trying to escape legal prosecutions. (Nichols finally moved to New York City where he died after several years as a printseller, and during which time he published a volume of bogus drawings he attributed to the then dead artist Aubrey Beardsley).

The author of *Life on Board a Yacht* is still unknown. He was definitely an Englishman, as evidenced by the characteristic spellings used (such as 'colour'), and the extensive use of British slang and argot. He was familiar with the jaded world of his society's 'upper crust', and had an intimate knowledge of leisure sailing. The novel is similar in mien and plot to such then contemporary works as *Maudie*, *Pleasure Bound*, *Nemisis Hunt* and the 'Charles Sackville' novels, (which latter have been attributed by Kearney, in his *Private Case: An Annotated Bibliography*, to George R. Bacchus, an English journalist and *bon vivant*.

Life on Board a Yacht is very much a reflection of the decadent sensuality rampant in Edwardian England. Lead by the King himself, the aristocracy and the wealthy set broke free from decades of Victorian sexual prudery with an Epicureanism and lasciviousness limited only by the size of the fortunes to be squandered. Life was a continuous attempt to gratify the senses; sexual morality was discarded. If the characters in this novel seem familiar to the modern reader, it is because our current counterparts are written up daily in gossip columns and scandal magazines. The jet setters of the 1980s and 1990s are mere imitators of these licentious celebrities of eighty years ago. For the privileged Edwardians, pursuit of carnal pleasure was a never-ending quest (as was so vividly dramatised in the BBC production *Upstairs, Downstairs*).

How well this book captures that atmosphere! The novel is set at the turn of the century aboard a private luxury vessel travelling the Mediterranean coast. The tale is told from an outsider's point of view, that of a male secretary to one of the onboard guests. The host for the floating orgy is the eccentric Lord Seacomb, a man of wealth by inheritance rather than any hard work or talent. His co-participants are nine men of title and property, each one a libertine of the highest order. Their female accomplices were well chosen to be equally devoid of moral scruples. Through the secretary's eyes we see this sexual menagerie engage in its randy excesses. Costume balls become salacious contests of female vanity. The atmosphere of frenetic lust becomes overpowering as the men try to outdo each other with acts of reckless virility.

In the hands of a lesser author such a plot could quickly become a tedious repetition of sexual gymnastics. The author, obviously himself a sophisticated and well-travelled man of the world, realises that the sensations of eroticism and unbridled sexuality are poorly served by mere strings of blunt four-letter obscenities. So instead the plot and characters develop through scenes described in clear, unambiguous terms, but with just enough of the fine detail left to the reader's imagination to allow for a personalised interpretation of the action. To highlight the lasciviousness of the partyers, the author introduces a foil, in the form of a virgin sold to the narrator by her aunt for 'the Count'. This girl is a true innocent, yet possessed of an enormous innate sensuality. Her sexual initiation germinates the development of a coquette able both to give and receive sexual ecstasy and spiritual love, in sharp contrast to the band of jaded seafaring bawds whose self-indulgent, egotistic lusts progress to scenes of self-destructive flagellation worthy of *Dolly Morton*.

Although the author's sympathies are obvious, *Life on Board a Yacht* should not be read as a merely political or social critique. It is first and foremost an erotic novel. However, like D. H. Lawrence's *Lady Chatterley's Lover*, the nature and quality and quantity of the sex is very much a product of its social milieu. The yacht is a microcosm for the world of pre-World-War-I Europe. Just as the excesses of the then power élite led to a cataclysm that resulted in the demise of their Golden Age, so do the sea voyagers here carry within themselves the seeds of their own destruction.

〜 from *Life on Board a Yacht*

The girl was very docile. Was it ingenuousness or vice? I cannot say. The fact is she followed me without hesitating. I explained to her that I was obliged to make her pass for my sister, that she would have to sleep in the same room with me, but in her own separate bed.

She made no objection and all went on without a hitch, until we came into the bedroom.

It was time for us now to go to bed, and the poor lass began to show the first signs of hesitation.

She stood there, without making a movement, like a statue, and not daring to undress.

'Come, Giovanina,' I said – her name was Giovanina Metelli. 'Come, don't be foolish. What will you do when you are asked to sit as a model?'

'All naked?' she asked in curious consternation.

'Certainly! Quite naked!'

She looked me straight in the face and, shrugging her shoulders with an air of incredulity, she demanded: 'Is that true – the honest truth?'

I assured her once more that it was so. She then uttered a sigh and, no doubt accustomed to passive obedience, murmured in Italian: 'Since it must be!'

And she began to undress. I wanted to help her, but she would not permit it, pushing me gently away.

I then seated myself on the edge of my bed and quietly prepared to contemplate the enticing spectacle that I surely expected.

In the meanwhile, she had taken off her bodice and, her arms bare, her glorious breasts set off by a chemise, perfectly white though of coarse material, she stopped and, looking at me, suddenly said: 'But you also – are you not going to take your things off?'

I may be mistaken, but it seemed to me as if I could discern in the eyes of the lovely child that unseemly curiosity to which the first desires of the ripe virgin give birth.

Without saying a word, I started undressing in my turn, and the damsel continued also to divest herself of her clothing, revealing to me little by little all her secret charms. When we were both of us half nude, I, in my shirt, and she in her chemise, one in front of the other we stopped, looking at each other, asking as it were: 'Well, and what next?'

I could not withstand the temptation to kiss the charming creature, and I did it deliberately without her opposing the least resistance.

She then begged of me to get into bed, which I did at once, so much was I disconcerted. She then slipped between her sheets, and I blew out the light. But I could not sleep and I soon became aware that Giovanina also had not closed her eyes.

Then, being no longer able to resist, I lit the candle again, boldly got out of my bed, and approached that of the beautiful girl.

'What do you want?' she asked with exquisite simplicity.

Without long fishing about for a pretext, I replied: 'I feel cold. I think we should be better together. Be good enough to make a little room for me.'

'But how can you think of such a thing?' she objected. 'A man in bed with me?'

'Oh, that does not matter!' I replied. 'You will sooner or later have to sleep with a man.'

'Yes, but that will be my husband!' was her reply.

Without adding a word, I lifted up the bedclothes and slipped into the bed, taking good care to avoid touching her.

At the end of the moment, a first involuntary rub of my knee against her thigh was inevitable.

A sort of electric shock ensued, and then there was a closer approach. Little by little, in spite of some slight resistance on her part, I held her in my arms.

Seeing, now, that for me the game was almost won, I began to kiss and embrace her. She let me continue without protesting in the least, but also without returning me a single touch of her lips. She was altogether passive. I became emboldened, and caressed her full throat, and her little bubbies, quite firm, solid as marble. I kissed her soft belly and my hand strayed as far as her pussy. She had progressively undergone these different sensations without making any opposition, and I thought that I could even perceive that she found a certain pleasure in this game – evidently new to her. I succeeded in making her enjoy by means of my finger, and then for the first time she went so far as to press her mouth to my moustache.

She had become like a toy in my arms. I was burning with the desire of possessing her and, seeing that she did not quite comprehend the situation, I managed at last to make her understand that what I wanted was something more than those little games which she seemed to think was all there was to be done. She made some timid protests, but they did not seem heartfelt, as her actions showed otherwise. And I reminded her of the words of her aunt, according to which she was to make every attempt to make me happy in everything.

'What am I to do?' she asked.

'I will show you,' I said.

Stretching her out on the bed, I had her open her thighs. She made no resistance. But when I laid myself atop of her, and placed in her little hand my big tool, as stiff as a rod of iron, she became hesitant.

'Put it inside your body,' said I to her. She could not make up her mind to that, but I was too randy not to go ahead. With one brisk gesture, I seized her in my arms, and sought to introduce my member into her slit. I partly succeeded, but perhaps I had undertaken the job awkwardly, for she cried out. I stopped immediately.

'Well then, let me do it to you gently,' said I.

After a short embrace, she gave in, and, enraptured, all shaken with voluptuous tremors, she for the first time received the essential baptism, the only one that gives tangible fruits – sometimes, but not always.

She remained in a partial swoon for about half an hour. I contemplated her tranquilly, with the pride of a cock who has just been treading a hen without defence – but perchance none too unwilling after all!

My eyes, dilated with desire, never ceased staring at her loveliness.

It was some time before she recovered her full consciousness, and then her first gesture was to lay feverishly hold of my weapon. She instinctively guided it to her nest of love. I required no other invitation. I possessed her. I took and embraced her again and again until the morning – and I did the same the next day, having found a pretext for making the Count wait. But when I conducted Giovanina Metelli, the all lovely and adorable Piedmontese lassie, to the Count, her rightful owner – for was he not her purchaser? – she was no longer a virgin.

Furthermore, I had made her believe that all sorts of annoying troubles would be her lot if she lost her innocence.

I was not wrong in acting thus, for up to the present day the beautiful girl is still mine, and I know pertinently that she has never been possessed by anyone else, I took my precautions far too well.

* * *

I cannot say how the ball ended, for I had retired, leaving the gentlemen to their voluptuous amusements. My readers will understand that all I had witnessed, all the unbridled episodes that had followed in such rapid succession, had contributed not a little to rouse within me an amount of desire and lustful appetite which I promised myself largely to glut with my little darling – Giovanina.

Free at last and without apprehension, I wended my way towards her cabin, or rather towards mine, for it was there that she had been installed, while I had settled down as well as I could in other quarters.

I tapped at the door but no response was made. On knocking again, I could hear my little Venus replying to me in her jargon – half French and half Italian.

'Wait a bit, sir! A couple of minutes only, and I will open the door!'

Why did she not open at once? I was still putting that question to myself, when I again heard her voice – this time ringing out clearly, in silvery tones: 'All right! Come in – but in one minute only, I beg of you!'

At the same time, I could hear the bolt being drawn back.

Despite my impatience, I waited two minutes, and then, throwing open the door, I advanced boldly within.

I have already had occasion to mention that after the Count had disinterestedly given Giovanina up to me, I purchased for her clothing and underlinen according to my taste.

Guess my amazement when I perceived Giovanina, her hair hanging down. She was stretched upon a small, low divan, and was lightly clad in a gauzy, rose-coloured dressing gown. It was trimmed with cream ribbons and lace. Besides being half open, the *peignoir*, cut very low in front, permitted vague glimpses of the openwork upper part of a white cambric chemise, edged with coquettish sky-blue ribbon and bows.

Negligently extended, she reclined swinging her small feet, daintily fitted into clinging, white satin slippers. Her slender ankles, encased in black silk stockings through the fine meshes of which the skin could be seen, were pink and tempting and fully exposed. This contrasted clearly with the lily-white slippers.

Her attitude was so languidly suggestive, the picture before me was so enticing, that I could not do otherwise than glue my lips to those of the lovely girl, at the same time dropping on my knees in adoration at the foot of the divan.

I began to caress her. I kissed the open space between her youthful breasts, so full of vigour and so dainty to the eye and taste. I gingerly devoured her voluptuous mouth, and she let me dwell upon her melting, luscious lips. I slipped my hand stealthily under her dressing gown, intending to caress her slender ankles and elegant calves. Mounting gradually higher, I started, suddenly meeting with naked flesh. I then discovered that Giovanina, by a refinement of coquetry, had put on a pair of my socks.

I cannot tell whether she read my astonishment in my looks, but she spontaneously confessed to me that, stimulated by curiosity, she had witnessed, through the keyhole, a great part of the licentious debauchery in the saloon and, overexcited by what she had seen, had determined to prepare a surprise for me. Knowing that I had taken no active part in the proceedings, she had decked herself to receive me.

In her girlish imagination – yet so refined – the sensual child had sought to give more piquancy to our meeting; to render herself more desirable and more seductive. That was the reason for her putting on my socks. They fitted her, as luck would have it, to perfection and made her beautiful skin stand out more conspicuously.

I listened to her, more and more delighted as she innocently unfolded the story of her harmless scheme. I could no longer contain myself. I felt I must possess her! In my eyes, she seemed more lovely than all those whom I had just seen wallowing in the salacious orgy.

But when I wanted to clasp Giovanina in my arms and make her taste supreme delight, I was forced to abate my pretensions. By an inexplicable caprice, she would not let herself be taken and enjoyed. She rebelled, and her resistance served to excite my ardour still further. I begged and prayed; I almost crushed her in my arms. All to no purpose! She still resisted.

What could be the matter with her? Was it woman's whims or any other sentiment? Was it voluptuous refinement? I could not tell.

But most certainly, I was that night obliged to possess her.

Reluctantly grasping the fact that I must put forth my desire, I manoeuvred and teased her.

She told me plainly that she would not have me. I was embarrassed by my clothing, so that, all in a fever, I left her to herself and quickly undressed.

Quite naked, without a vestige of clothing or underwear to impede my movements, I returned to her, more maddened with the most acute desire than ever before in my life.

She had watched me tearing off my garments, following my movements with looks as if to provoke me, an indefinable smile on her lips, and when I approached her, she said to me passionately, in panting accents: 'Oh come! Come then!'

She drove me crazy and, like a stallion in heat, I threw myself upon her. Her half-opened *peignoir* surrendered to my ardent kisses her voluptuously tempting breasts. Through the fine cambric of her chemise, I could lengthily breathe the intoxicating, fragrant emanations of her moist flesh, palpitating beneath the pressure of my feverish, trembling fingers. I hardly remember what I did in my state of mad desire – but certainly many wildly fantastical acts of loving lewdness.

She lent herself without demur to all my fancies, and even experienced great pleasure, as I could often feel her floodgates of sexual sap freely opening, and the tight folds of her warm sheath throbbing on the column of my straining shaft. Giovanina let herself be futtered in front, from behind, dog-fashion, kneeling – in fact, in every possible manner; the more she got, the more she appeared to desire, until at last, exhausted and worn out with fatigue, we fell asleep, locked in each other's arms.

* * *

The temptation was too great. I had before me a beautiful girl, nineteen years old, in the full bloom of her youth, offering herself to my caresses, so as to escape those of an older man who filled her with disgust.

Without another word, I took her round the waist. I drew her to me, and on her trembling lips I imprinted a burning kiss. Then I led her away.

She allowed herself to be helped along like a lamb to the shambles.

We passed unnoticed to my cabin, and I hastened to close the door after us. Then I found myself in presence of the lovely lass – alone with her – who was voluntarily giving herself to me; who had of her own free will made the offer. The situation was for me altogether a new one, and certainly not devoid of charm.

She abandoned herself resignedly. I pressed her to me, kissing her downcast eyelids and her voluptuous mouth; passing my lips over the silky curls playing about her white neck and rosy ears.

Falling back on a divan, I drew her on my knees and contemplated her for a few instants.

She gave herself up passively, with closed eyes, but through her long lashes her tears filtered – big, liquid pearls. I thought of the sacrifice of Iphigenia, and for one second felt remorse.

But my scruples soon faded away when I called to mind the features of the old captain. If she must undergo the sex-initiation, it were better that she should for the first time swoon from pleasure in my arms than in those of another.

With burning lips, I sucked the salt tears from her flushed cheeks. She nestled obediently in my arms and, one by one, I freed her from her various articles of dress – her bodice and stays, to begin with. My fingers trembled at the contact of her delicate and velvety skin, which under my touch was moist, warm and quivering. And that put me all in a fever!

Inert, Renée submitted to my will, without any resistance. She abandoned herself to my caresses. I felt quite dazed and confused. But my sensual excitement was only the more increased. Beneath the delicate lace trimming of her cambric chemise, her breasts swelled out, heaving with emotions, and her nipples stood up temptingly.

I had removed her blouse and her beautiful, plump and dimpled arms, that I made her put round my neck, gave me another voluptuous thrill. In her low corset, her exuberant breasts, under the satin and lace, and her sculptural shoulders, rendered her desirable and irresistible in the highest degree. I covered her with kisses, to which she did not seem insensible. Still keeping her on my knees, panting and beside myself, so much had the abandonment of her virgin body excited my senses, I undid her tiny shoes and threw off her white silk stockings that she had fancied to wear that day.

Then, no longer able to restrain myself, I finished undressing her and carried her to my couch. It was not difficult for me to lift her chemise and open her drawers, and the mere contact of my fingers with the silk and lace of these mysterious articles of underwear set my blood on fire. I had denuded her down to her chemise. I could see her beautiful thighs, so firm and white, and had pressed my burning lips upon them. She had continued to submit without the least emotion.

Her passivity began to tire me – I had even allowed my hands to explore the secret regions between her thighs which did not oppose my indiscreet probing.

'Are you made of marble?' I asked her, feeling myself incapable of enduring her silent resignation. 'Do you then feel nothing? Look here, I prefer not to have you! I won't have you – I refuse to make you a real woman if you care no more than this for what I am doing!'

Her sole reply was to draw me to her. She seized my head in her hands, kissed my lips, and then said in a murmuring whisper: 'Undress!'

I clasped her in my arms and, leaving her for a moment, I took off all my clothes, down to my shirt, and then came back to her, reclining on my bed awaiting me.

Pressed by my impatience, I was about to commence at once my attack on the fortress which it was no longer necessary for me to besiege – and, without flattering myself, I was well prepared to come out with flying colours – when, contrary to my expectations, Renée gently pushed me on one side as she whispered faintly: 'Not yet! Not like that just yet! Oh, come – do! No, not yet!'

Until that moment, by a supreme effort of her will she had restrained herself, but she no longer had the strength to resist the agitation of her senses now at the boiling point and, as she was not carved out of stone, she submitted to nature's laws and gave free course to her feelings. In her turn, she clasped me in her arms, reciprocated my caresses, and was even bold enough to put her hand down – from curiosity probably – as far as my organ of generation. On touching it, she gave a little start which I perceived quite distinctly, but she said nothing.

What appears to me now very foolish and unreasonable is the fact that only a few broken utterances and indistinct words were exchanged between us.

At last, by mutual consent, we prepared fully to consummate the carnal act.

'What must I do?' she murmured coyly.

'Come, darling!' I replied.

For one moment, she experienced a sudden upheaval of recoiling rebellion, but with gentle words and soothing caresses and kisses, I persuaded her to let me do as I chose with her. So she submitted to the supreme embrace of the sexes.

Quite exhausted, almost fainting, after I had plucked the flower of her maidenhood and ejaculated freely within her throbbing cleft, she had a slight fit of hysterics. Then she regained her senses and began to cry bitterly. I tried to pacify and console her, and she laughed through her tears.

When I returned to the charge, she gave herself willingly, with all her heart and soul, joyously, and without manifesting the slightest opposition to my desires, as if she felt the necessity of calming her overwrought nerves by total abandonment to the shower of virile elixir bringing peace to her womb, and quieting her racked brain.

Bibliography

The following standard bibliographies and sources were utilised for some of the bibliographic information contained in this book.

Apollinaire, *et al.*, *L'Enfer de la Bibliothèque Nationale*, 1913
Ashbee, *Bibliography of Prohibited Books*, Brussel, New York 1962
Bécourt, *Livres Condamnés, Livres Interdit*, Cercle de la Libraire, 1961
Bilderlexicon der Erotik, Verlag für Kulturforschung, Vienna & Hamburg 1928–1931 (Supplement, 1965)
Chanover, *The Marquis de Sade: A Bibliography*, 1973
Clowes, *Bibliotheca Arcana*, Redway, 1884
Cohen–De Ricci, *Guide de l'Amateur de Livres Gravures du XVIIIe Siecle*, sixth edition, 1973 reprint
Dawes, *A Study of the Erotic Literature in England*, Gothingham 1943
Deakin, *Catalogi Librorum Eroticorum*, Woolf, 1964
Englisch, *Geschichte der Erotischen Literatur*, Püttmann, 1927
Englisch, *Irrgarten der Erotik*, Lykeion, Leipzig 1931
Forbidden Books . . . by an Old Bibliophile, Carrington, Paris 1902
Fryer, *Forbidden Books of the Victorians*, Odyssey, London 1970
Fryer, *Private Case, Public Scandal*, Secker & Warburg, 1966
Galitzin Catalogue, 1887
Gay, *Bibliographie des ouvrages Relatifs à l'Amour . . .* , 1864
Gay, *Bibliographie . . .* , third edition, 1871–3
Gay–Lemonneyer, *Bibliographie . . .* , fourth edition, 1894–1900
Gillete & Dicks, *The Encyclopedia of Erotica*, Award Books, 1969
Girodias, *The Olympia Reader*, Grove Press, 1965
Girodias, *The New Olympia Reader*, Olympia Press, New York 1970
Goodland, *A Bibliography of Sex Rites and Customs*, 1931
Hayn & Gotendorf, *Bibliotheca Germanorum Erotica & Curiosa*, 1912–14 and 1929
Hoffmann, *Anglo-American Traditional Erotica*, Popular Press, 1973
Kearney, *A History of Erotic Literature*, London 1982
Kearney, *Private Case: An Annotated Bibliography*, London 1981

Kearney, *The Olympia Press: A Handlist*, London 1975

Kronhausen, *Pornography and the Law*, Ballantine, 1959

Legman, *The Horn Book*, University Press, 1964

Legman, Introduction in Kearney, *Private Case: An Annotated Bibliography*, London 1981

Marcus, *The Other Victorians*, Basic Books, 1964

Obliques, Nos. 12–13, 1977 (special de Sade issues)

Parke-Bernet Catalogue, No. 3194, *Libertine Literature*, compiled by J. B. Rund, 1971

Perceau, *Bibliographie du Roman Erotique au XIXe Siècle*, 1930

Perkins, *The Secret Record*, Morrow, 1976

Pia, *Les Livres de l'Enfer*, Coulet & Faure, 1978

Plesch, *Bibliothèque la Leonia* III, Monte Carlo 1955

Rose, *Registrum Librorum Eroticorum*, London 1936

Scheiner, *Compendium: Being a List . . .* , New York 1989

Stern–Szana, *Bibliotheca Erotica et Curiosa*, 1921

Thomas, *A Long Time Burning*, Praeger, 1969

Notes

Sources for text excerpts in *The Essential Guide to Erotic Literature*. All texts in this work are somewhat edited from any previously appearing texts, for reasons discussed in the Introduction.

1. Aretino, *Sonetti Lussuriosi*, *c.*1527. This original translation by C. J. Scheiner is based on three sources: an explicit English translation, attributed to Oscar Wilde but most likely by Samuel Putnam, *c.*1920; the more euphemistic Sam Putnam English translation printed in *The Works of Aretino*, Covici, 1926; and the original text in the unique *c.*1527 copy.
2. Chorier, *The Dialogues of Luisea Sigea*, *c.*1660. Text from the *c.*1925 Jack Brussel offset reprint of the *c.*1893 continental piracy of the 1890 Liseux edition.
3. Cleland, *Fanny Hill*, 1748–9. Text from the complete and unexpurgated Liseux edition of 1888.
4. Musset, *Gamiani*, 1833. Text from the 1923 Dorian Club edition.
5. Rochefoucault, de la, *The Cavendish Divorce Case Letters*, 1859. Text from the *c.*1891 offprint.
6. Anonymous, *Nunnery Tales*, 1866–88. Text from the *c.*1935 US edition.
7. Sellon, *The Ups and Downs of Life*, 1867. Text from the first edition.
8. Schroeder-Devrient (?), *Pauline the Prima Donna* I, 1868. Text predominantly from the *c.*1925 US edition, by an unknown translator, and also the 1960 Olympia Press edition.
9. Schroeder-Devrient (?), *Pauline the Prima Donna* II, 1875. Text from the *c.*1925 US edition, by an unknown translator, but predominantly the 1960 Olympia Press edition.
10. Potter, *et al.*, *The Romance of Lust*, 1873-6. Text from the first edition.

11. Anonymous, *The Pearl*, 1879. Text from the *c.*1890 Brancart edition.

12. Anonymous, *The Pearl, Christmas Annual*, 1881. Text from the first edition.

13. Anonymous, *The Boudoir*, 1883. Text from the first edition.

14. Rhodes, *The Autobiography of a Flea*, 1887. Text from the first edition.

15. 'Walter', *My Secret Life*, 1888–94. Text from the first edition.

16. Belot, *Parisian Frolics*, 1889–94. Text from the *c.*1912 first English-language edition.

17. Anonymous, *The Simple Tale of Susan Aked*, *c.*1892. Text from the first edition.

18. Wilde *et al.*, *Teleny*, 1893. Text from the Olympia Press, Paris, 1958 edition.

19. Anonymous, *Lascivious Scenes in the Convent*, 1898. Text from the first edition.

20. Jem, *Wide Open*, 1899. Text from the *c.*1935 American first English translation.

21. Anonymous, *The Initiation of Aurora Trill*, 1903. Text from the 1932 US edition.

22. Bacchus, *The Confessions of Marie Carey*, 1902. Text from the *c.*1935 US edition.

23. Bacchus, *The Romances of Blanche la Mare*, 1903. Text from the *c.*1935 US edition.

24. Bacchus, *The Story of Nemesis Hunt*, 1906. Text from the *c.*1935 US edition.

25. Salten, *Josefine Mutzenbacher*, 1906. Text from an anonymously translated *c.*1925 US edition.

26. Kirkwood, *Sadopaideia*, 1907. Text from the first edition.

27. Bleichröder(?), *James Grunnert*, 1908. Text from an anonymously translated *c.*1930 US edition.

28. Anonymous, *The Way of a Man with a Maid*, 1908. Text from the *c.*1933 US Psyche & Erros edition.

29. Anonymous, *Life on Board a Yacht*, c.1908. Text from the first edition.